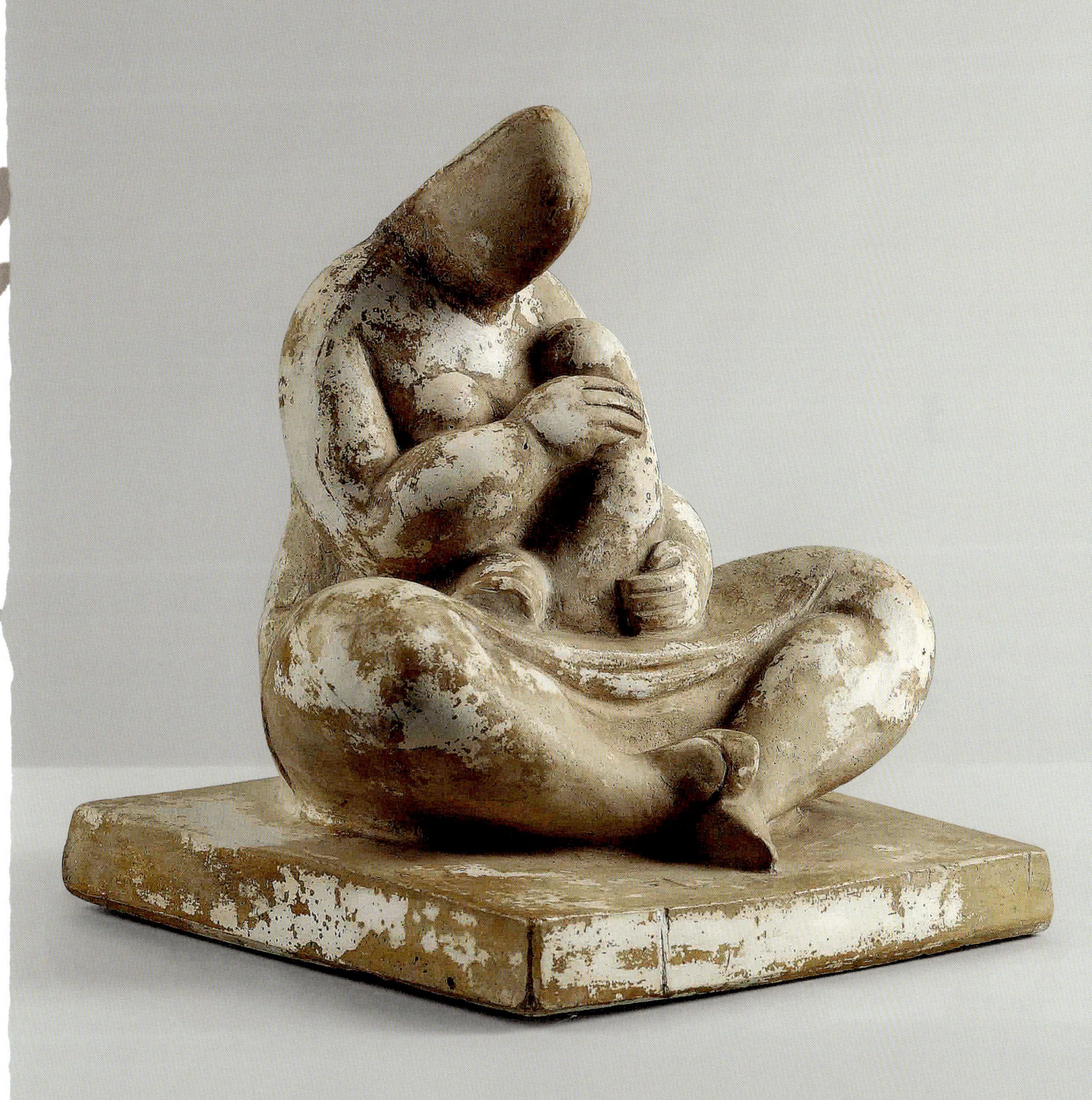

Maternità
1926
glazed plaster
25,5 × 20 × 18,5 cm
26 A 2
Courtesy Sergio Casoli

Ballerina
n.d.
plaster
25 cm
1785/199
Courtesy Sergio Casoli

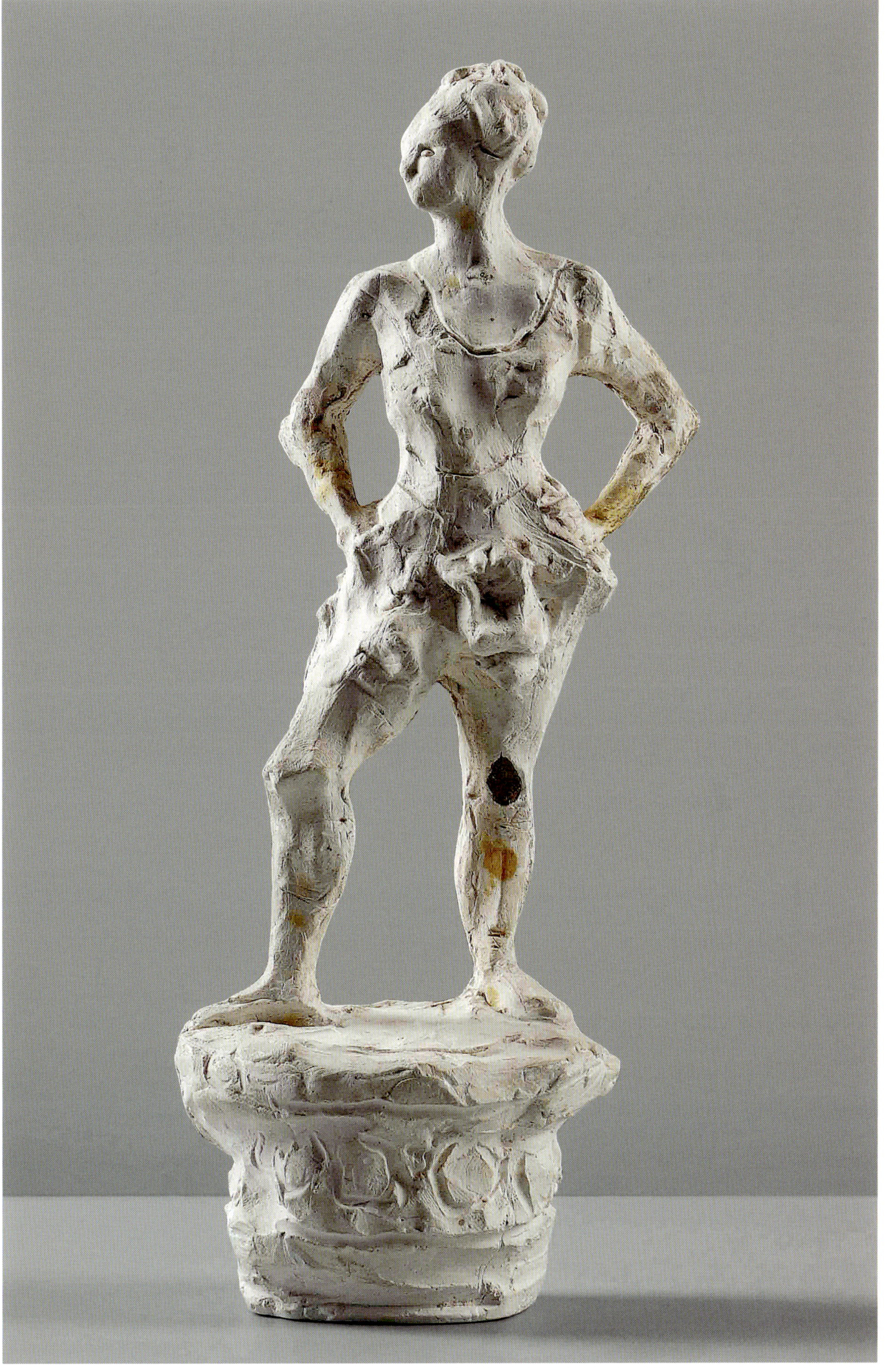

Figure nere
1931
scratched cold-coloured
terracotta, black and white
41 × 30 × 12,5 cm
31 SC 7
Courtesy Fondazione
Lucio Fontana

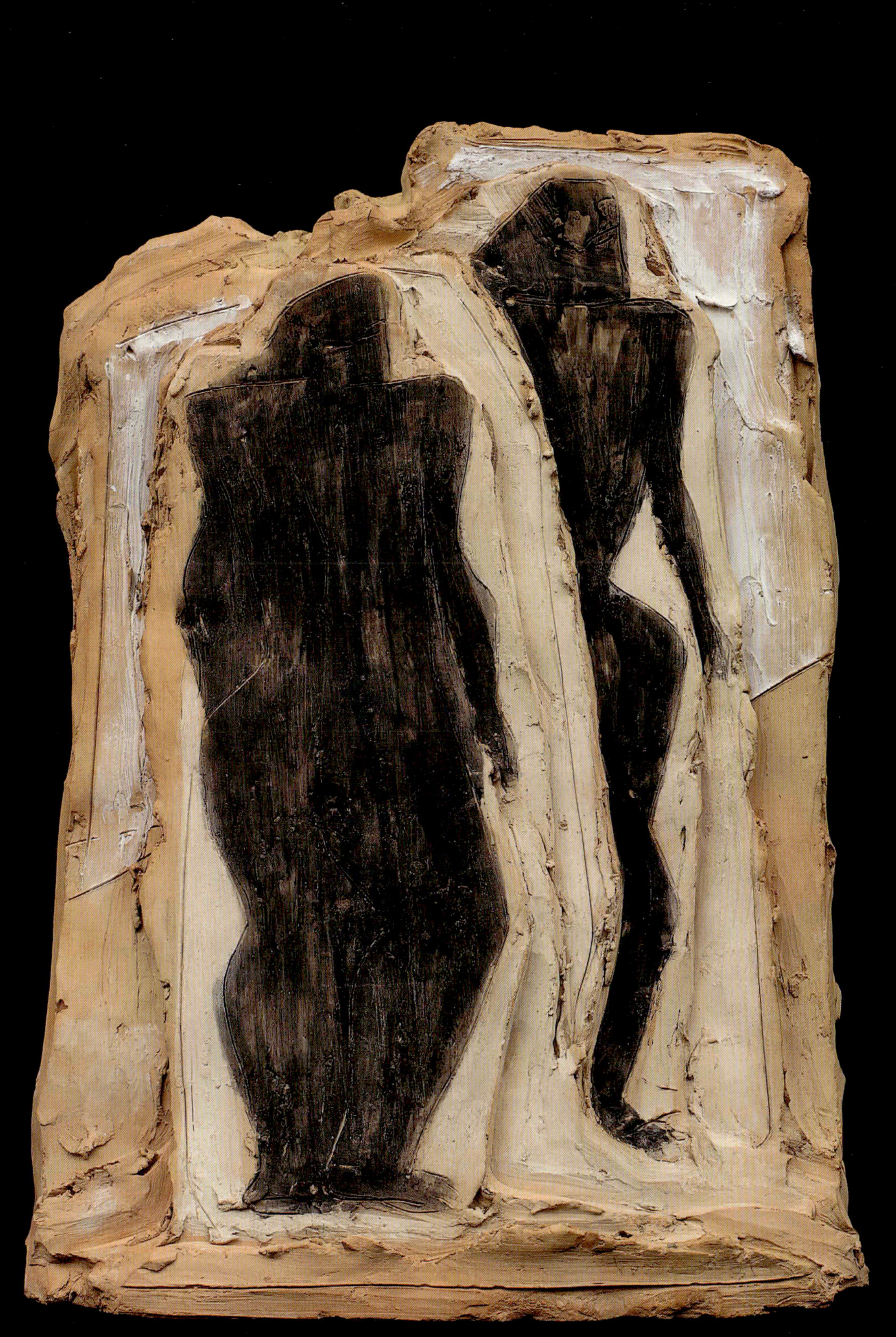

Figura sdraiata
1938
coloured ceramic
11 × 45,5 × 26 cm
38 SC 31
Courtesy Collezioni Civiche
gift Alberto Della Ragione
Firenze

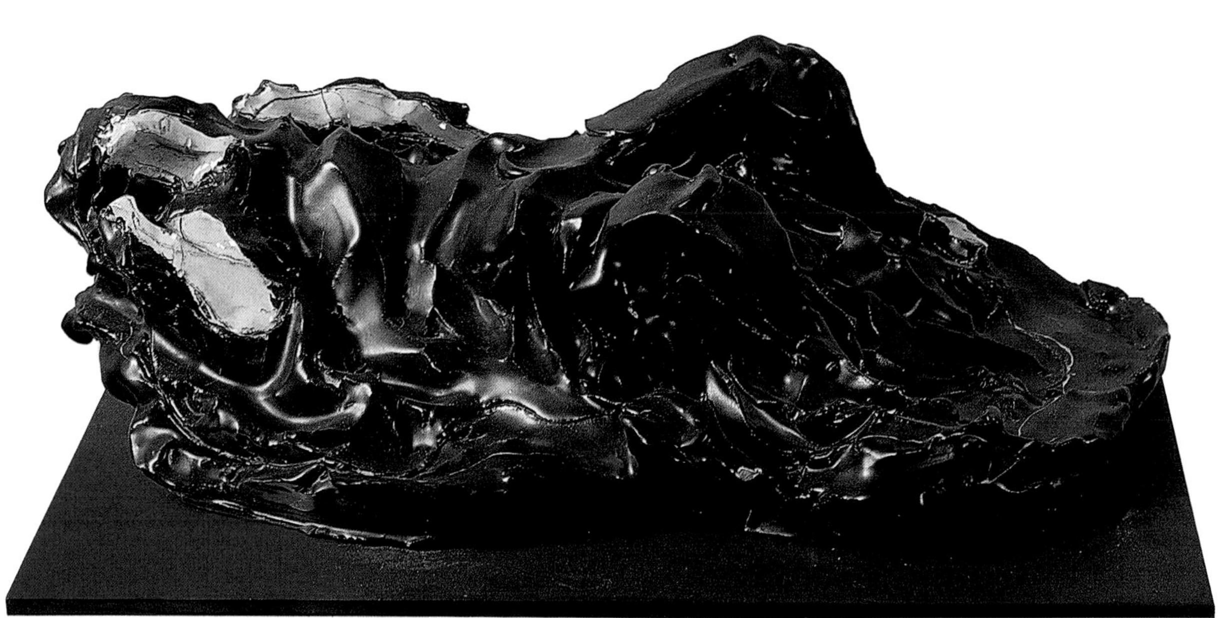

Mujeres ante el espejo
(Women in front of a mirror)
1940
coloured plaster
40 × 28 × 20 cm
40 SC 15
Courtesy Sergio Casoli

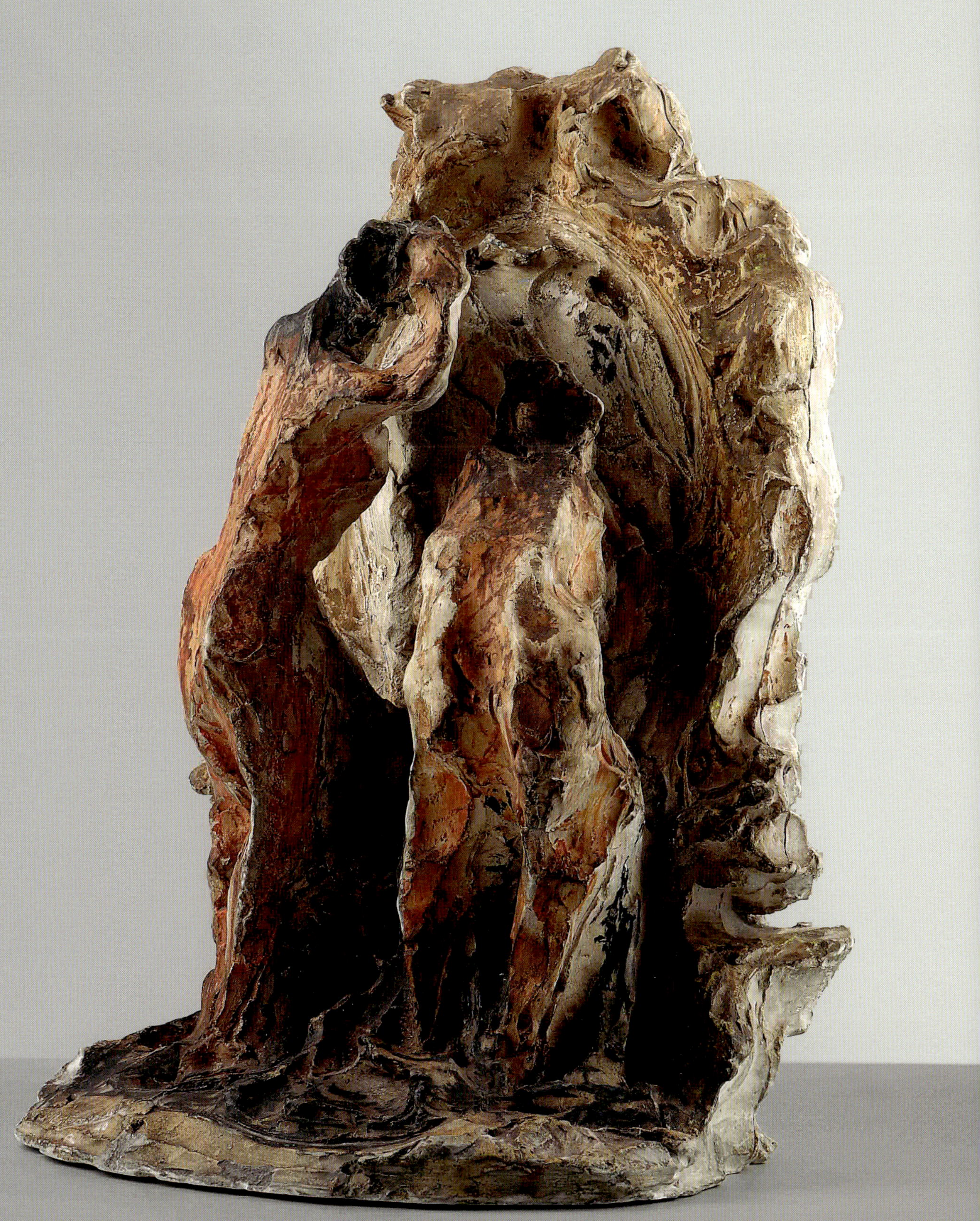

Nudo femminile seduto
1940
natural red terracotta
22,6 × 21 × 24 cm
40 SC 18
Courtesy Sergio Casoli

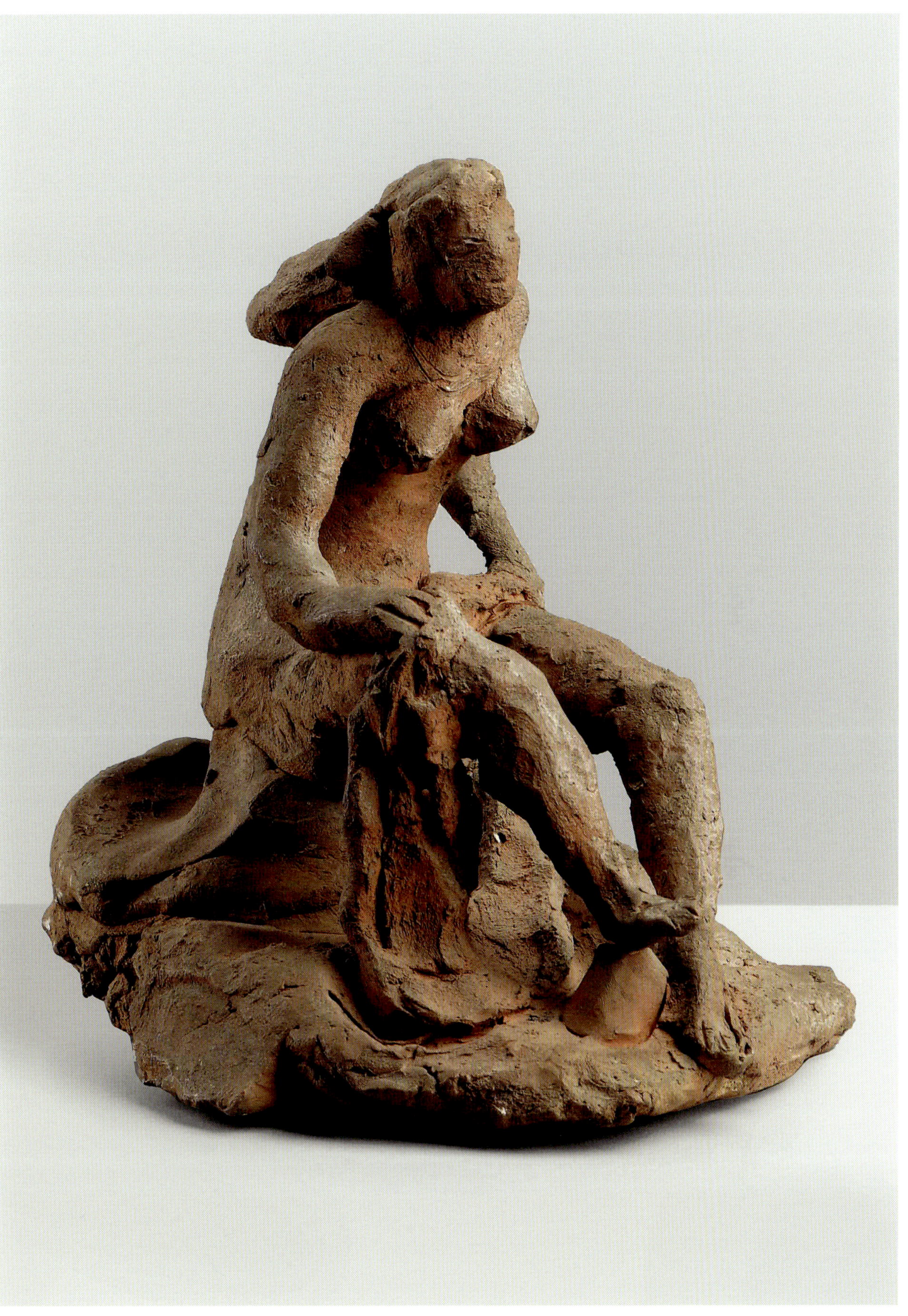

Concetto spaziale. Natura
1959-60
bronze, 42 × 58 cm
59-60 N 25
Courtesy Fondazione
Lucio Fontana

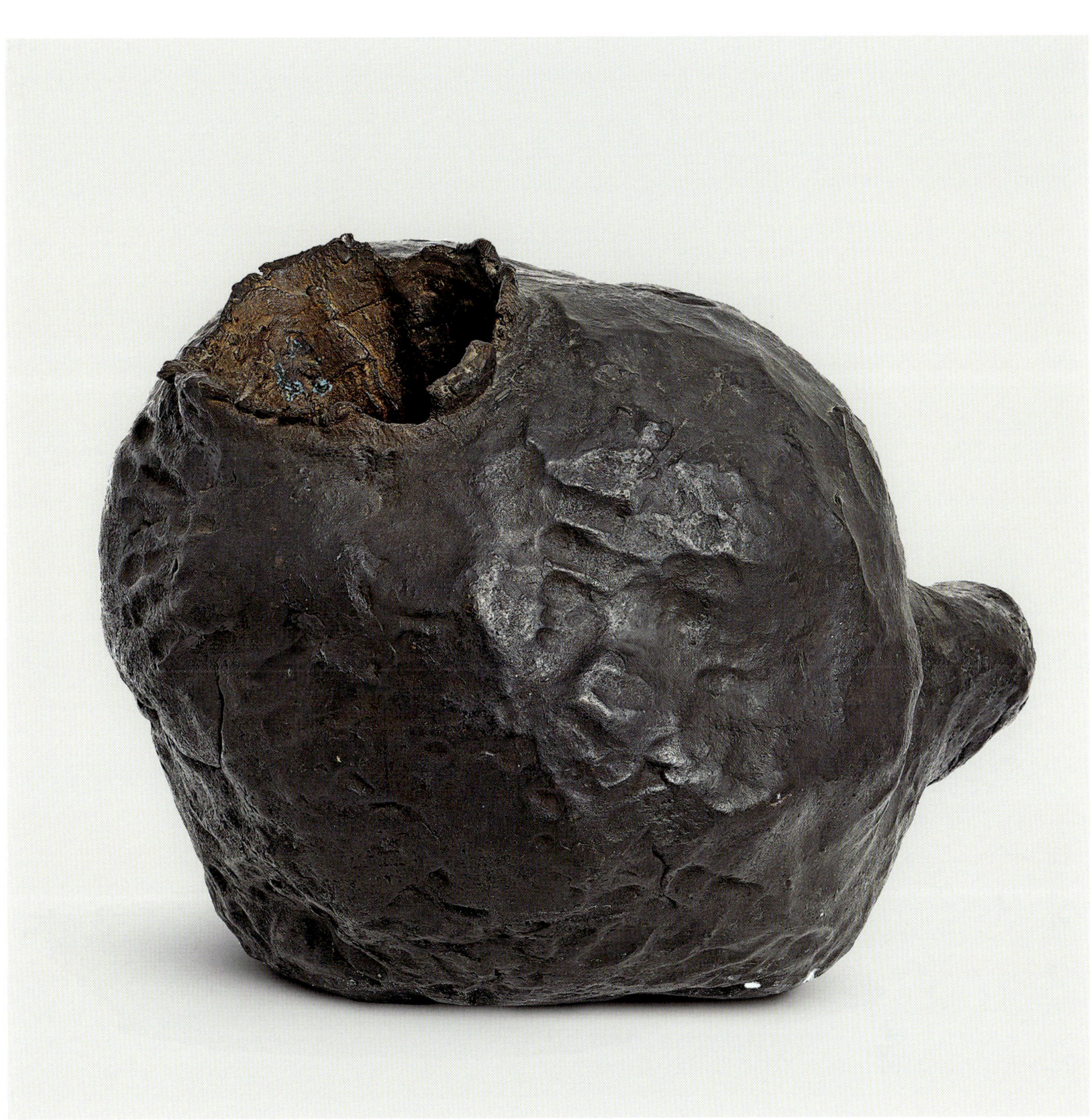

Nudo femminile
1960 – 64
china on paper
100 × 70 cm
60 – 64 DF 279
Courtesy Fondazione
Lucio Fontana

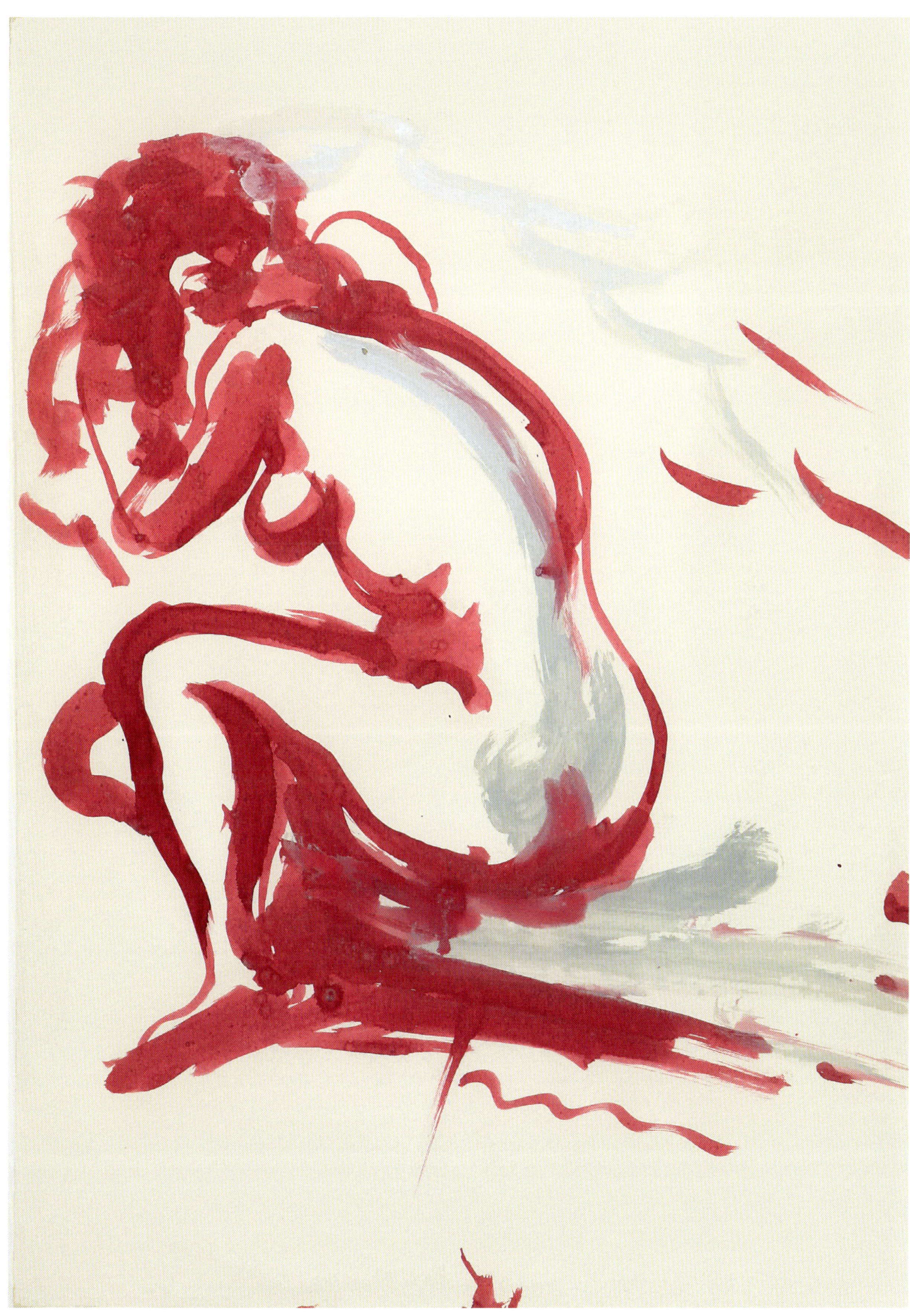

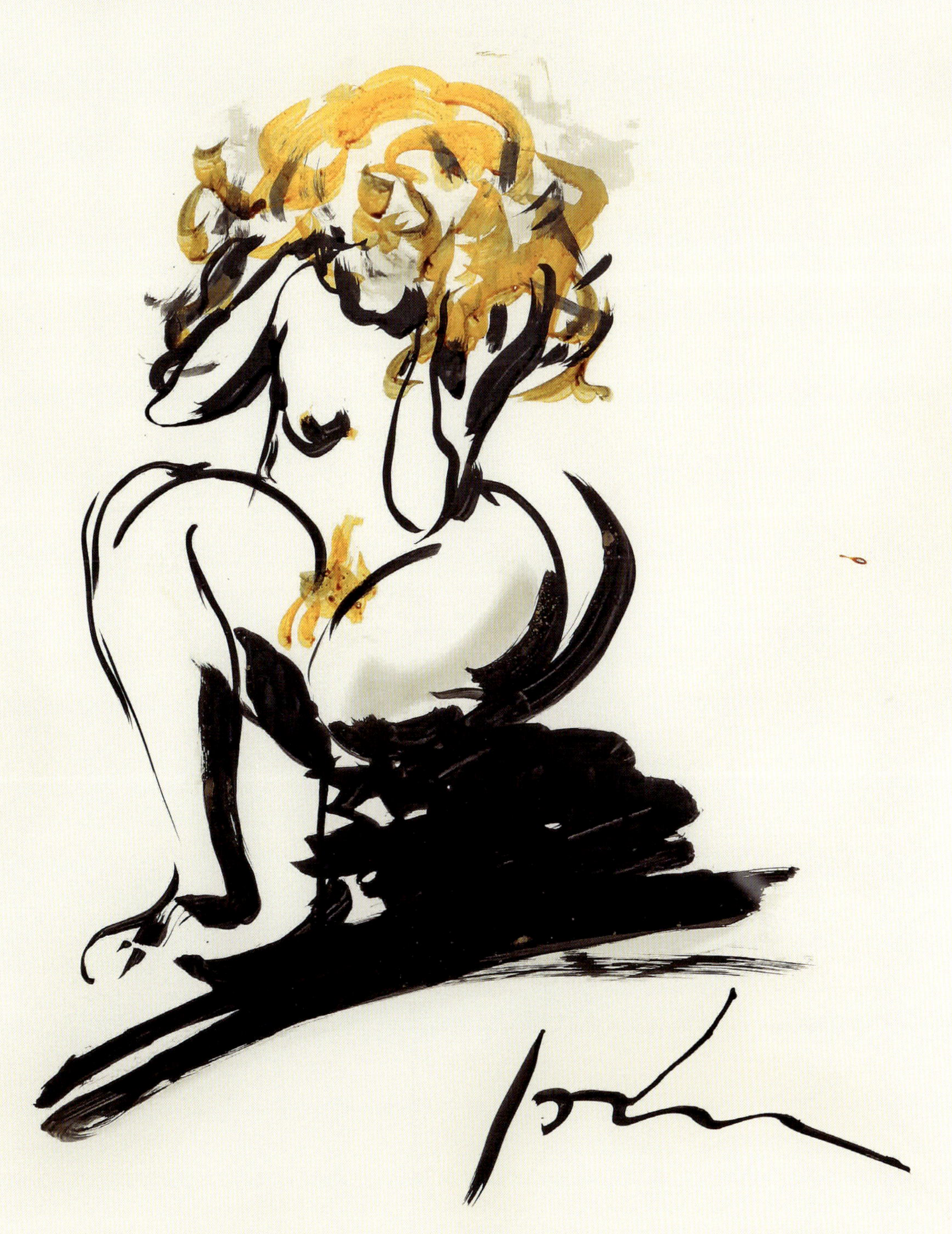

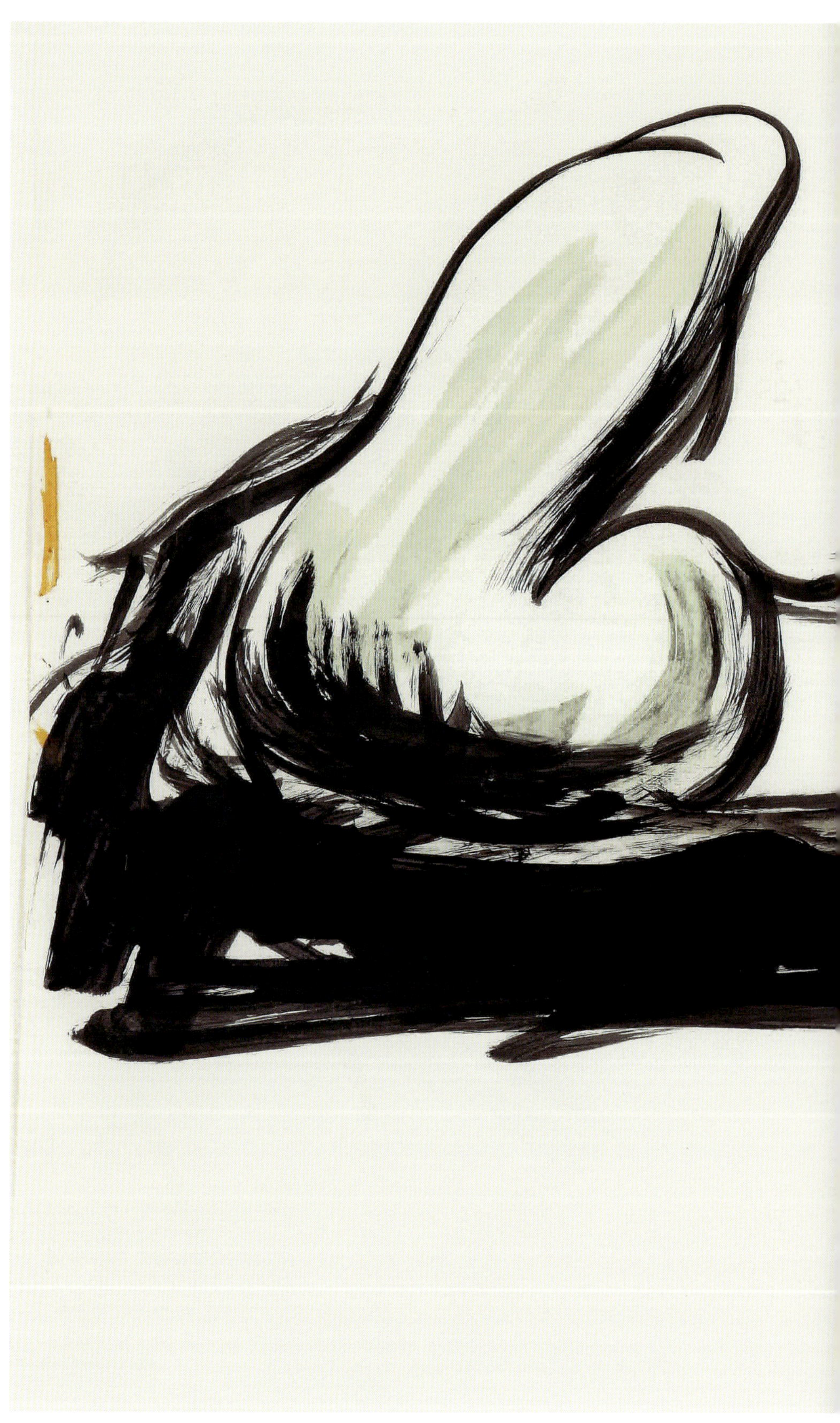

Nudo femminile
1960–64
china on cardboard
70 × 100 cm
60–64 DF 281
Courtesy Fondazione
Lucio Fontana

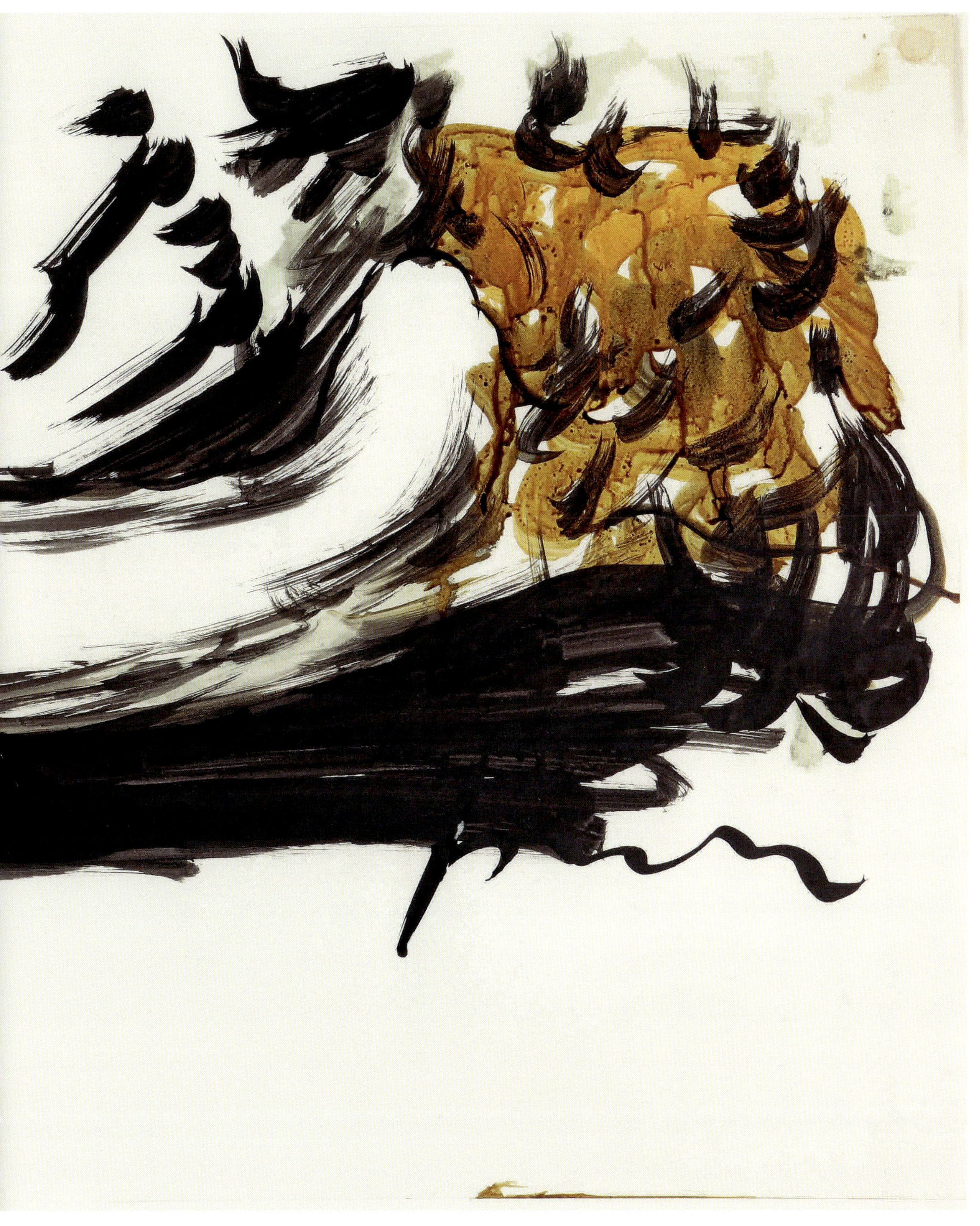

Nudo femminile
1960–64
china on cardboard
50 × 70 cm
60–64 DF 172
Courtesy Fondazione
Lucio Fontana

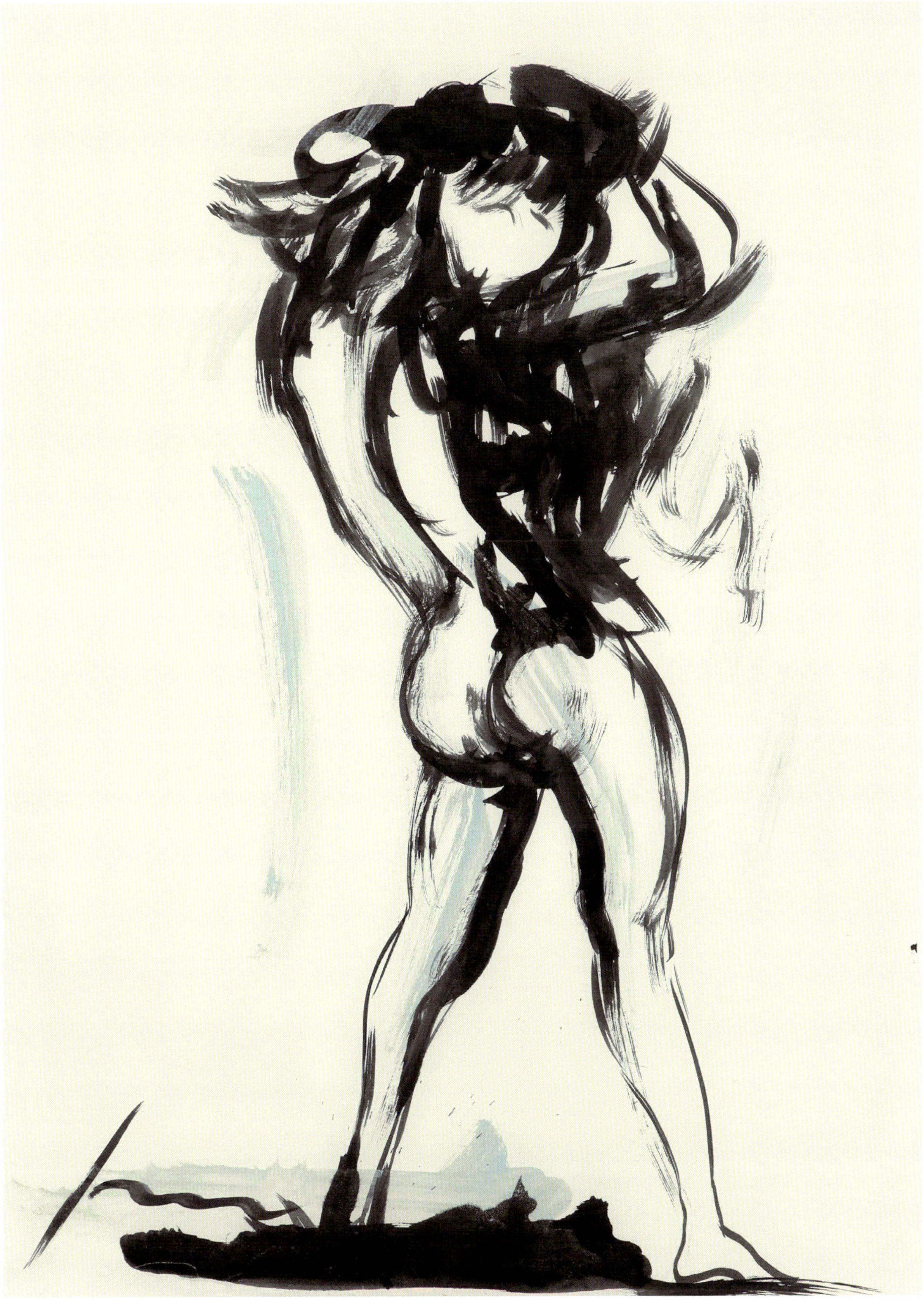

Nudo femminile
1960-64
china on cardboard
70 × 50 cm
60-64 DF 236
Courtesy Fondazione
Lucio Fontana

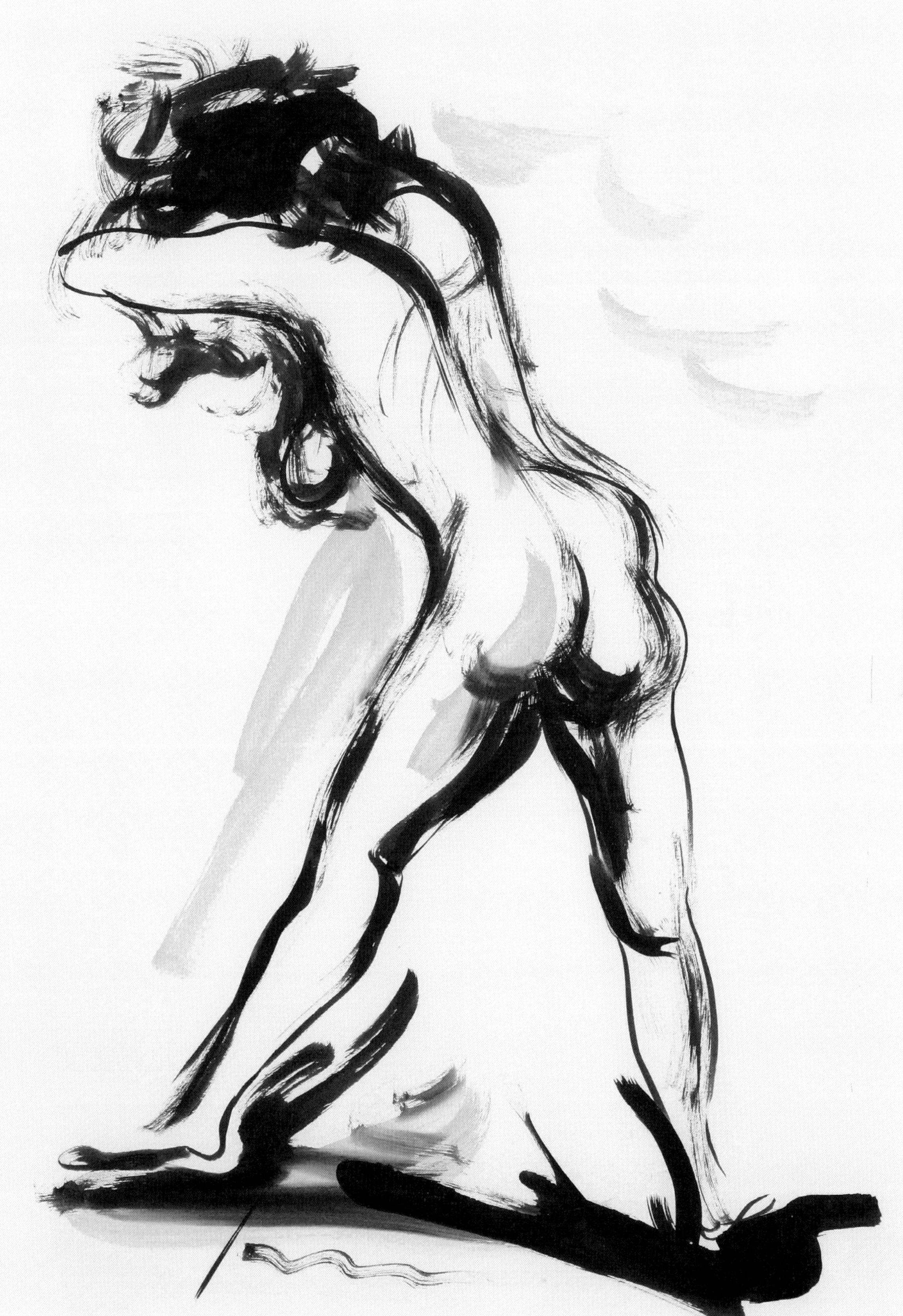

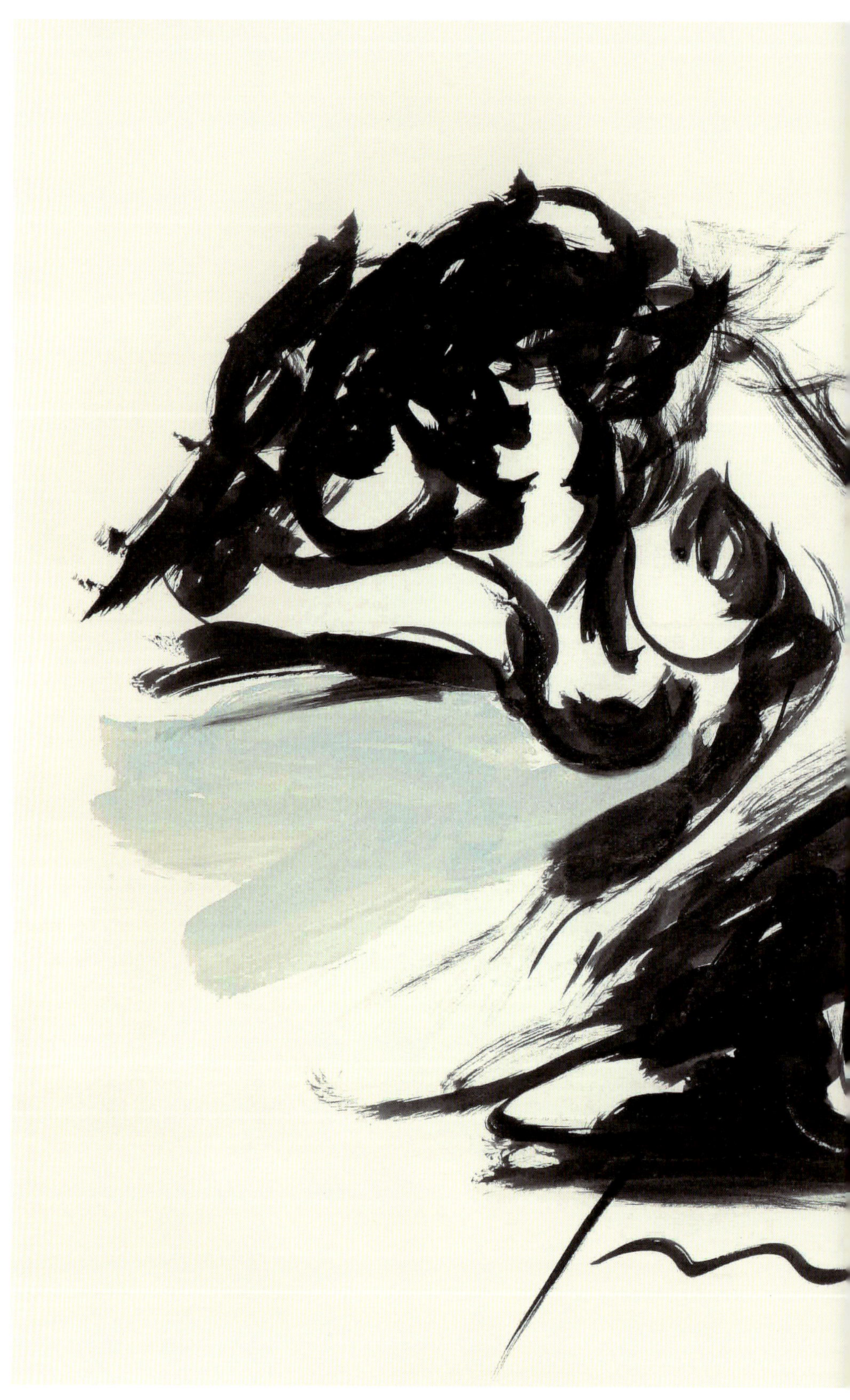

Nudo femminile
1960-64
china on cardboard
50 × 70 cm
60-64 DF 171
Courtesy Fondazione
Lucio Fontana

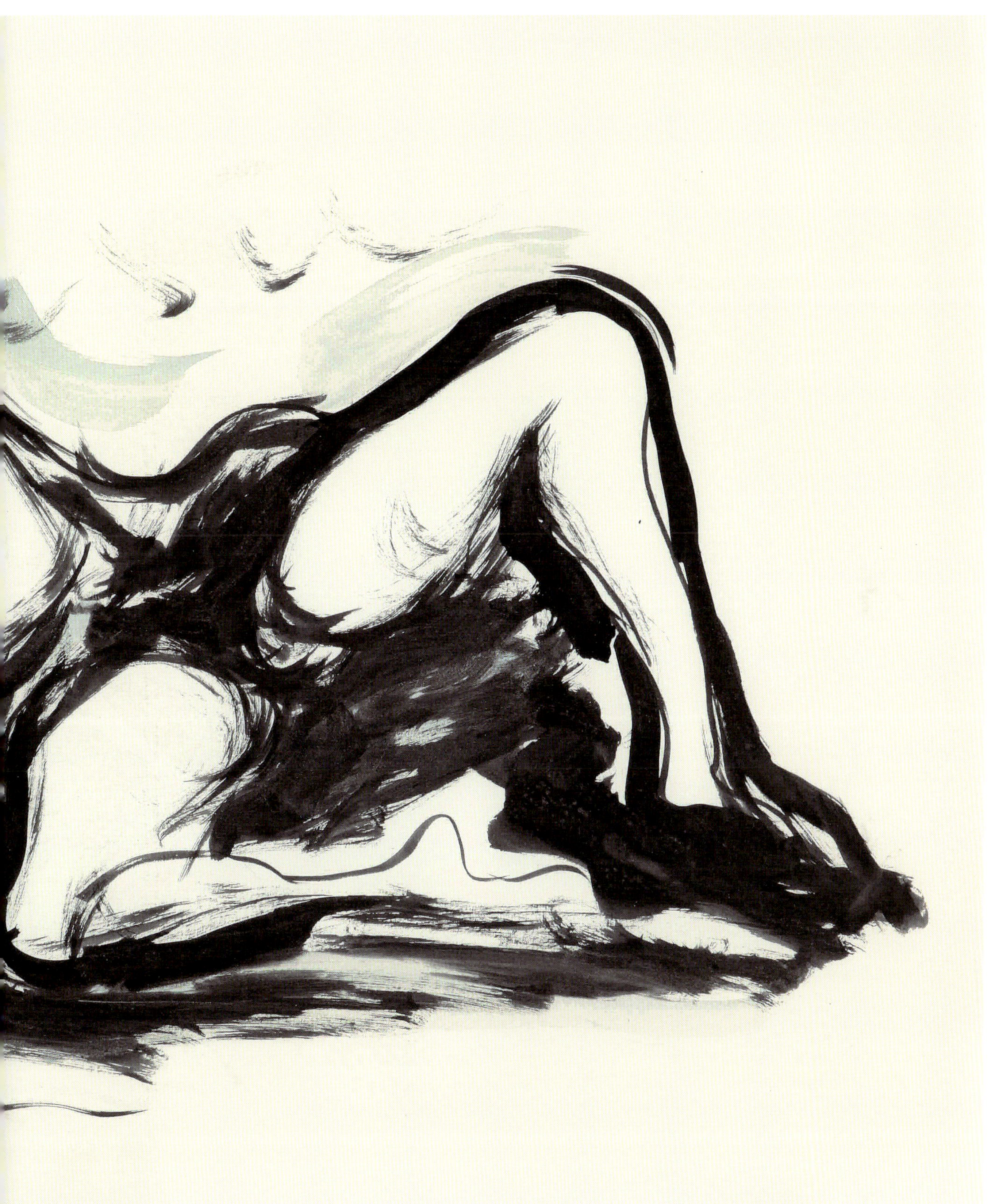

Nudi
1960-64
coloured tempera and gold
on cardboard
50 × 23,5 cm
60-64 DF 20
Courtesy Fondazione
Lucio Fontana

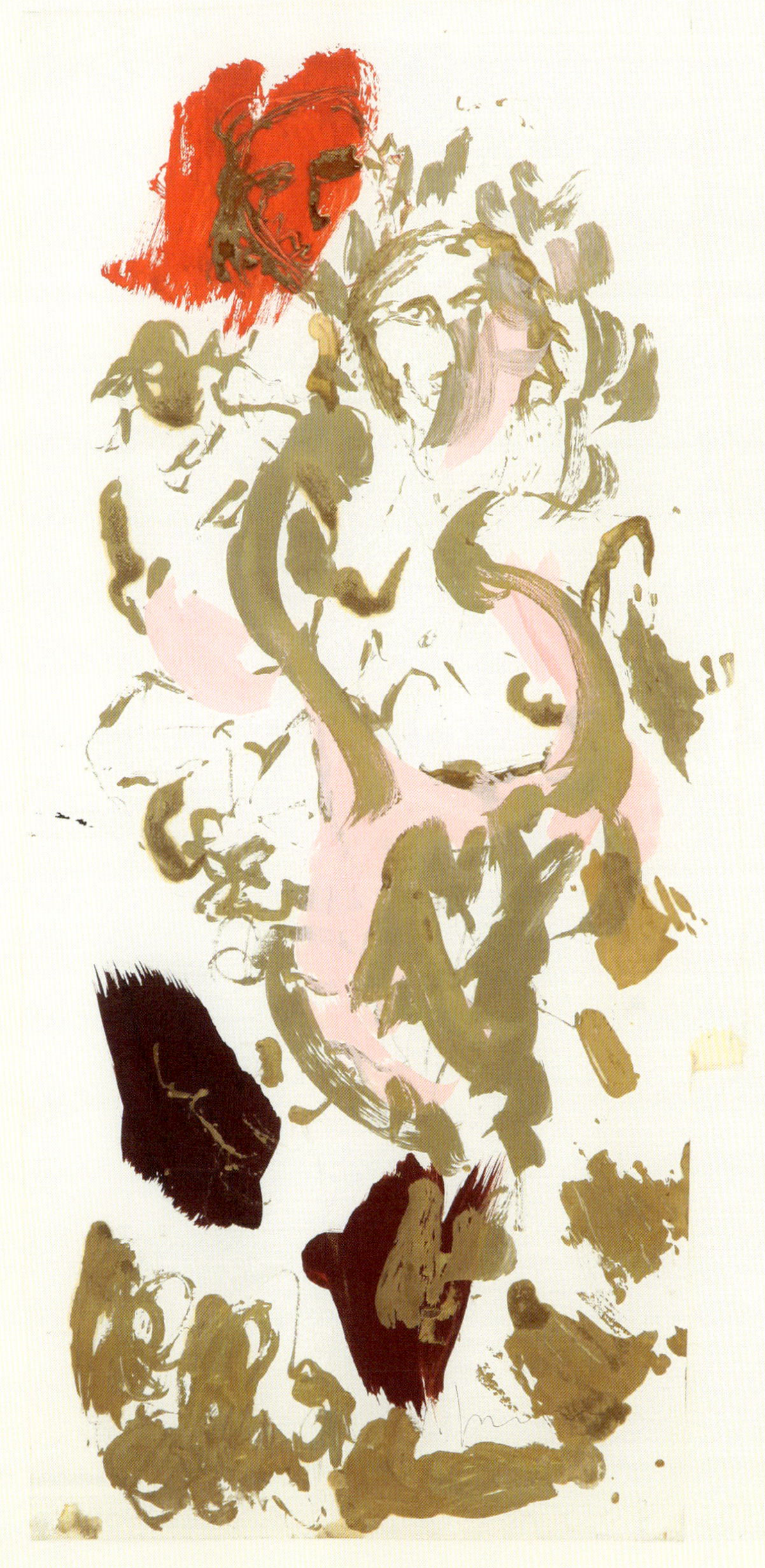

Nudo femminile
1960-64
china on cardboard
100 × 70 cm
60-64 DF 278
Courtesy Fondazione
Lucio Fontana

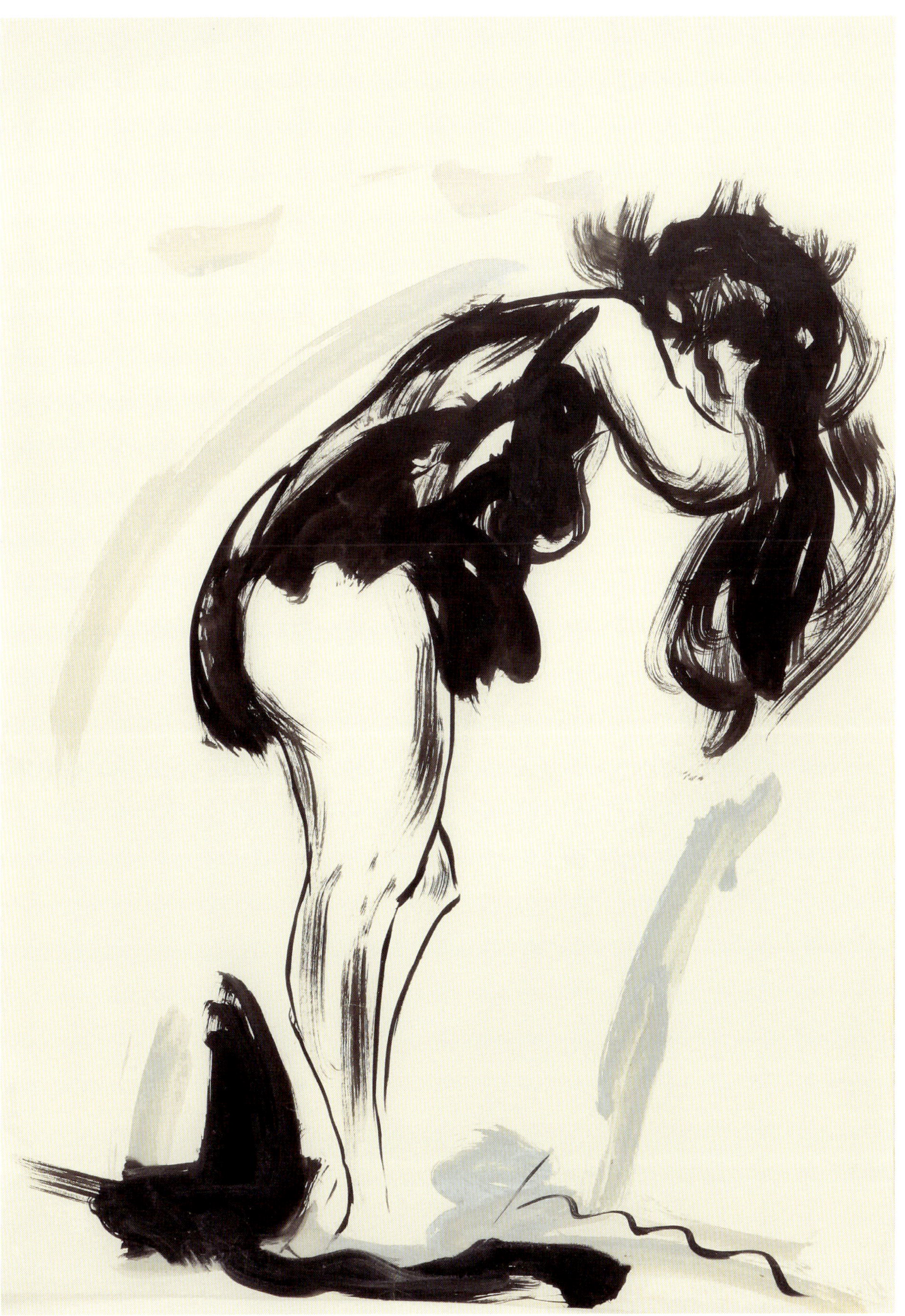

Nudo femminile
1960–64
china on cardboard
50 × 35 cm
60–64 DF 59
Courtesy Fondazione
Lucio Fontana

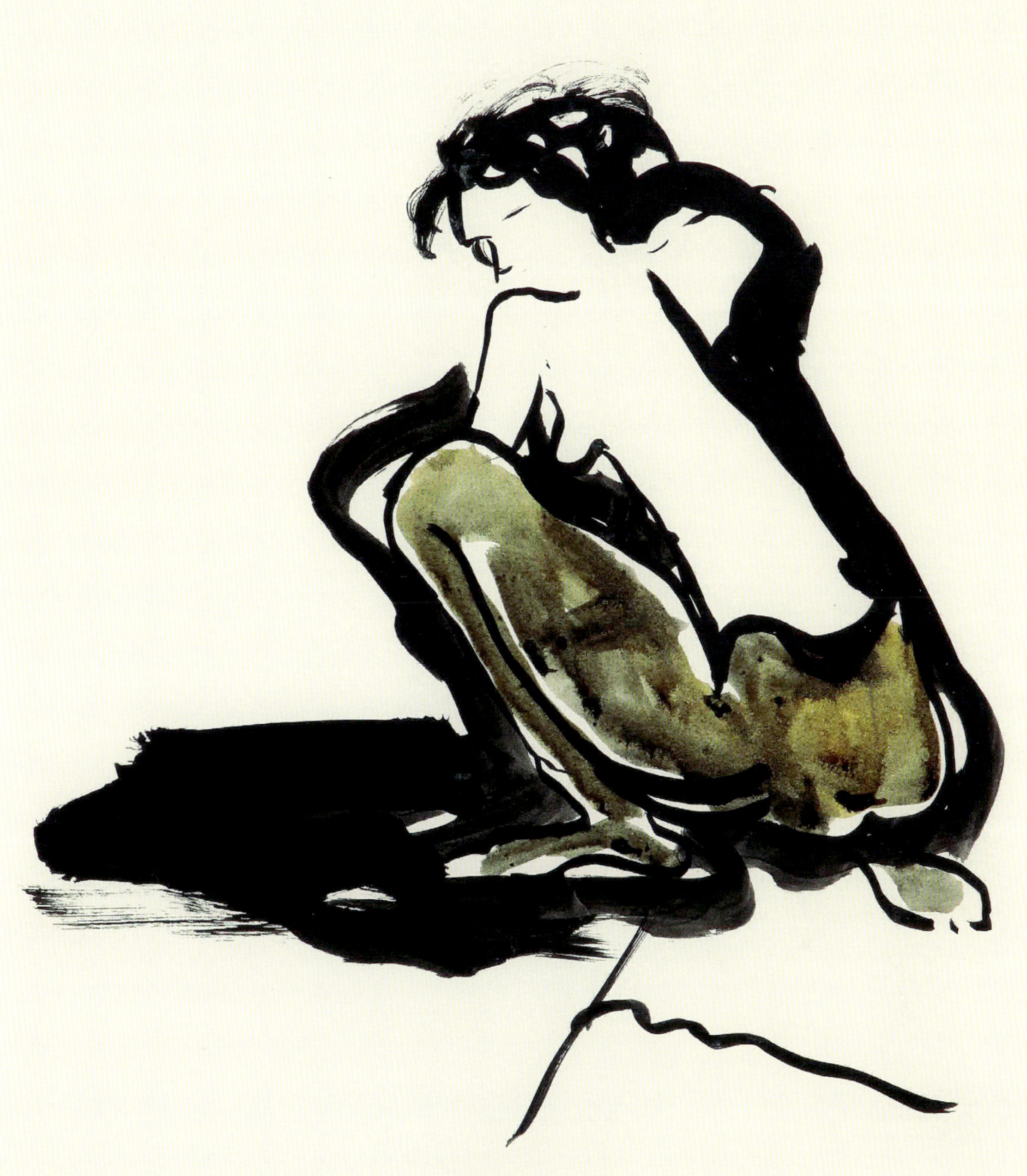

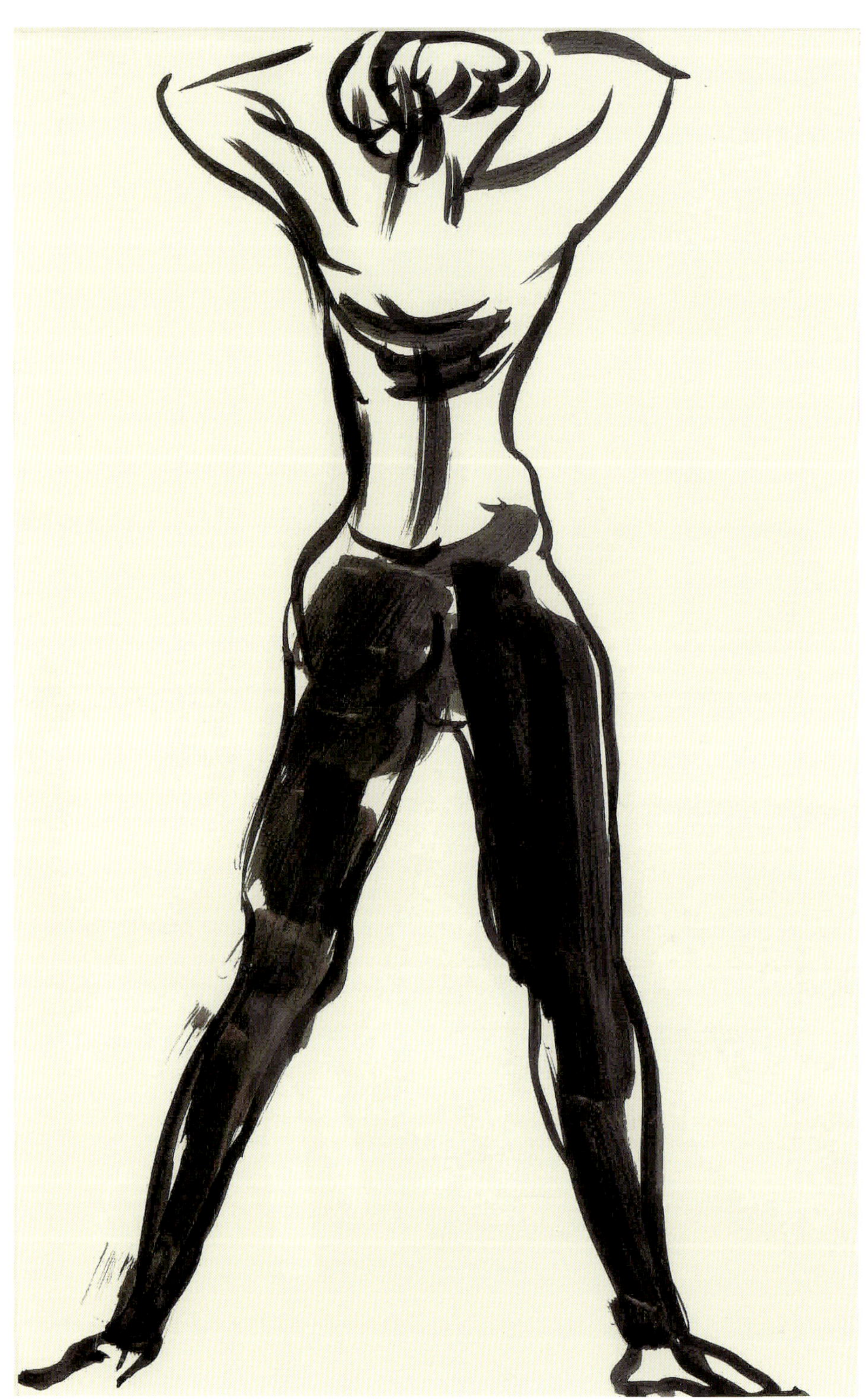

Figura femminile
1960-64
china on paper
55 × 33,5 cm
60-64 DF 50
Private collection
Courtesy Gió Marconi
Milano

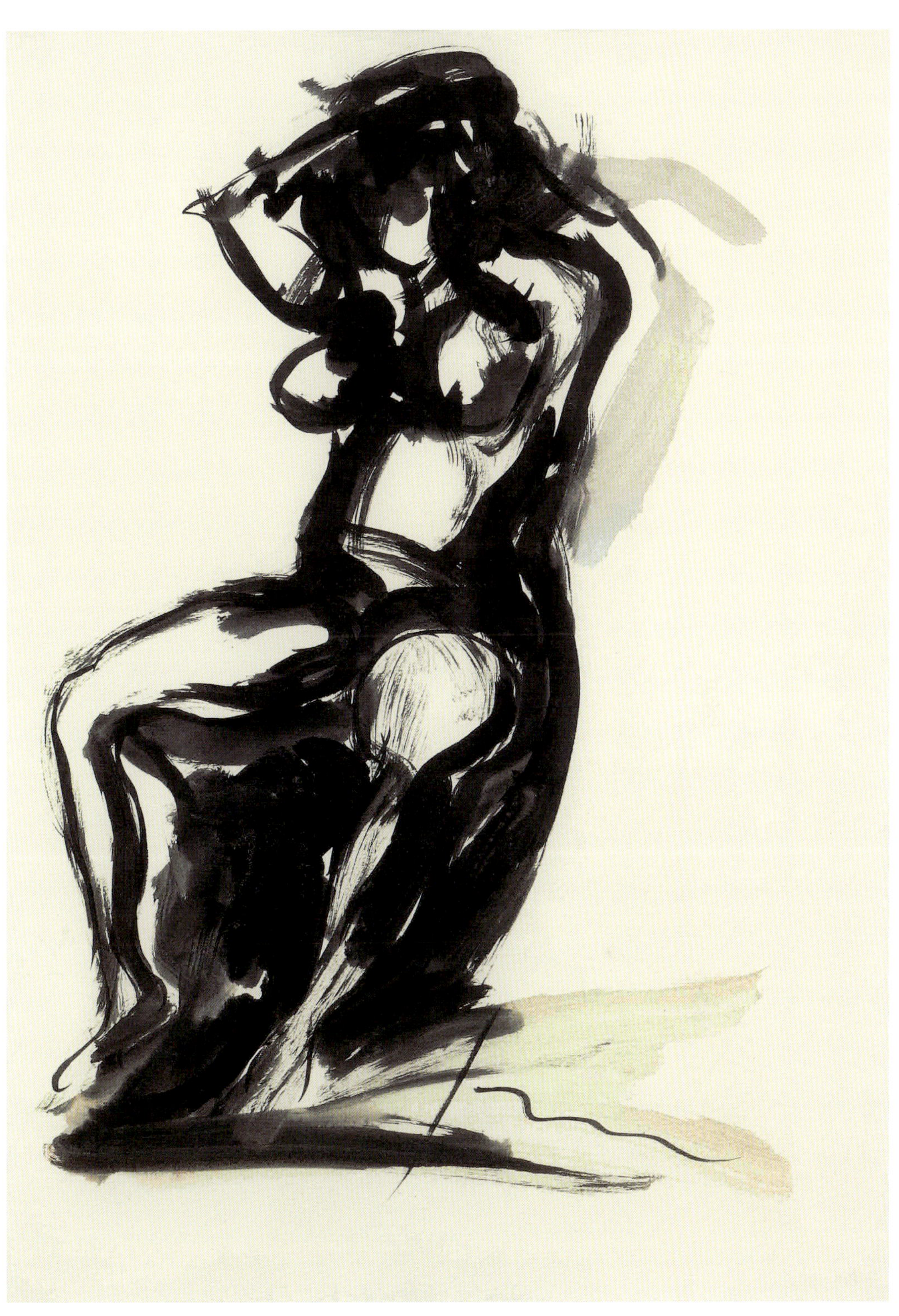

Nudo femminile
1960–64
china on paper
70 × 50 cm
60–64 DF 237
Private collection
Courtesy Gió Marconi
Milano

Nudo femminile
1960 – 64
china on paper
69,5 × 49,5 cm
60 – 64 DF 238
Private collection
Courtesy Gió Marconi
Milano

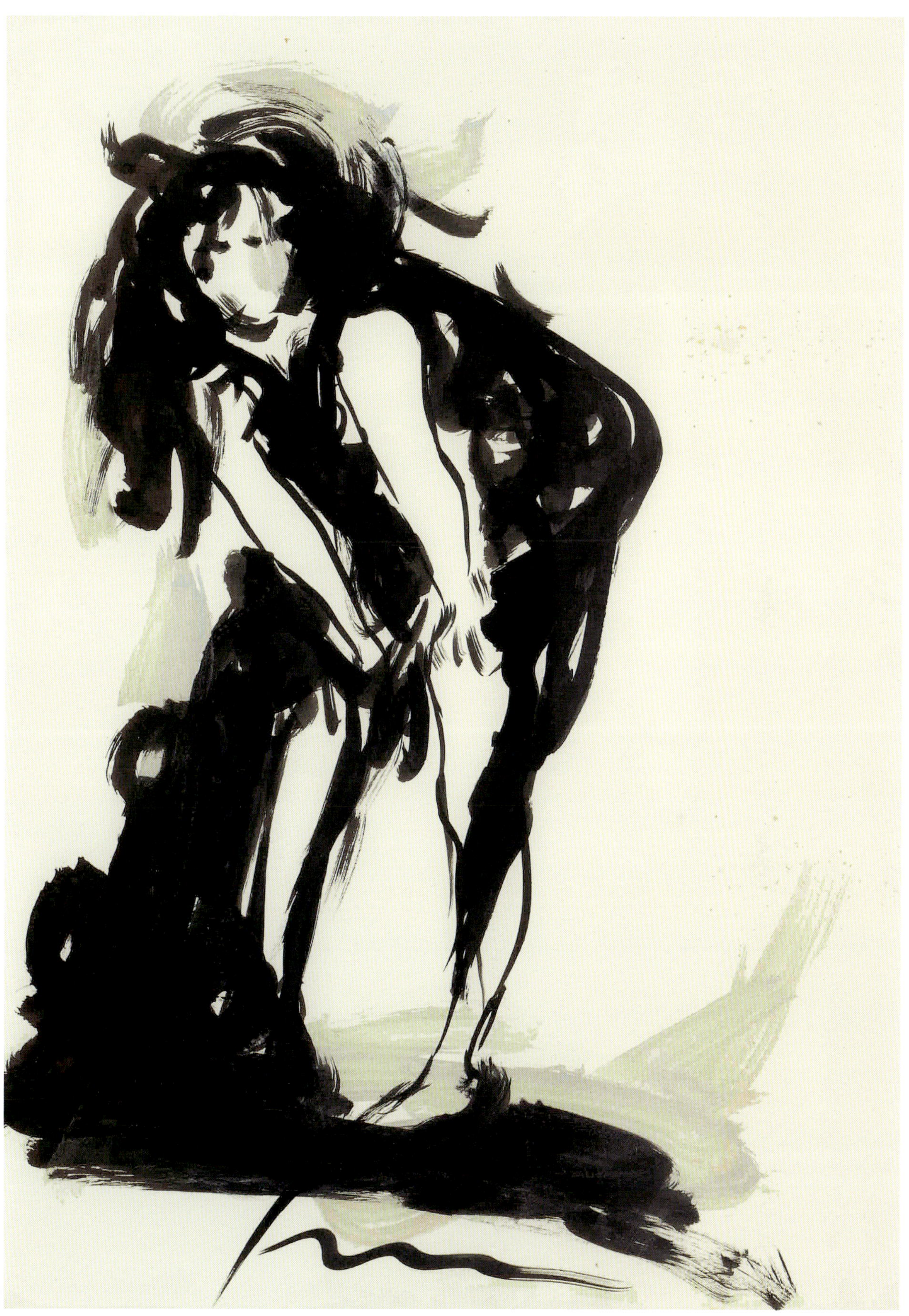

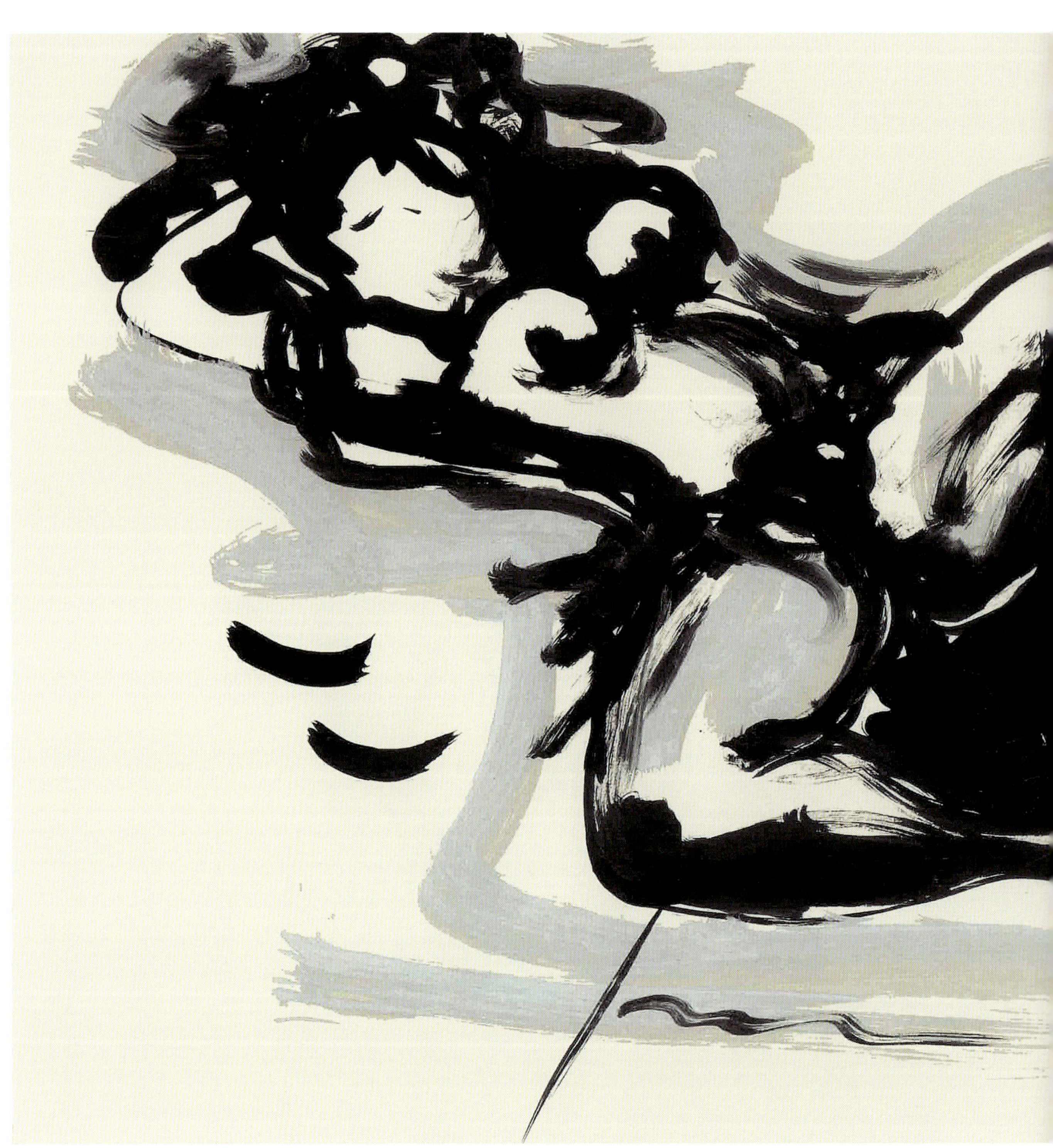

Concetto spaziale
1962
oil on canvas
44,6 × 57,4 cm
62 O 61
Private collection

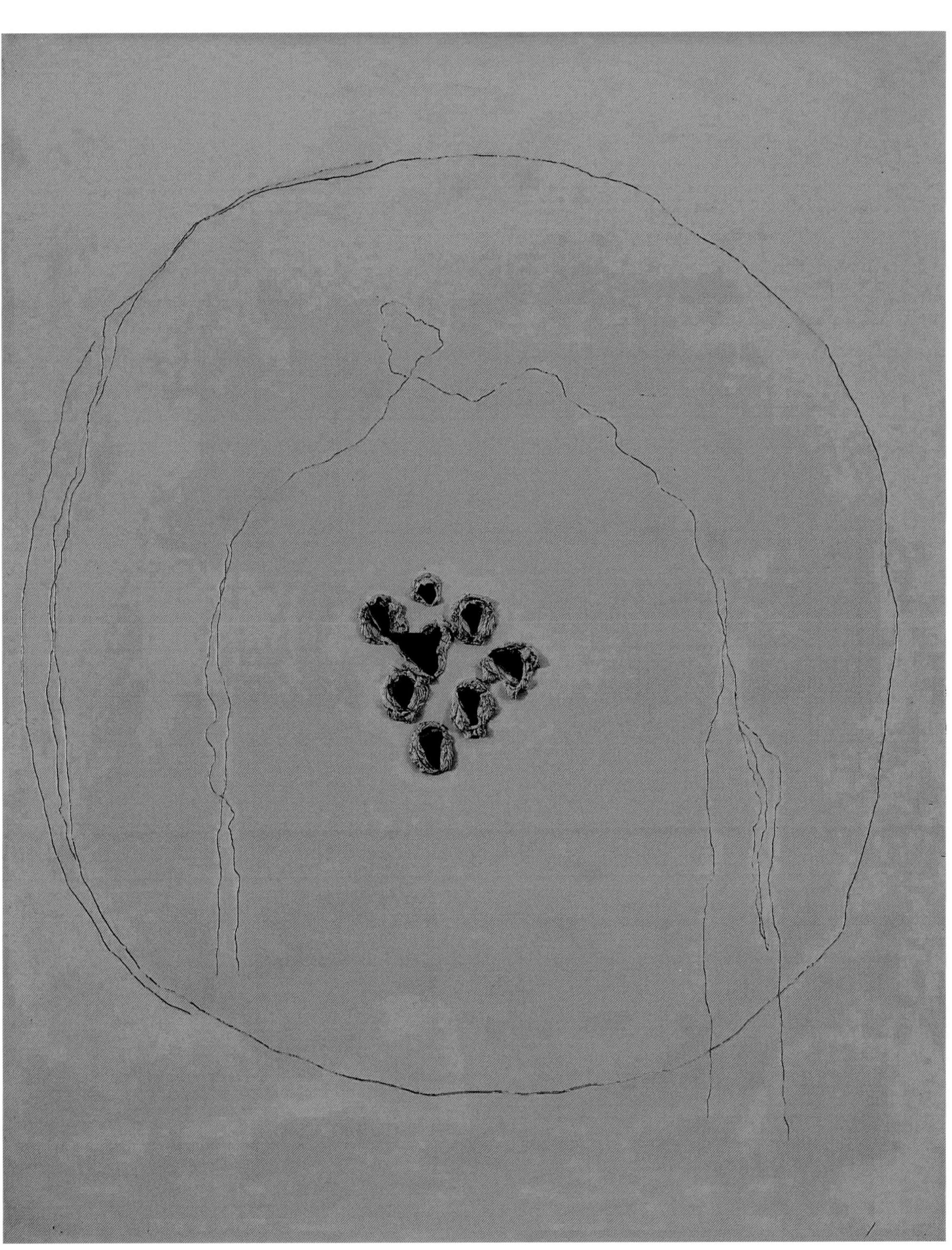

Ugo Mulas

Lucio Fontana, 1962
1962
Modern print. Gelatin silver print
on baryta paper
37 × 25 cm
Courtesy Robilant+Voena

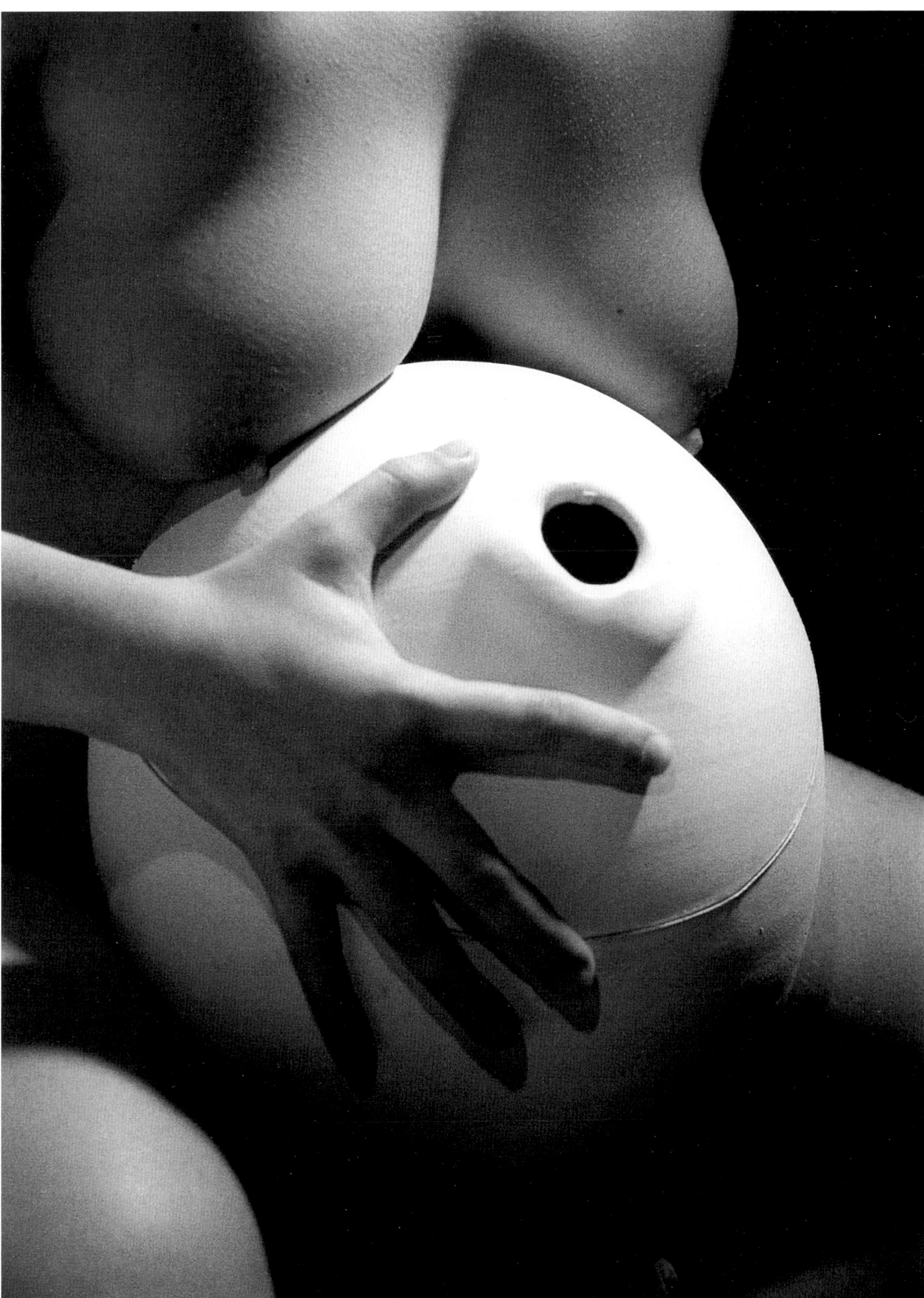

Scultura astratta
1934
reinforced concrete
58,5 × 43 × 12,5 cm
(work and base)
34 SC 6
Courtesy Fondazione
Lucio Fontana

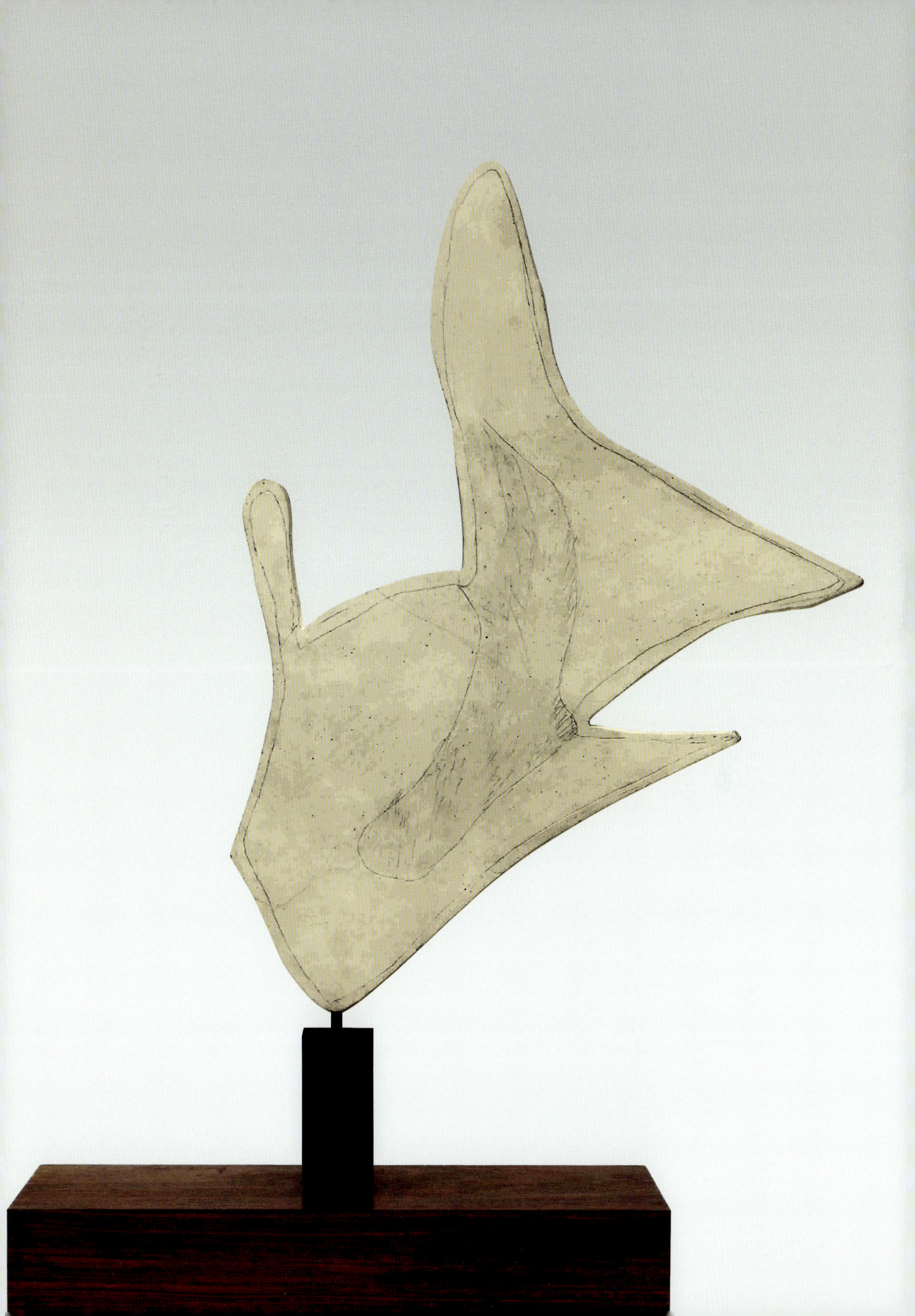

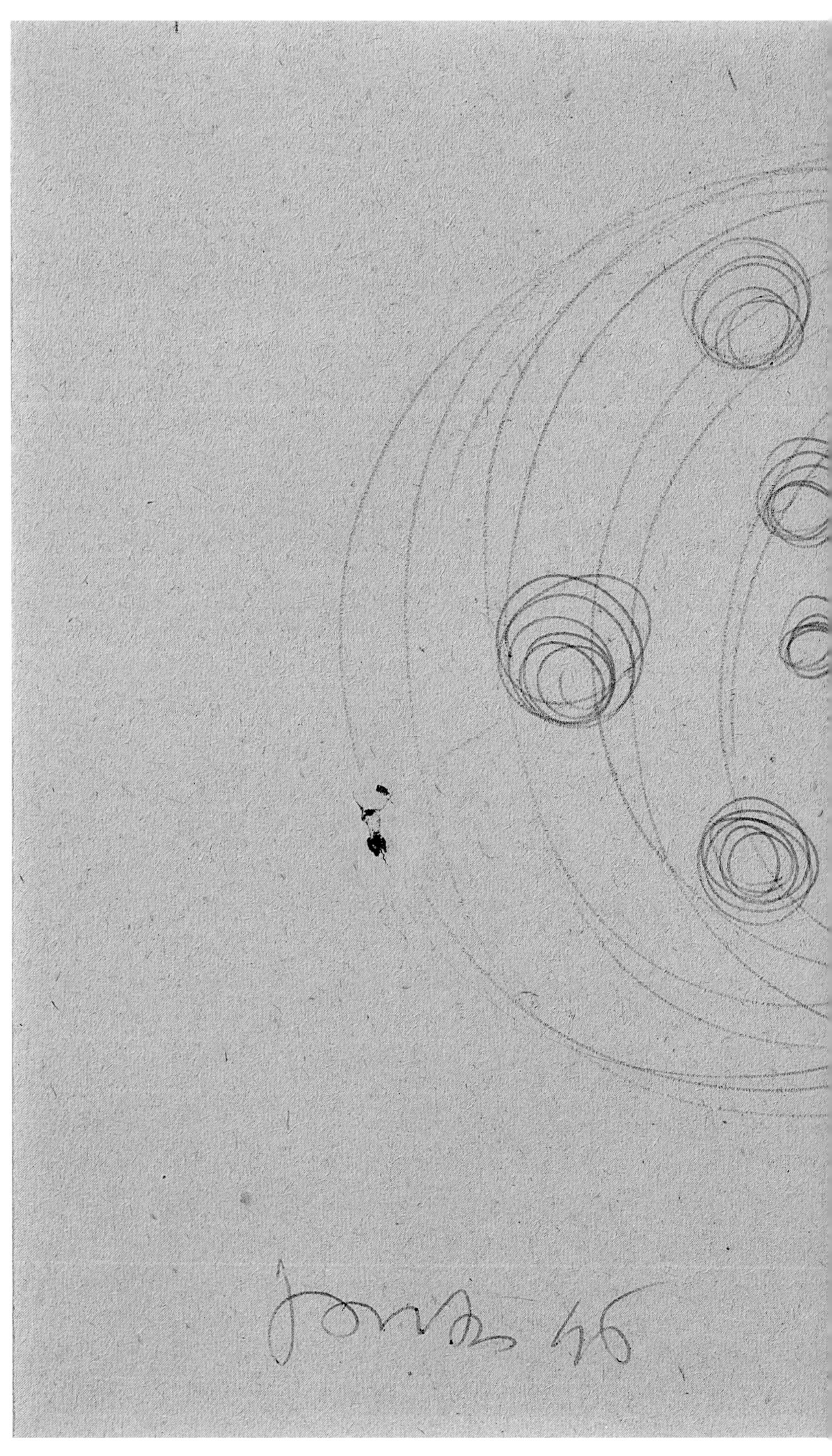

Concetto spaziale
1946
ballpoint pen on paper
20,2 × 27,5 cm
46 DSP 45
Courtesy Fondazione
Lucio Fontana

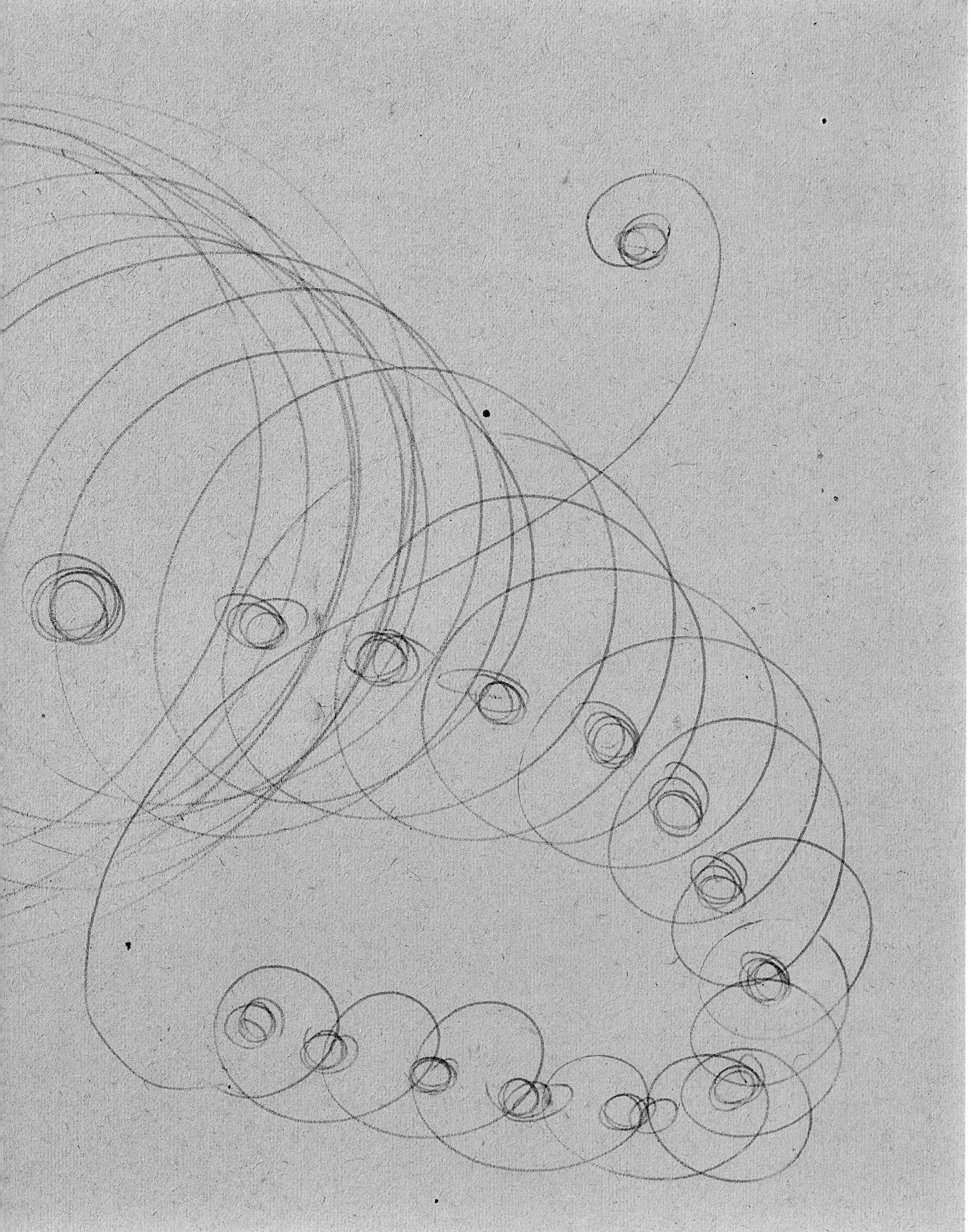

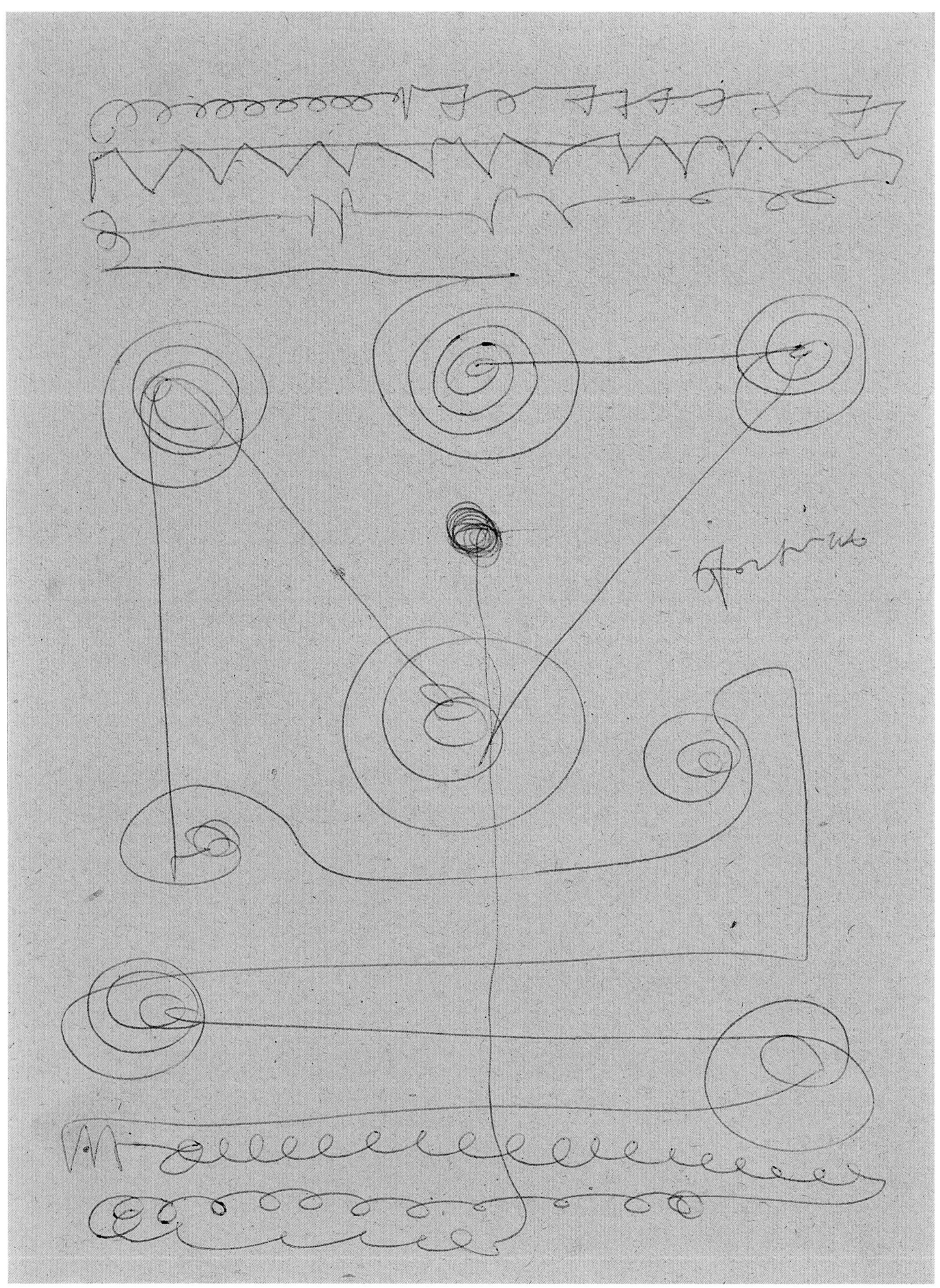

Concetto spaziale
1946
ballpoint pen on paper
27,5 × 22 cm
46 DSP 44
Courtesy Fondazione
Lucio Fontana

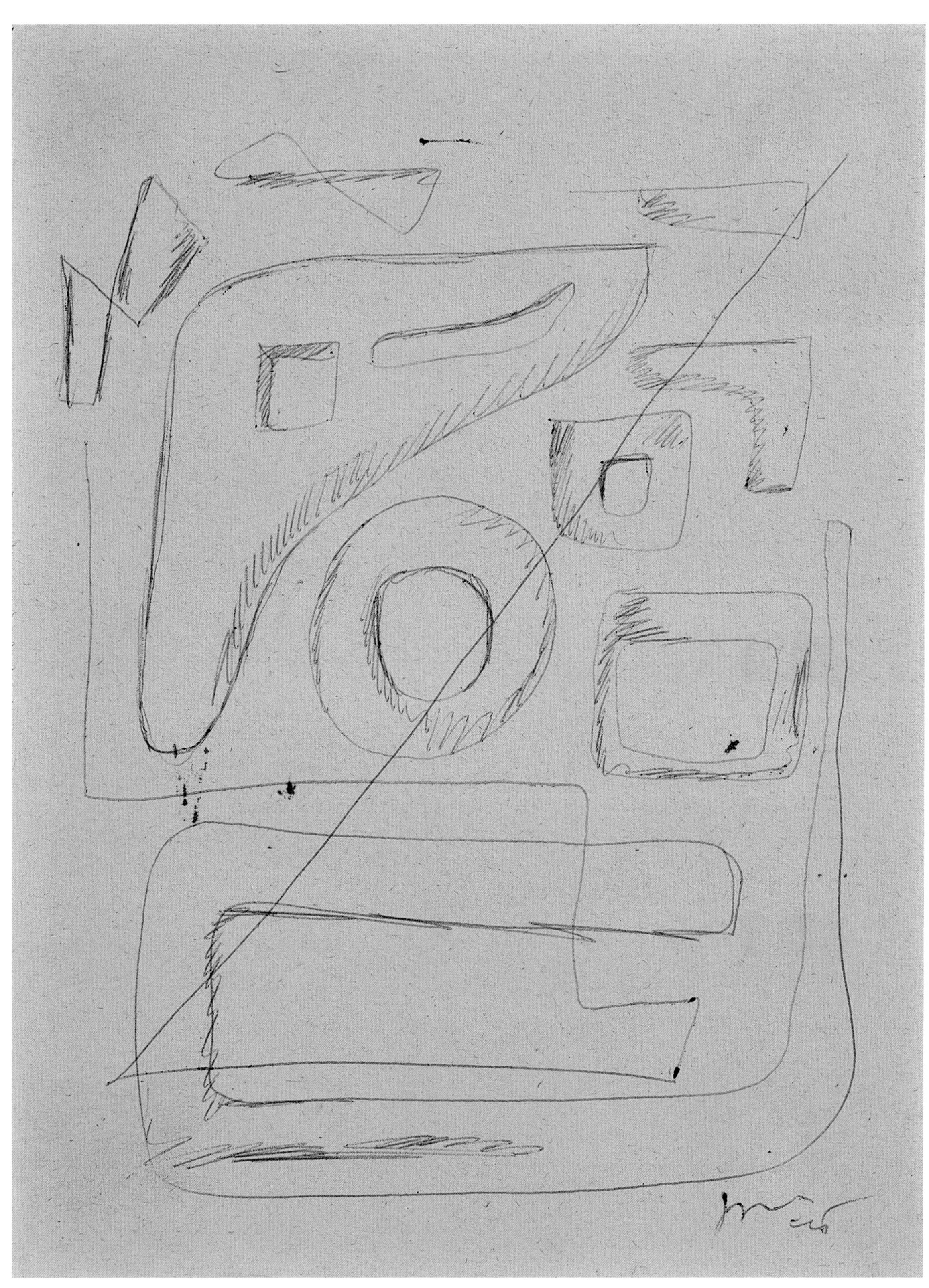

Concetto spaziale
1946
ballpoint pen on paper
27,5 × 22 cm
46 DSP 37
Courtesy Fondazione
Lucio Fontana

Concetto spaziale
1946
ballpoint pen on paper
27,5 × 22 cm
46 DSP 32
Courtesy Fondazione
Lucio Fontana

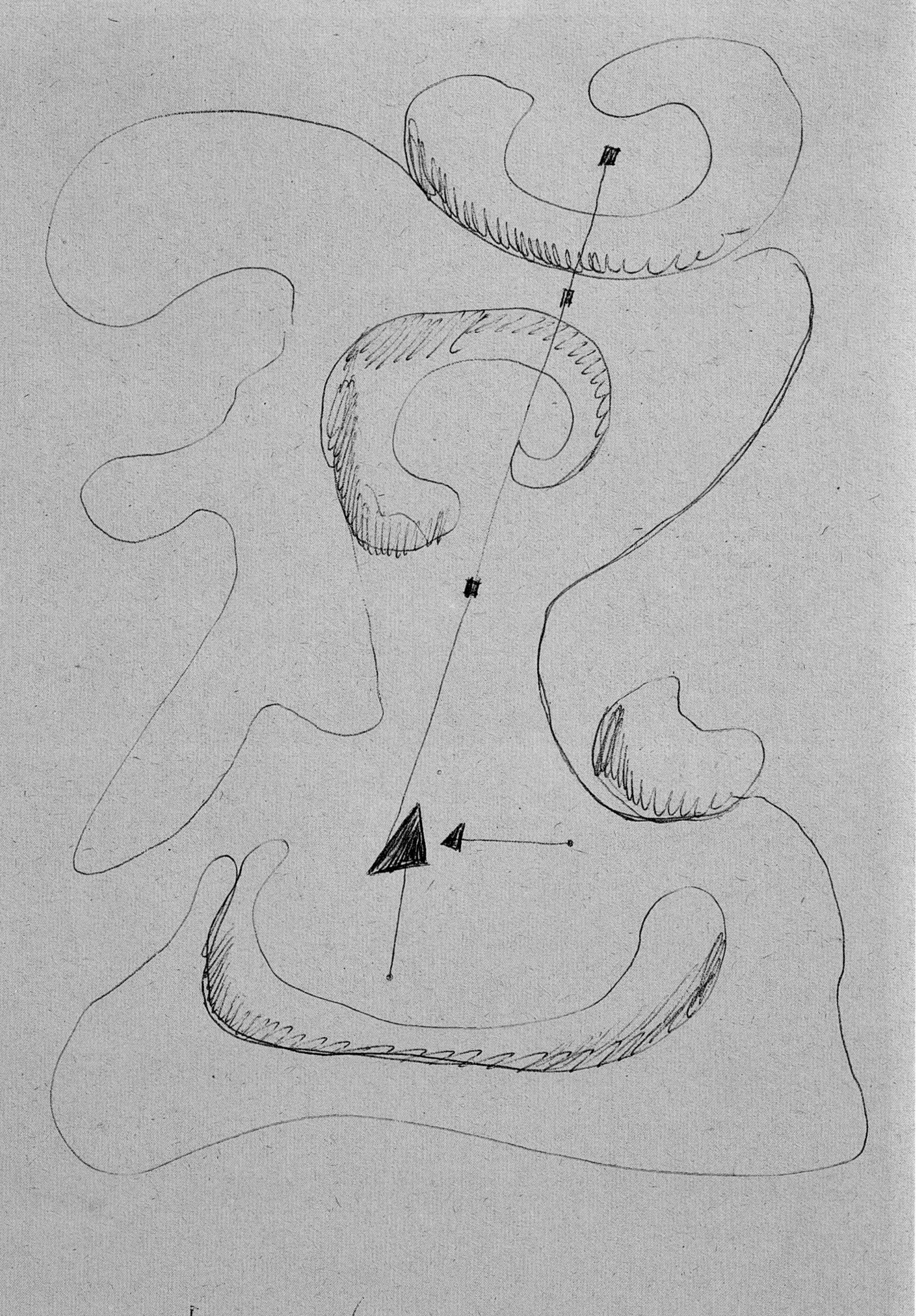

Concetto spaziale
1946
ballpoint pen on paper
27,5 × 22 cm
46 DSP 33
Courtesy Fondazione
Lucio Fontana

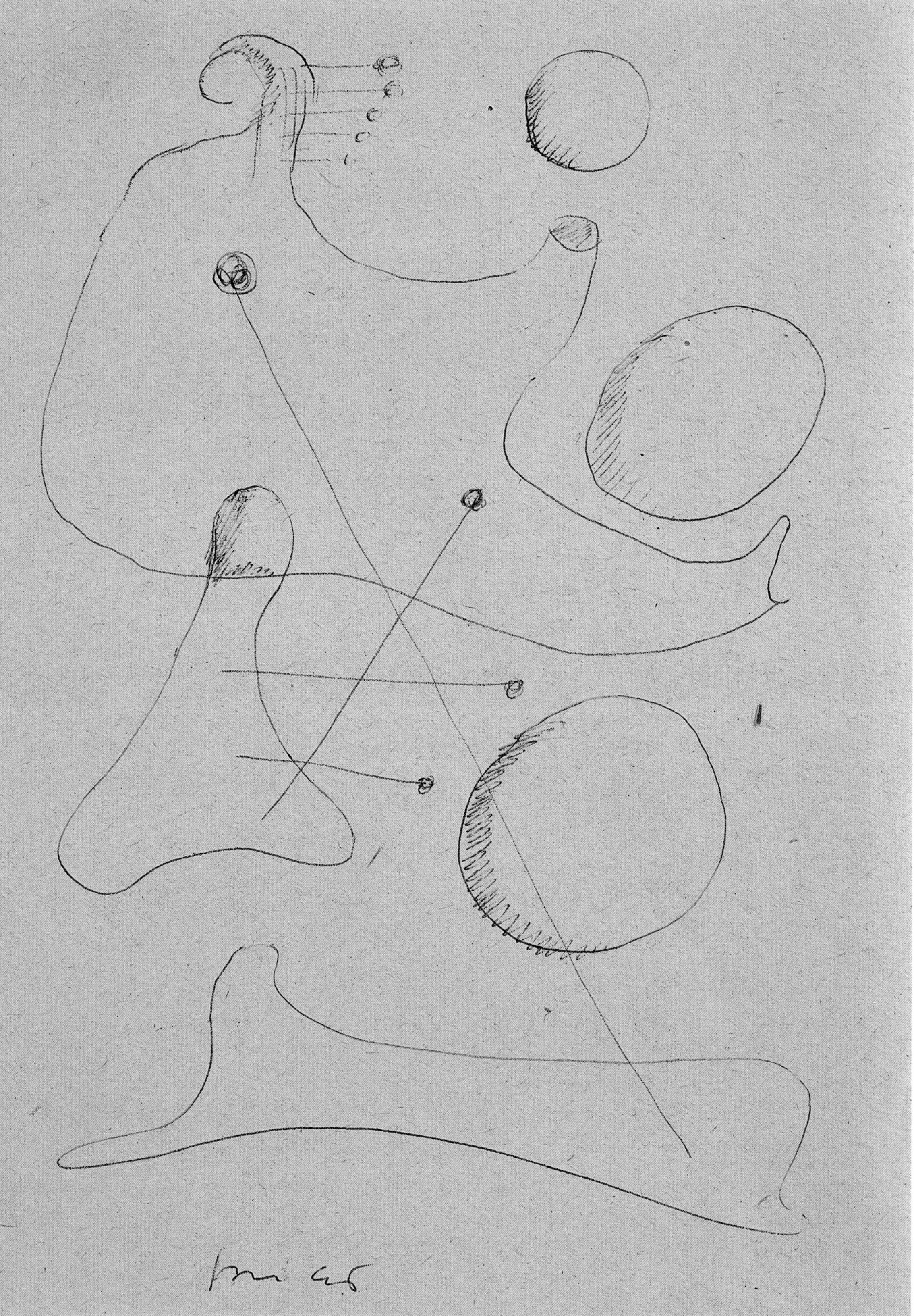

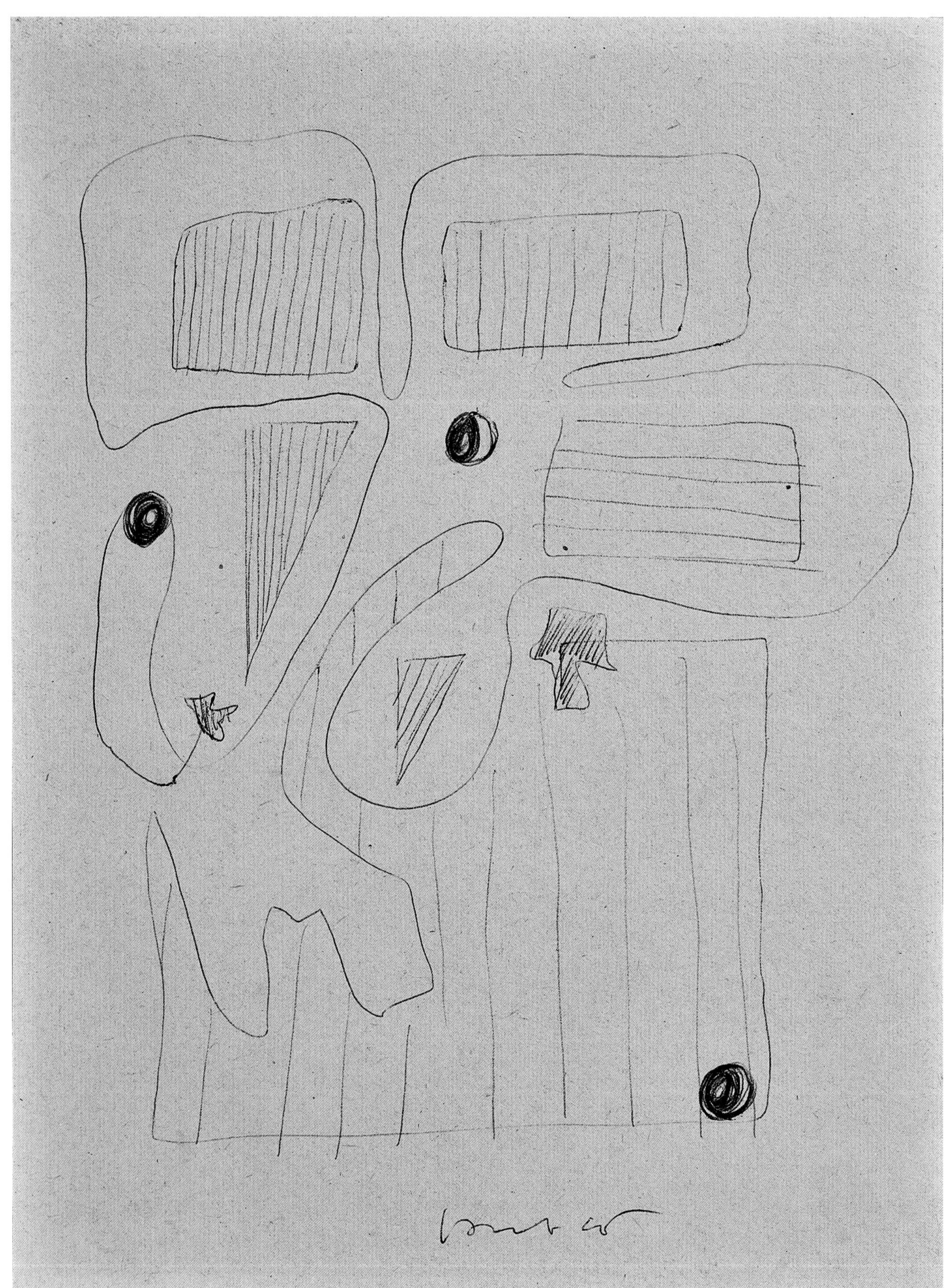

Concetto spaziale
1946
ballpoint pen on paper
27,5 × 22 cm
46 DSP 31
Courtesy Fondazione
Lucio Fontana

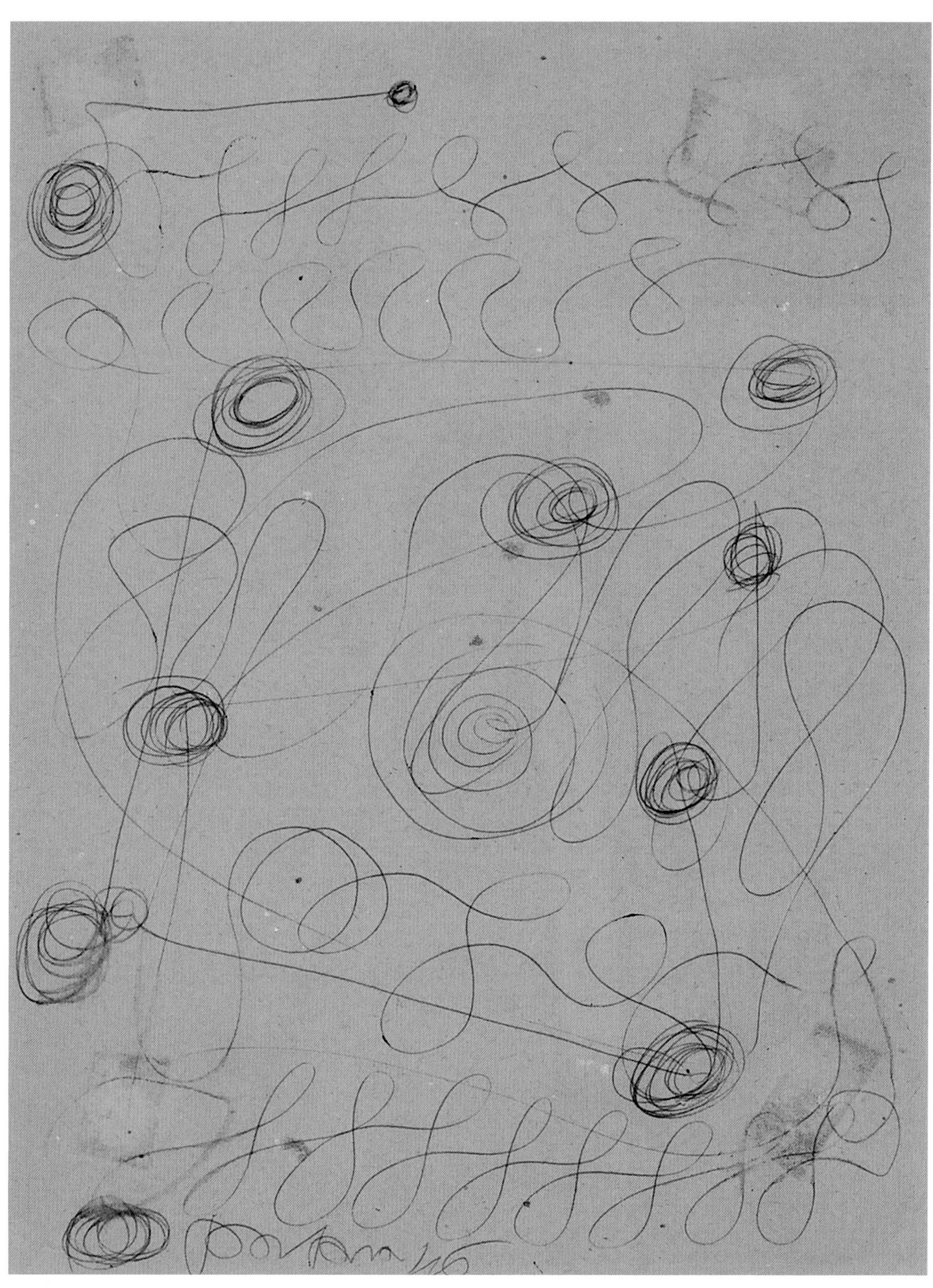

Concetto spaziale
1946
ballpoint pen on paper
27,5 × 20,5 cm
46 DSP 50
Private collection
Courtesy Gió Marconi
Milano

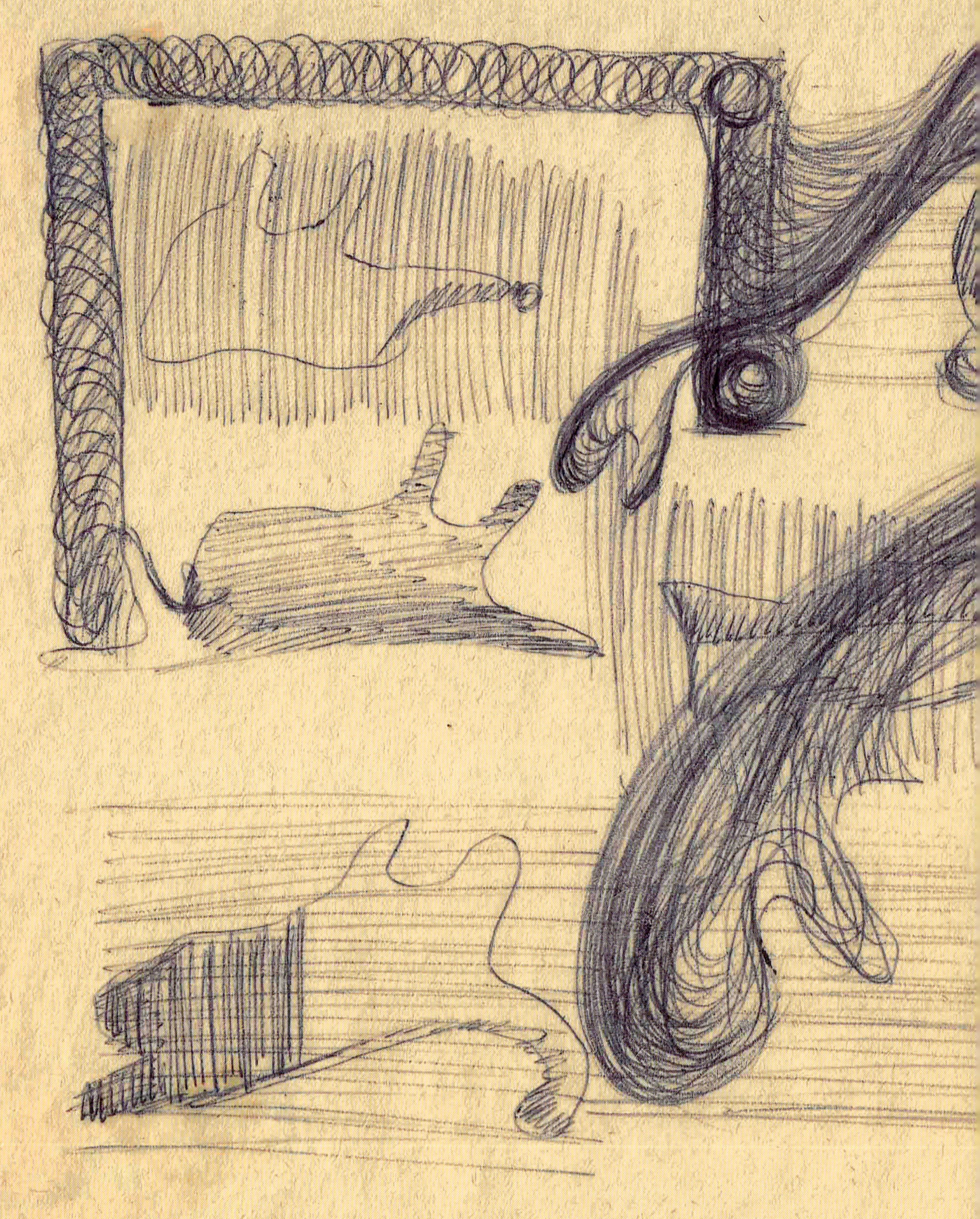

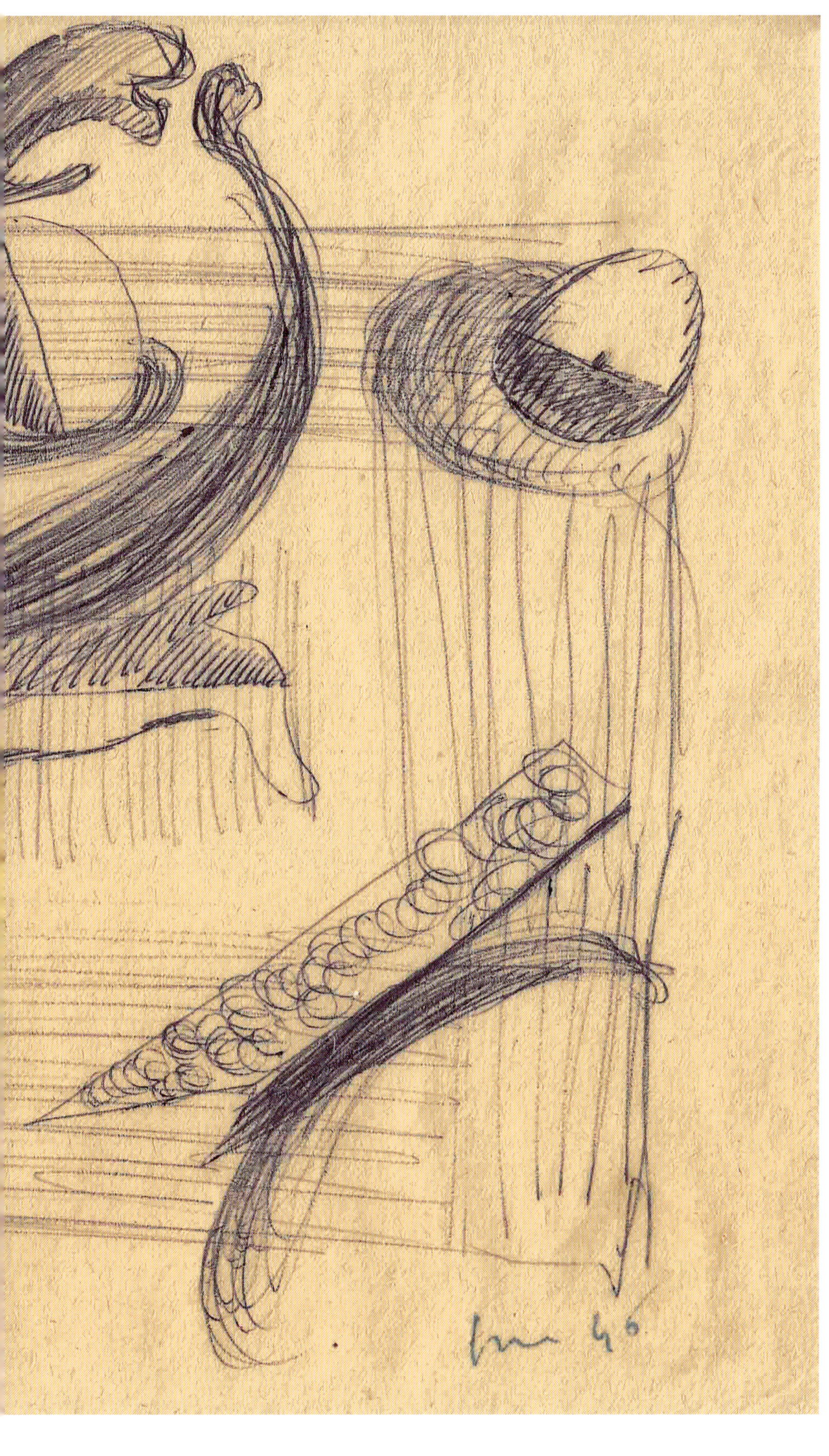

Concetto spaziale
1946
ballpoint pen on paper
20,2 × 27,4 cm
46 DSP 35
Courtesy Fondazione
Lucio Fontana

Ambiente spaziale
1948
gouache on paper
37,7 × 22,5 cm
48 DCSA 42
Courtesy Fondazione
Lucio Fontana

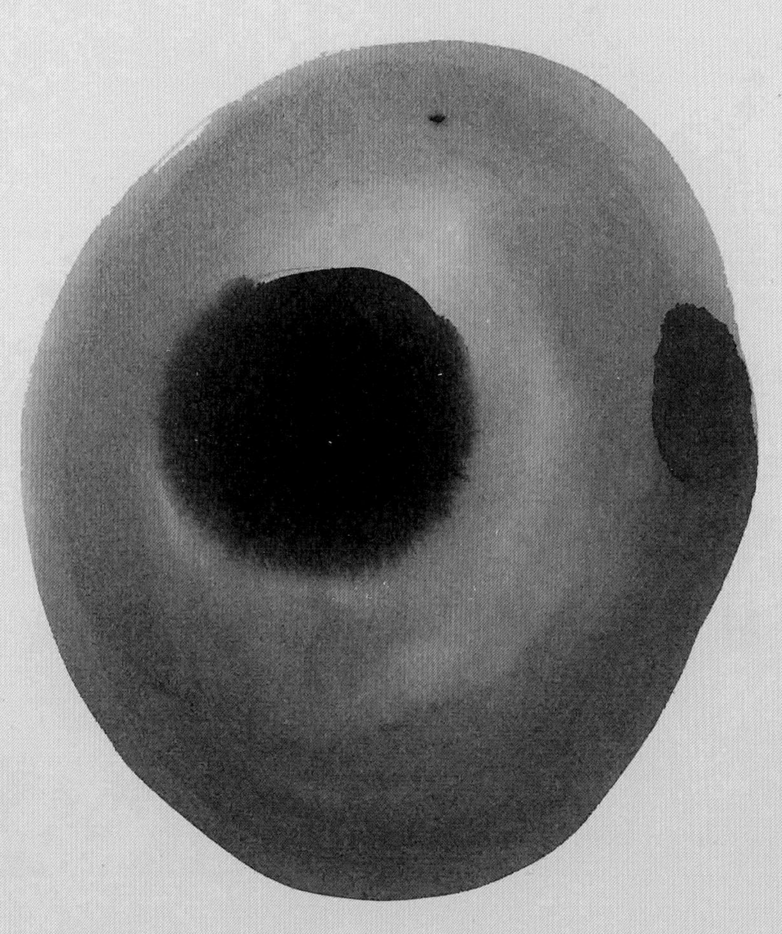

Ambiente spaziale
1949
china on paper
46,5 × 37,5 cm
49 DCSA 3
Courtesy Fondazione
Lucio Fontana

AMBIENTE SPAZIALE

di LUCIO FONTANA

Ambiente spaziale
1949
gouache on paper
44,5 × 37 cm
49 DCSA 28
Private collection
Courtesy Gió Marconi
Milano

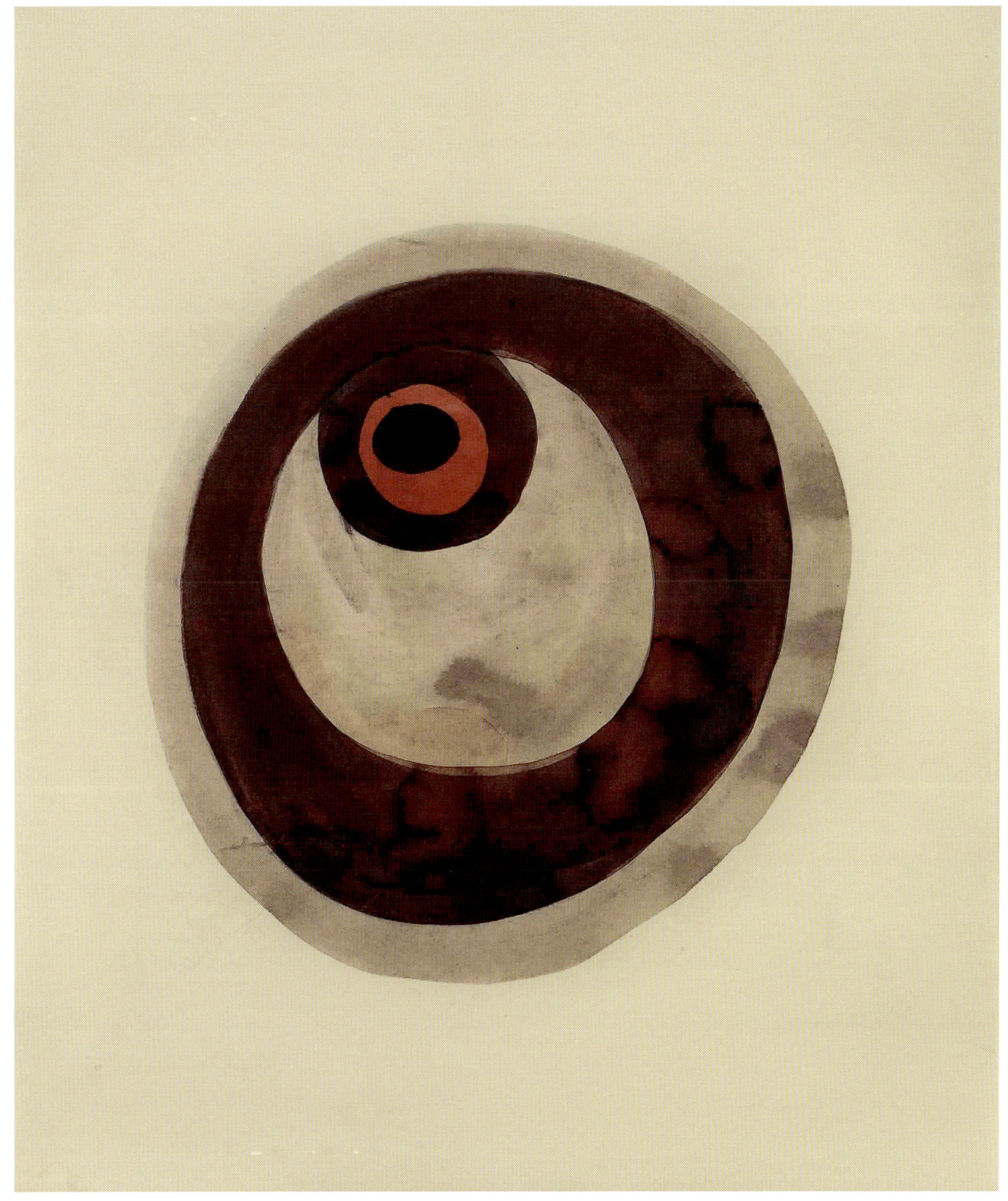

Ambiente spaziale
1949
gouache on paper
30 × 23 cm
49 DCSA 5
Courtesy Fondazione
Lucio Fontana

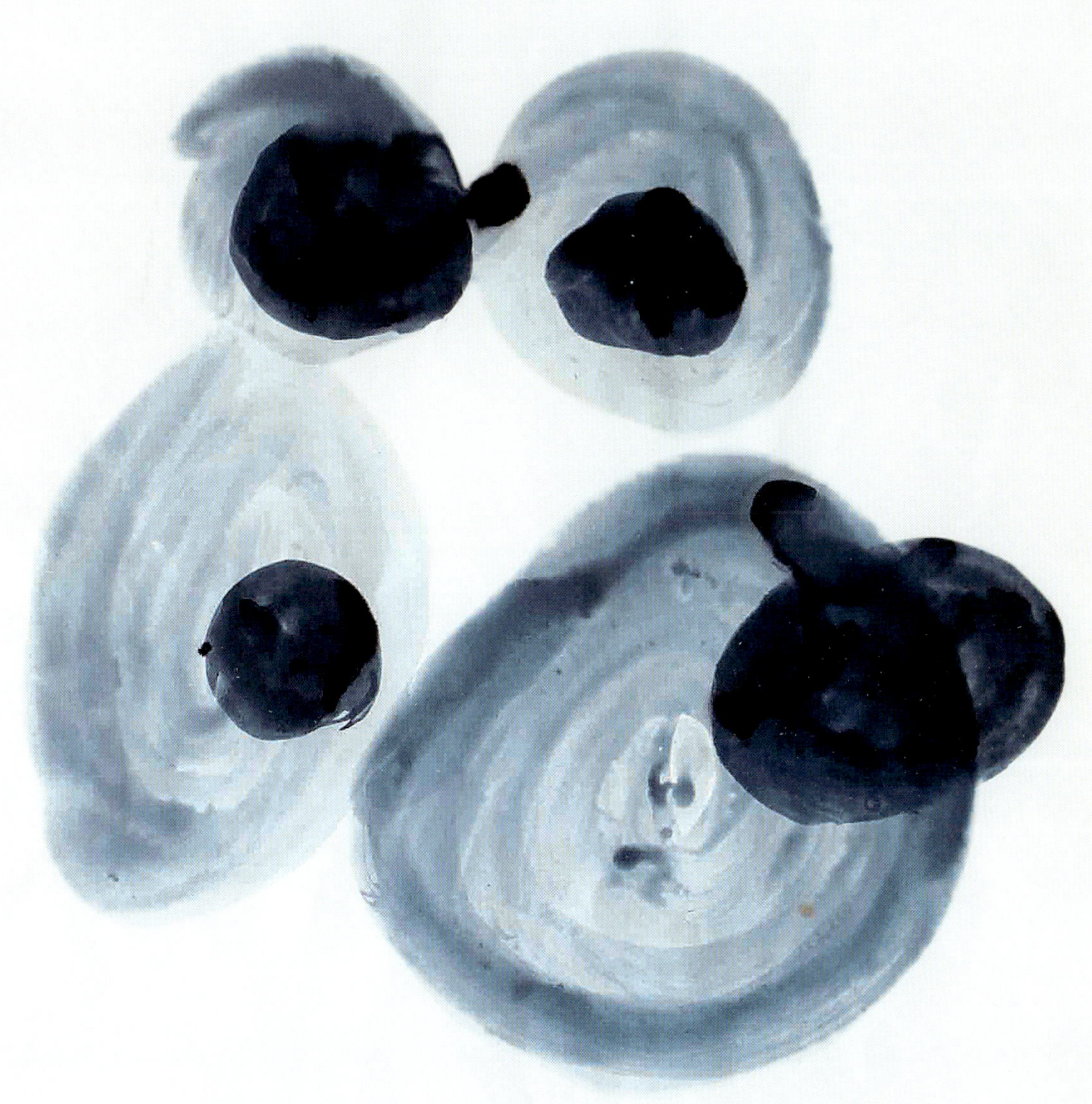

Ambiente spaziale
1949
gouache on paper
30 × 23 cm
49 DCSA 4
Courtesy Fondazione
Lucio Fontana

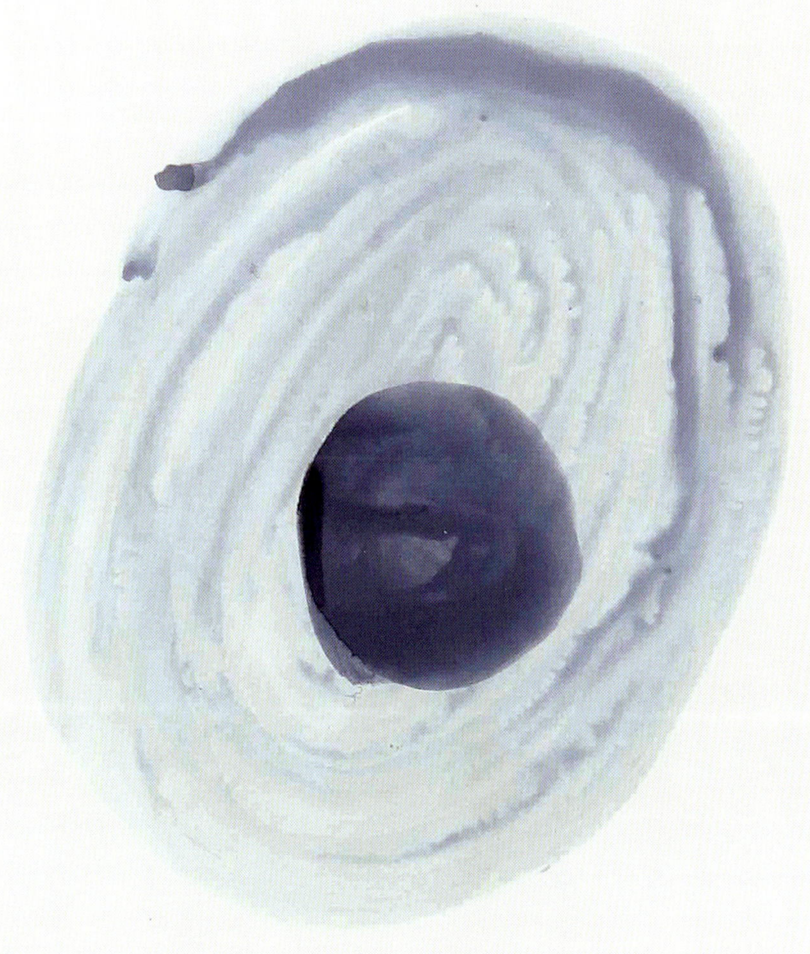

Concetto spaziale
1950
gouache on canvas paper
48 × 33 cm
50 DCSA 10
Courtesy Fondazione
Lucio Fontana

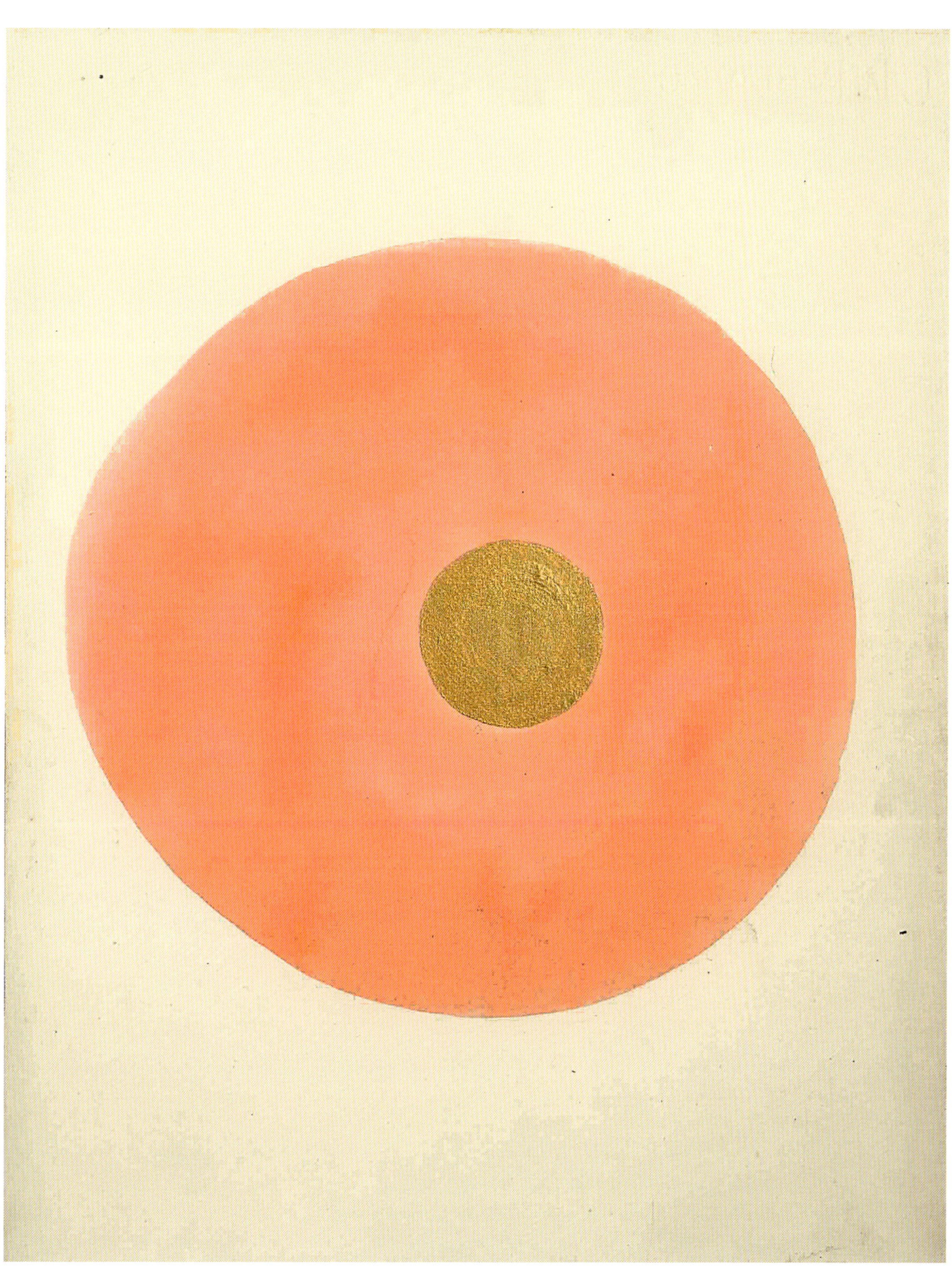

Concetto spaziale
1950
gouache on canvas paper
48 × 33 cm
50 DCSA 9
Courtesy Fondazione
Lucio Fontana

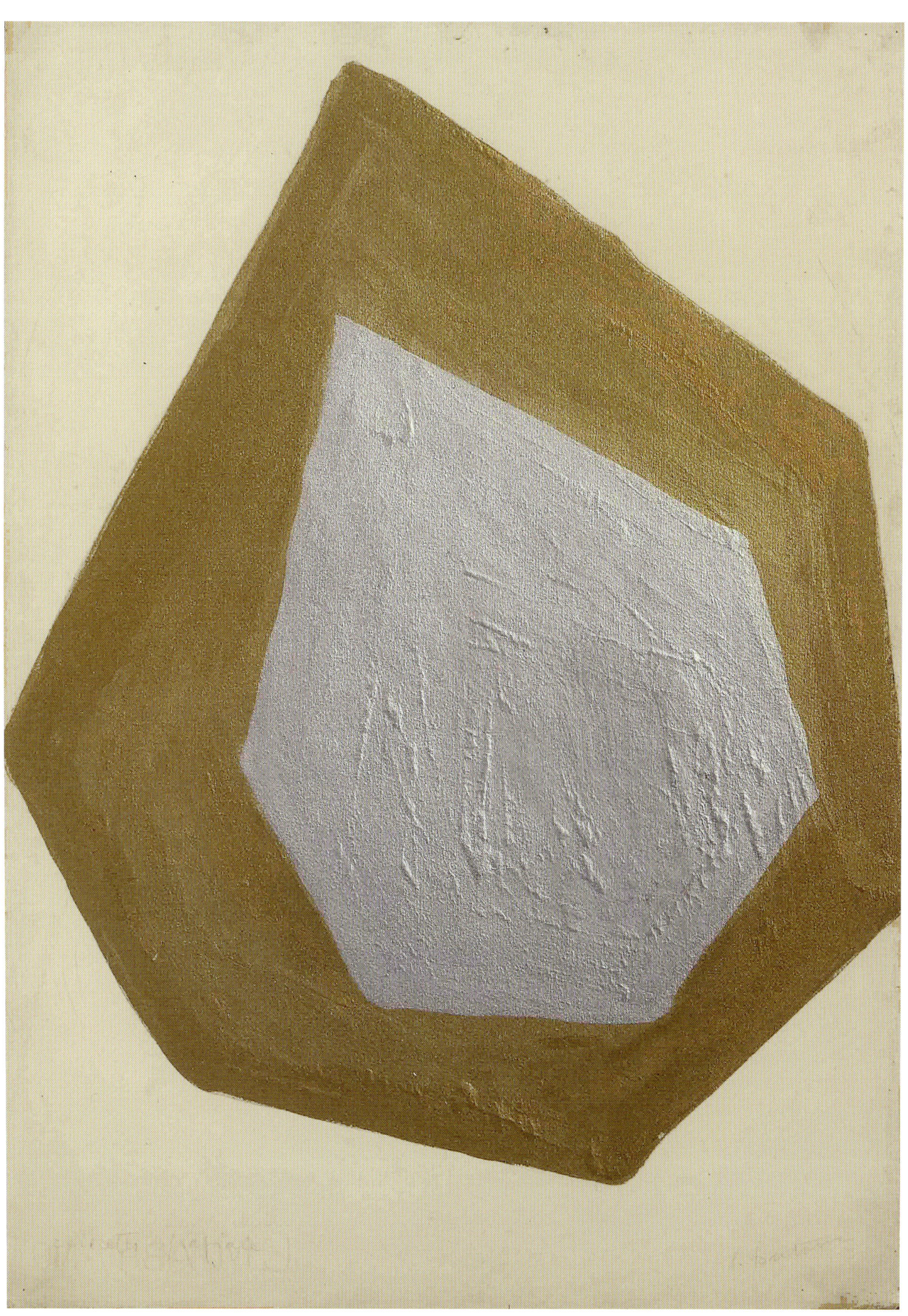

Concetto spaziale
1950
gouache on canvas paper
48 × 33 cm
50 DCSA 7
Courtesy Fondazione
Lucio Fontana

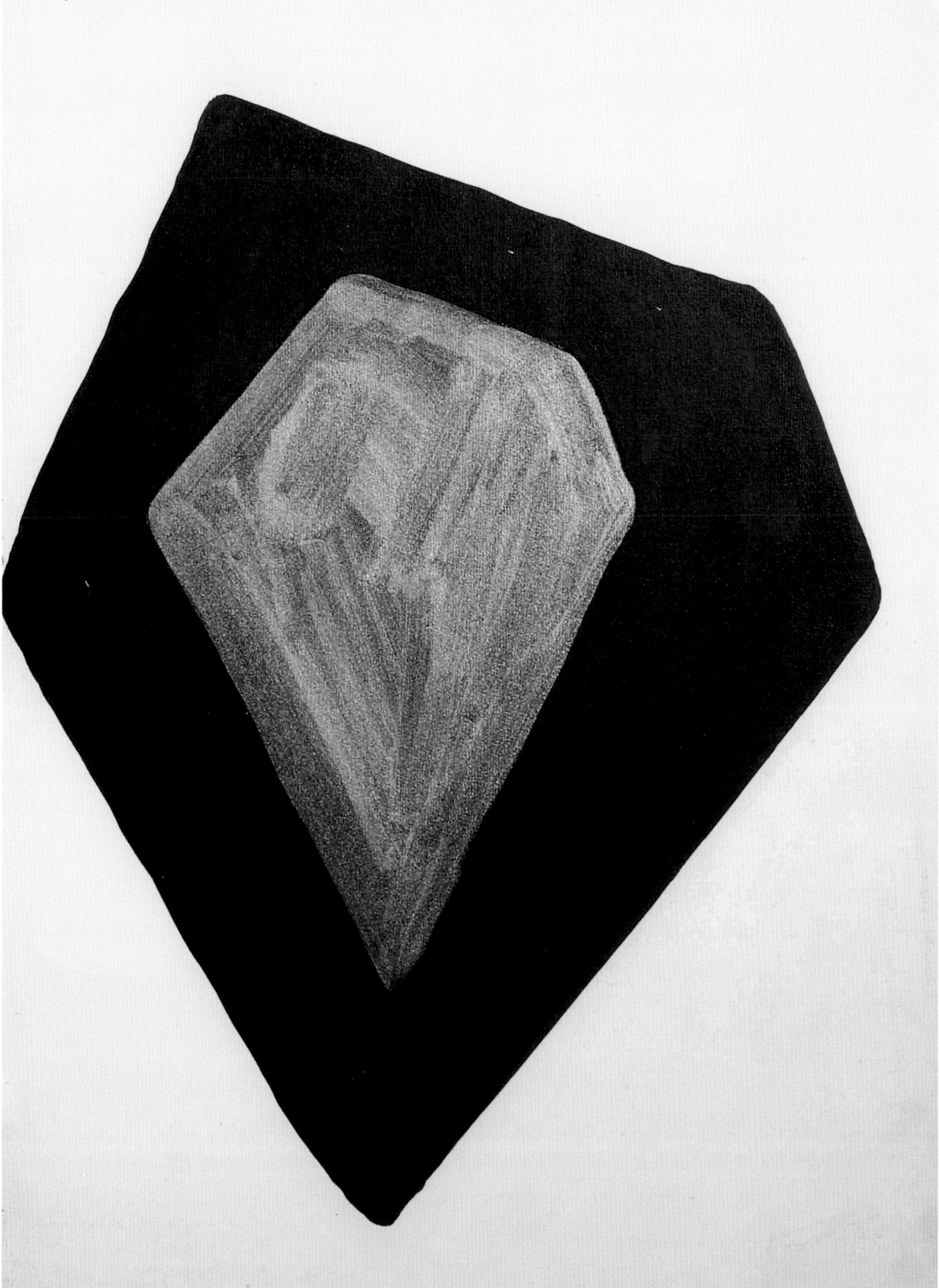

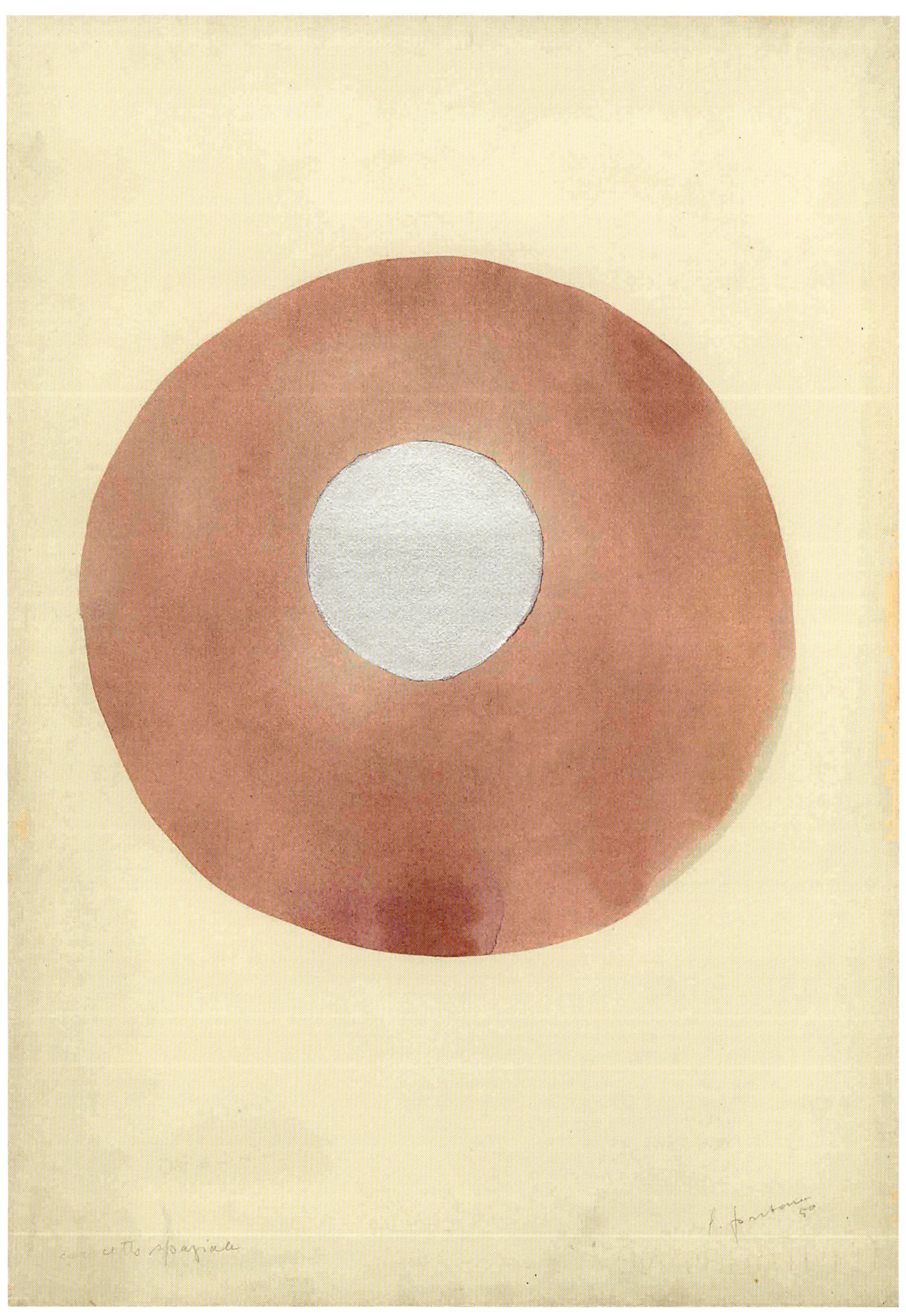

Concetto spaziale
1950
gouache on canvas paper
48 × 33 cm
50 DCSA 3
Courtesy Fondazione
Lucio Fontana

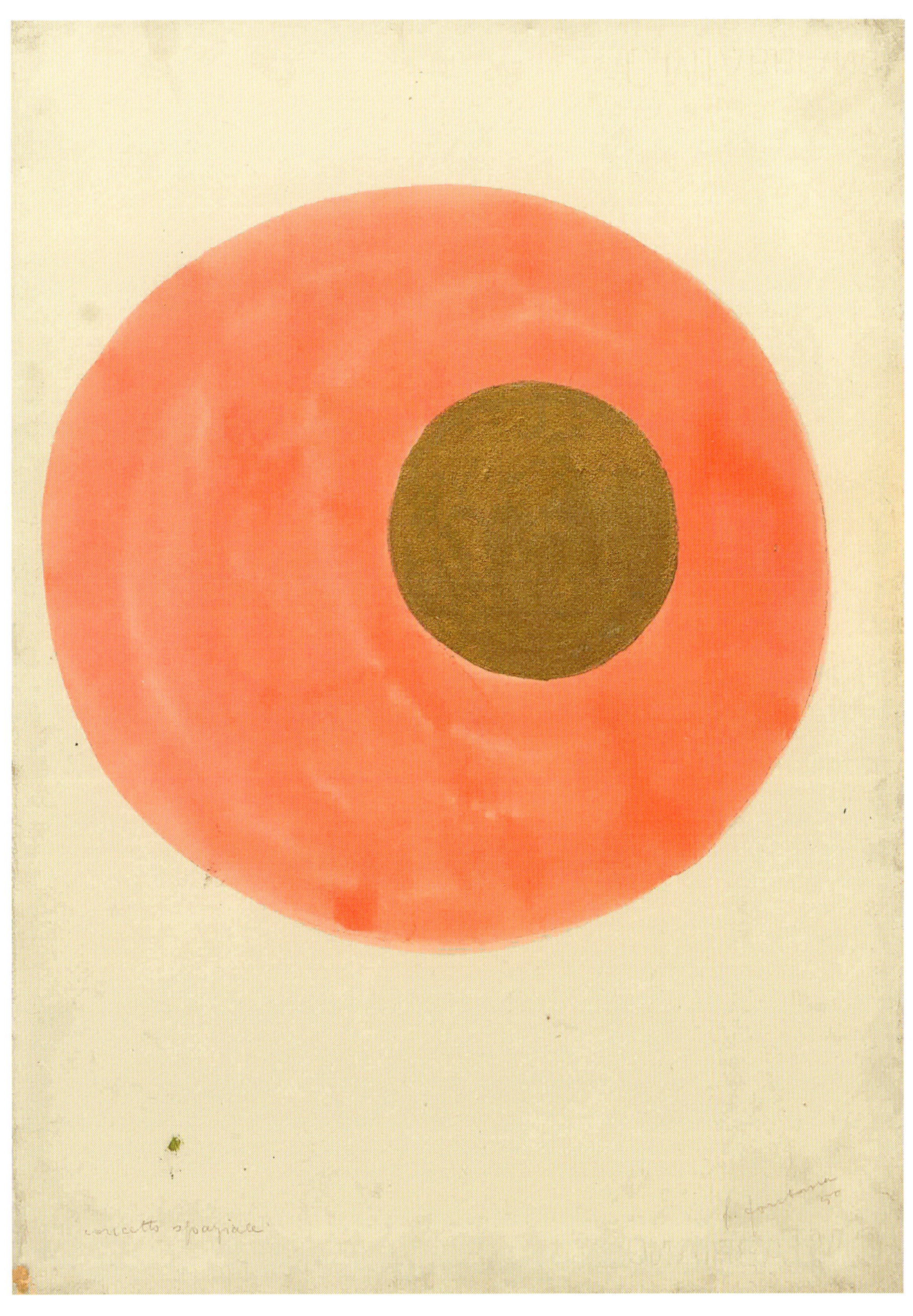

Concetto spaziale
1950
gouache on canvas paper
48 × 33 cm
50 DCSA 2
Courtesy Fondazione
Lucio Fontana

Concetto spaziale
1950
ink on paper
29 × 21,3 cm
50 DSP 5
Courtesy Fondazione
Lucio Fontana

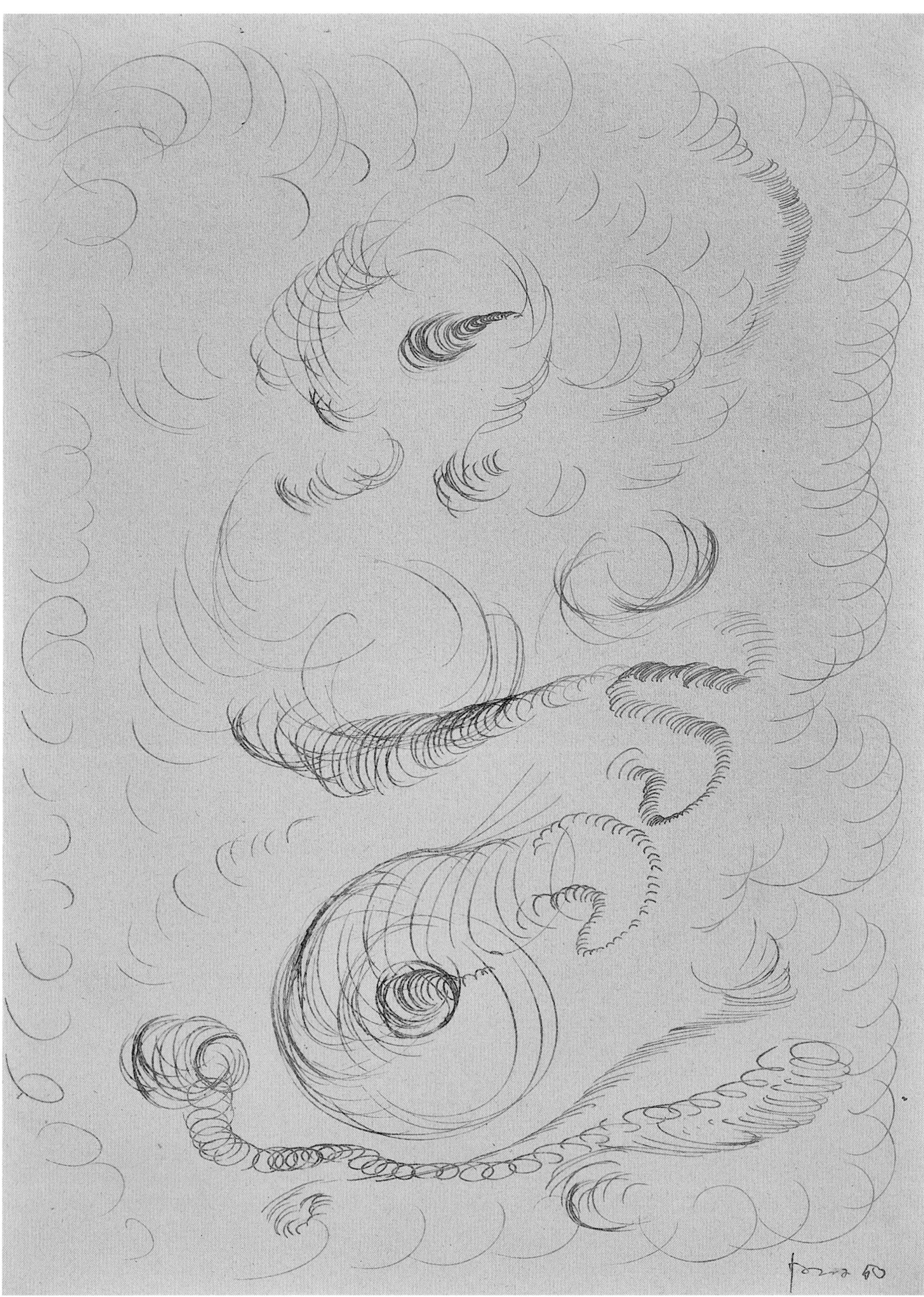

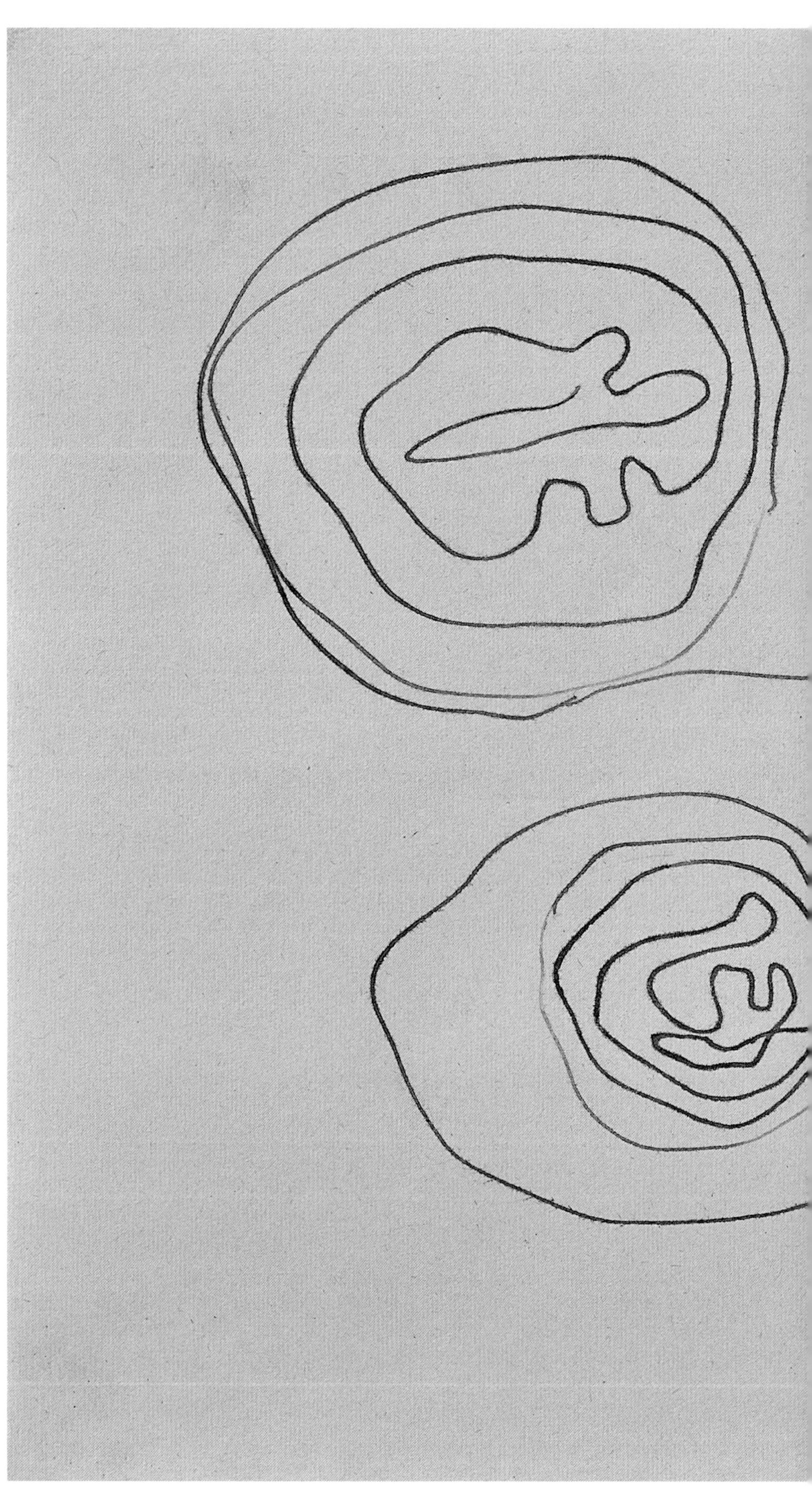

Concetto spaziale
1950
china on paper
21 × 29,5 cm
50 DSP 11
Courtesy Fondazione
Lucio Fontana

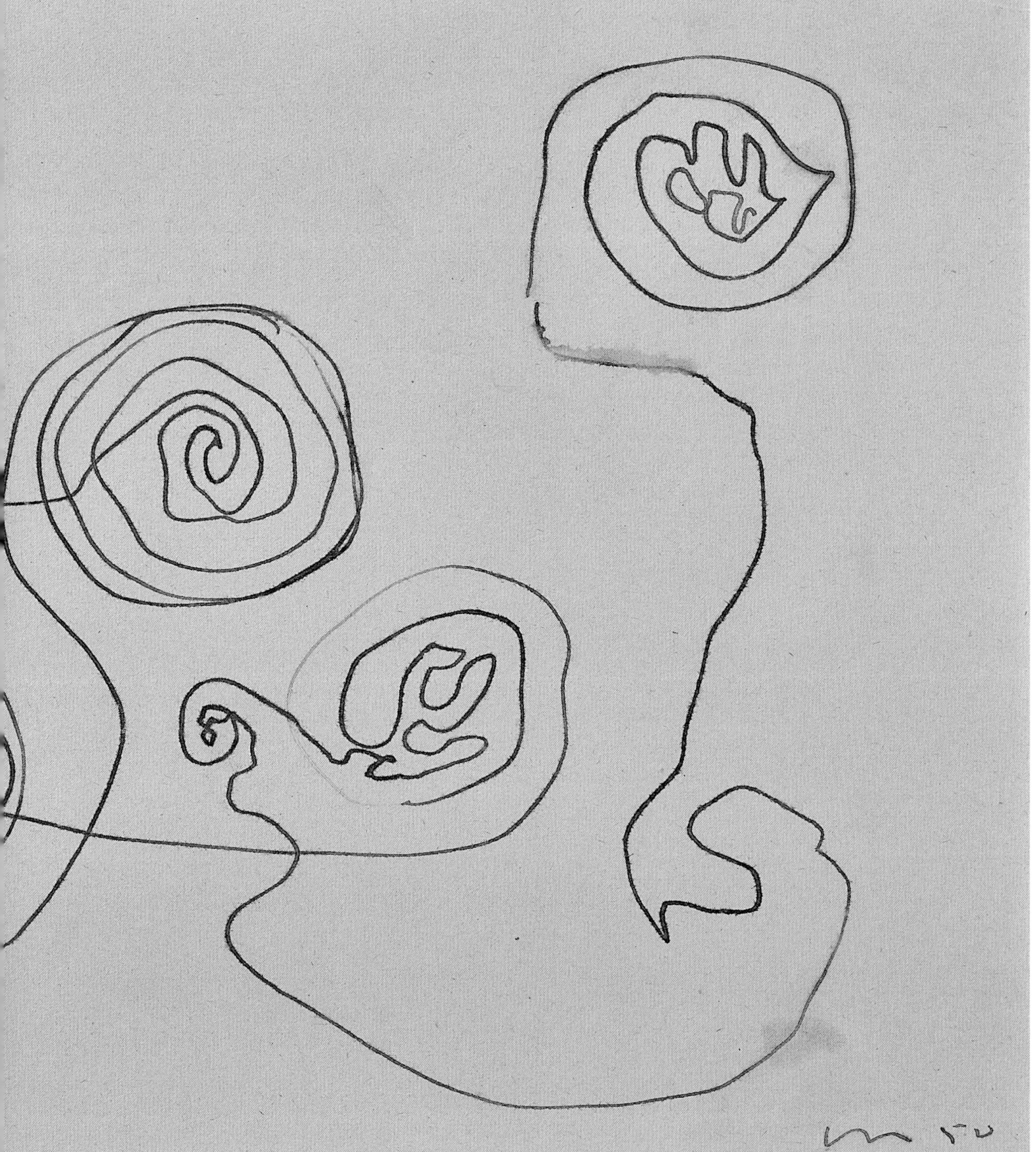

Concetto spaziale
1950
holes on tin
74,5 × 64 cm
50 B 9
Courtesy Fondazione
Lucio Fontana

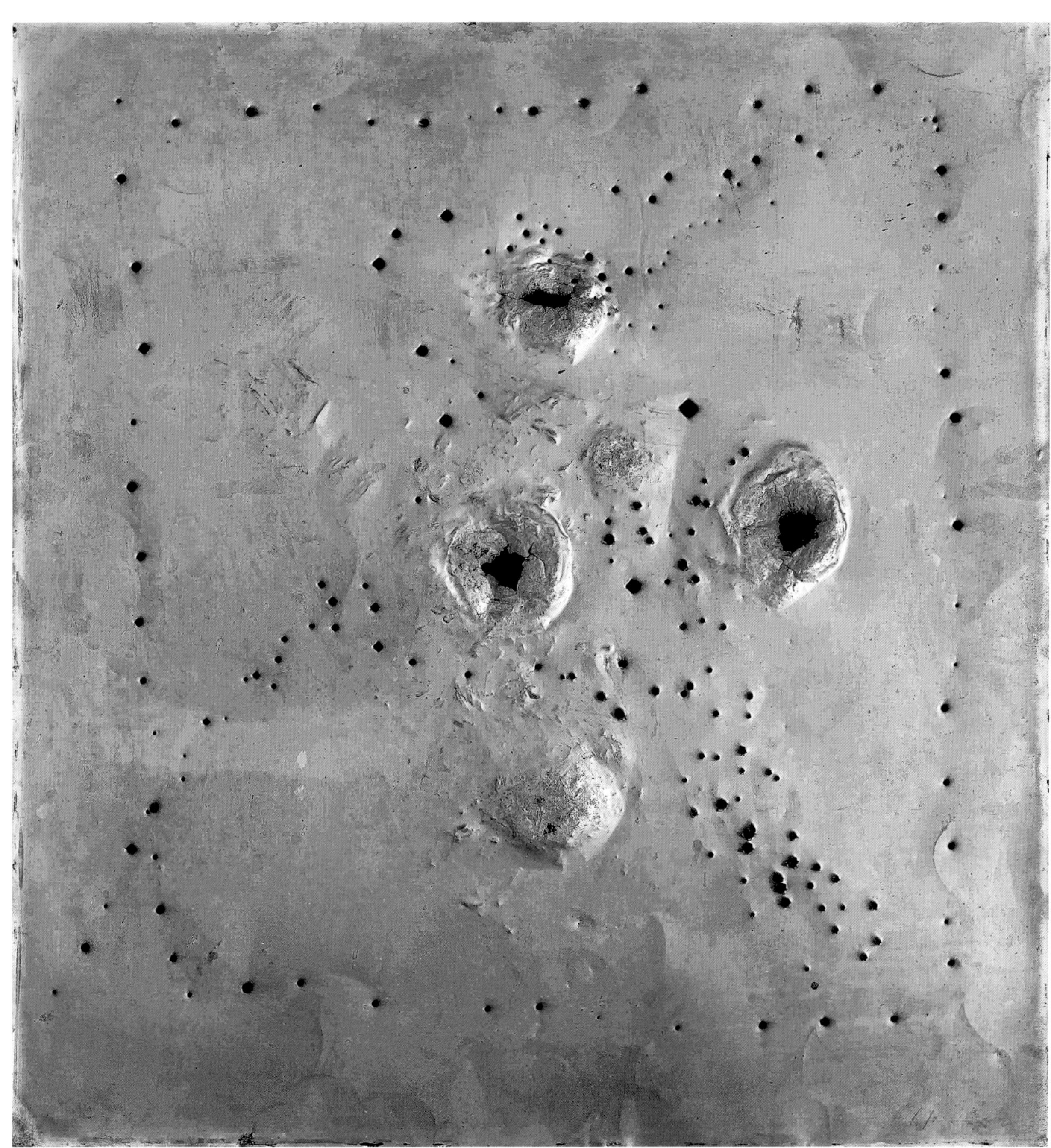

Concetto spaziale
1951
oil, sand and holes on canvas
60 × 59 cm
51 B 17
Courtesy Fondazione
Lucio Fontana

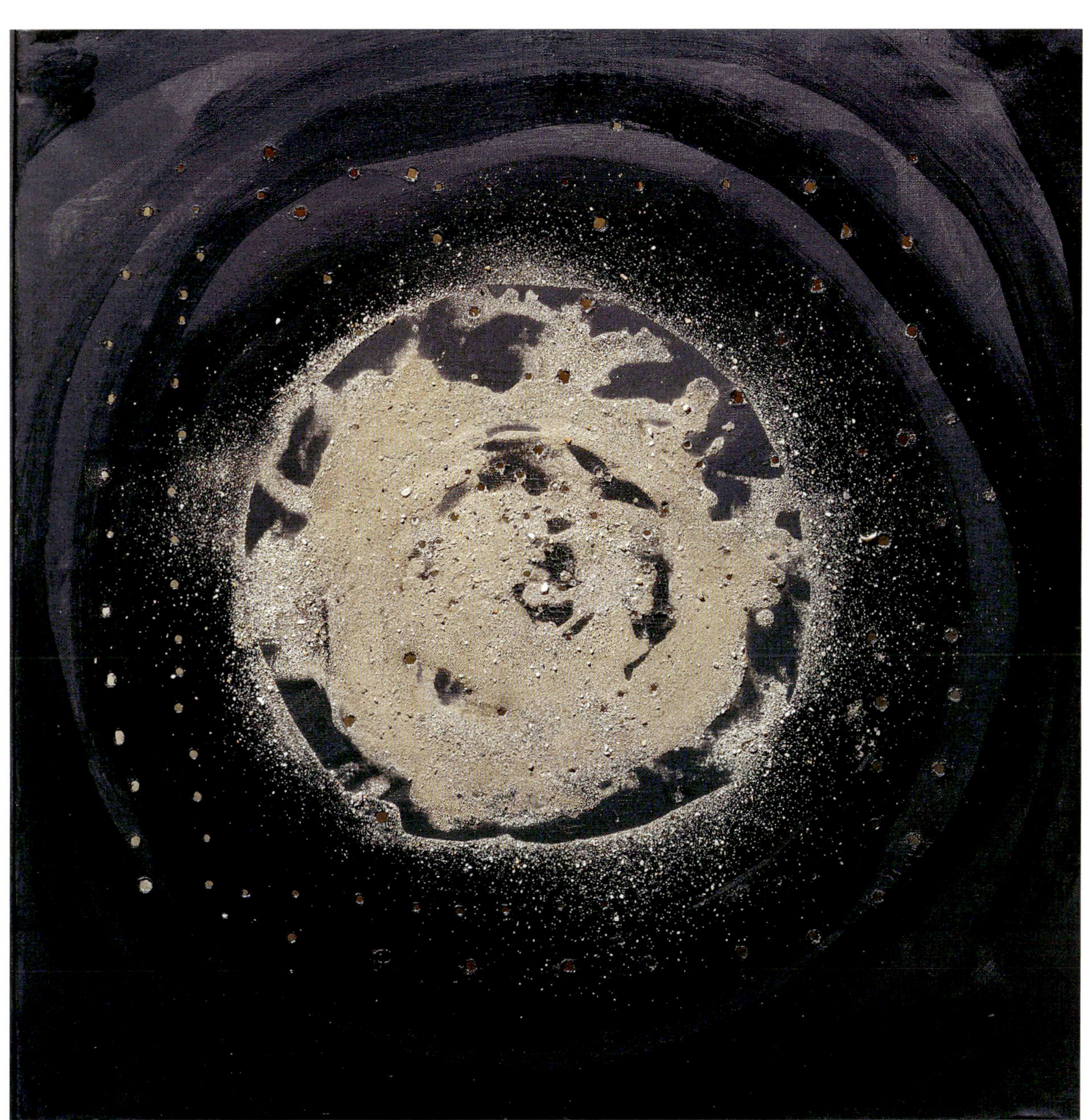

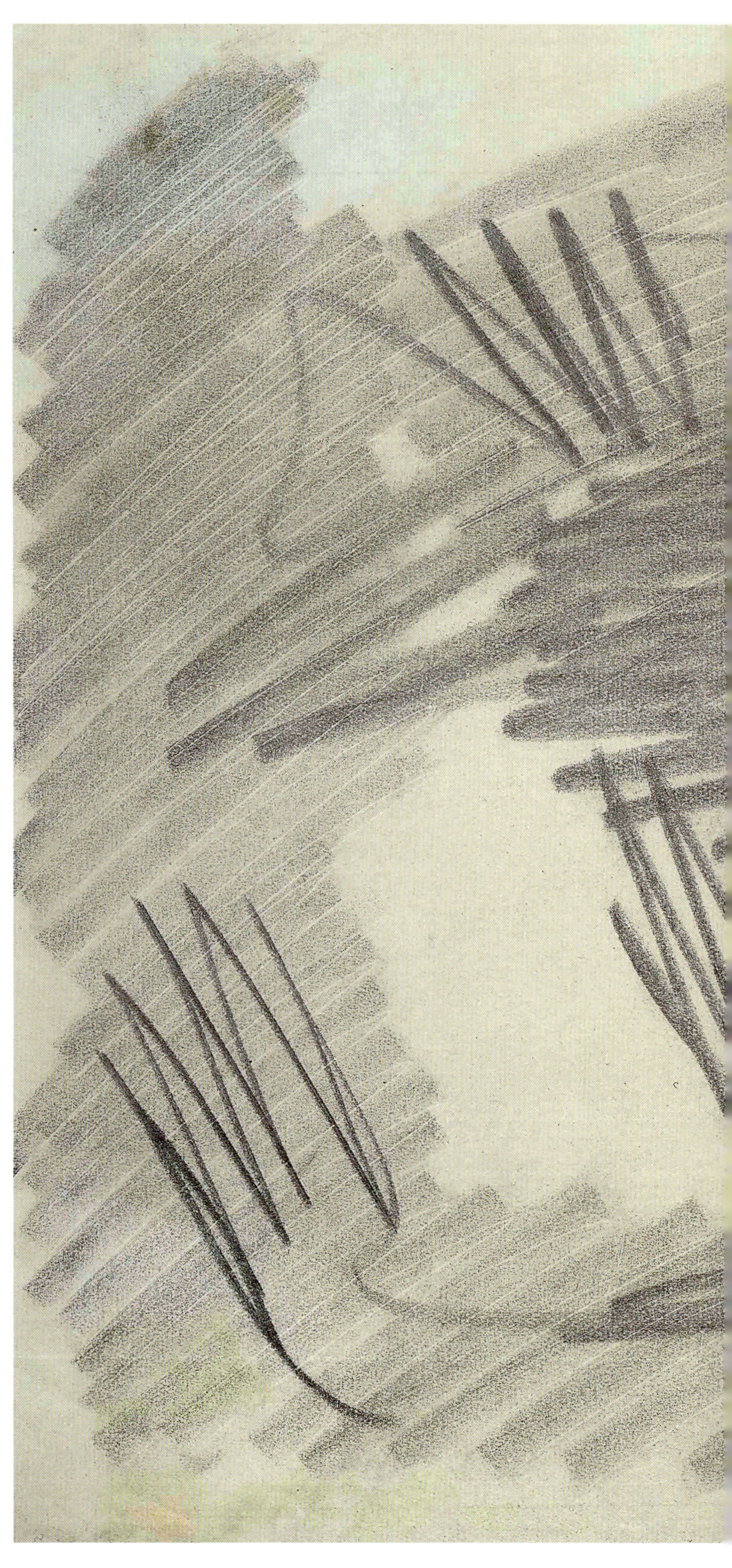

Concetto spaziale
1951
pencil on paper
21 × 29 cm
51 DSP 26
Courtesy Fondazione
Lucio Fontana

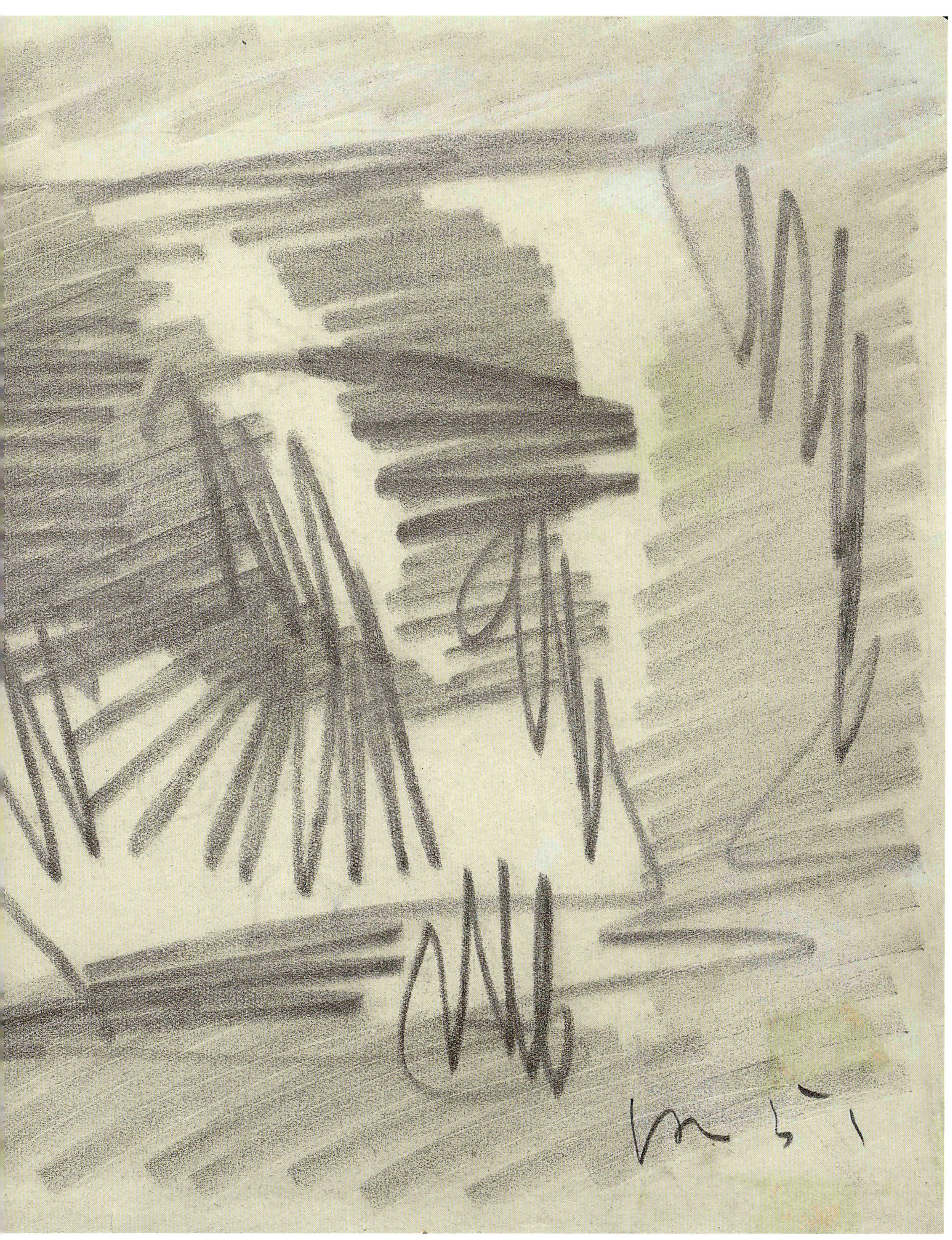

Concetto spaziale
1951
china on paper
29 × 23 cm
51 DSP 5
Courtesy Fondazione
Lucio Fontana

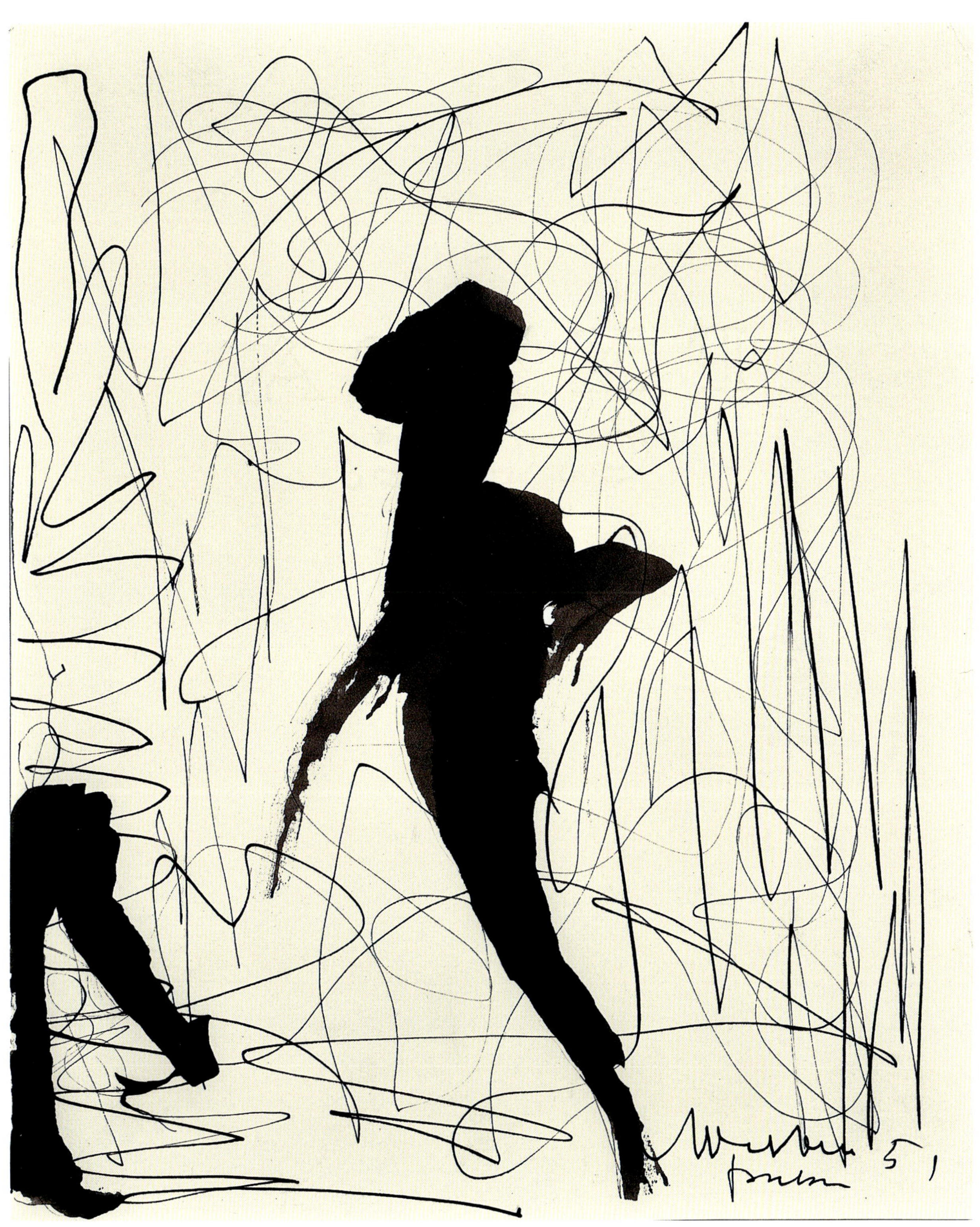

Concetto spaziale
1951
pencil on paper
29 × 21 cm
51 DSP 25
Courtesy Fondazione
Lucio Fontana

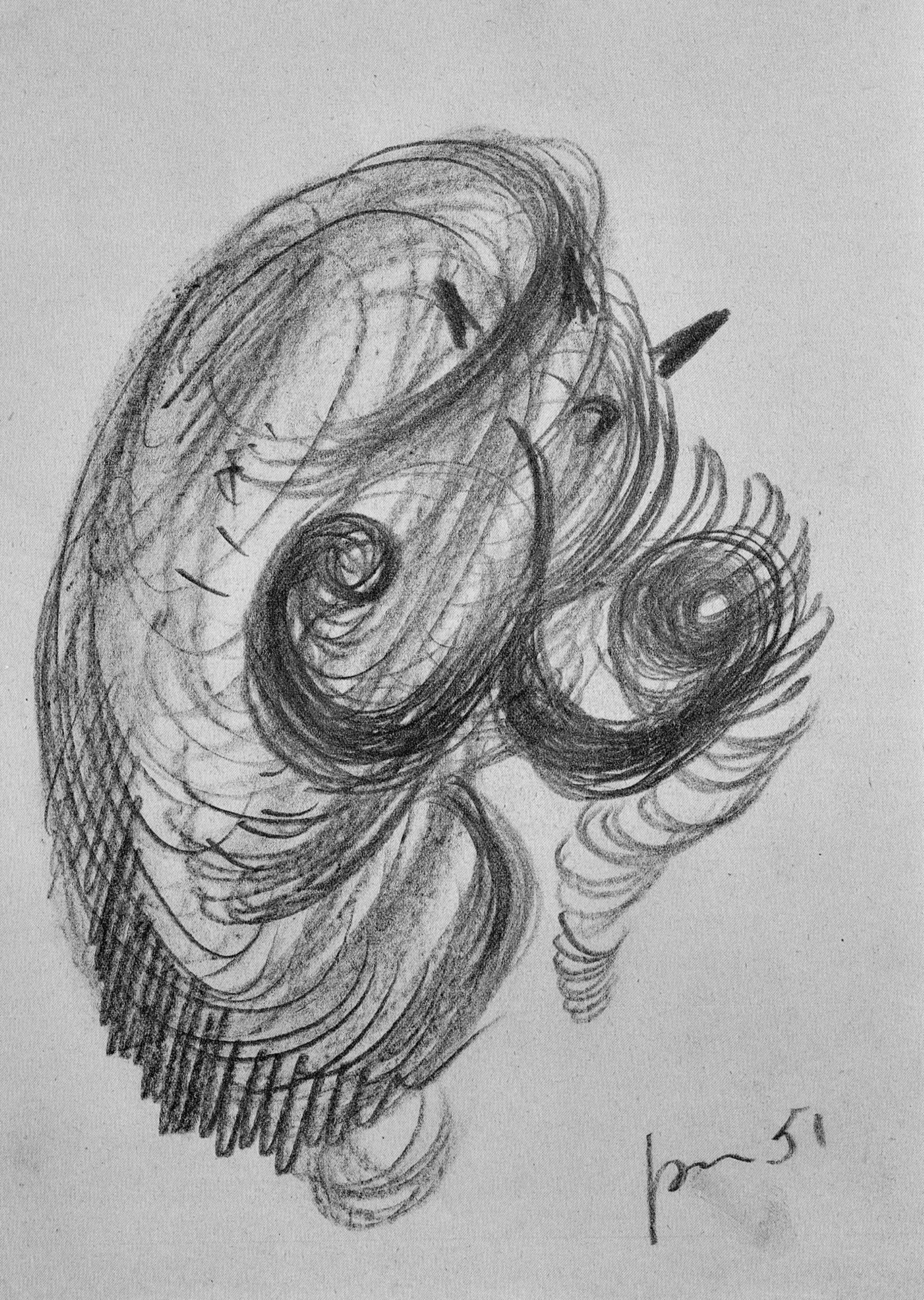

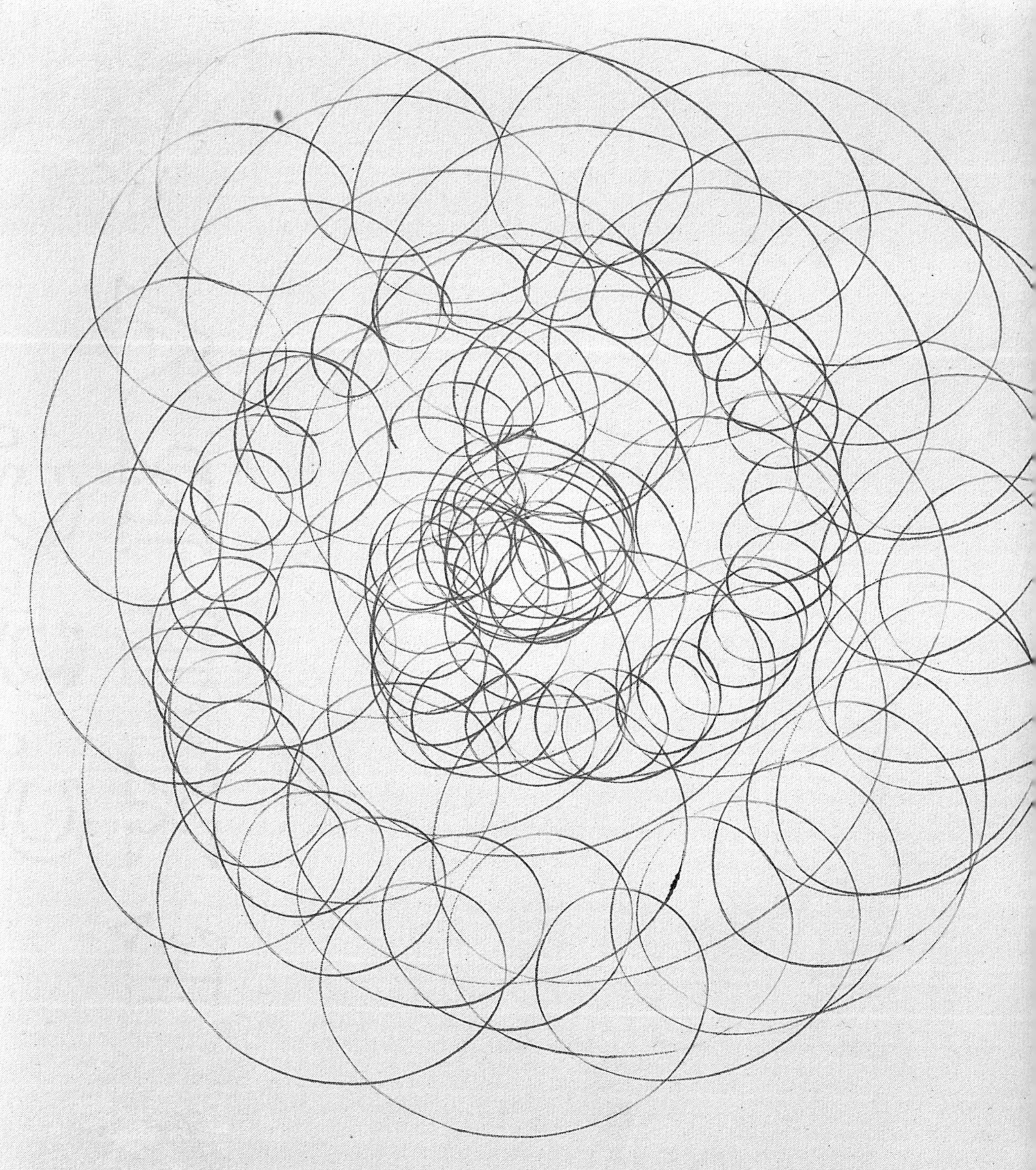

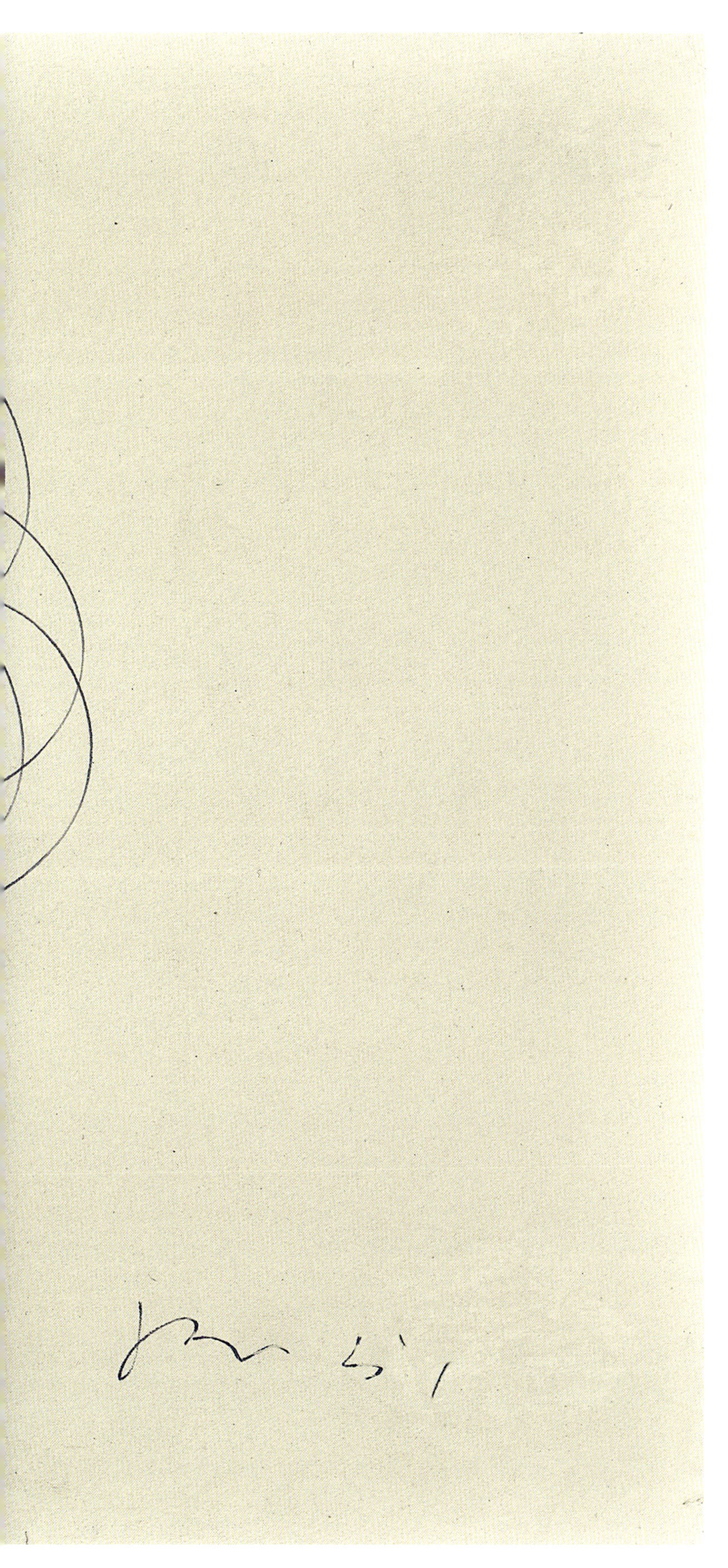

Concetto spaziale
1951
ballpoint pen on paper
23 × 29 cm
51 DSP 18
Courtesy Fondazione
Lucio Fontana

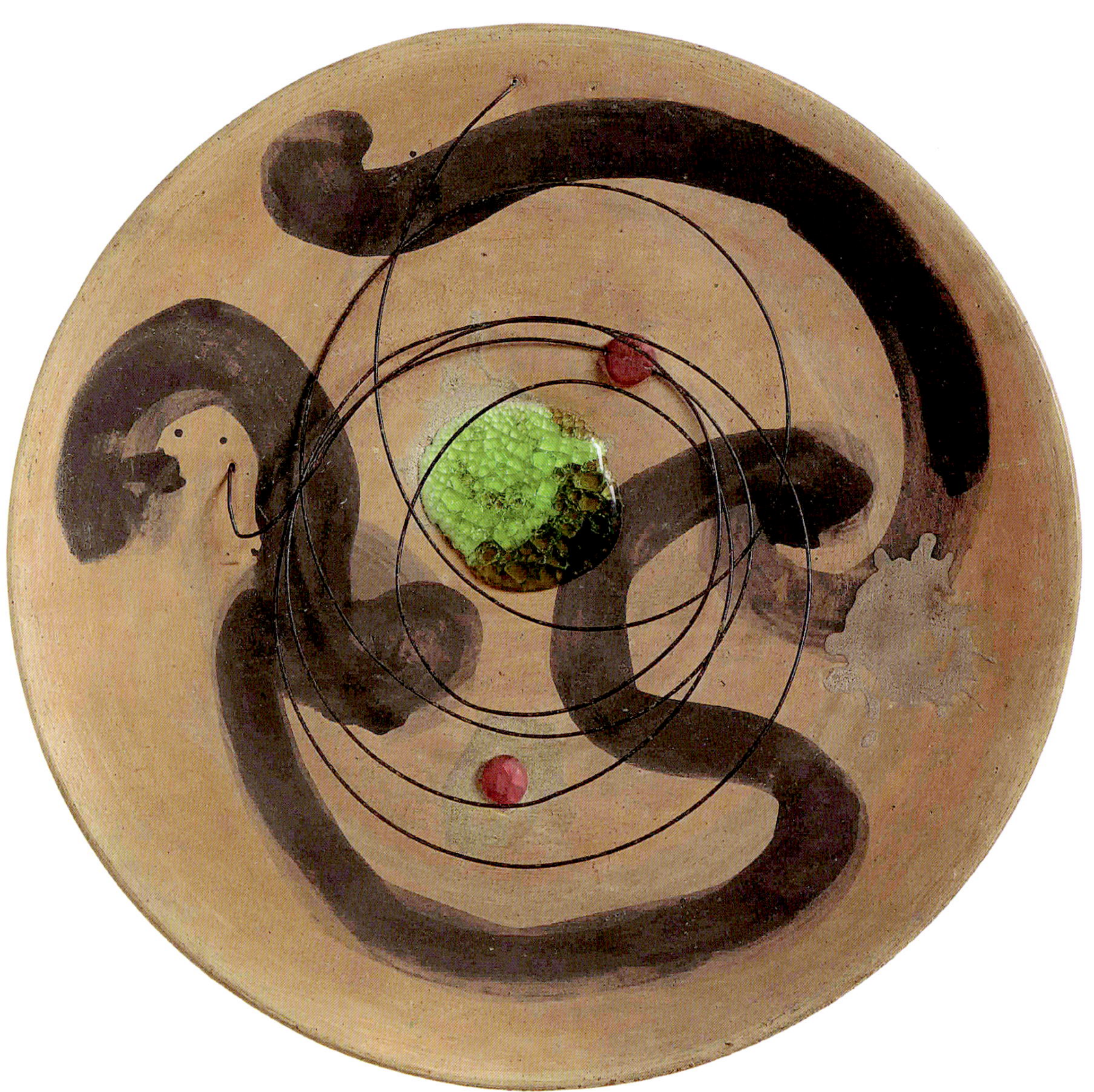

Concetto spaziale
1951
engobed, painted terracotta,
wire and glass paste
diameter 35 cm
51 SPC 1
Courtesy Fondazione
Lucio Fontana

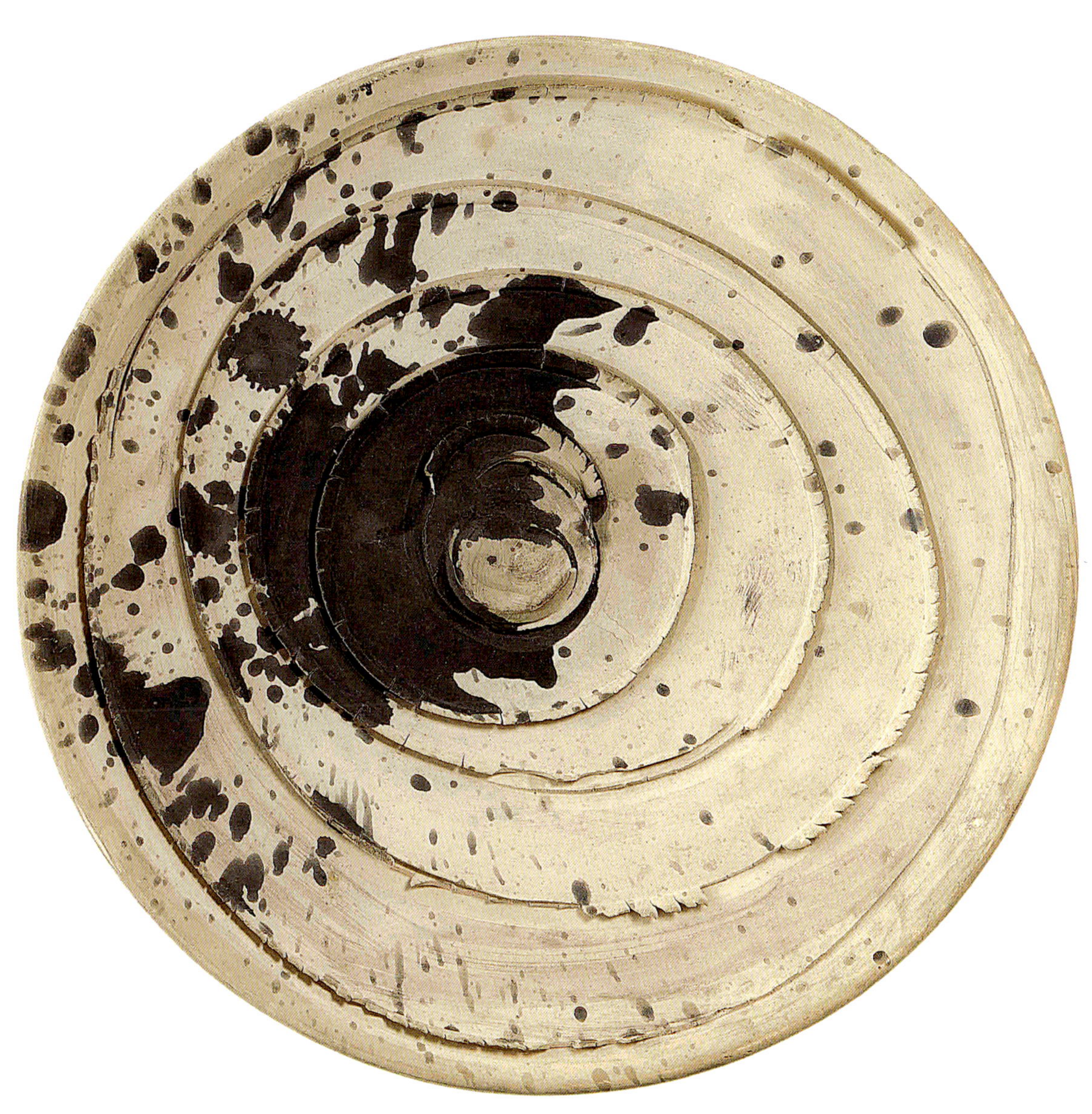

Concetto spaziale
1952
engobed, painted
and scratched terracotta
diameter 36 cm
52 SPC 4
Courtesy Fondazione
Lucio Fontana

Concetto spaziale
1952
coloured terracotta, yellow
and black
diameter 25 cm
52 SPC 2
Courtesy Sergio Casoli

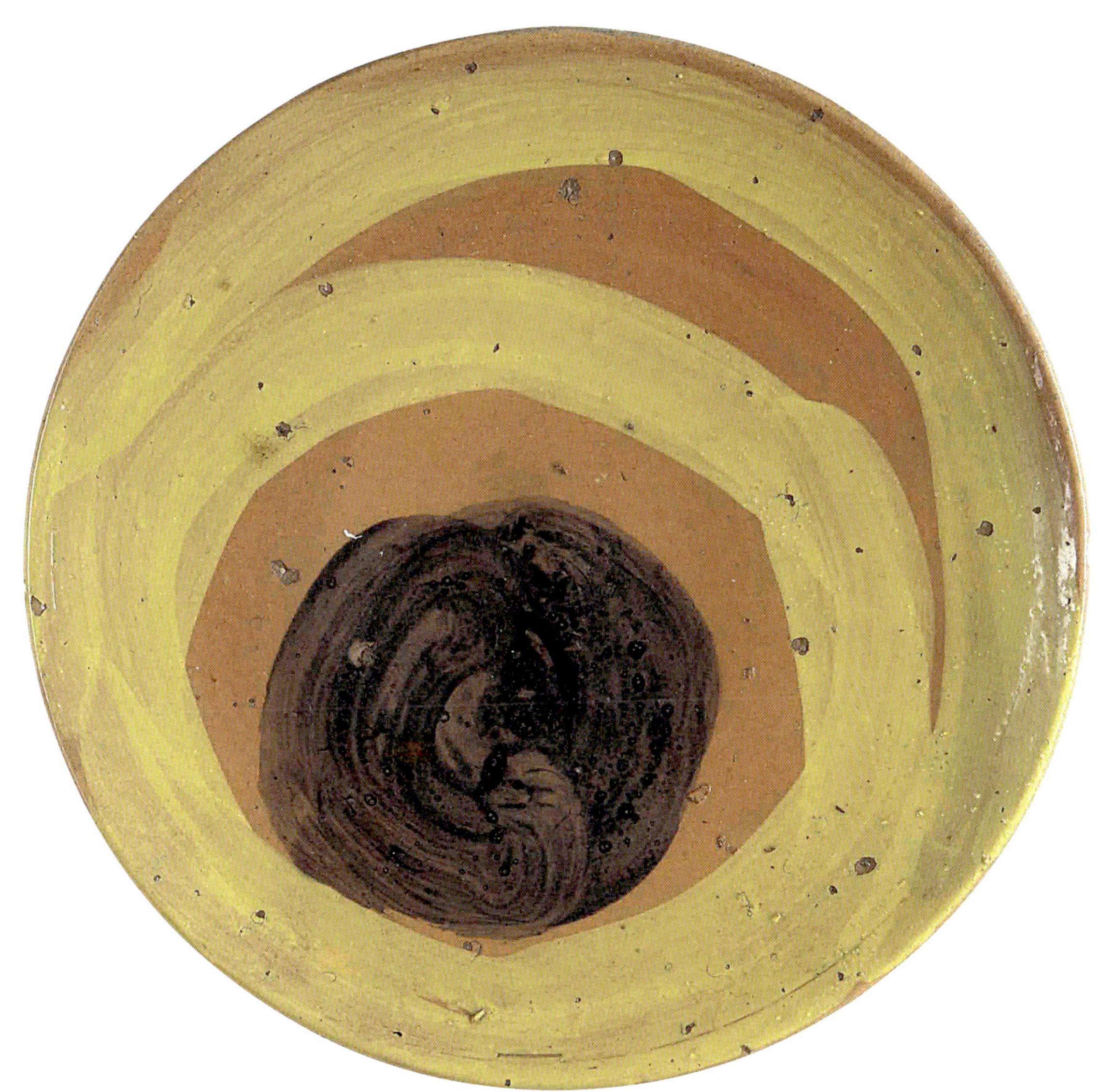

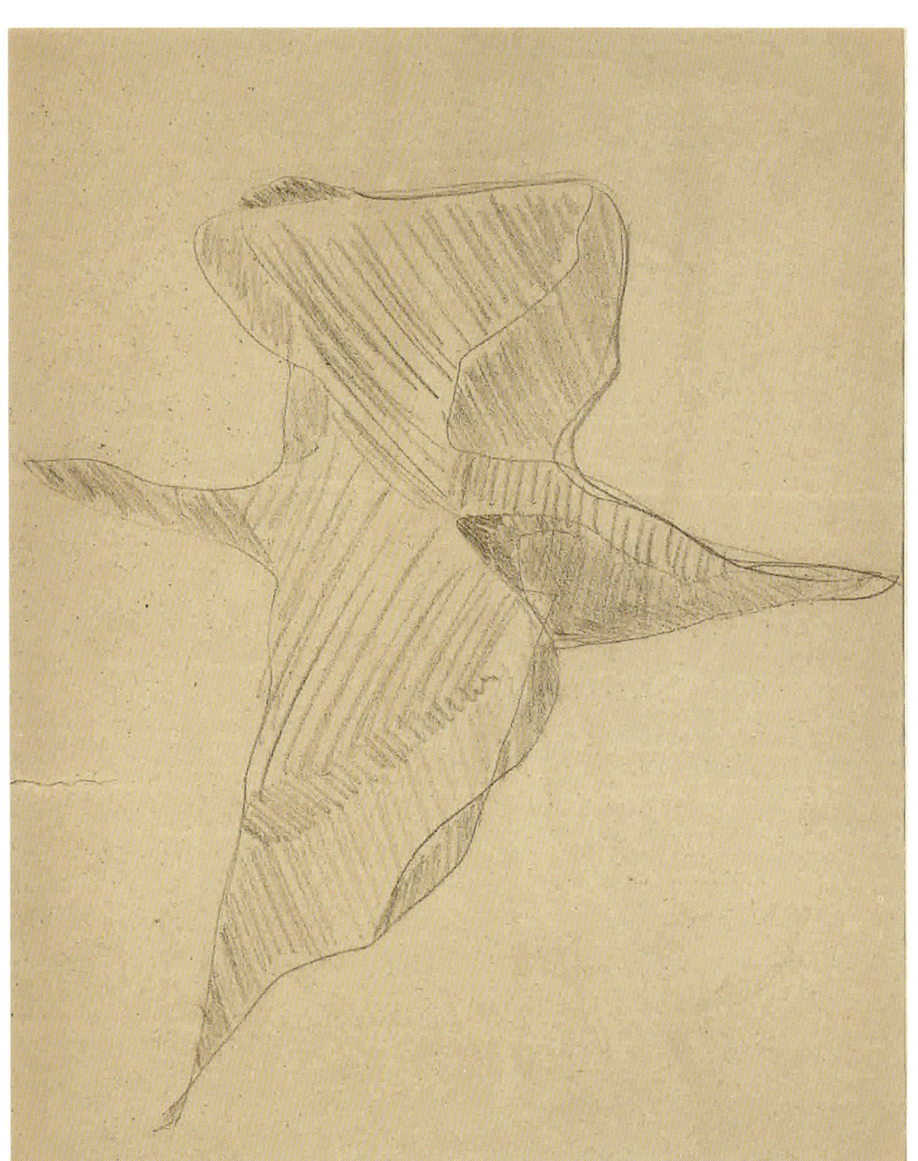

Concetto spaziale
recto and verso
1952-54
pen on paper
32,5 × 25,5 cm
Archivio Fontana
57 DSP 22 v
57 DSP 22 r
Private collection
Courtesy Gió Marconi
Milano

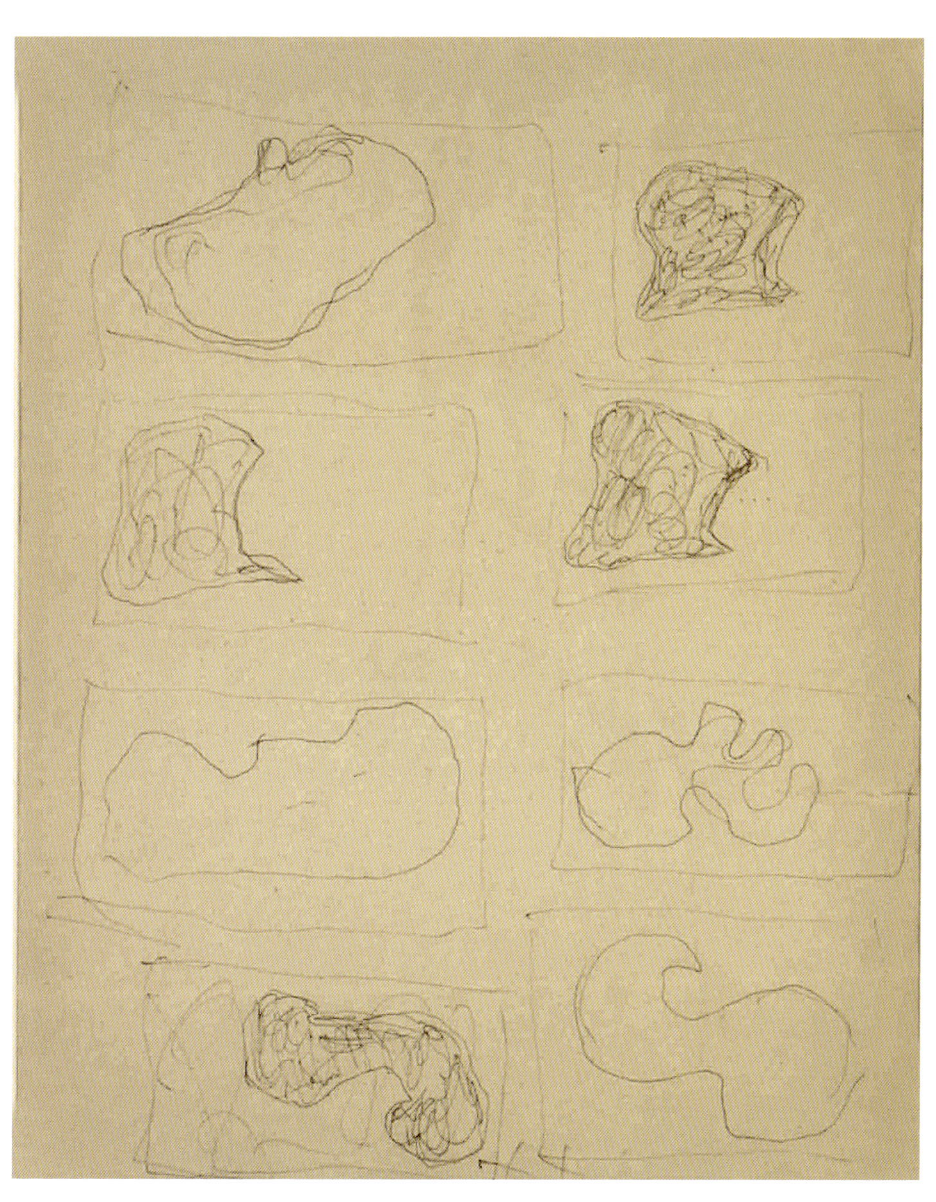

Concetto spaziale
1955
holes and china on orange paper
32,5 × 22 cm
55 DSP 19
Private collection
Courtesy Gió Marconi
Milano

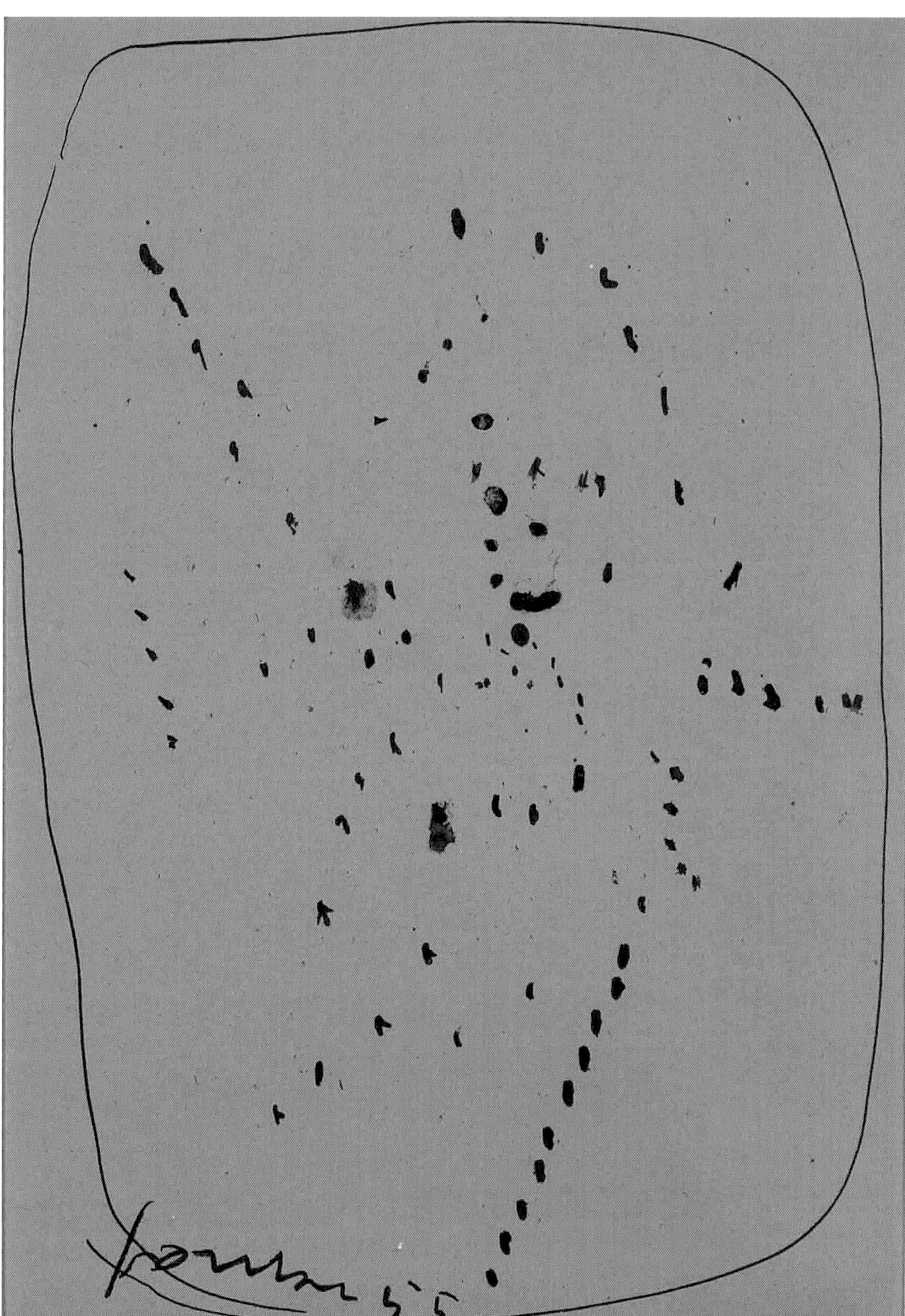

Concetto spaziale
1956
oil, mixed technique and glass
on canvas
80 × 70 cm
56 P 14
Private collection

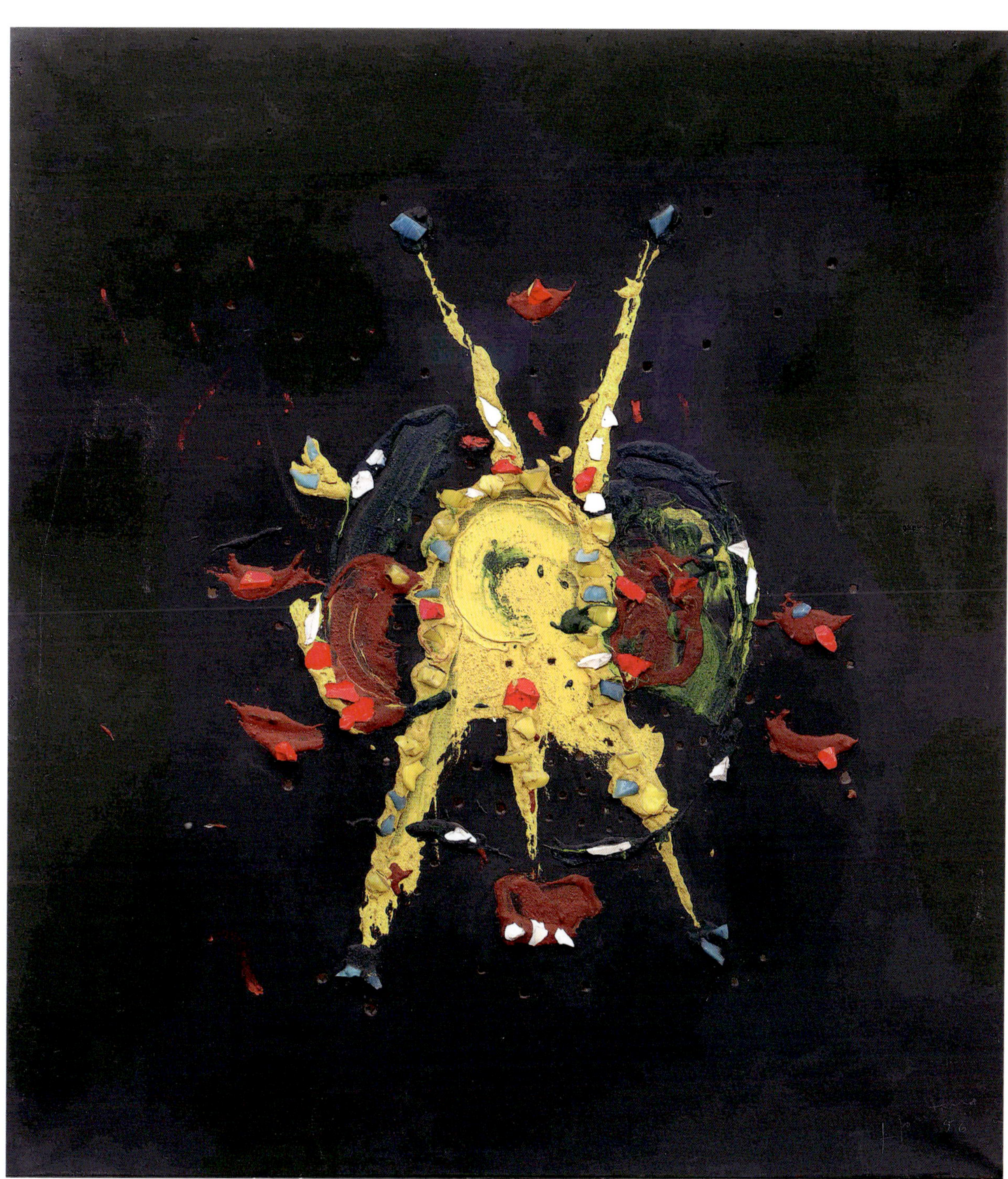

Concetto spaziale
1956
oil on canvas
100 × 70 cm
56 B 1
Courtesy Sergio Casoli

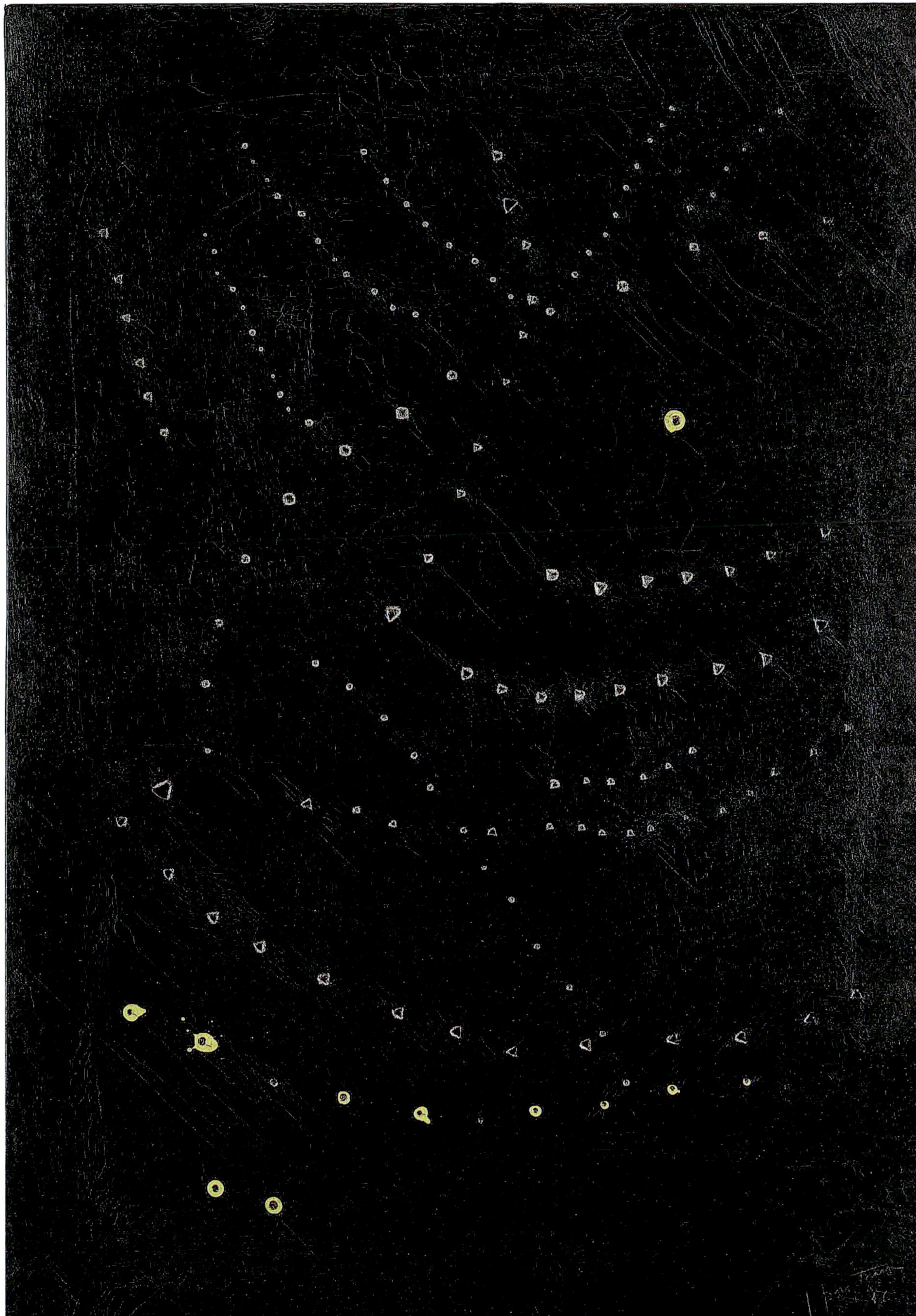

Studi per "Concetti spaziali"
1957
ballpoint pen on paper
32,5 × 25,5 cm
57 DSP 85 r e v
Private collection
Courtesy Gió Marconi
Milano

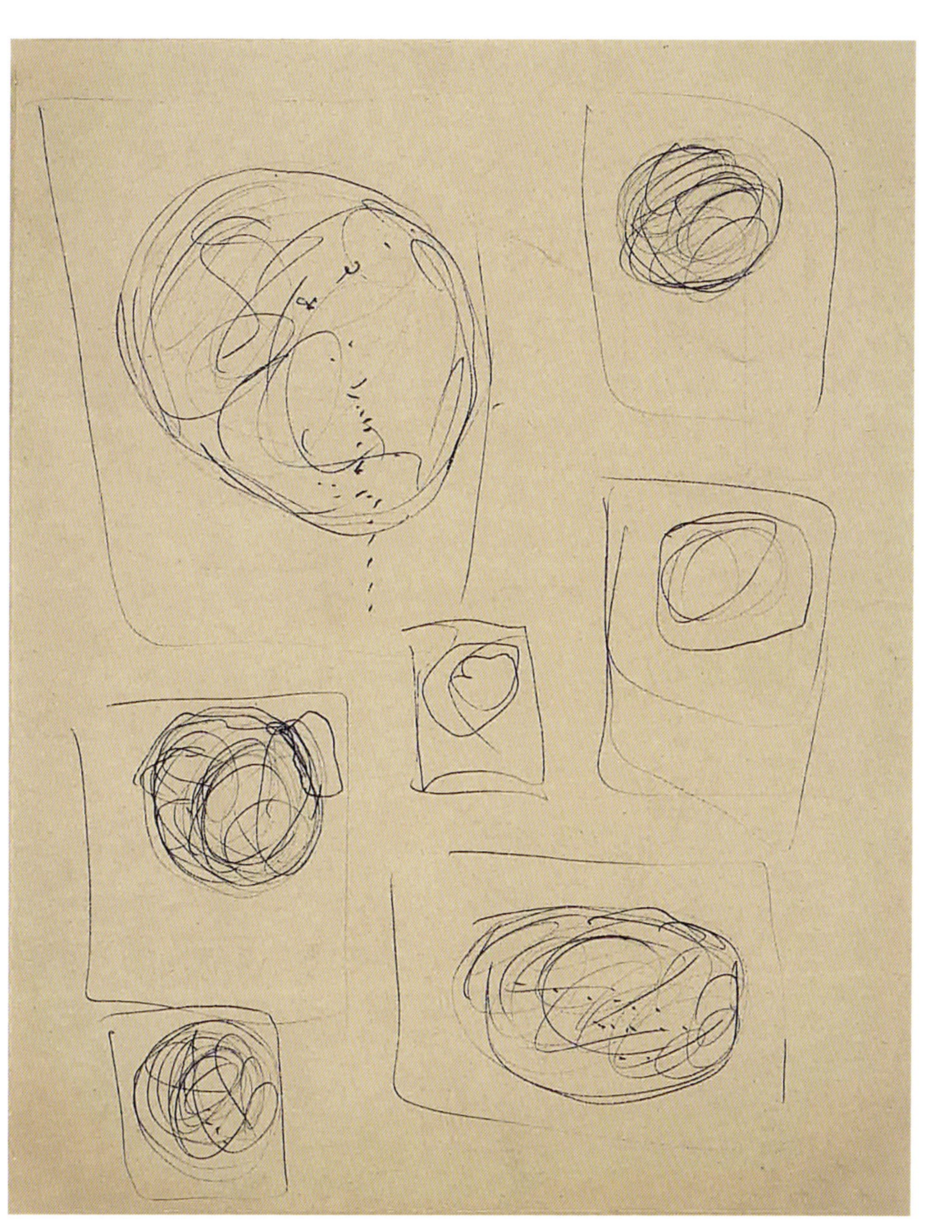

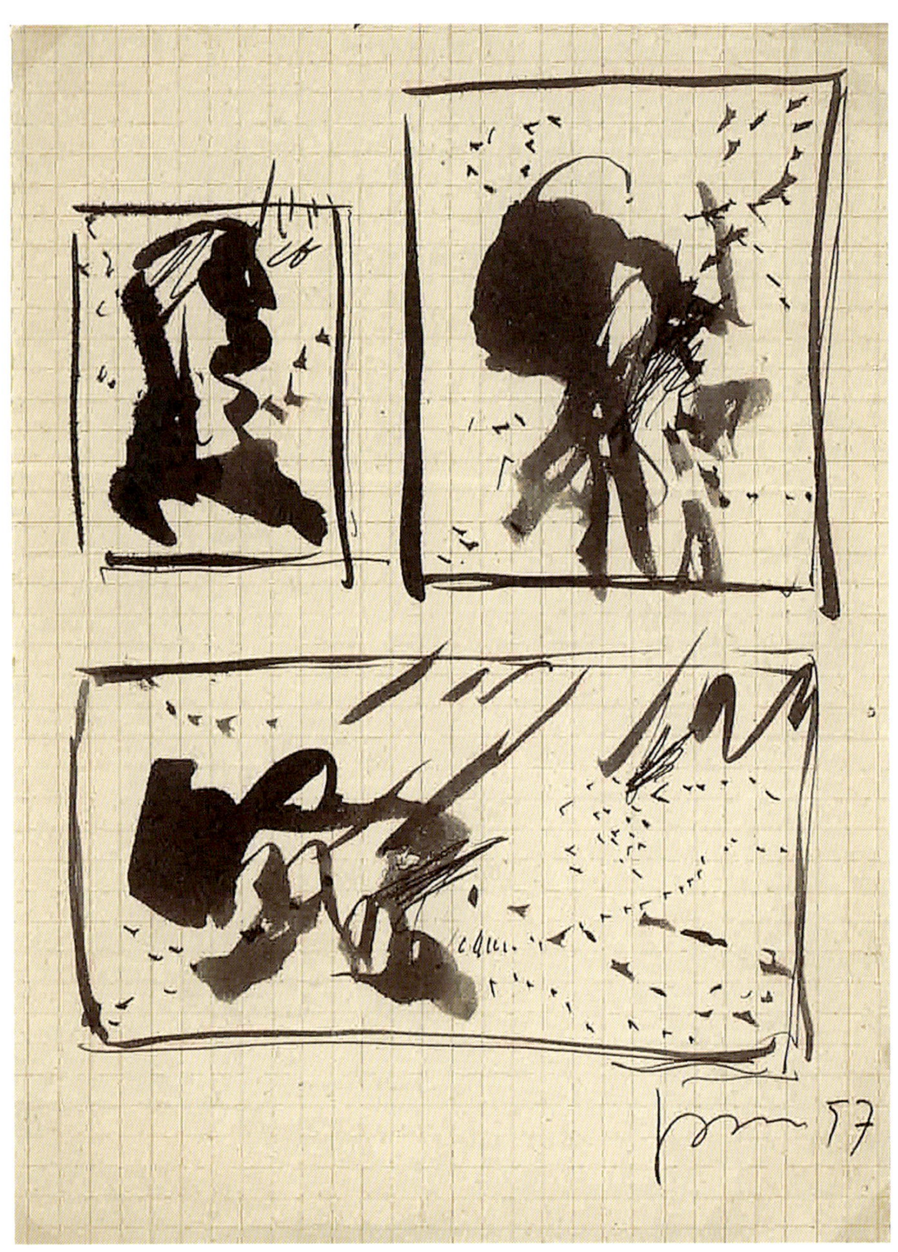

Studi per "Concetti spaziali"
1957
ink on squared paper
20 × 15 cm
57 DSP 38
Private collection
Courtesy Gió Marconi
Milano

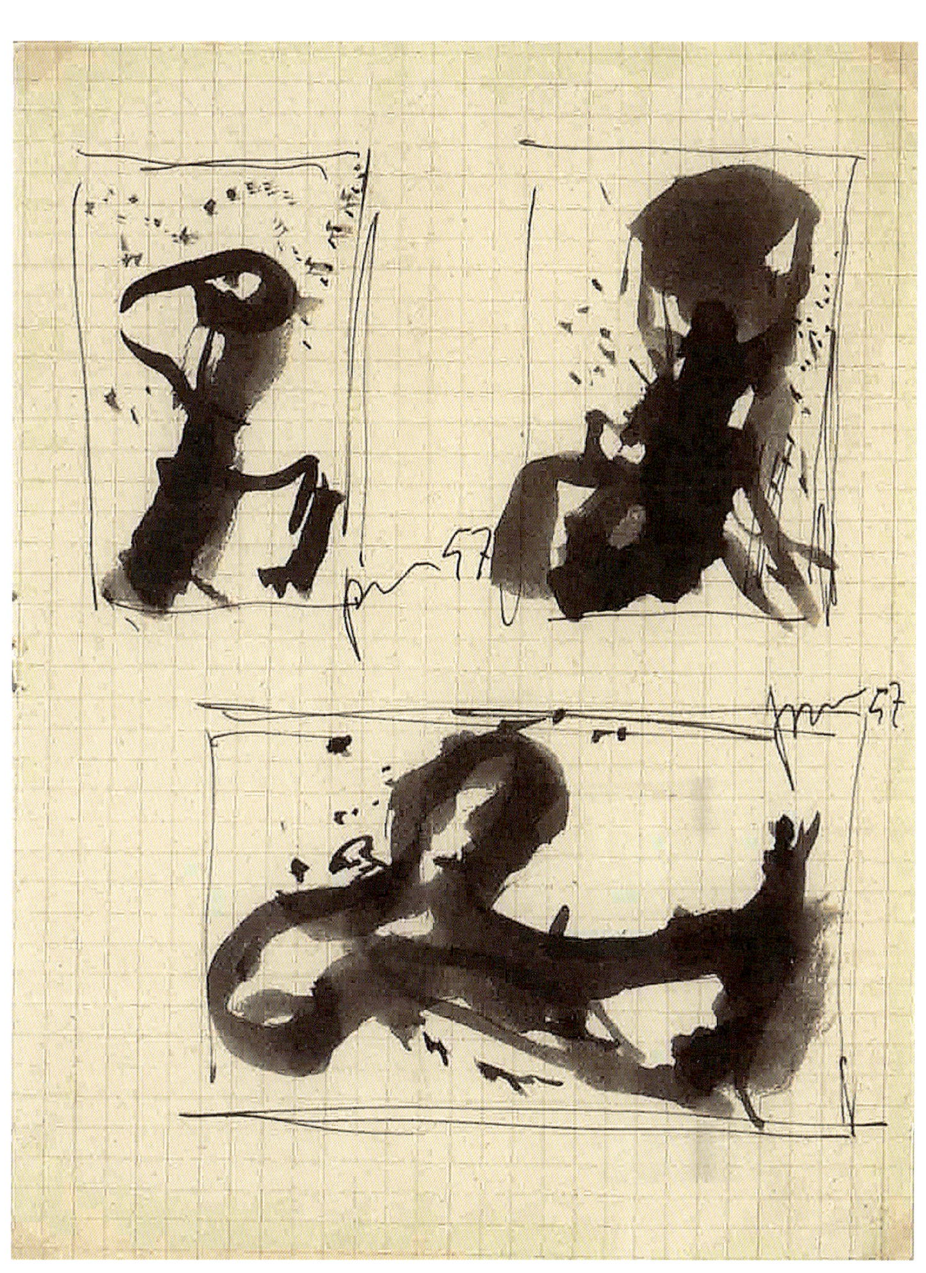

Studi per "Concetti spaziali"
1957
ink on squared paper
22 × 15 cm
Archivio Fontana
57 DSP 37
Private collection
Courtesy Gió Marconi
Milano

Concetto spaziale
1957
crayons and collage on canvas
125 × 101 cm
57 G 26
Courtesy Fondazione
Lucio Fontana

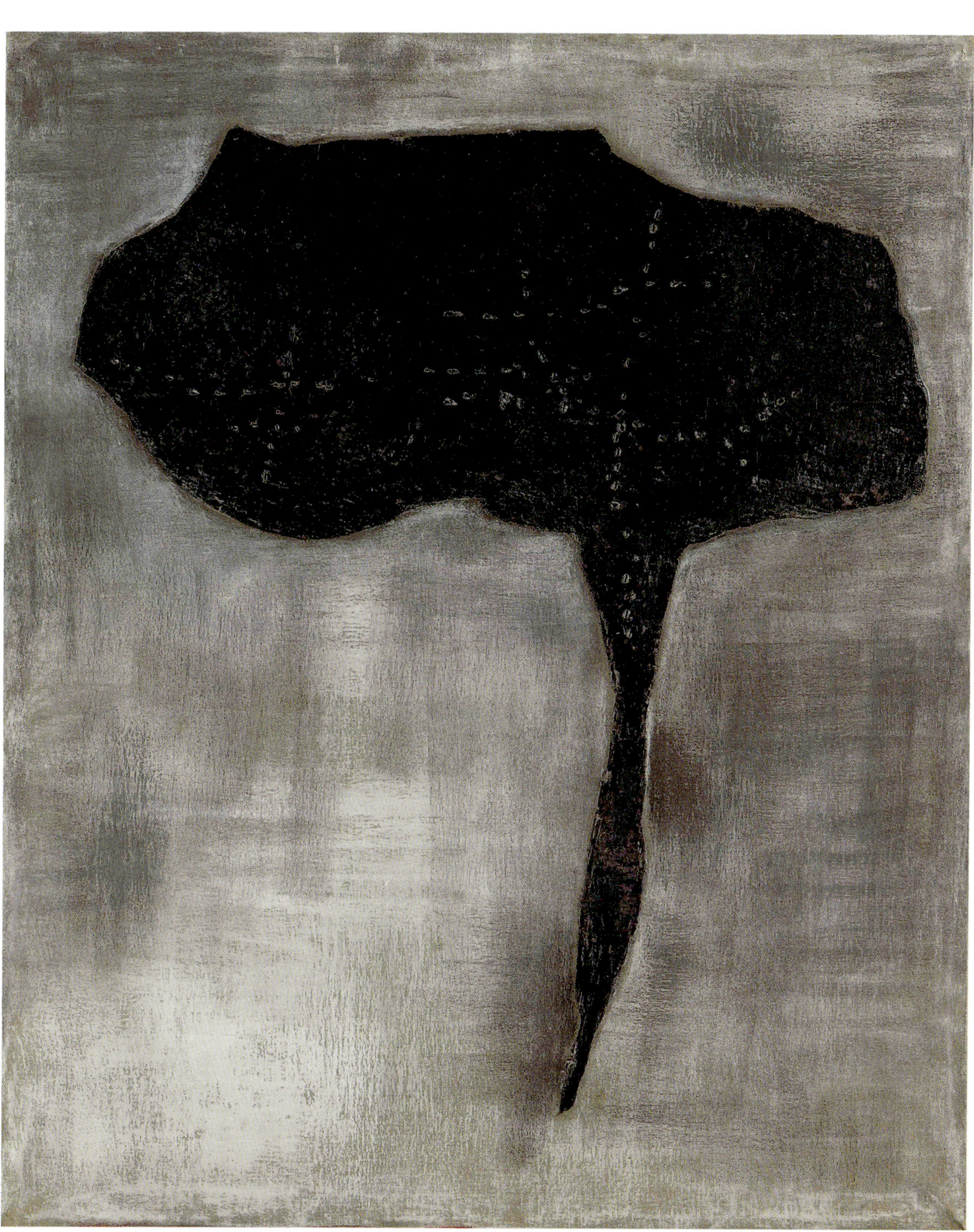

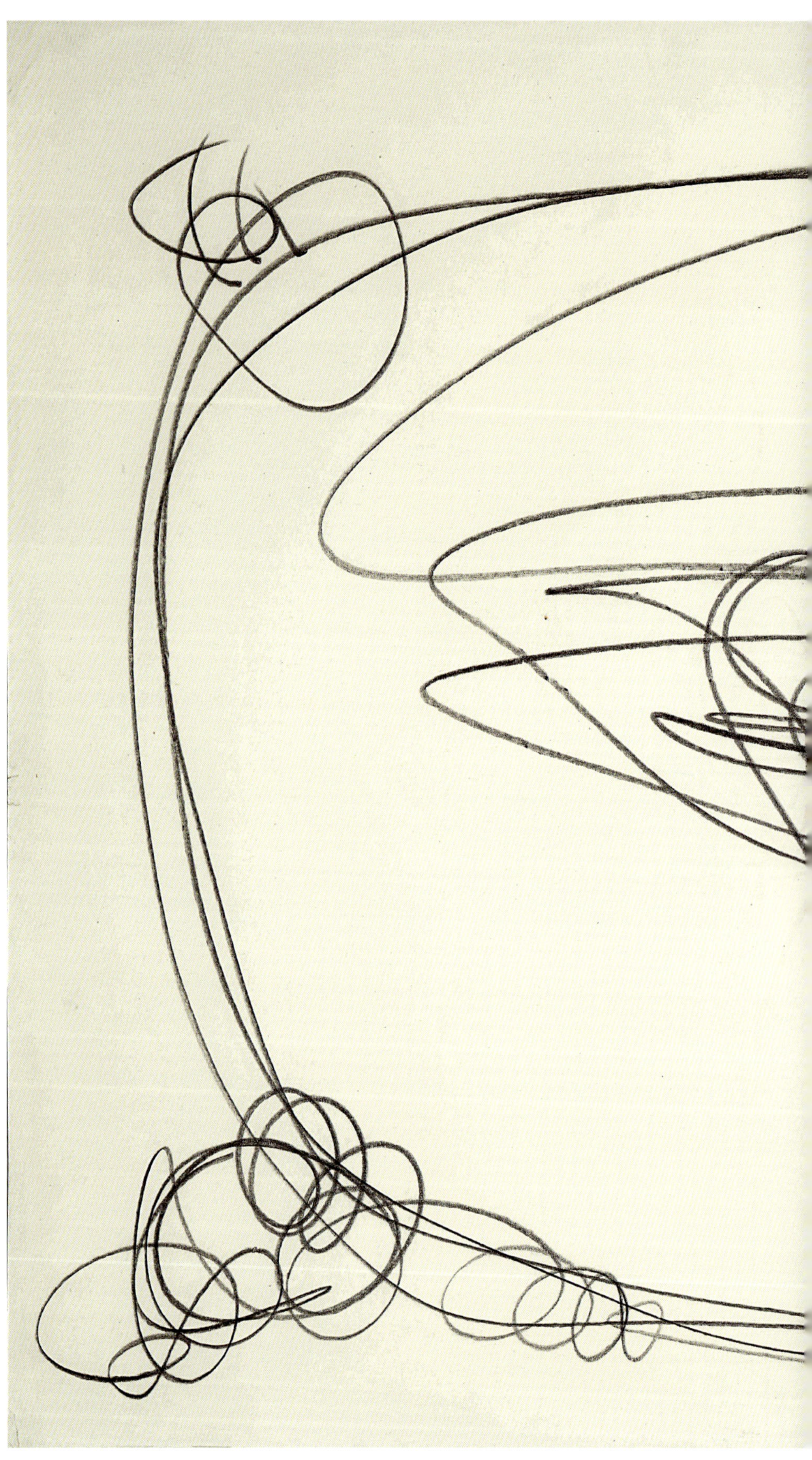

Concetto spaziale
1958
pencil and tempera
on cardboard
49,7 × 67 cm
58 DSP 40
Courtesy Fondazione
Lucio Fontana

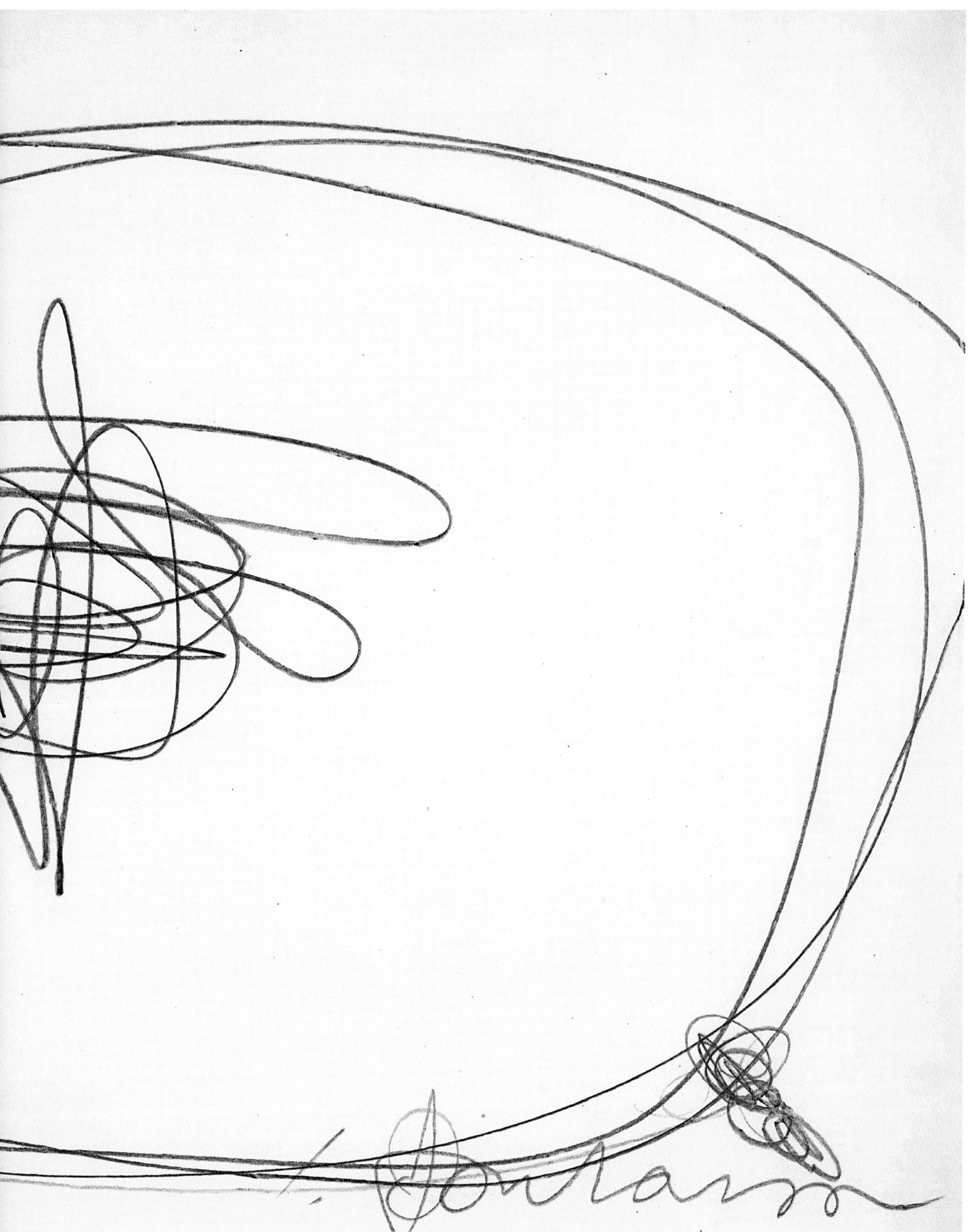

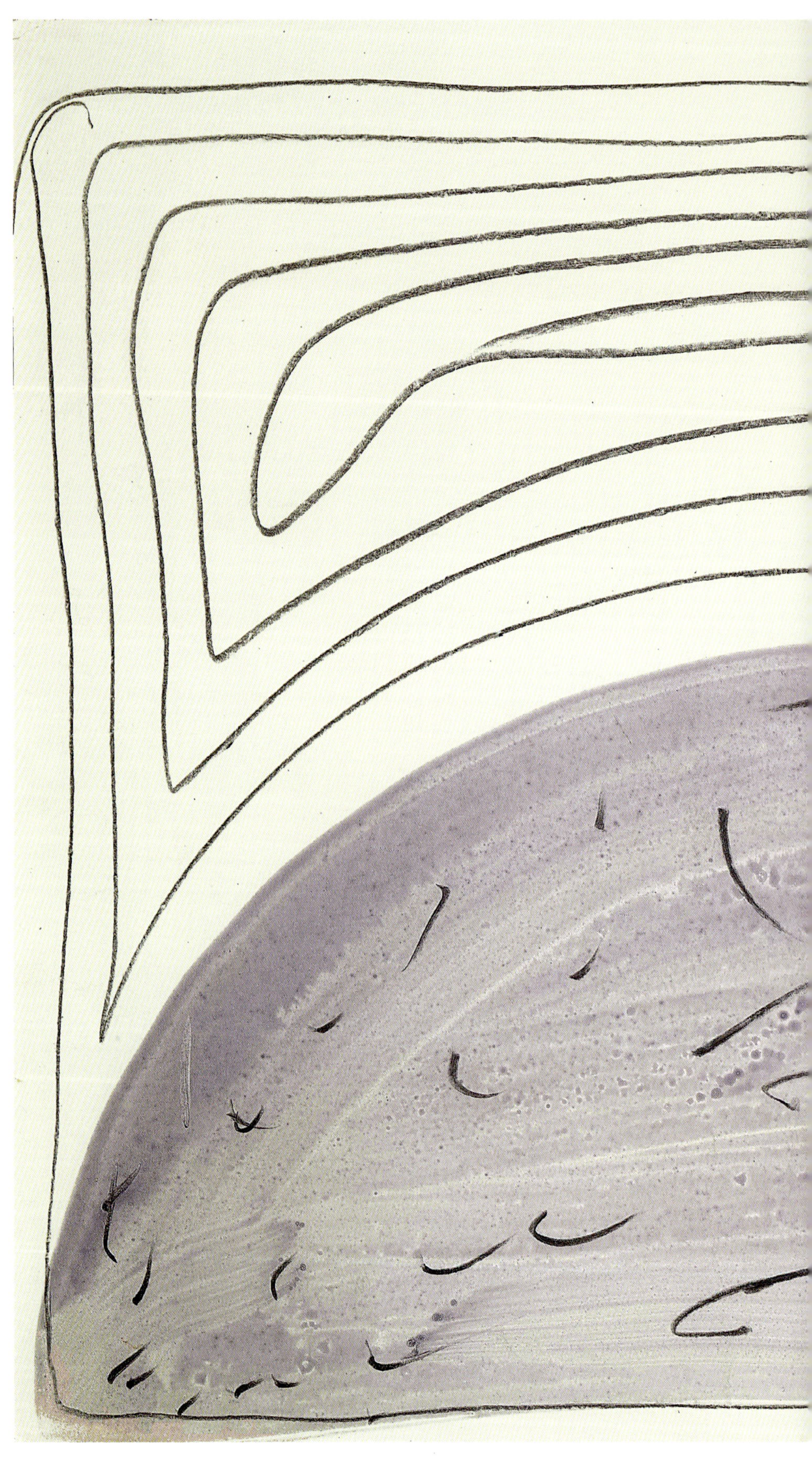

Concetto spaziale
1958
pencil and tempera on cardboard
49,7 × 67 cm
58 DSP 39
Courtesy Fondazione
Lucio Fontana

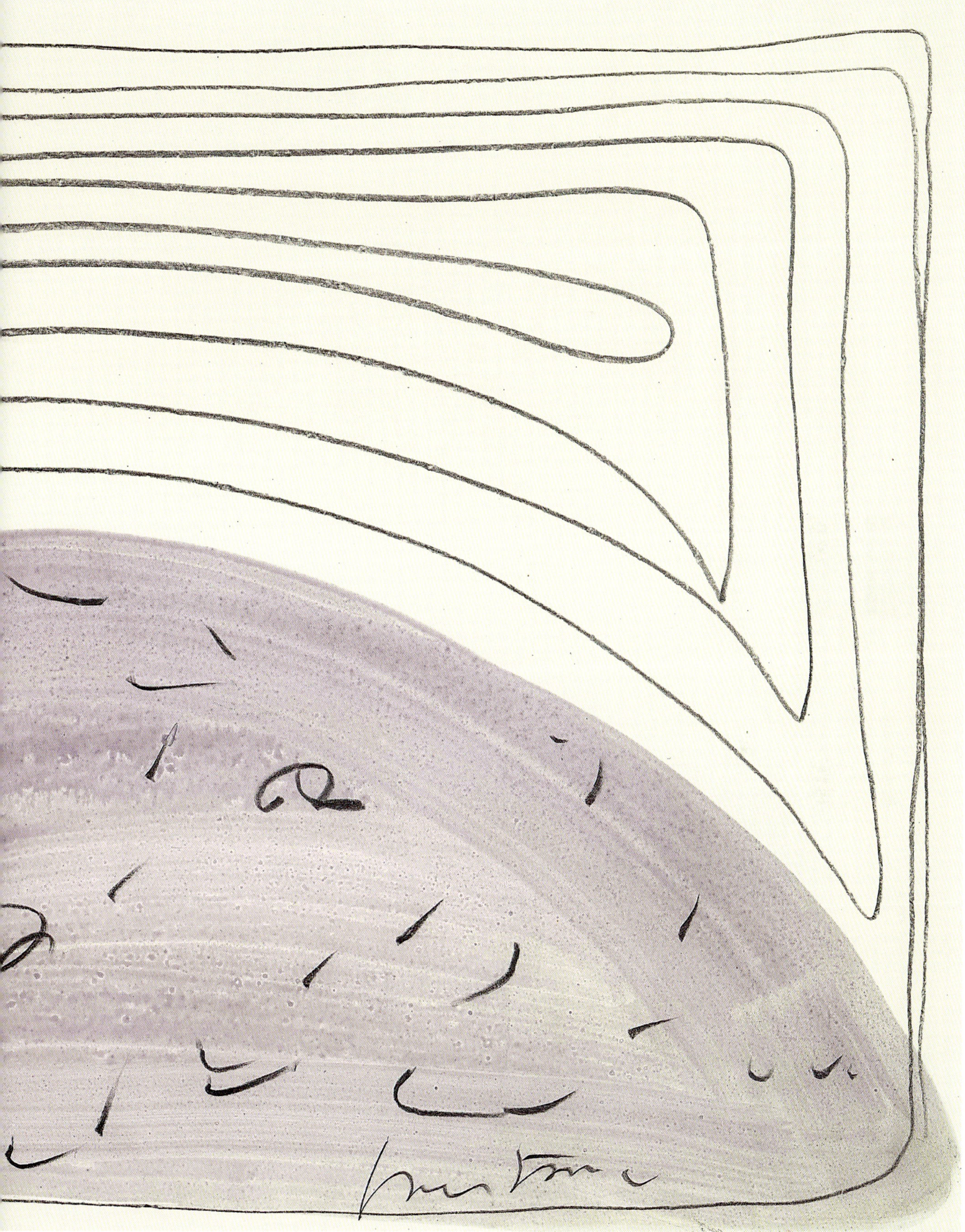

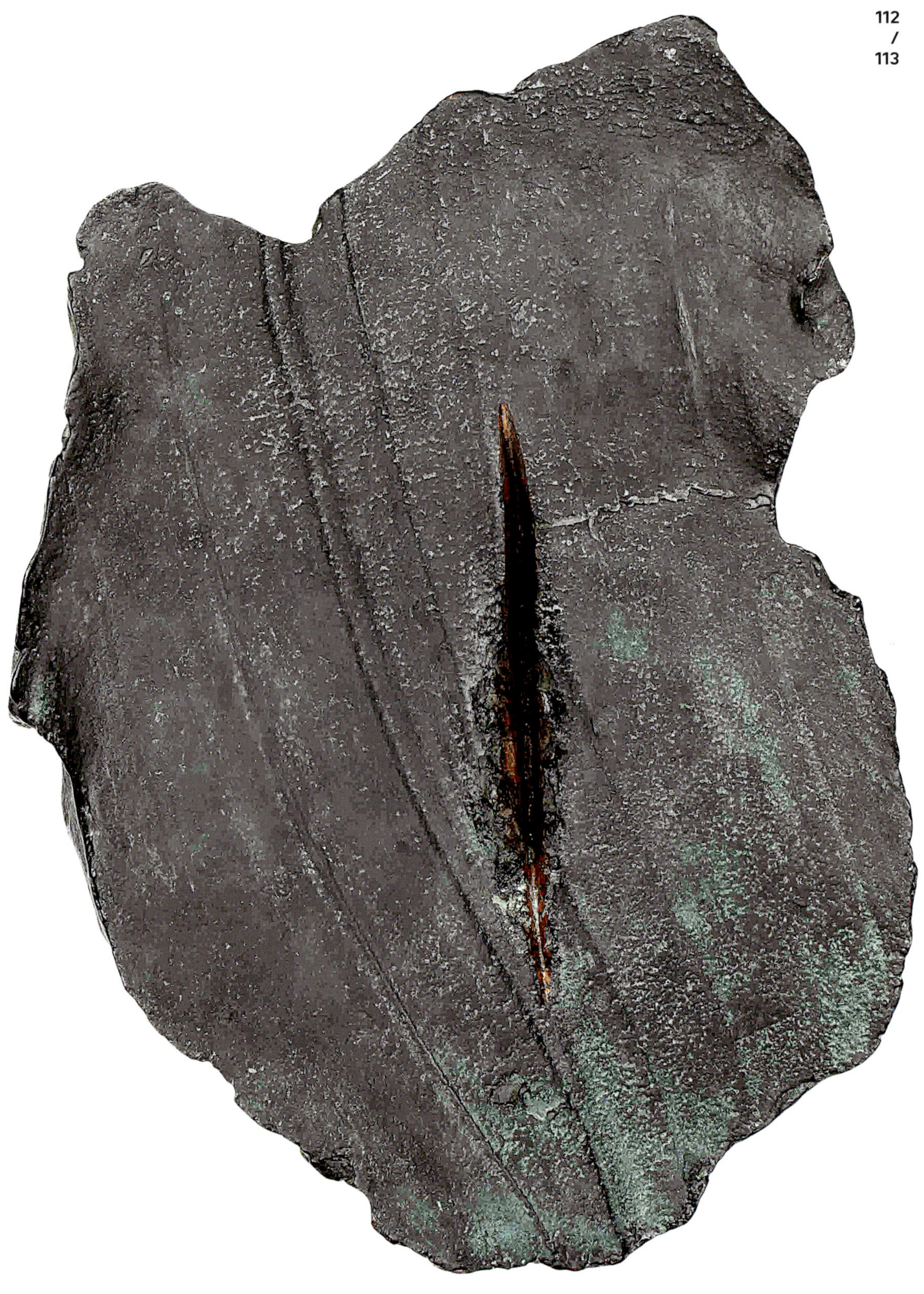

Concetto spaziale
Nature
1959
bronze
50 × 34 × 13 cm
49 × 34 × 8 cm
59 N 4 and 5
Courtesy Fondazione
Lucio Fontana

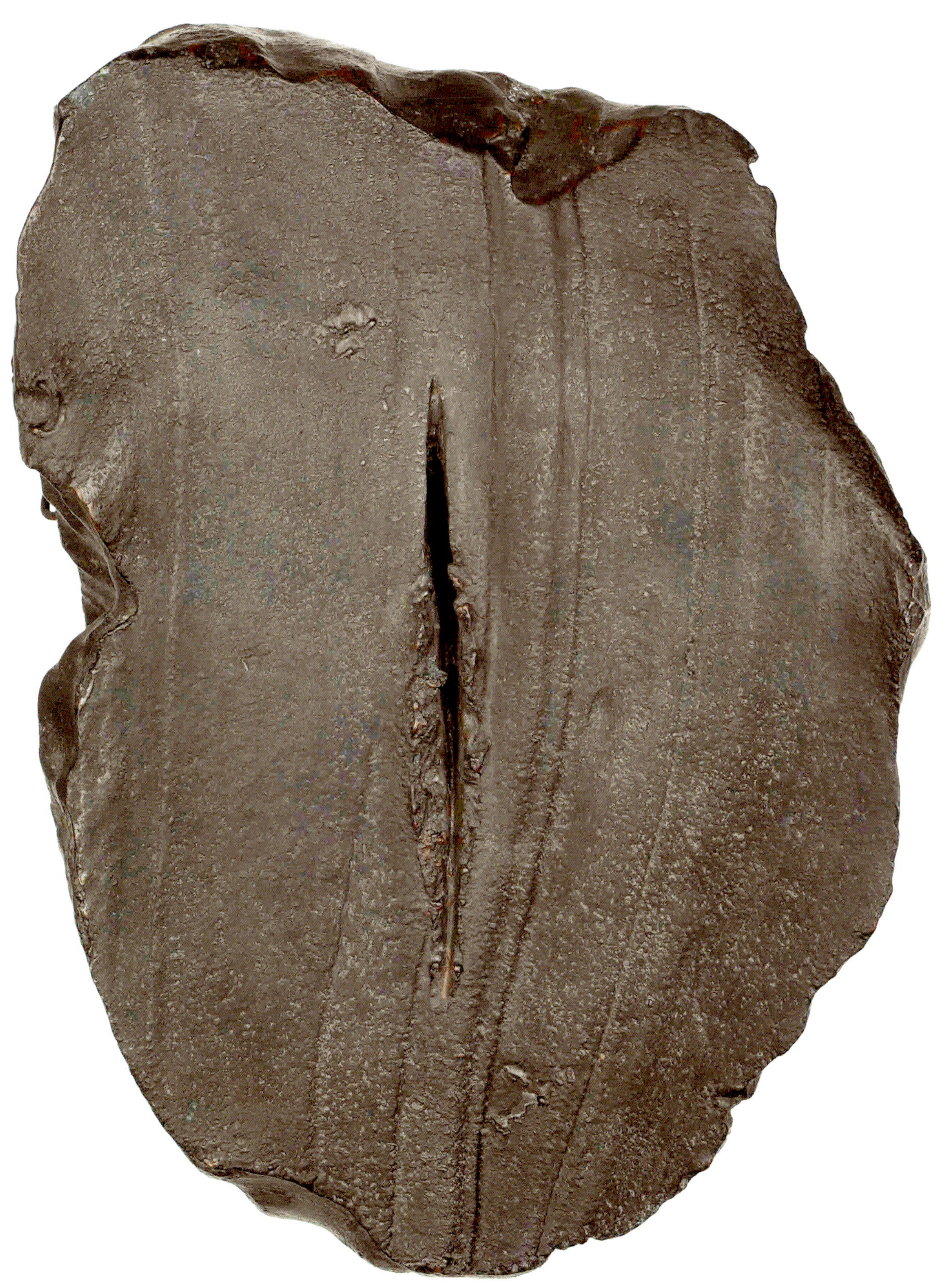

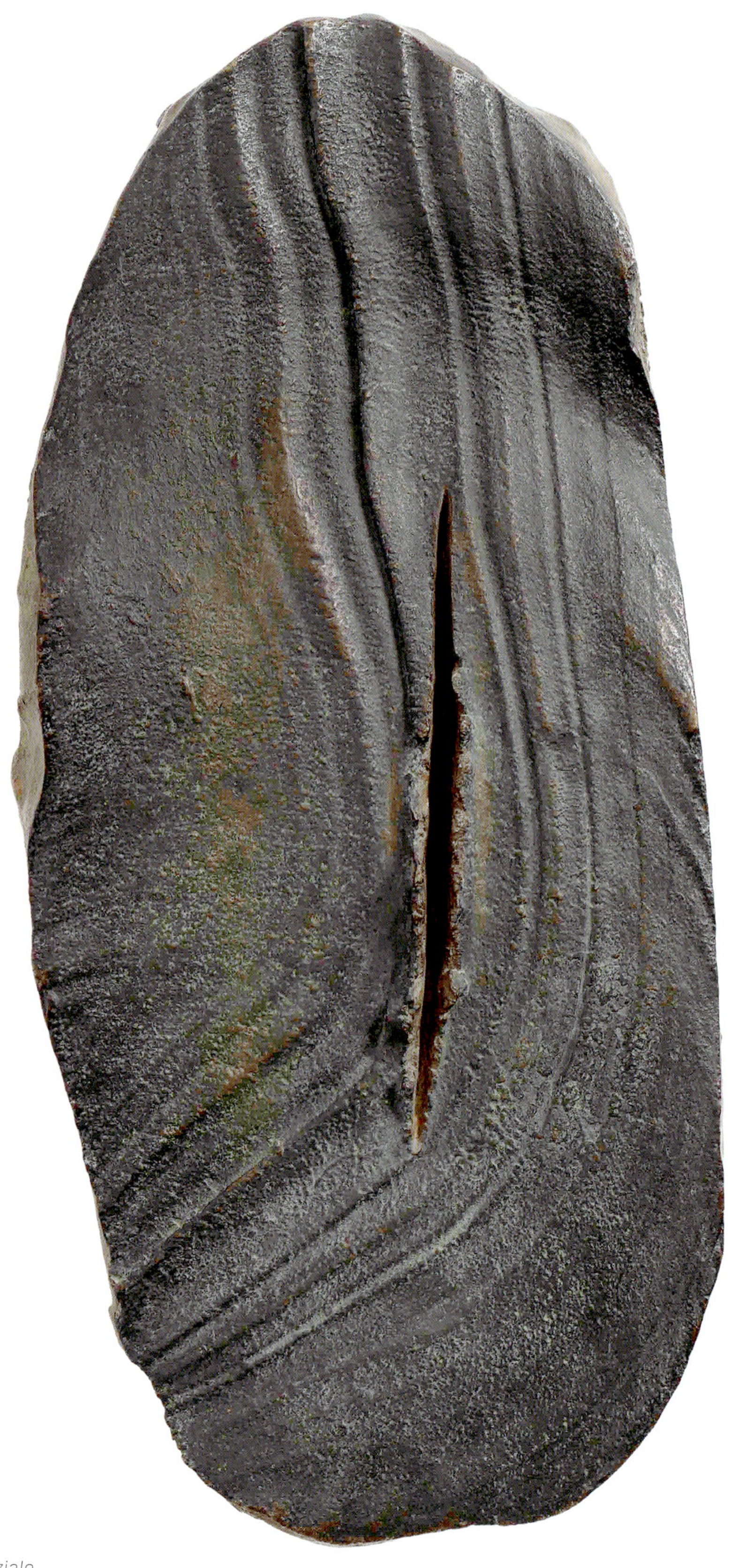

Concetto spaziale
Nature
1959
bronze
64 × 29 × 15 cm
63 × 28 × 15 cm
59 N 25 e 33
Courtesy Fondazione
Lucio Fontana

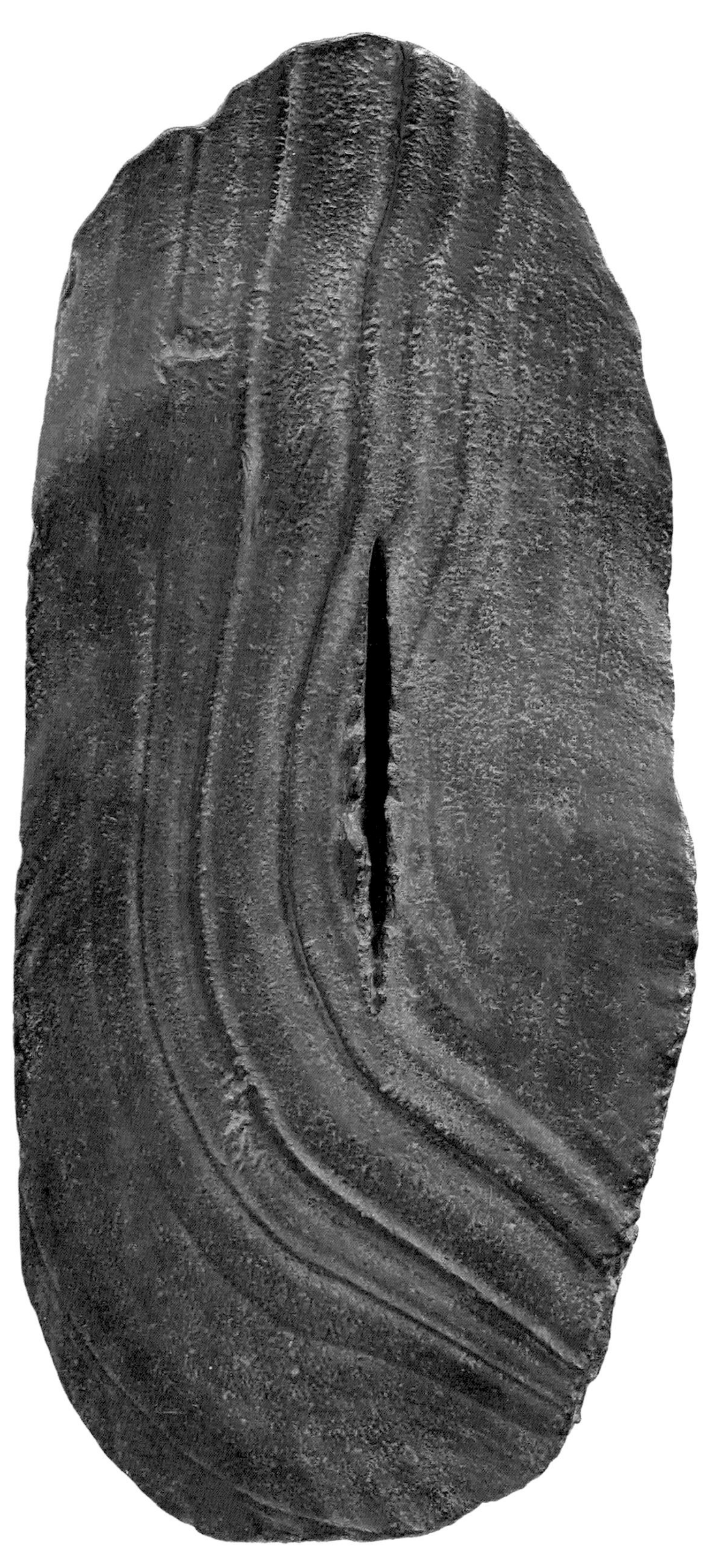

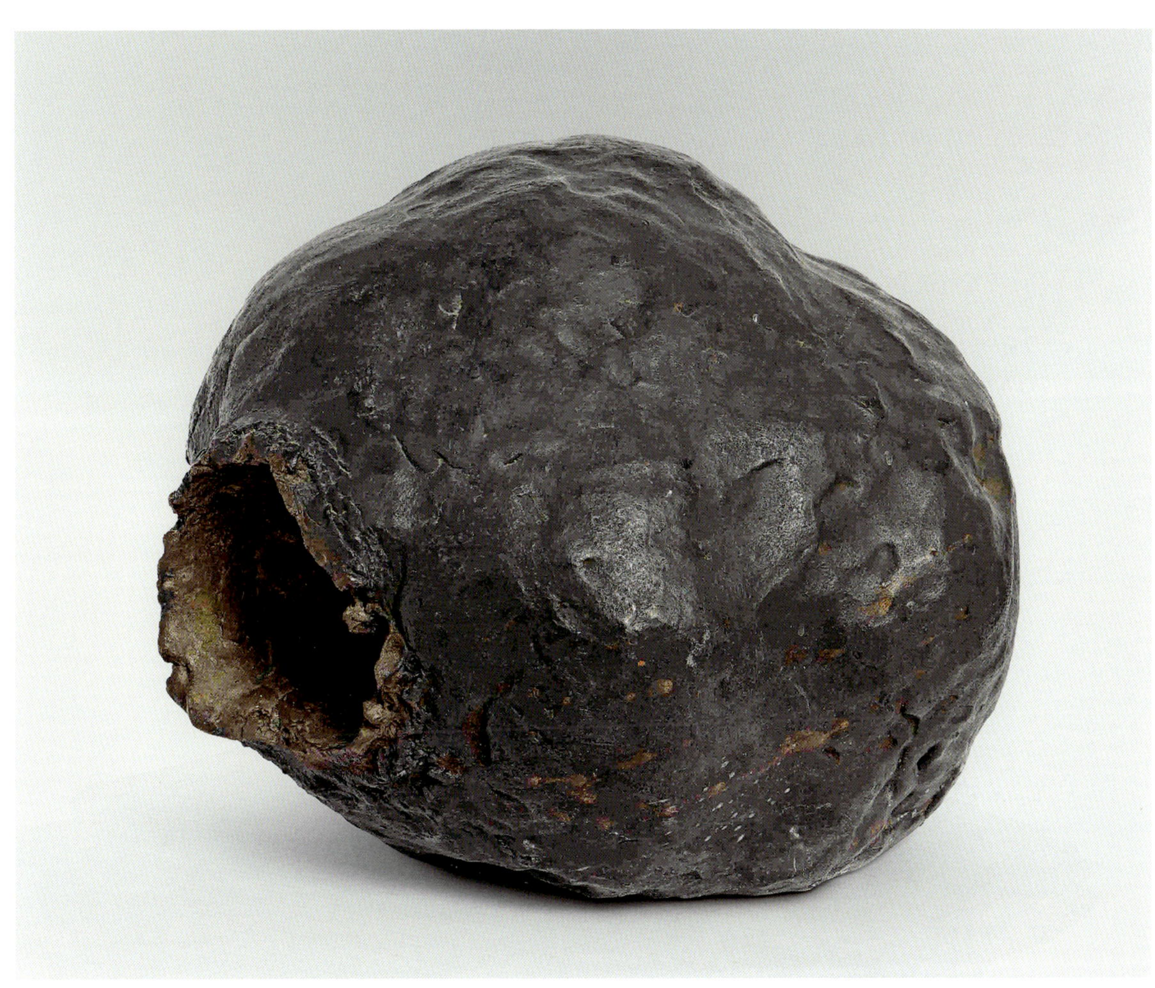

Concetto spaziale. Natura
1959-60
bronze
40 × 48 cm
59-60 N 31
Courtesy Fondazione
Lucio Fontana

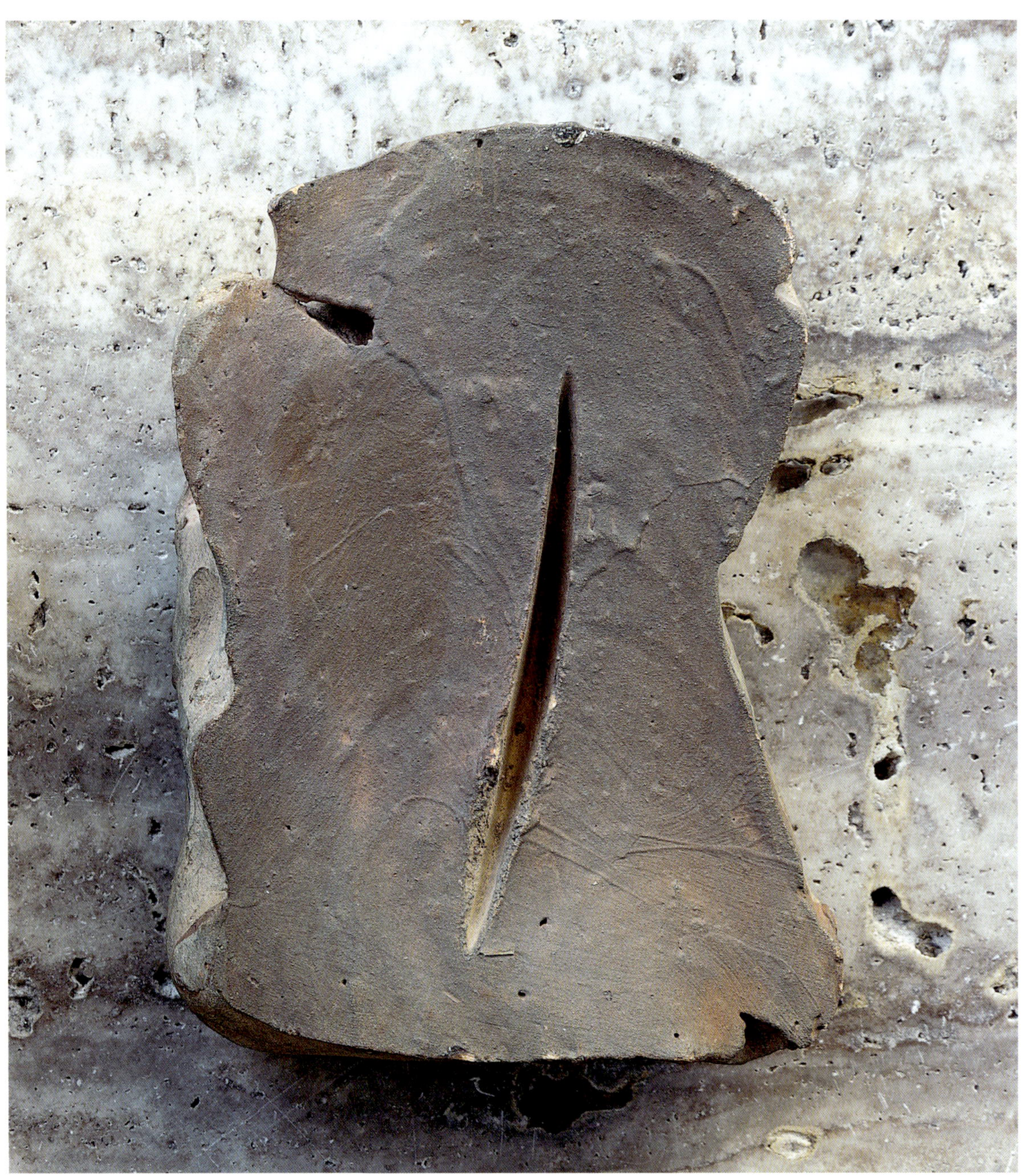

Concetto spaziale. Nature
1959
painted terracotta
14,5 × 10,5 × 5,5 cm
59 N 34 and 35
Courtesy Private collection

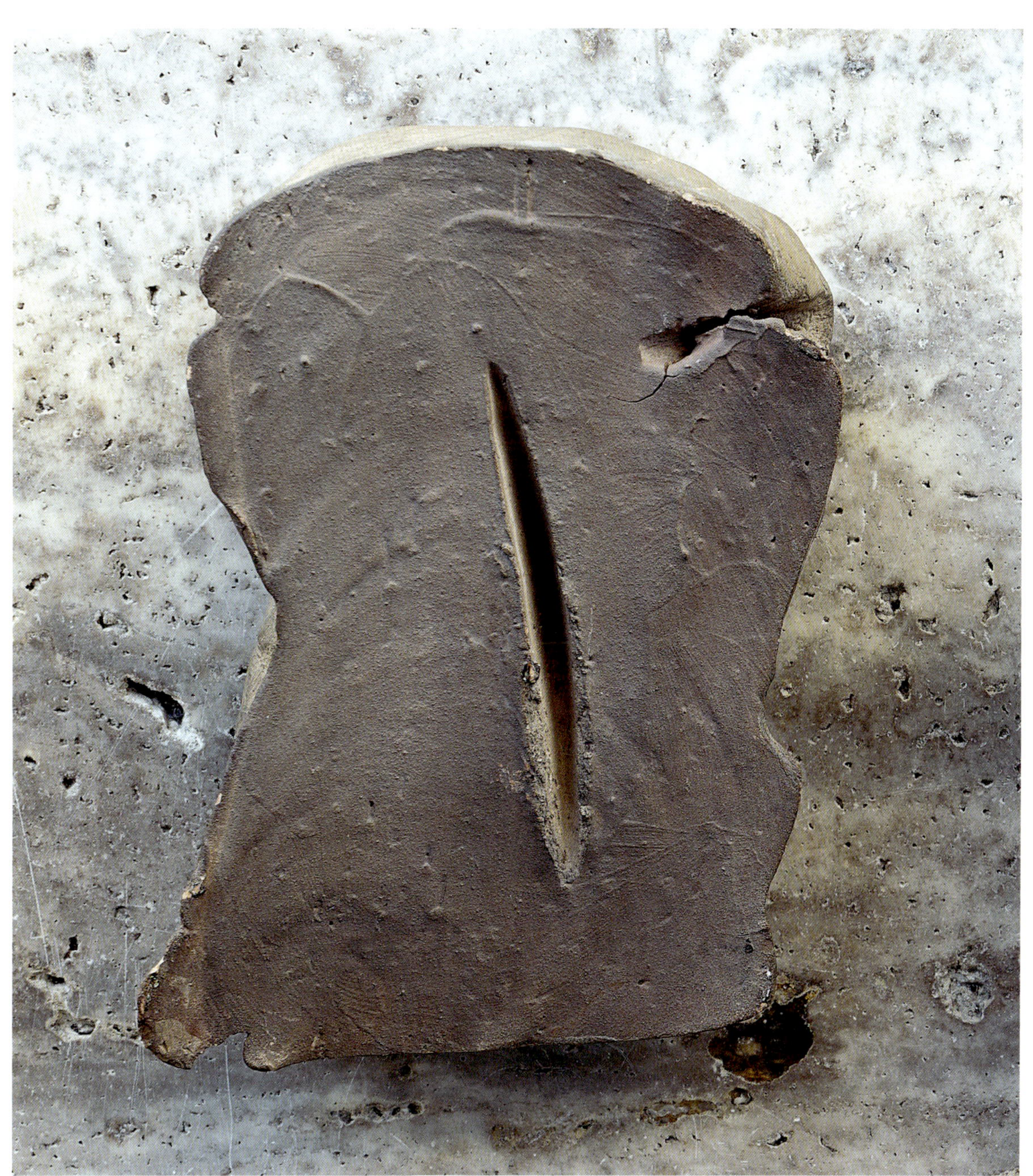

Concetto spaziale
1964 – 65
holes, graffiti, gashes and black
tempera on white blotting paper
65 × 45 cm
64 – 65 DSP 120
Private collection
Courtesy Gió Marconi
Milano

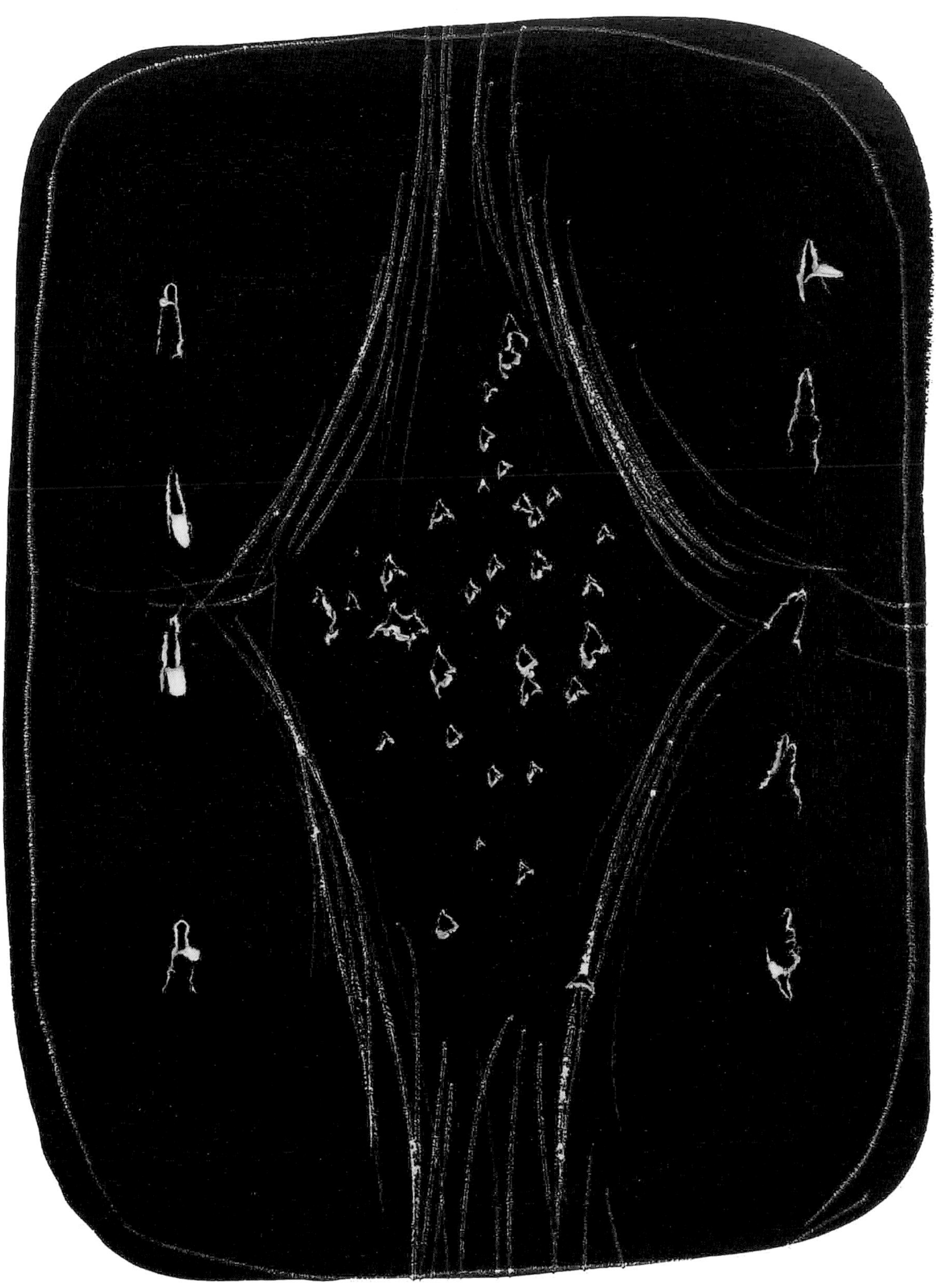

Concetto spaziale
1965 ca.
holes and graffiti on white
absorbent paper
45 × 58 cm
2436/211
Private collection
Courtesy Gió Marconi
Milano

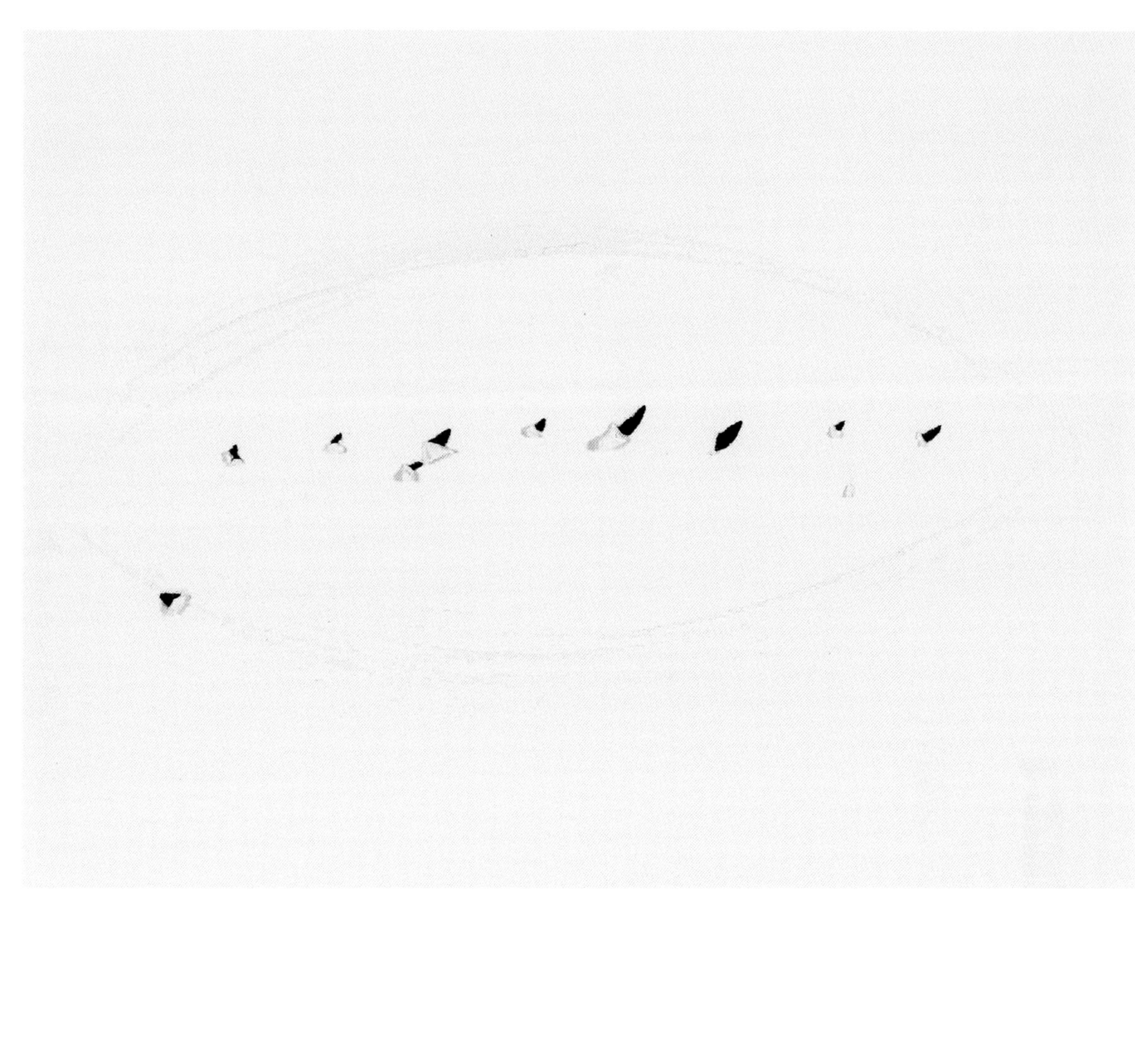

Concetto spaziale
1964 - 66
holes and graffiti on black paper
45 × 32 cm
64 - 65 DSP 47
Private collection
Courtesy Gió Marconi
Milano

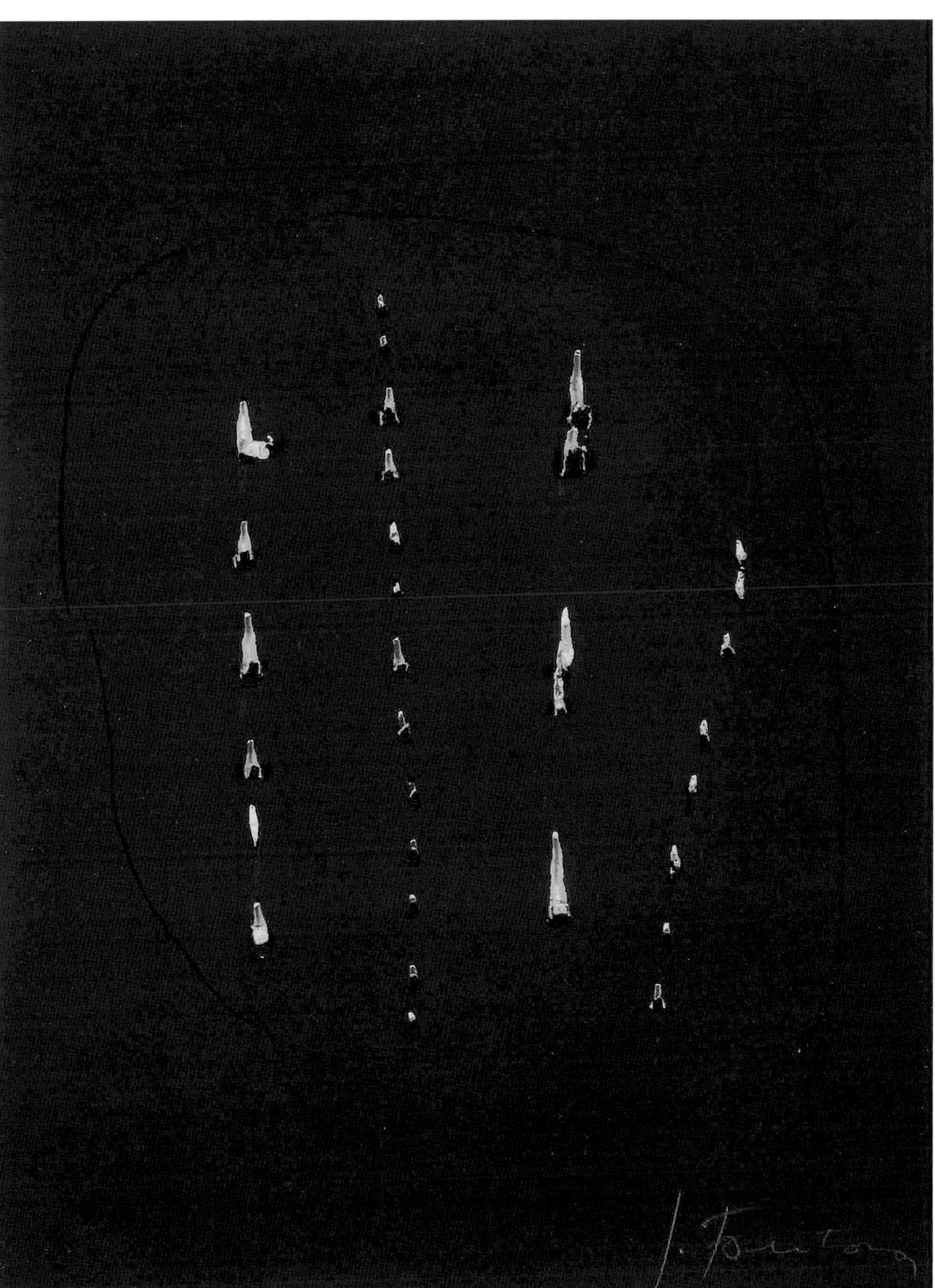

Concetto spaziale
1964–67
gashes and graffiti on white
absorbent paper
45,5 × 58 cm
64–65 DSP 136 E
Private collection
Courtesy Gió Marconi
Milano

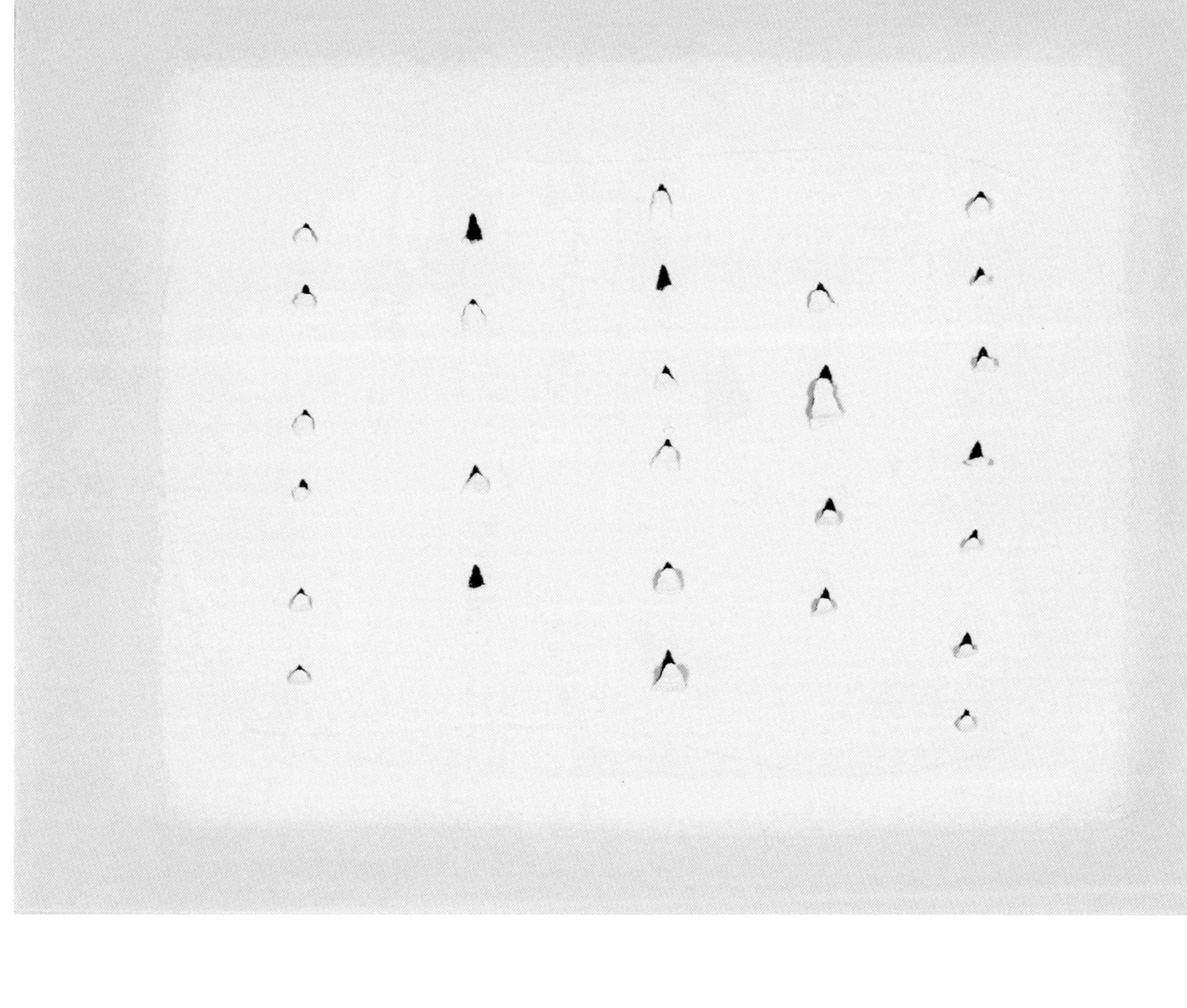

Concetto spaziale
1966-68
holes and graffiti on white
absorbent paper
44 × 56 cm
66-68 DSP 40
Private collection
Courtesy Gió Marconi
Milano

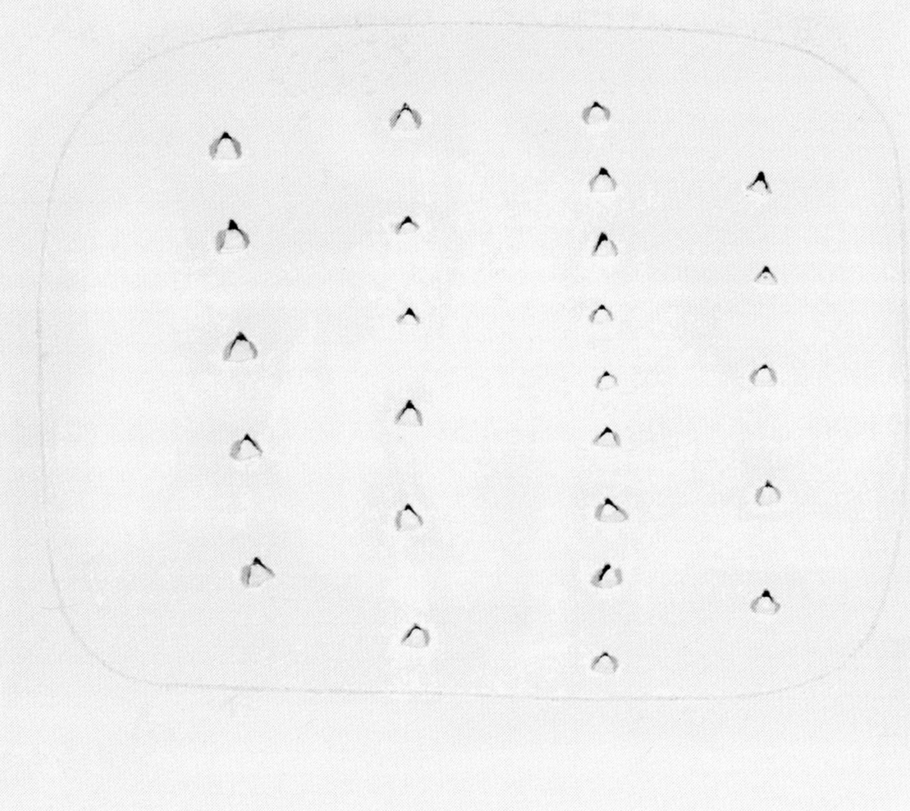

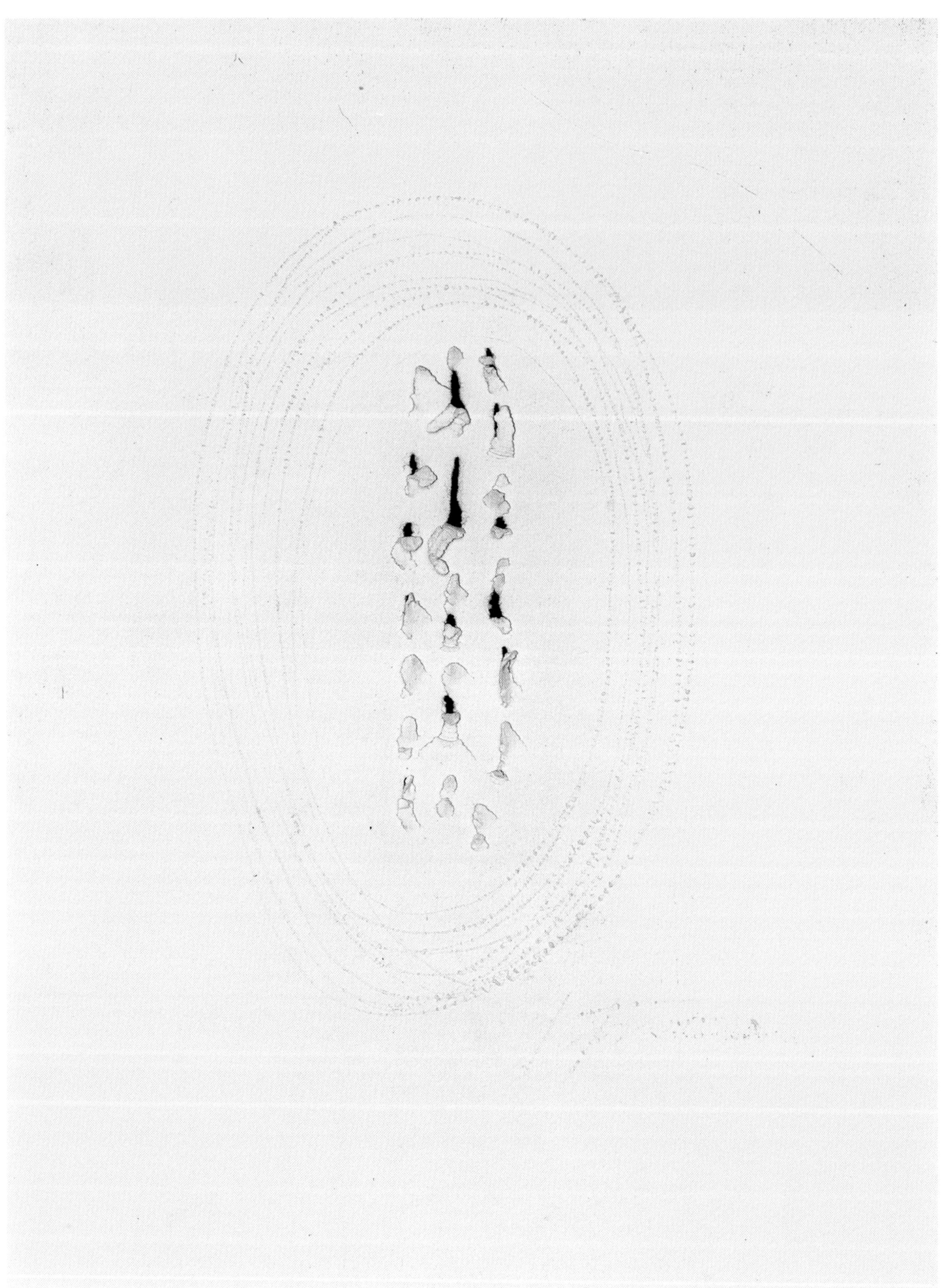

Concetto spaziale
1966-68
graffiti and gashes on white
absorbent paper
66 × 48 cm
66-68 DSP 239
Private collection
Courtesy Gió Marconi
Milano

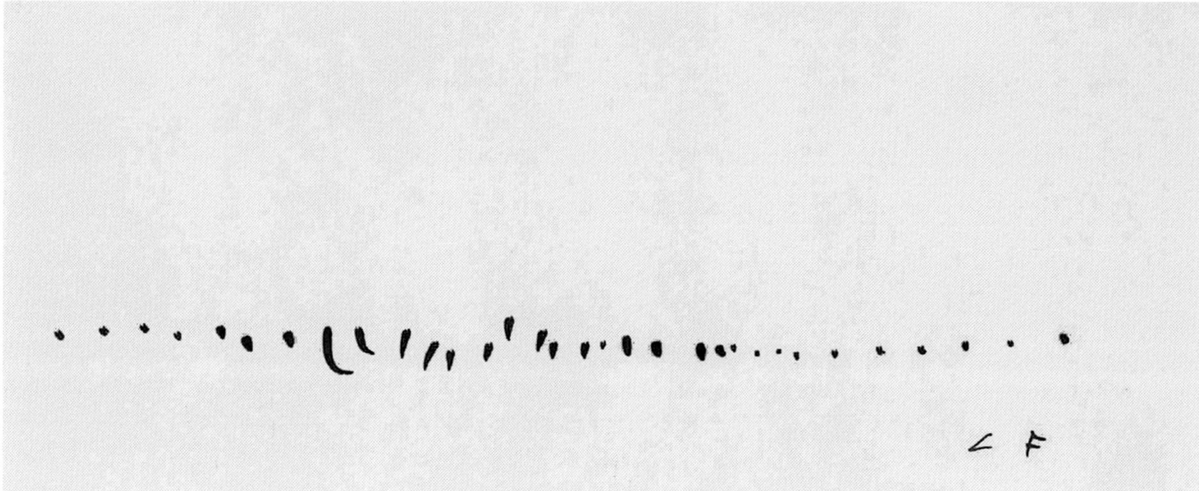

Concetto spaziale
1967-68
ink on paper
9,4 × 22 cm
Archivio Fontana
inv. 2436/215
Private collection
Courtesy Gió Marconi
Milano

Concetto spaziale
1966-67
oil and holes on canvas
200 × 150 cm
66-67 B 18
Private collection

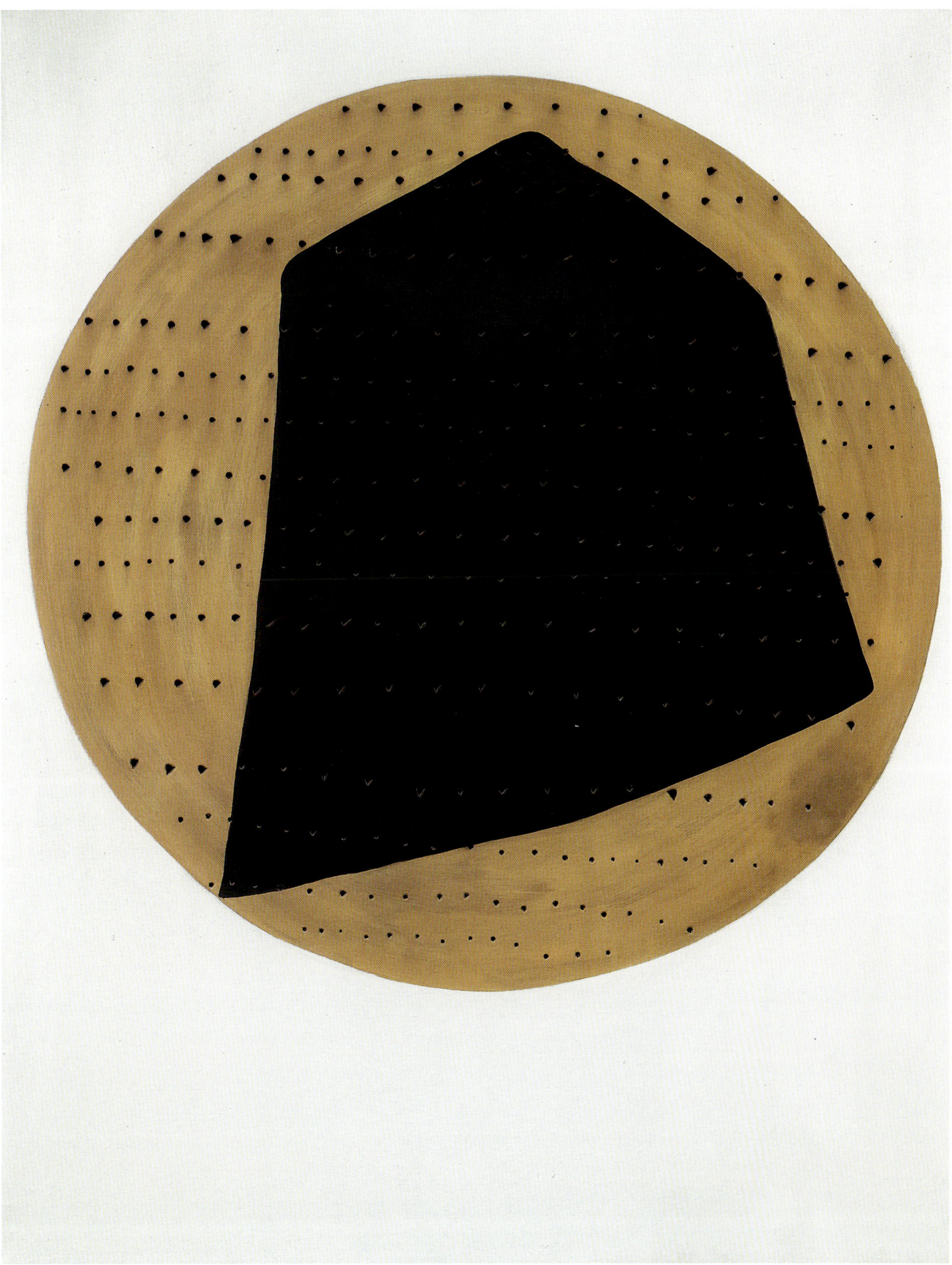

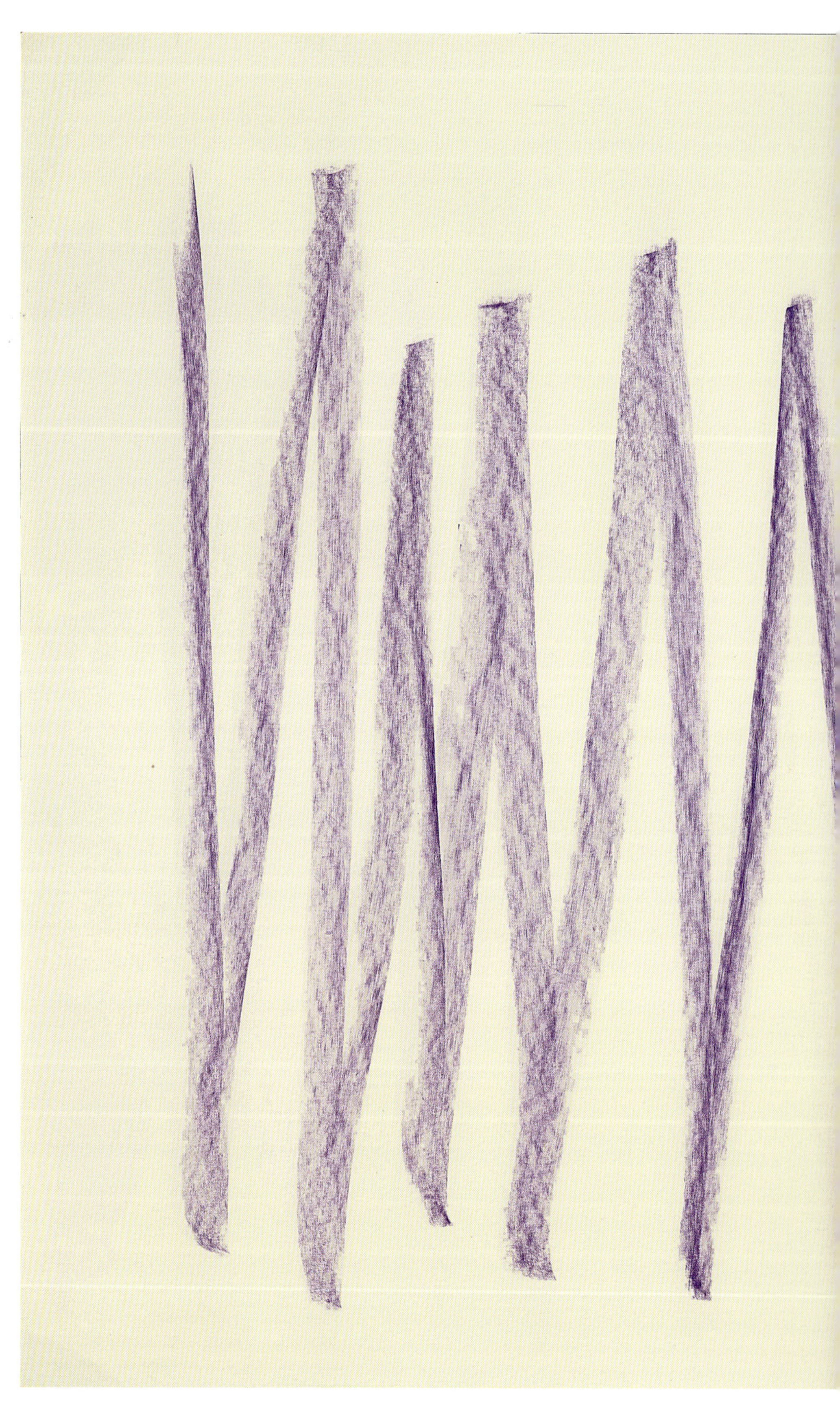

Concetto spaziale
1966–68
grease pastel on cardboard
70 × 100 cm
66–68 DVA 1
Courtesy Fondazione
Lucio Fontana

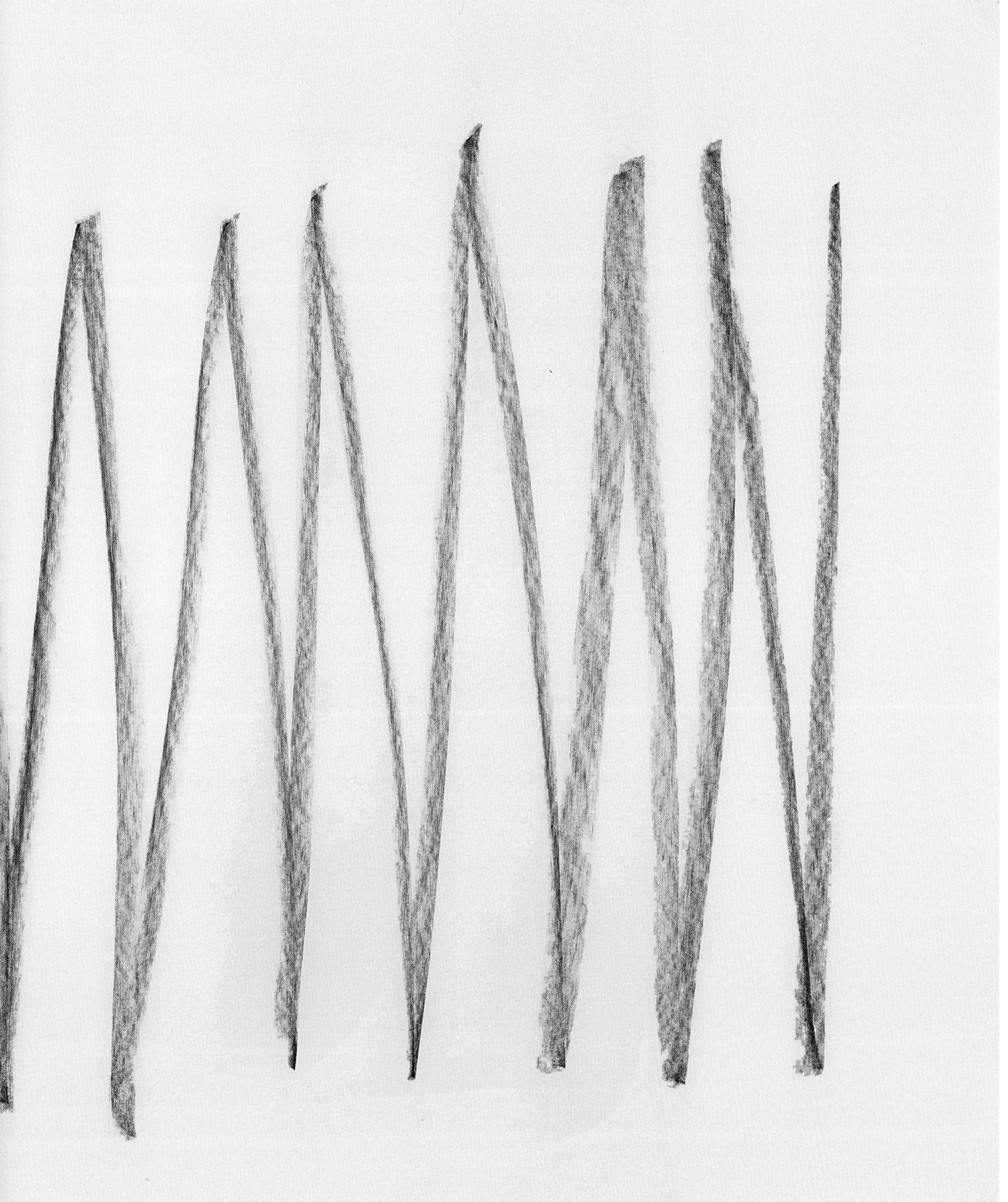

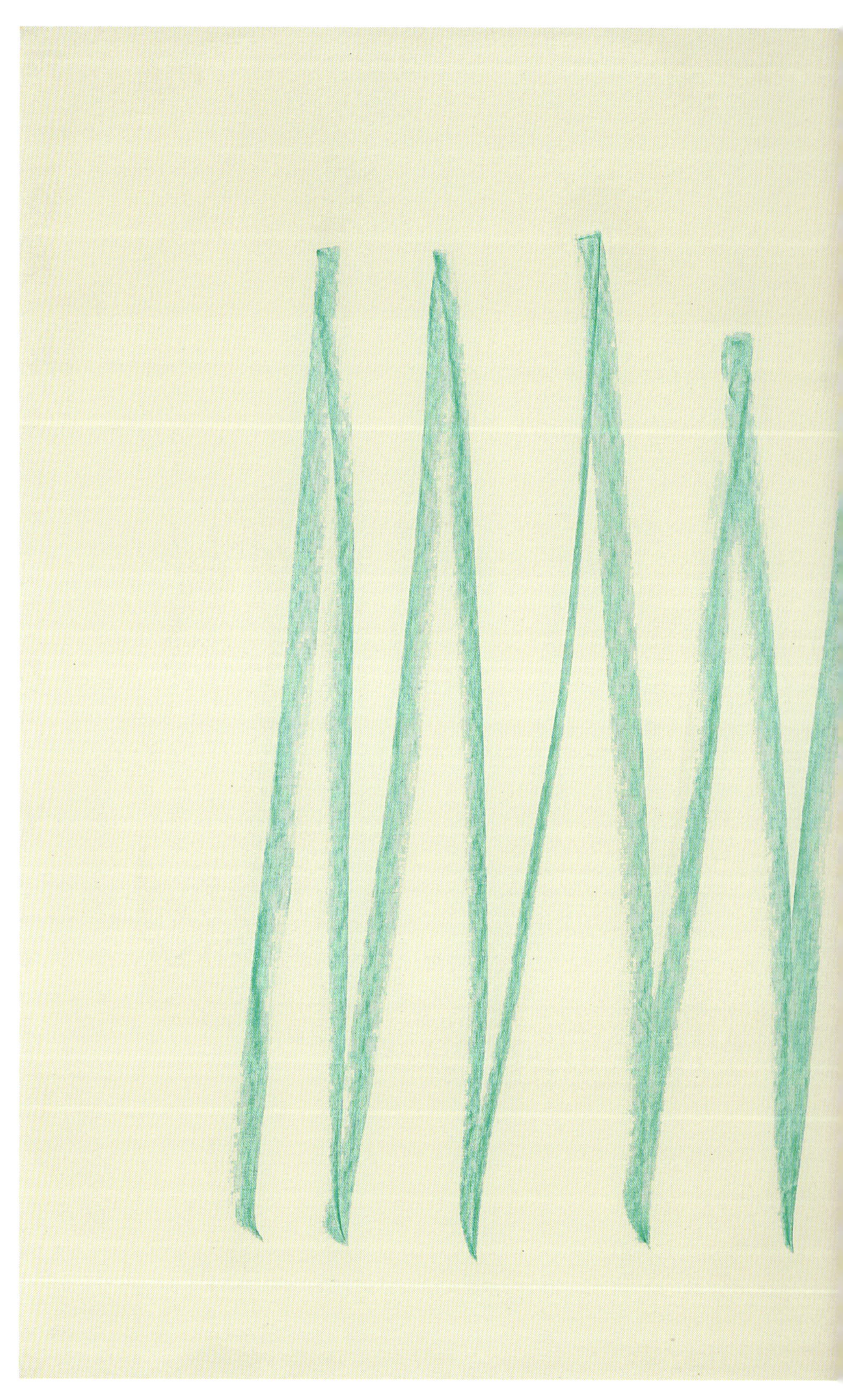

Concetto spaziale
1966–68
grease pastel on cardboard
70 × 100 cm
66–68 DVA 3
Courtesy Fondazione
Lucio Fontana

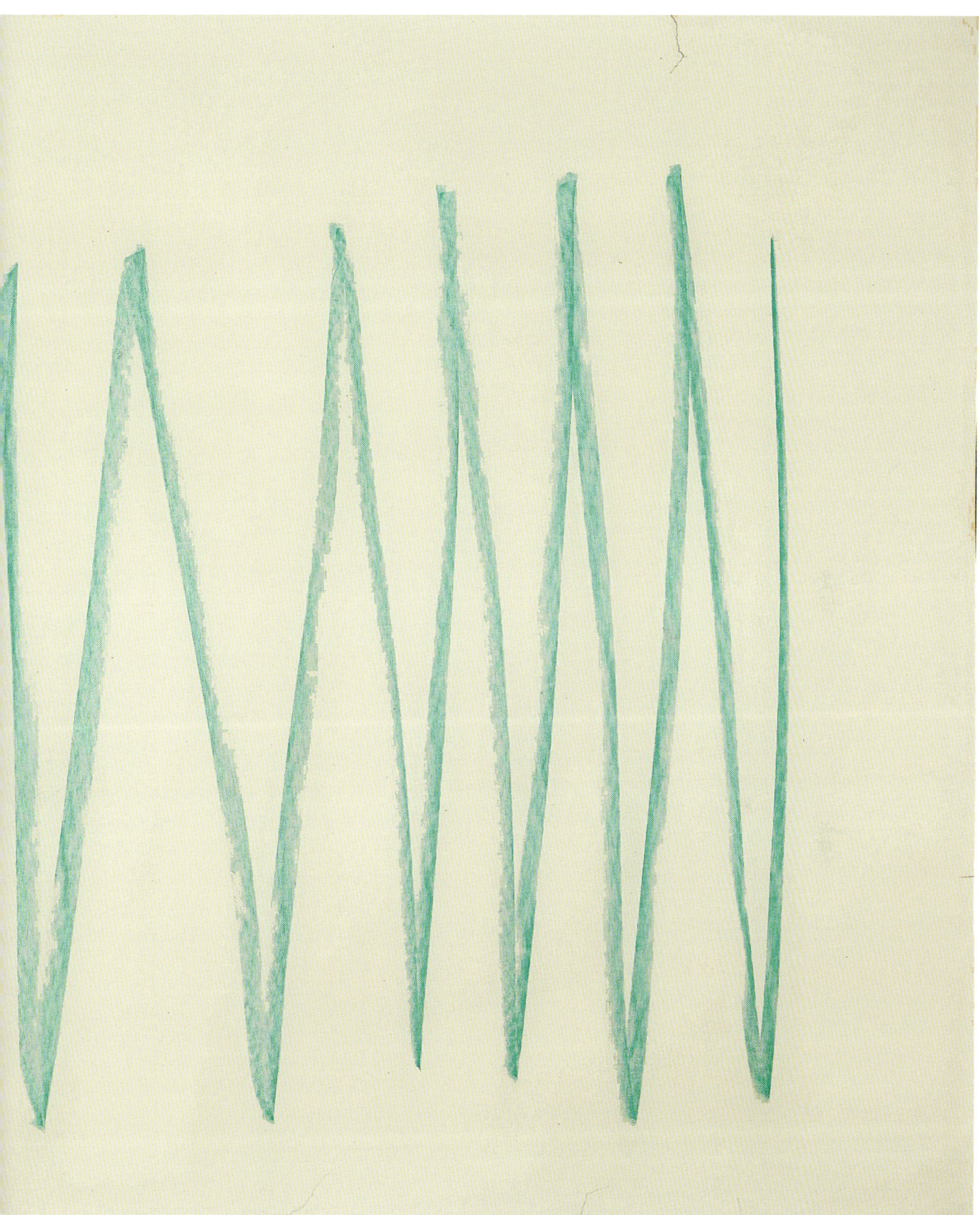

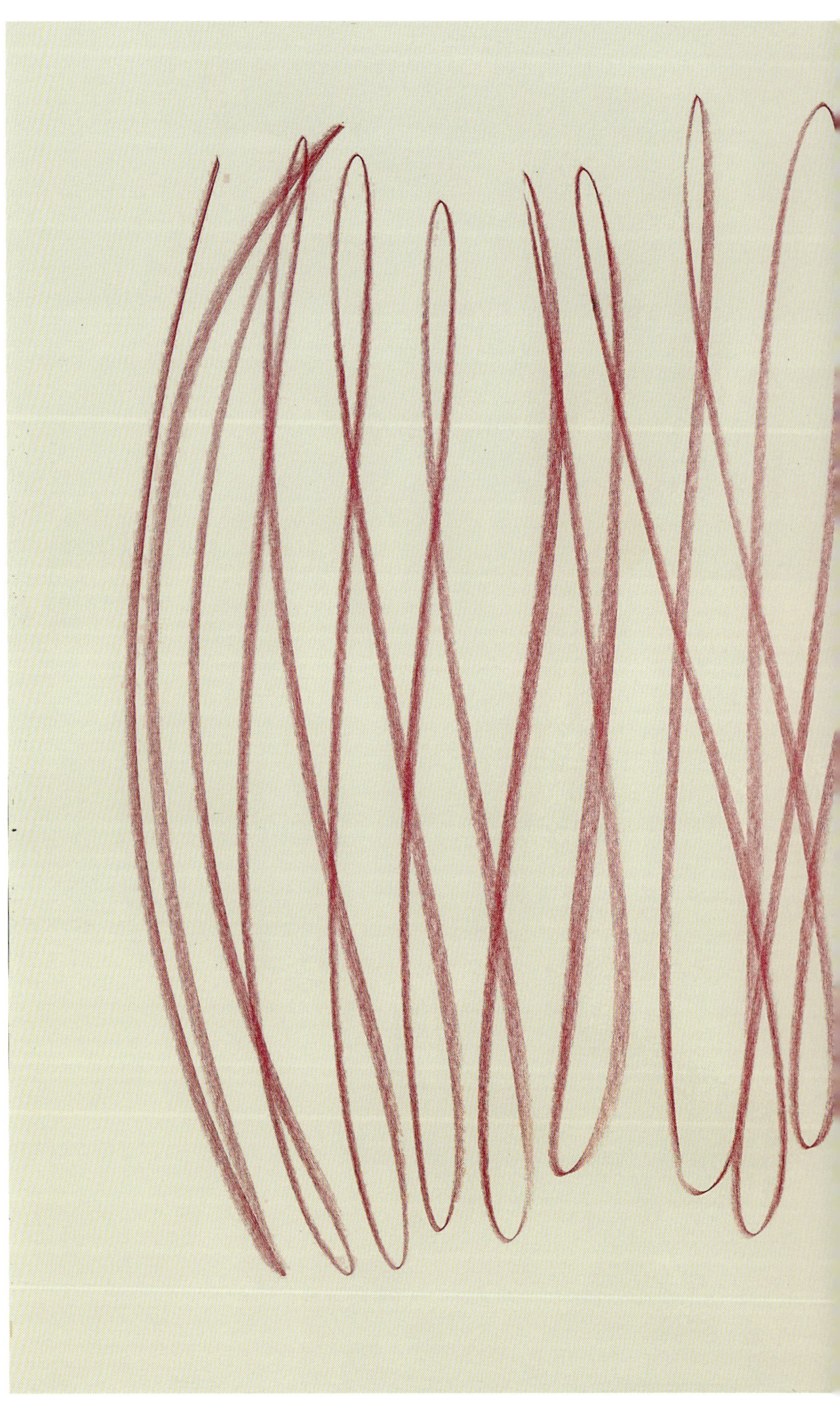

Concetto spaziale
1966–68
grease pastel on cardboard
70 × 100 cm
66–68 DVA 2
Courtesy Fondazione
Lucio Fontana

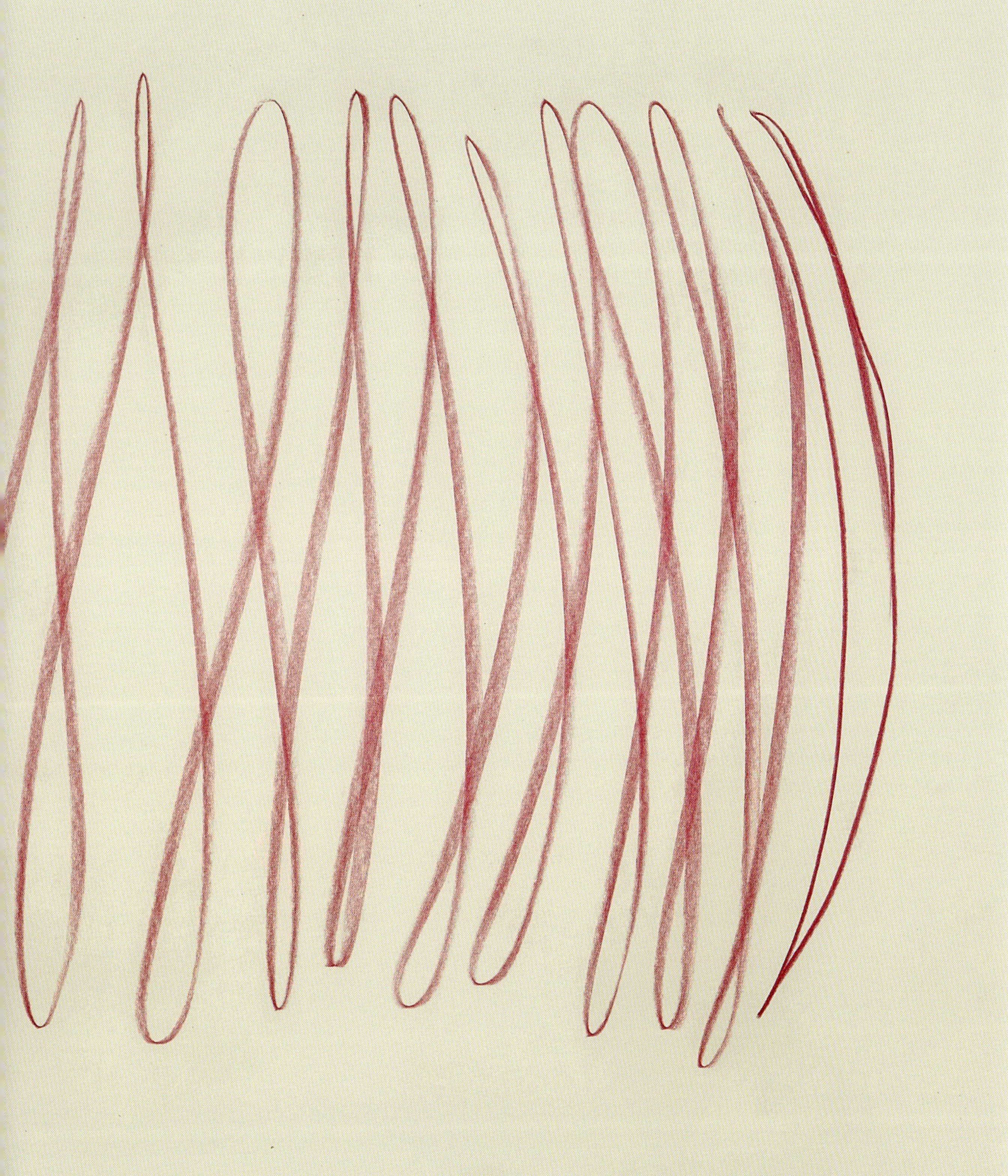

Concetto spaziale. Attesa
1965
water paint on canvas
149,8 × 116,7 × 7,5 cm
65 T 154
Courtesy Collezioni civiche
Raccolta MIAC
Museo Novecento
Firenze

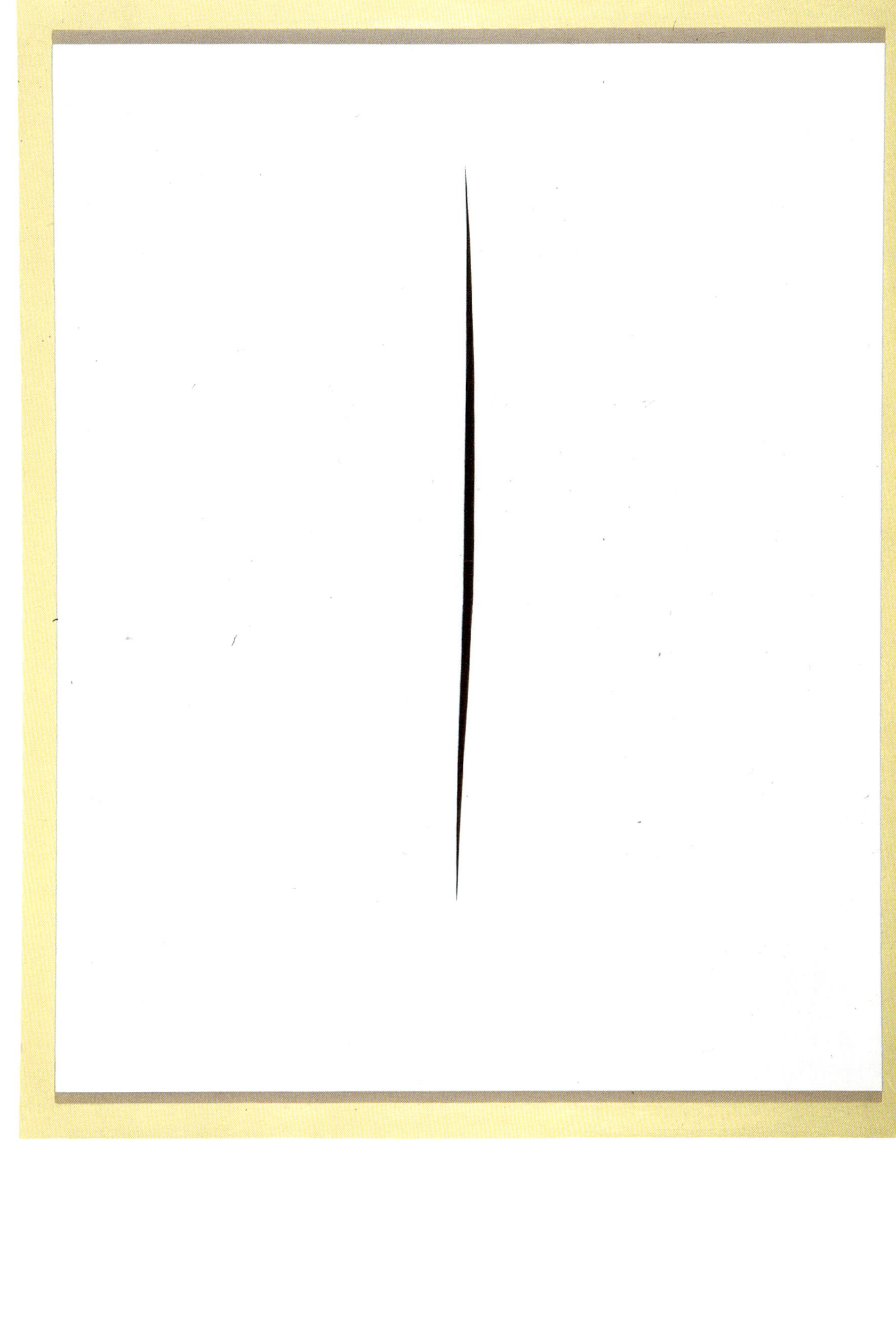

Multiplo Pillola:
Concetto spaziale
1967
fuchsia lacquered copper with cut
on black metal pedestal
20 × 20 × 38 cm
n. 321/56
Private collection

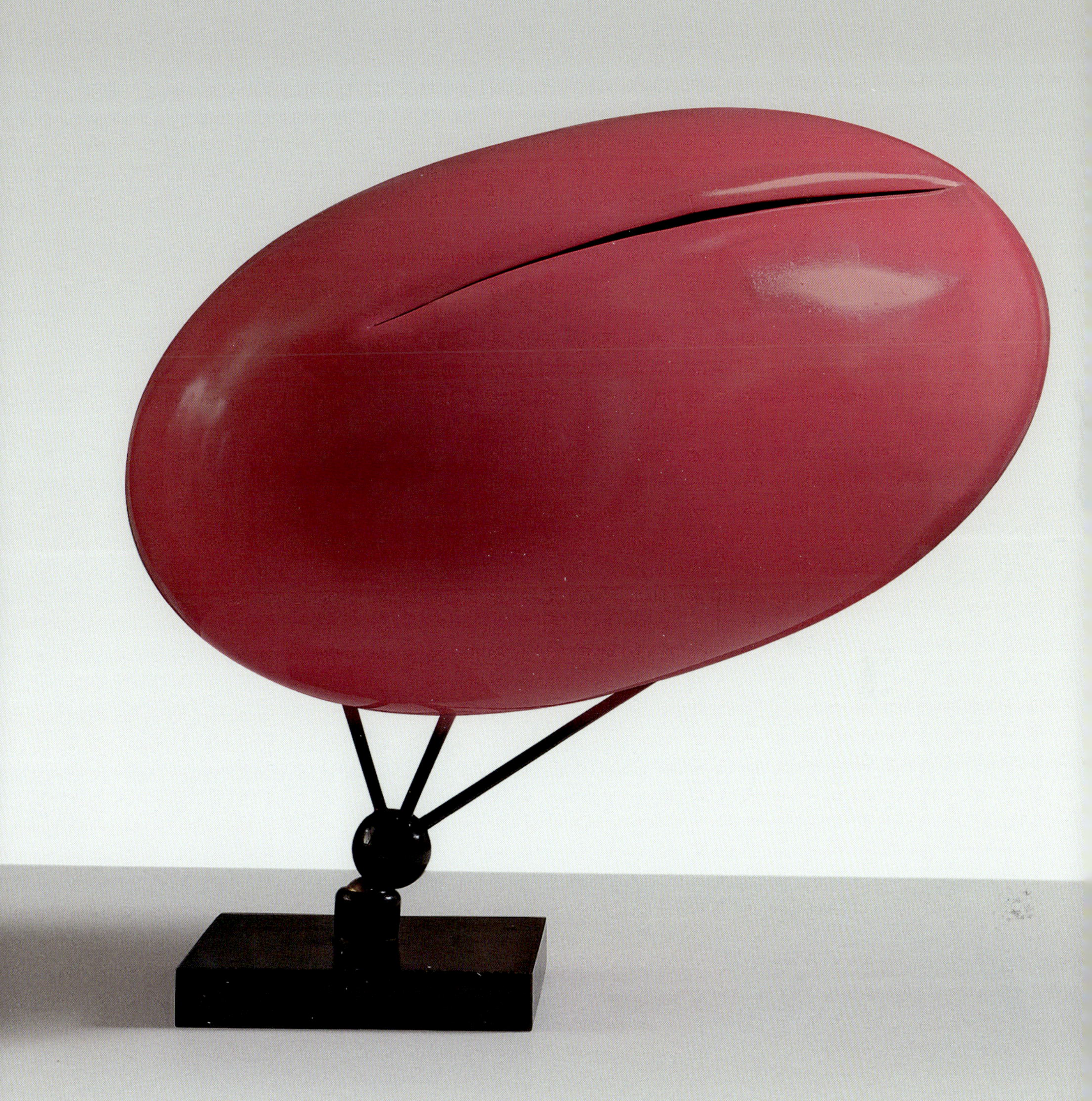

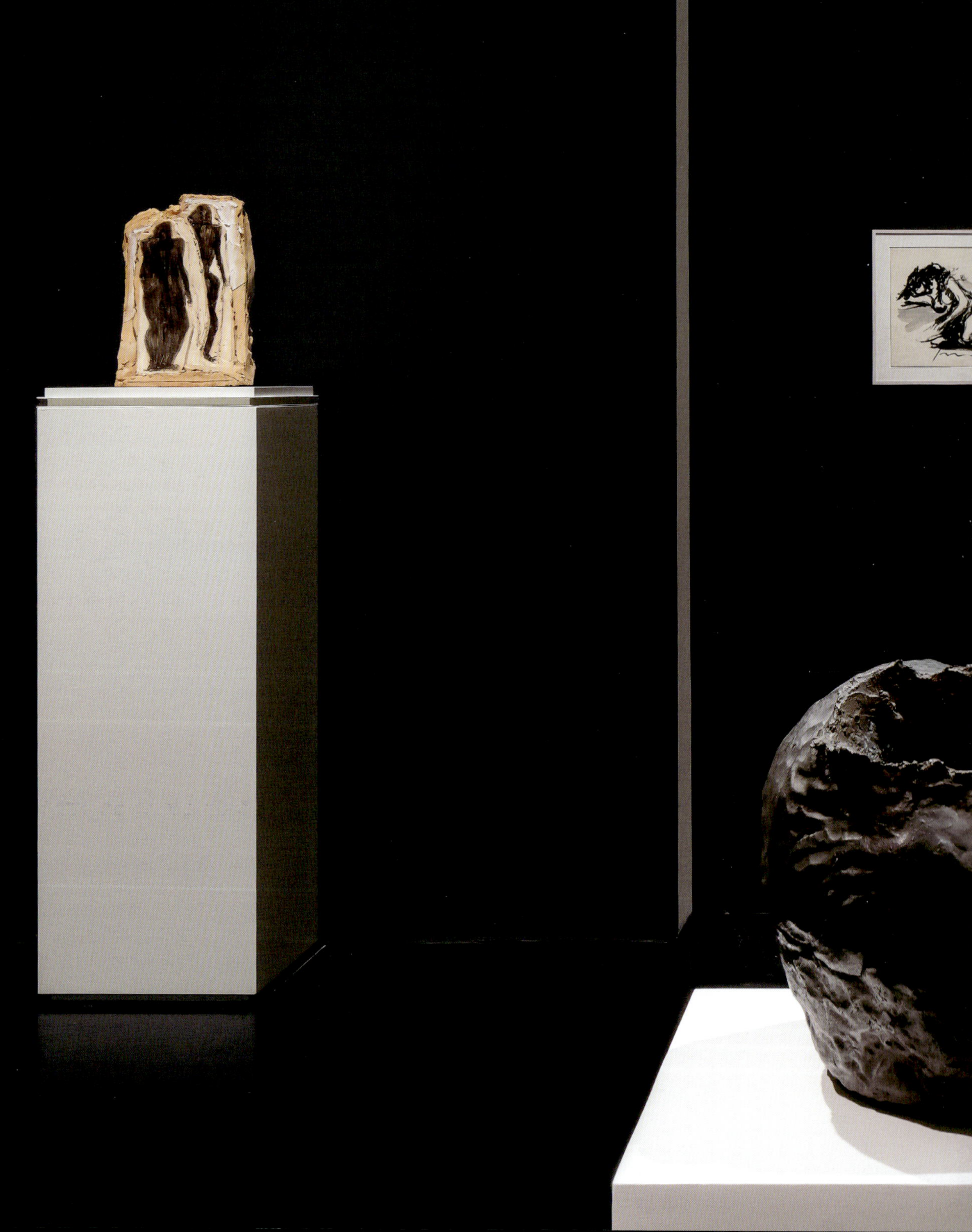
LUCIO FONTANA
L'origine du monde
02.03 — 13.09.2023
Ideazione Sergio Risaliti

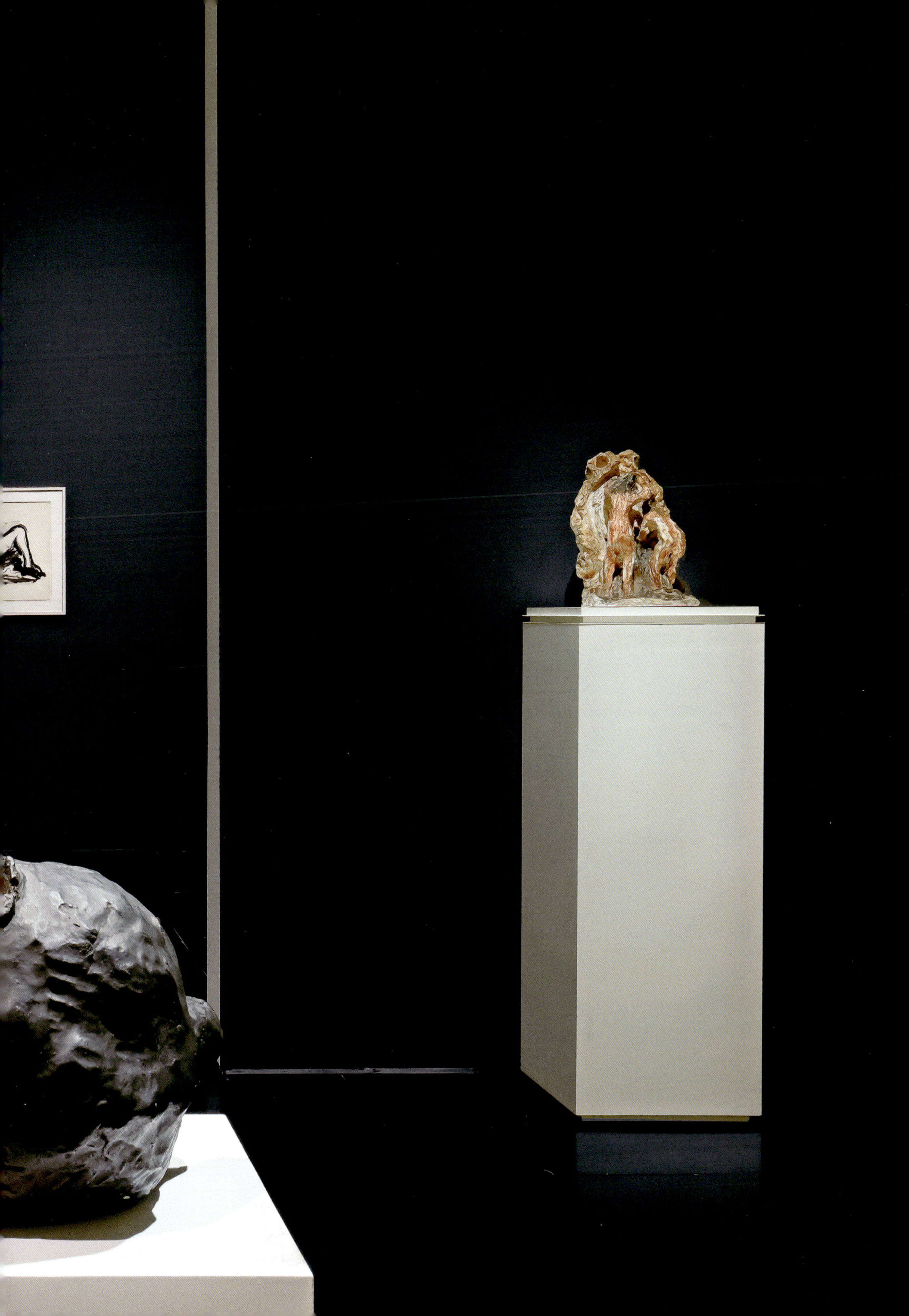

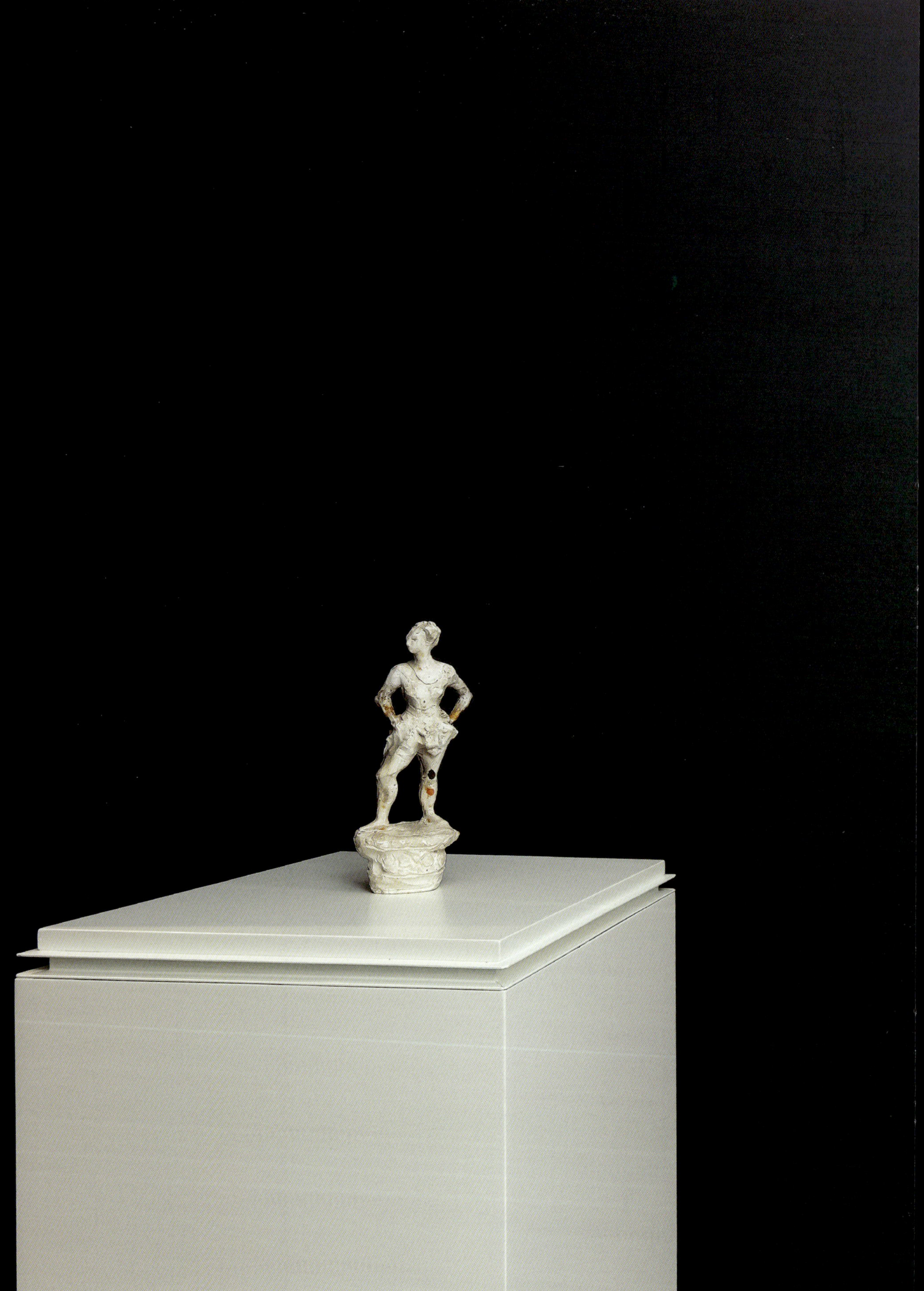

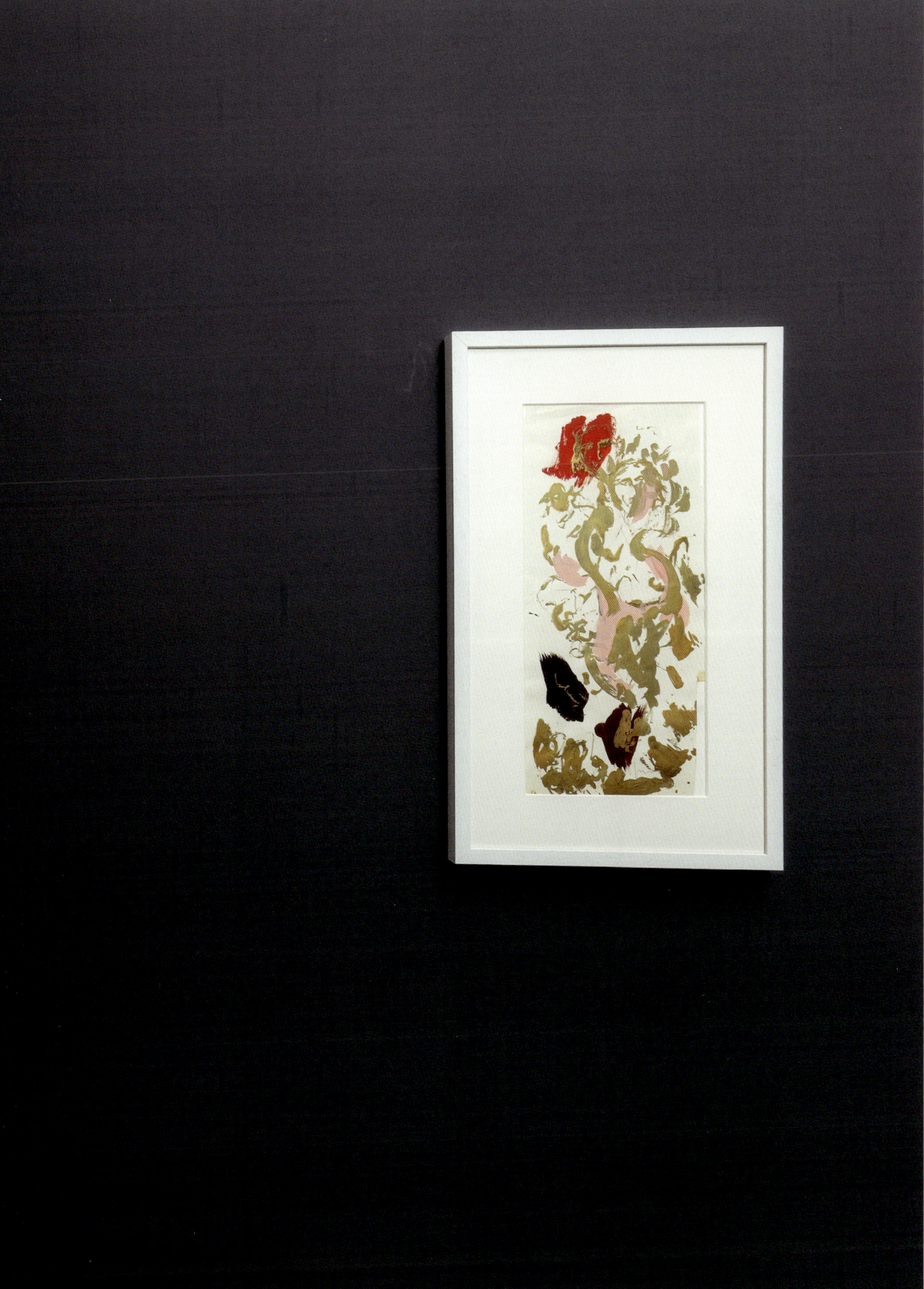

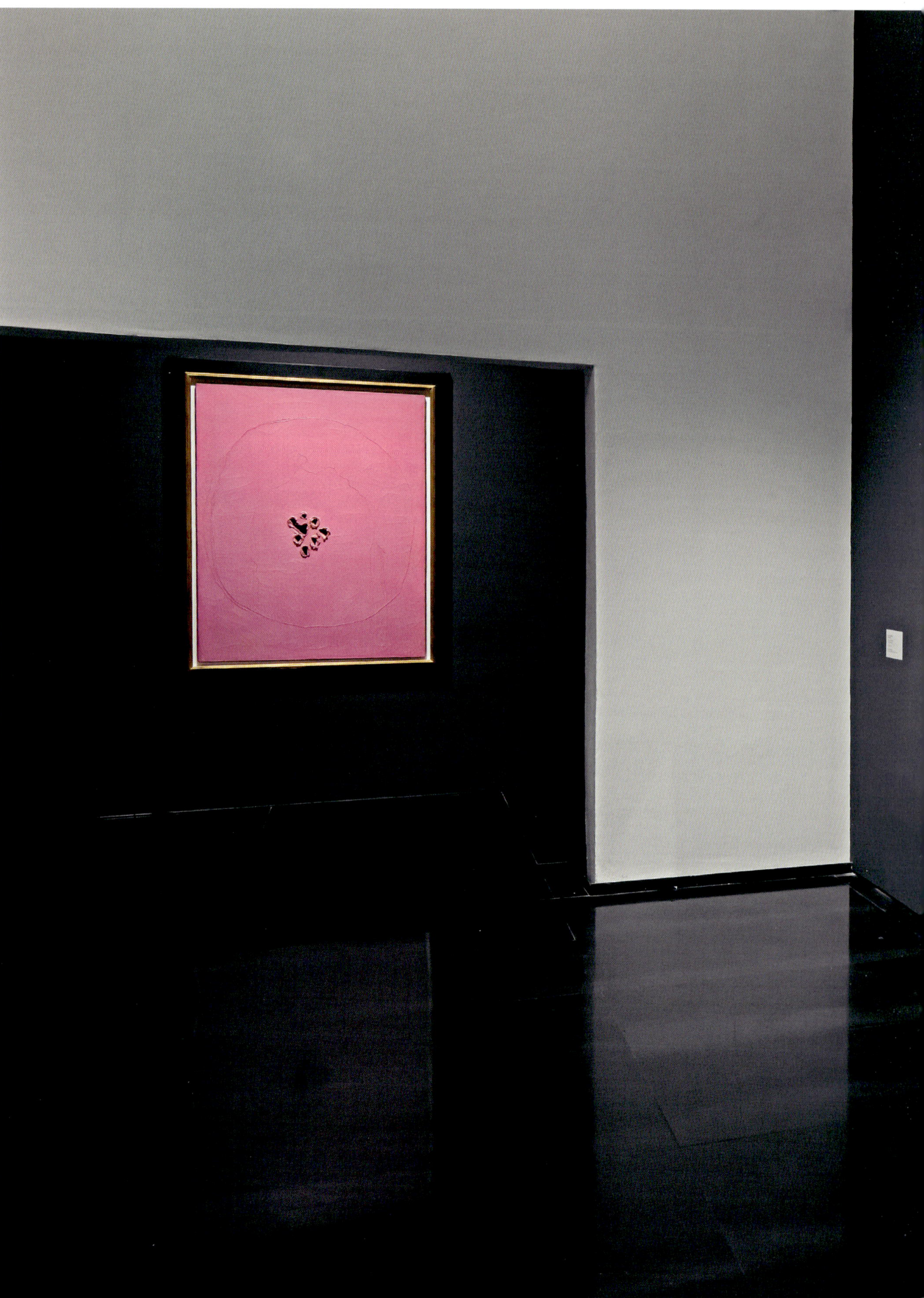

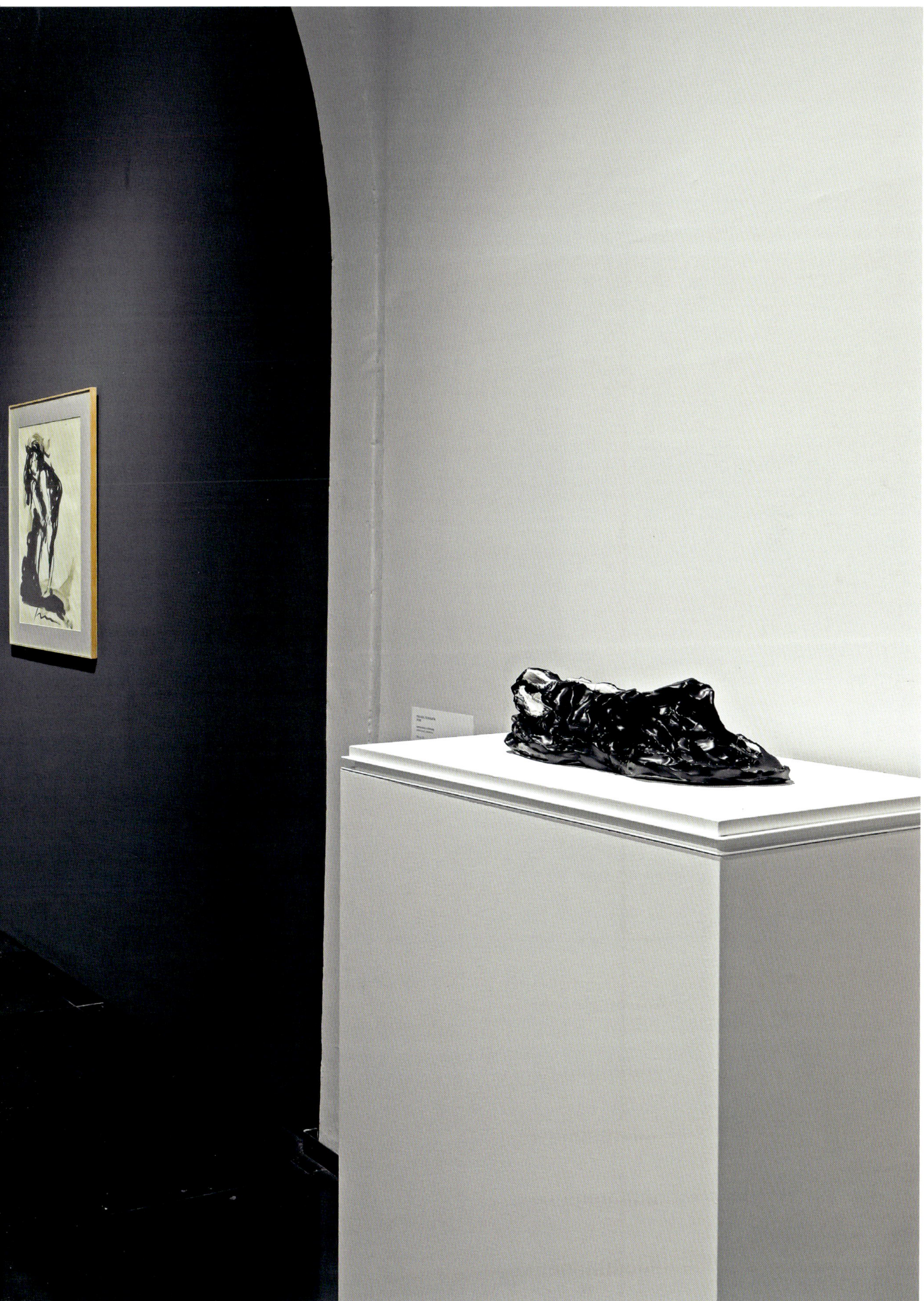

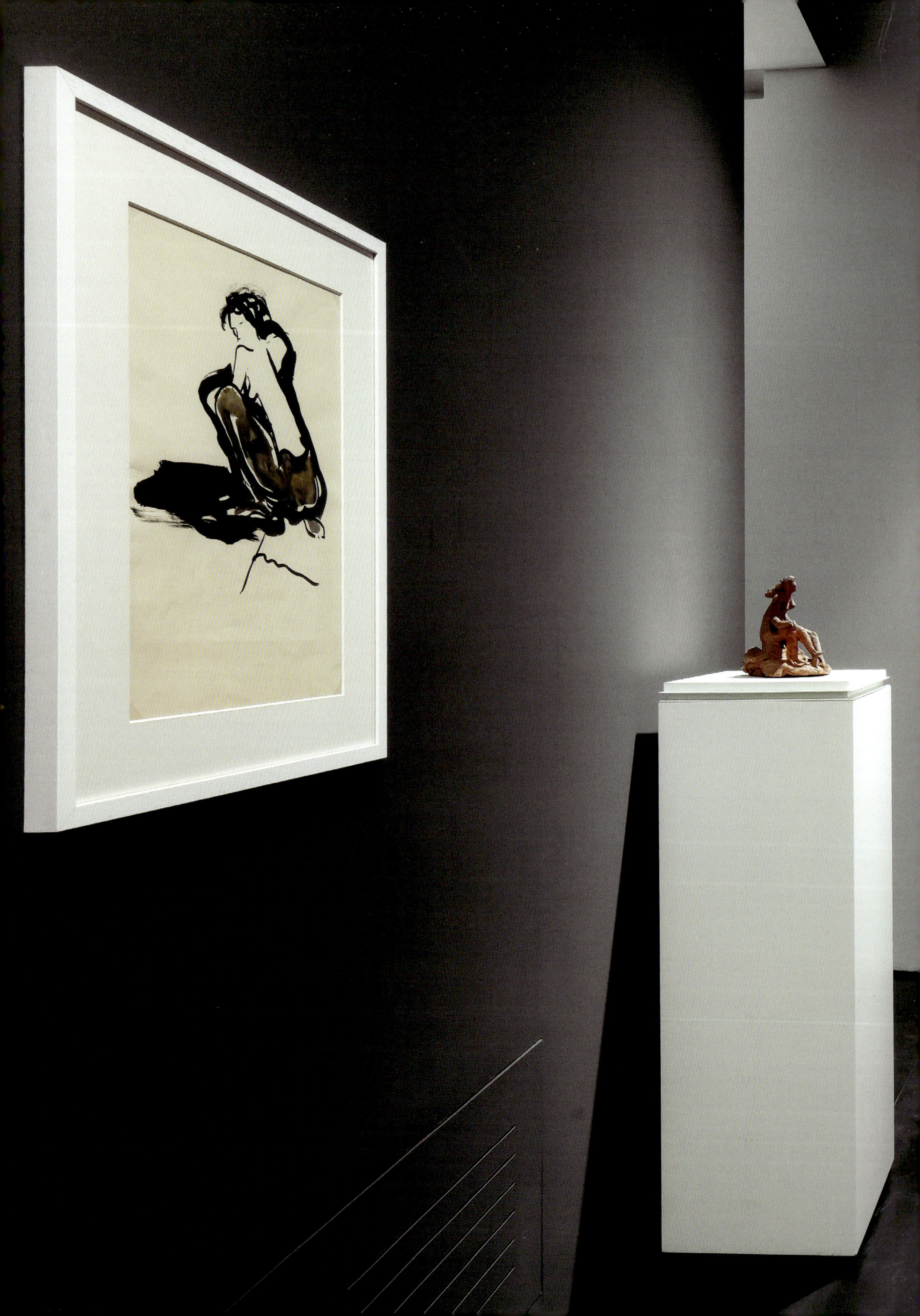

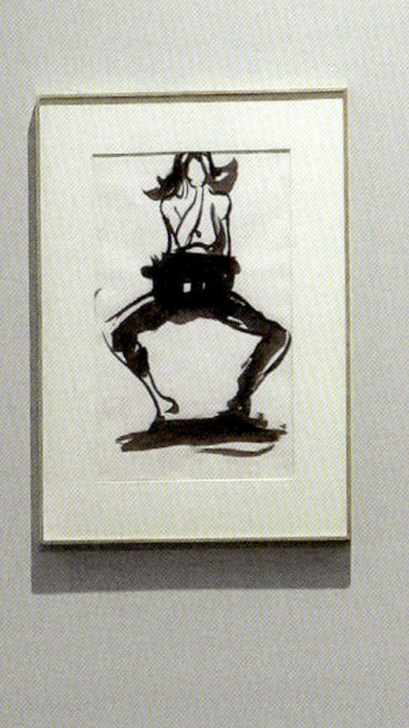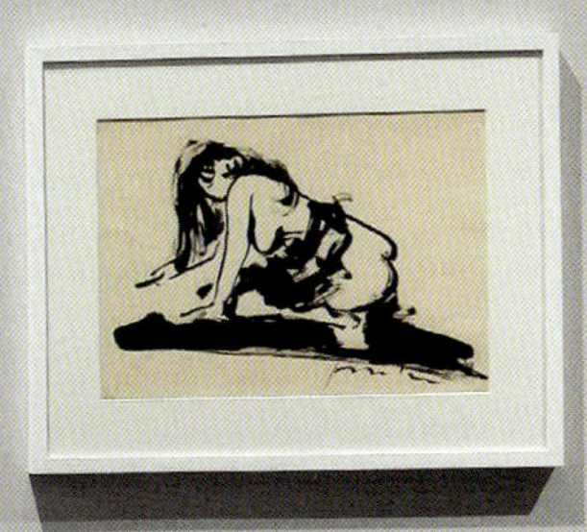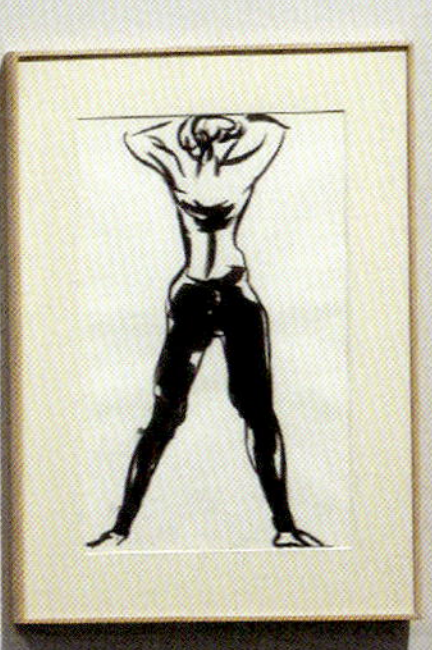

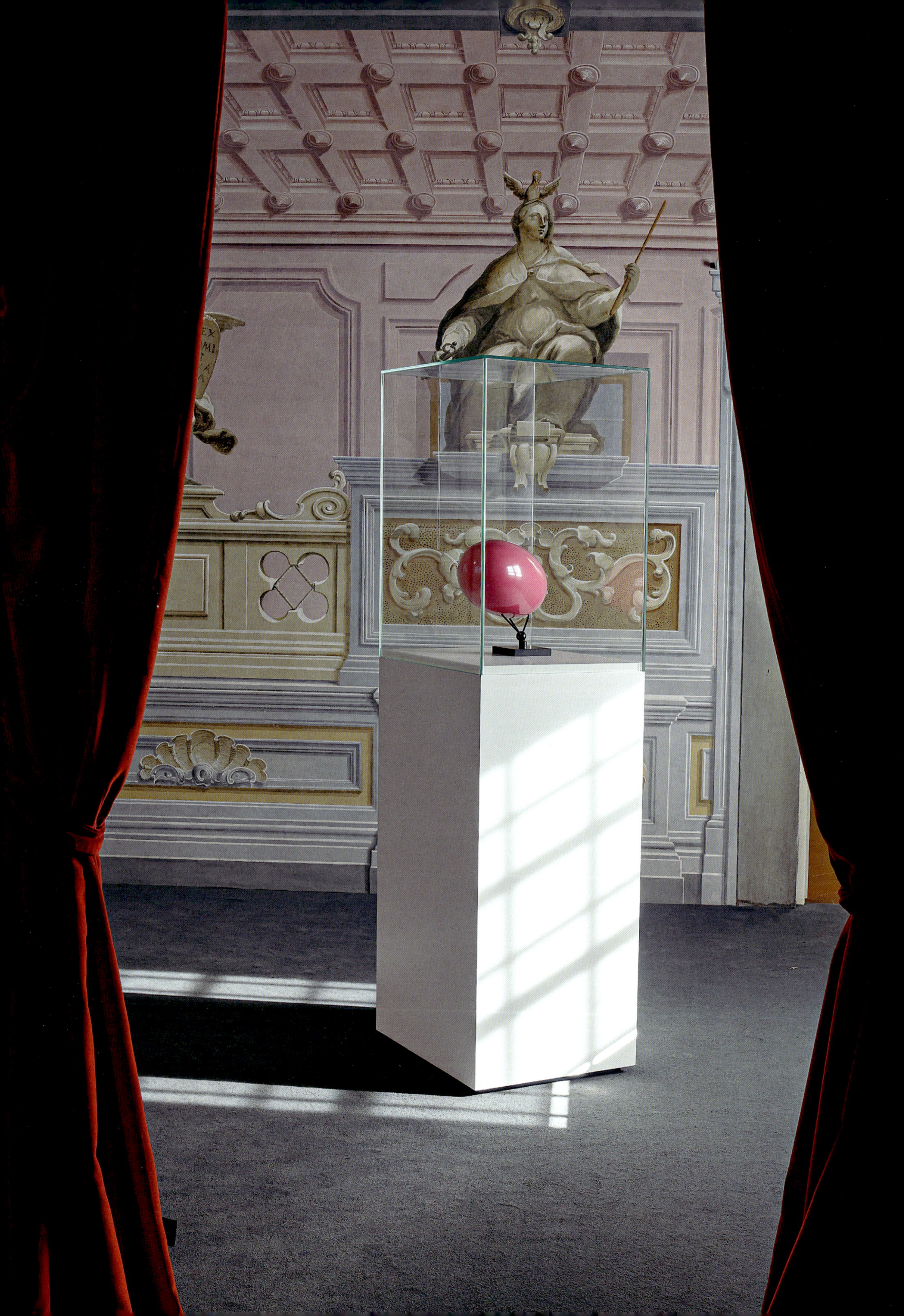

LUCIO FONTANA

The Origin of the World

edited by
Sergio Risaliti

SilvanaEditoriale

"I could have done that too". How many times have we heard this phrase, even from friends or relatives, when talking about a work of contemporary art? And how many times have we gone along with it, unaware perhaps of the research, the study, the mastery, the groundwork behind that piece?

Lucio Fontana's art often lends itself to such comments, followed by discussions on the alleged inconsistency and excessive abstraction, not to use more drastic terms, of today's art.

An exhibition such as *L'origine du monde* at the Museo Novecento in Florence has the merit of bringing us closer to Fontana's art, and taking us beyond the famous and equally mistreated cuts on canvas.

The museum is dedicating a vast retrospective to him that takes up two entire floors of the former Leopoldine complex in Santa Maria Novella, complementing the other exhibition on Lucio Fontana, in Palazzo Vecchio, which presents works by the Italo-Argentine master along with works by Alberto Giacometti: a project that brings together for the first time these extraordinary contemporary artists in an intense visual and sensorial one-on-one challenge.

The exhibition at the Museo Novecento, including drawings and sculptures, narrates the artist's development not only through his studies of space and time, but also his interest in the human figure and female nude. The exhibition offers a fully-rounded profile, capturing his vision, innovation and versatility. The figures hosted in the rooms are geometric one moment, and swirling the next, or they are barely roughed-out forms, yet filled with sensuality and primordial qualities.

At the end of the itinerary, Fontana appears less abstruse and more familiar.

For some years now, Florence has been committed to promoting, researching and workshopping contemporary art, with exhibitions that have drawn some of the greatest artists of our time to Florence. Retrospectives and site-specific works by artists like Jan Fabre, Jeff Koons, Giuseppe Penone, Urs Fischer, Jenny Saville and Henry Moore have offered a stream of cross-references and enrichment, making our city an attractive hotbed for new styles and trends, and a major hub for public art.

No one claims to hold the key to teaching people how to appreciate art, let alone contemporary art. But to try to get to know it, to approach it, to take a first-hand look at it and not just know it through hearsay or through a smartphone screen, is the first step to approaching it without bias or arrogance. Or without the usual comment, "I could have done that too".

Dario
Nardella

**MAYOR
OF FLORENCE**

Lucio Fontana, Female Figures, Nature and Cuts at the Origin of the World

Sergio
Risaliti

Lucio Fontana's creative horizon is so extensive that it is sometimes perplexing, making it impossible to gather the many inventions, variations and linguistic deviations under a single ideological umbrella. On this level, the only comparison that holds up is that with Pablo Picasso, whose brilliant artistic frenzy hindered him from lingering on any one style, driven as he was to win his daily battle against death, tackling non-being with his painter's and sculptor's tools. Picasso repeatedly spoke of art as a form of exorcism to be used against any force that opposed the creative impulse, which he had in spades. Fontana also had something of an initiation into the experience of death, which probably conditioned his career from the outset. His father owned a business that produced commemorative monuments, portraits and in particular, funerary sculptures, in Rosario di Santa Fe. Otherwise, how could we understand his attraction to the darkest and crudest formlessness, found, for example, in the Promethean inventions such as the *Nature*, so seemingly far removed from his more aseptic and iconic works such as the famous "cuts". As much as those seem to be compromised with mud and telluric material, the others are much more purified and dematerialised. And yet this dialectic seems to have been as original as it was crucial to the development of his research, starting in his youth, as in the project for the De Medici Tomb of 1929–30 and the famous, singular *Pillole [Pills]* of 1967. According to the artist himself, with those "missile-like ovular sculptures" in metal, he wanted to confirm the death of God. This experience of death, a vitalistic response and a dialectical process between reality and unreality, presence and absence, was noted by Germano Celant, who wrote: "...in his funerary sculpture, which marks the beginnings of his artistic experience, death inhabits life, just as darkness inhabits light, and the two entities, in positive and negative, in colour and in black, must always be connected. The aspiration is to transcend their antagonism, so that life goes beyond all limits, like the tomb group that leans towards a broader conception of living in time.... In the period between 1925 and 1930 the artist relied on transcendence, on intertwining experience and religiosity, which is signified by the serenity of the nude body lying down, placated by death but still sleeping, as in the project for the De Medici Tomb... Here the subject of death is perceived as an attempt to take possession of an unknown nullity through a known dimension: the human body. A kind of living that seeks to integrate eternal sleep without losing its singularity. A reflection on the transcendent, on the afterlife that defines Fontana's intention of immobilising the surface or volume of the living on the boundary with the nothingness and emptiness of death. An immobilisation in *the between*, an attempt to place both polarities on the plane of their exchange between reality and unreality, presence and absence. A shared boundary that assumes the nude as a suspended moment of being and beingness: the luminous snapshot of a gesture to be deciphered that stands at the edge of something erotic and authentic, anatomical and epidermic like all of Fontana's art". To those unable to navigate Fontana's creative vitalism, including the oxymoronic polarities in his imagery of materialism and metaphysics, all we can do is define him as an eclectic, all too nonchalant and eccentric in leaping from a figurative language to an aniconic and conceptual one, from a baroque exuberance to a decidedly orthodox attitude, like that of a painter of golden icons. How then should certain drawings of female nudes executed after 1960 be approached? And how do we compare them with those of a Spatialist matrix, developed from the 1940s to 1968, the year of his death. Fontana insisted on the female nude with an interest that goes beyond the mere daily exercise of drawing from the academic model, an obsession and involvement between eros and a creative vocation that rivals the one he had towards the universe, the cosmos, space and infinite time. A confrontation with the naked female body, an uninhibited focus on 'nature' as the organ of birth and fertility, which goes hand in hand with the experience of death and nothingness. Discovering these drawings, and assuming a relationship between the upper and lower parts of our bodies, between skin and cavernousness, between transcendental imagination and sexual impulse, we could easily fall into the kind of banal interpretation that associates the cuts with female genitalia, a trace of uninhibited erotic impulse or - in Freudian terms - a gesture that sublimates the irrepressible pressure of the libido in a clean stroke. This subject has certainly not left critics indifferent. It has often presented a challenge, having to find a plausible synthesis between "sensual illusion" and "abstraction of an archetype". That clearly recognisable 'crevice', which escapes any sexual simplification or conceptual purification, is the same 'nature' that Gustave Courbet, or whoever, understood as the 'origin of the world'. In fact, the series of drawings made on large sheets says much about this openness to the origin of creative, existential drives, and the connection between female fecundity and cosmological genesis. Meanwhile, it should be noted that these drawings were made with an 'eagerness' that has nothing of the academic study. These drawings are almost performative, revealing an instinctive, impulsive departure; drawings connected to deep areas of the subconscious. Two details arouse some interest. The first is the insistence on the genitalia of the models, always well exposed, and usually covered by a deep black, almost fluid or organic material leaking from the body, a placenta sliding between the thighs or around the buttocks. The second recurring element is the erasure of the face with decisive strokes, or erasing of the features. As if the artist had deliberately avoided looking into the model's face, or rather the woman's, retreating from the power of that gaze and that body.

From his youth, Fontana had an attraction for life, its bursting from the woman's body, and for its opposite, death. Life as genesis, springing from sexual energy and the ether, from cosmic matter as well as from

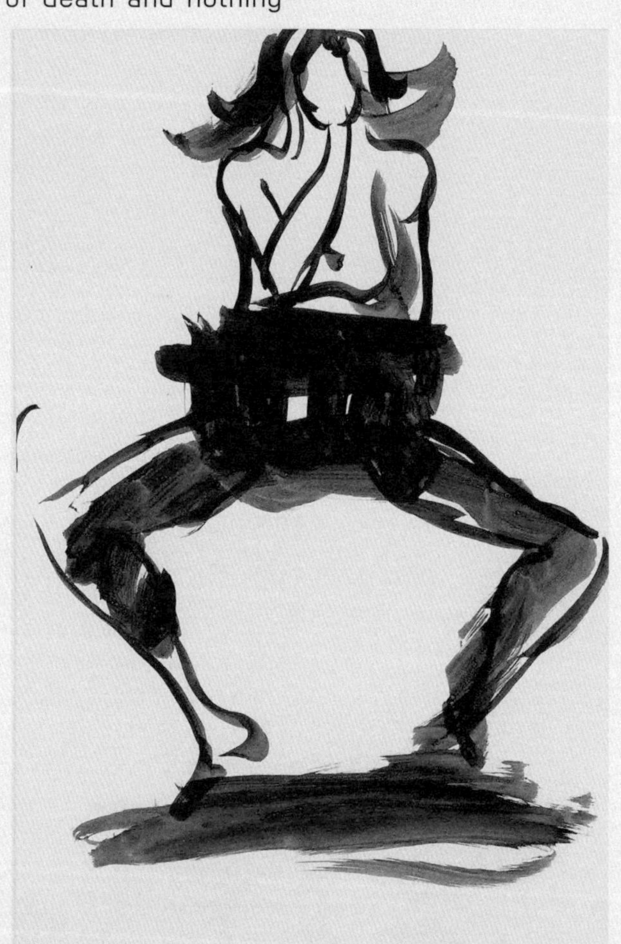

Figura femminile
1960-64
china on paper
50 × 35,5 cm
60-64 DF 49
Private collection
Courtesy Gió Marconi
Milano

human flesh, and life as light in infinite space, and as a procreative and fertile force in the earth and in female flesh. The female nude, her body stretched out, and sex as the origin of the world; the crevice on display would always be the site of an experience of recognition of the limitation and its transcendence. The creative and erotic experience that can take place in contact with the body of mother earth and woman the procreator. Woman, her body, her exhibited sexuality, are the place where life is generated, with its mystery and the possibility of transcending mortal destiny. For Fontana then, female sexuality and eros were experiences of a generative power that inhabits the earth and is connected to the cosmos. Therefore, it is already the place for an encounter between the embodiment of energy and its most visionary abstraction, dark, telluric grim depths and transcendence into luminous ecstasy, an energy that expands in spiral motions or is discovered penetrating the flesh, between ecstasy and enjoyment. Beyond the crevice, the cut, this energy unfolds and reproduces itself, expanding infinitely into the universe for all eternity. There is a photograph, taken by Ugo Mulas, that could help stitch together separate and distant pieces of language. This image was undoubtedly also directed by Fontana himself, and therefore required some preparation, because it is, after all, a staging used to convey a message. It is an assertive photo, a statement. The photo in question shows a naked woman with florid breasts, hugging an ovoid on her lap. The angle of the image is designed to emphasise and enhance the relationship between the woman's breasts and the object held in her lap as if it were her favourite child. The pose is certainly reminiscent of motherhood. It undoubtedly evokes iconographies from Christian art: Mary nursing the Only-Begotten, that is, God incarnate, the infiniteness of the Being in the finiteness of human nature, in being. However, the woman's prosperous shape recalls a Palaeolithic figure, those evoking female fertility equated with mother earth and connected to the cycles of the moon and the cosmos. As Giulio Carlo Argan wrote: " We have arrived at the chthonic myth, at the origins, where the steatopygian form of the first woman is confused with that of the seed". And this is the way forward, a deeper, more anthropological interpretation of Fontana's work, of certain *nature* and drawings of female nudes, as proposed by Maria Grazia Messina in the catalogue dedicated to *Giacometti-Fontana. La ricerca dell'assoluto [Giacometti-Fontana. The Quest for the Absolute]*. We would like to recall here *L'ordine dei tempi e delle forme in natura* [*The Order of Times and Forms in Nature*], published in Bologna in 1928-'29, on the moon and lunar rhythms, the hebdomadar cycles in the organic world and in human pathology, a text cited by Mircea Eliade in his *Une nouvelle philosophie de la lune*. Eliade himself explains how the "fécondité de la terre et celle de la femme est exprimée par des rythmes et des nombres lunaires". Therefore, from the beginnings of human history, life and death are connected to the moon, which remains three days in darkness and is then reborn. From the 1930s, Fontana was concerned with taking art, or rather sculpture, back to its origins, freeing it from all the cultural trappings and superfetations, from ideological and symbolic superstructures. Proof of this is the *Uomo nero [Black Man]*, inspired by an unequivocal primitivism that nevertheless connects the most remote to the most distant future. Fontana intended to go beyond history, for a return to the origins, which is that of civilisation, the earth and the cosmos. It is also an origin of art that stems from the immediate response to instincts and drives, such as sexual drives or death wishes. As Campiglio writes in this catalogue: "In those first investigations, which began in 1930 and continued over the next few years, especially in his drawings, the motifs of inspiration appear to have been the first terrestrial loves of men and women – the isolated male figure, the female nude in a desert landscape, the man and the horse, the woman and the horse, the virgins. Primitive loves, core instincts, not experienced nostalgically. The atmospherics of these pieces allude to a time in which there is no awareness of an afterwards, and the "waiting" figures (a condition that takes on meaning in the light of the best-known appellative that the artist would use for his "cuts") are mute presences in an anti-history dilated within an undefinable time frame". The egg is the cosmic egg behind the origin of the world, which contains and symbolises infinite space and time. An egg that refers to that ovoid of shiny metal made by Constantin Brancusi and titled the *Inizio del mondo [Beginning of the World]*. Brancusi made several ovoid forms, the heads of new-borns, muses or mythological figures. The series that began with the portrait of a sleeping child, which already has the shape of an egg without facial features, quickly progresses towards ground zero of the ovoid form that is both sculpture for the blind and the beginning of the world. Brancusi's work should not be confused with Courbet's painting known as *L'origine du monde [The Origin of the World]*, a provocative, shocking canvas that caused a great scandal among the Parisian public at its first exhibition. And yet it is not improper to recognise obvious allusions to the erotic sphere and sexuality in Brancusi's sculpture as well. The artist must have thought of divine and human, astral and terrestrial fertilisation and procreation when he created this ovoid form, and in terms of genealogy and cosmology, dwelling on the birth of a form in the very moment of the beginning of the world. Manifested in the egg - which incubates the later infinite expansion in this beginning - is the creative principle, which while being of a spiritual nature is a generative act, in terms of matter. The iconography of the primordial egg is vast and very remote. During the Middle Ages and Renaissance, the form symbolised the divine origin of the son of man, eternity, universal genesis. The egg is also symbolically synthesised in the almond, the *Deus ex machina* generator of reality. In alchemy, the egg contains the four original elements of creation. Eggs, such as ostrich eggs, together with ivory eggs, were displayed in the *Wunderkammer* and are often seen depicted as still life and vanitas, perhaps cracked, arranged on some table together with hourglasses, fruit, fish or skulls, to conceal stoic or epicurean thoughts on the eternal nature of time and the paucity of human life. Finally, eggs appear on modern stages like those that De Chirico designed for metaphysical representations. Then Carrà and Casorati also painted finely shaped eggs. How could Fontana fail to remember these forms or recognise in each of these alchemical objects symbolic connections to the sexual sphere and eros, as well as cosmology. Calvesi was so convinced of this that he devoted a weighty essay to the subject to illustrate the famous *Fine di Dio [End of God]*, which Fontana created in the last years of his life. In Fontana's life and art, woman was meant to arouse thoughts of both procreation and fertility as well as chthonic and cosmological power. Oneiric thoughts, archetypal and universal impressions, useful for figurative syntheses and material expressions. Much more than logical intuitions, they were scientific formulations for minimal creations. The general catalogue of Lucio Fontana's graphic works shows how the artist practised as an "academic" on the female body in classic studies involving varied but almost always academic poses. In certain cases his *ductum* takes on an ironic, almost satirical verve. Woman, however, is an outpost of death and nothingness. Or rather, sexuality, as Bataille argues, is closely related to death, and it defends us from it erotically by propelling us into transcendence through the ecstasy of the body. The fact that Fontana is oneiric and plays with reverie and archetypes is confirmed by a drawing from 1946, which will serve as a paradigm from now on. We recognise two forms in it: one phallic and the other ovarian, where one penetrates the other, and the other welcomes it by opening its extremities to receive it, and between the one and the other we recognise small seeds passing through, which, lost in outer space, then revolve like tiny planets. We are in a *mundo imaginalis*, a climate outside of climates that smacks of genesis, of origin, in this case of infinite space-time between the microcosm and macrocosm. An astonishing fantasy that narrates something seen, a rêverie of a universal and primordial kind, which depicts the imaginary and unimaginable birth of the cosmos, the interpenetration of male and female in an archetypal imagery. Those seeds appeared again over the years in a series of formidable imaginings that translated the microcosm of cells and atoms into the macrocosm of planets, stars, galaxies and black holes. Those early rotations multiplied, appearing unfettered first in squiggles and then in spirals and vortices to be contemplated on a cosmological scale. Only by understanding this profound binding of reverie and archetypes, between the female body, sexuality, earthly genesis and the cosmos, do we come to recognise the Cuts and Nature as complementary and proxemic. This is beyond any reductive exegesis either leaning towards a base materialism or formalism that relies on minimal and conceptual hypotheses, both phenomenological and poverist. And it was towards this imagery of forms and gestures originating from the most archetypal and universal unconscious that Fontana himself wanted to direct us: "An art based on forms created by the subconscious, balanced by reason, constitutes a real expression of being and a synthesis of the historical moment".

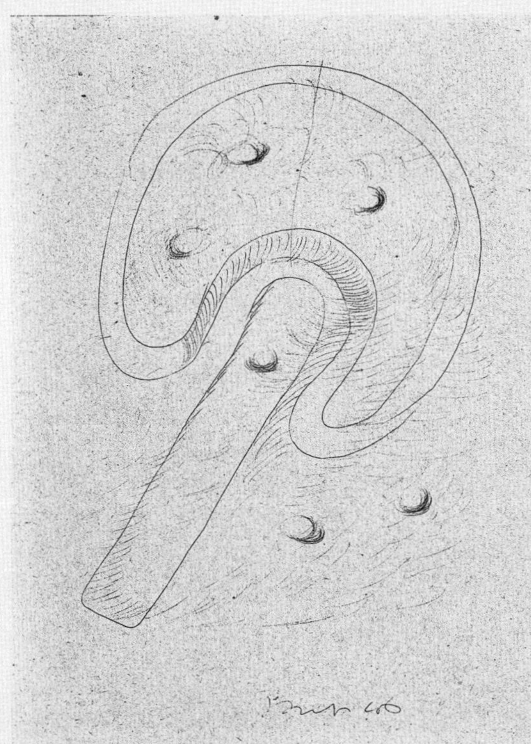

Concetto spaziale
1946
pen on paper
27,5 × 22 cm
46 DSP 34
Courtesy Fondazione
Lucio Fontana

L'origine du monde [The Origin of the World] by Courbet

<u>Sergio Risaliti</u>

I am fifty years old and I have always lived in freedom; let me end my life free; when I am dead let this be said of me: 'He belonged to no school, to no church, to no institution, to no academy, least of all to any régime except the régime of liberty'.

G. Courbet

Painting is an essentially concrete art and can only consist of the representation of real and existing things. An abstract, non-visible object does not fall within the domain of painting. Imagination in art consists in being able to find the most complete expression of an existing thing, but never in supposing or creating this same thing. Beauty is in nature, and is encountered in reality under the most diverse forms. As soon as it is found, it belongs to art or rather to the artist who knows how to see it. Beauty, like truth, is a thing relative to the time in which one lives and to the individual capable of conceiving it. The expression of beauty is in direct proportion to the power of perception acquired by the artist. There can be no schools, there are only painters.

G. Courbet

I

L'origine du monde by Gustave Courbet, one of the most scandalous paintings in the history of Western art, seems to have had a precedent in the *Song of Songs*, the most misunderstood poem in the Bible: "The curves of your hips are like jewels / The work of the hands of an artist / Your vulva a curved alembic / Of fragrant liquor never dry / A handful of wheat in a rose garden / Lies between your groins". Who knows if the images of the Canticle perhaps reached the painter through Charles Baudelaire, the author of *Flowers of Evil*. In one of his poems, *The Promises of a Face*, the poet begins by describing dark eyebrows, very black eyes, and an even blacker hair. Those eyes, however, invite the poet to acknowledge the truth of what he sees, almost to touch with his own hand that which is before him, something that must nevertheless remain untouchable in order to stay at the centre of desire: "You will be able to prove our truthfulness / From the navel to the buttocks / You will find at the tips of two heavy breasts / Two slack bronze medallions / And under a smooth belly, soft as velvet / Swarthy as the skin of a Buddhist / A rich fleece, which truly is the sister / Of this huge head of hair / Compliant and curly, its thickness equals / Black night, night without stars!".

The *Origin of the World* would appear to be something similar to a 'noche oscura' or black night. This is an inverted perspective on the origin of desire that goes far beyond sexual attraction. The way the attention zooms in on the painting, the biblical text, and the Parisian flower of evil, in all three cases, focuses on the same part of the female body. The image is composed at close range and invites us to look naturally at the impudent cleft, to recognise in it the origin of the world, reconciling the sacred and the profane, enjoyment and creation. The sumptuous soft, curly hair as it appears in the verses is also found in the painting. Courbet, unlike the others, has, however, cropped the framing of the female body so as to feature the female sex in the foreground, in "an exclusive frontal view". Provocation? Not only that. Until then, nothing similar had been seen in painting. Courbet gets rid of all the coy concealment, allusion, fiction. And he plays with the memory of ancient statuary. His image is constructed along ancient lines, working on an academic leitmotif: the statuary fragment. In fact, the female figure is reduced to a trunk, like a marble statue cast among other ruins; it is headless, armless, without lower limbs. In other words, we could say that Courbet has decapitated, or rather, literally torn the female body to pieces, certainly the body that had been idealised for centuries in its intact perfection. Should we then think of Courbet as a serial killer of similar female bodies, as unreal as dolls or mannequins insofar as they are idealised, in other words, increasingly emptied of their carnal truth? It is as if the painter-hunter had framed his pictorial prey by visiting those extraordinary game reserves that are the Museums and Academies of Fine Arts, always filled with Venuses, nude, bathing, crouching, or reclining nymphs. This memory, however, is corrected by another far more 'natural' association. Courbet left the academic world and headed for more wretched districts, the brothels, then went into those rooms to know women without prohibitions or inhibitions. We know that prostitutes were some of the fundamental subjects of modern art: think of Degas, Picasso, even Giacometti who confessed his predilection for the tenants of the Sphinx. For Courbet, the prey is not so much the woman as it is the classicist ideology, that set of rules and moral precepts that prevented one from approaching and appreciating the truth of the female nude, censoring 'nature', uninterested in the *Origine du monde*. So Courbet places the canvas at the end of the bed; just before or just after having sex, and by choosing the rhetorical figure of the synecdoche, shows us the part which stands for the whole. Courbet's painting is cinematic and already performative. After all, Courbet is a performer in paint. *Un metteur en scène*. Are paintings such as *Bonjour Monsieur Courbet* and *The Painter's Studio* not performative stagings? Rather than fictions they are portions of reality. Real presences. And what about works like *The Desperate Man - Self-Portrait* from around 1843, *A Burial at Ornans* from 1849-50, *The Sleepers* or *Stone Breakers*?

Since 1866, *L'origine du monde* – a small painting (46x55) that looms large in men's fantasies - has continued to spark philosophical interest that goes far beyond the fetishistic perversion of the porn cinema or porn video viewer. In all likelihood it is the title – *Origine du monde* [Origin of the World] - that short-circuits the mind of the 'user', divided between base and instinctive reactions and high intellectual questioning, between unconscious-libido and modesty-repression, between eros and *thanatos*. It should be remembered that the title was assigned to the work by Khalil-Bey, who commissioned it, almost certainly the only real creator of the iconographic project. Khalil-Bey was a collector of erotic paintings, afflicted with syphilis, a diplomat of the Ottoman Empire, who already owned Ingres' *The Turkish Bath* and *The Sleepers* by Courbet himself. In his gallery-harem-boudoir, perhaps a bathroom, the *Origine* was covered by a green curtain that only the owner could pull aside, sparking a voyeuristic relationship - as Daniel Arasse calls it in his *book Il dettaglio, la pittura vista da vicino* [*The Detail, Painting Seen Up Close*]. After various ups and downs, the painting came into the hands of Jacques Lacan, the famous psychoanalyst, who had bought it at an auction for more than a million francs in 1955 and who kept it hidden, concealed beneath another painting of the same size (*Terre érotique*), a surrealist landscape specially created by André Masson, transforming the truth according to Courbet into an elegant hieroglyphic, a surrealist calembour. The pleasure for Lacan consisted in studying the reaction of his friends when confronted with Courbet's "icon". The psychoanalyst sought to grasp the work's secret by putting under the magnifying glass not so much that detail as the cultural backgrounds of such people as Dora Maar, Marguerite Duras or Claude Lévi-Strauss. Voyeurs, despite themselves, at the service of psychoanalysis. So, for a long time the image was considered potentially dangerous, rather than obscene. And because it was believed to emanate a mysterious, uncontrollable energy, it

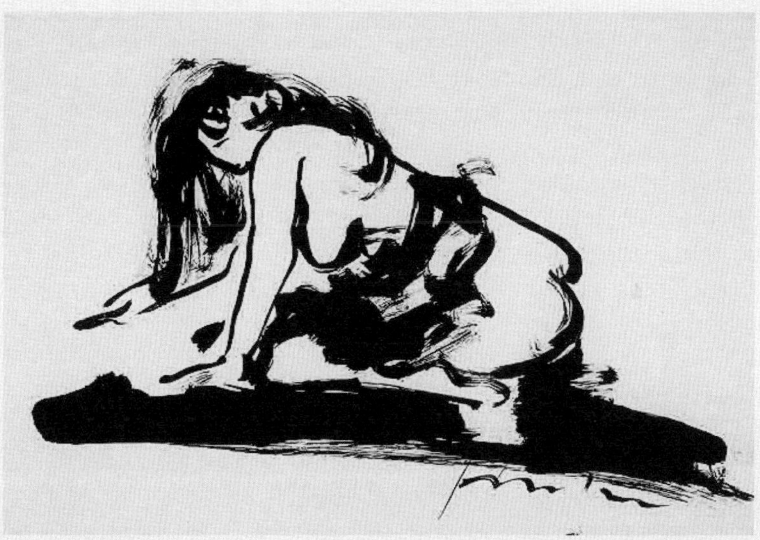

Nudo femminile
1960-64
china on cardboard
35 × 50 cm
60-64 DF 154
Courtesy Fondazione
Lucio Fontana

was incubated under other images; as if it were one of those archaeological relics endowed with extraordinary, thaumaturgic and apotropaic powers. Masson brought things forward, lowering the light on what was burning behind; he blurred the obscure power of Courbet's erotic image with a correct image, incorporating, in a sort of graceful and harmless arabesque, that fierce and savage painting, that image endowed with a cumbersome, even exorbitant realism, capable of emerging from the frame. A painting that is difficult to relate to aesthetics, and which rebels against mimesis. Yet Edmond de Goncourt, one of the most feared critics of the 19th century, appreciated its style, considering it worthy of the greatest masters of the Renaissance. In his dreaded *Journal*, he stated: "In front of this canvas that I had never seen before, I must make amends and honour Courbet: that belly is as beautiful as the flesh of a Correggio". The critic was probably thinking of works such as *Io and Jupiter*, *Leda and the Swan*, or *Venus and Cupid with a Satyr*. According to de Goncourt, *The Origin of the World* was the type of painting that even Stendhal could have appreciated, perceiving its velvety sensibility and fleshiness. This judgement tells us that the strength of Courbet's work lies in the perfect alchemy of iconography and painting style, to which the title was added, but only later. In truth, it was a test of bravura contained within an iconographic exercise that the artist respected and used to attack the academic culture, riddled with tired mythology and false modesty. Daniel Arasse explains this perfectly when he writes that Courbet's aesthetic project was "to make the work consist in the strength of its style; a style that is the trademark of the impulse… of the painter within the pictorial act". Courbet ultimately "offers to see the pictorial act, its physical action in the material, and the bodily involvement of the painter in his work". 'Nature', with its soft, curly fleece, confronts us and physically touches us as few other images in history have done, and this happens for two main reasons. The first lies in the fact that the dominant image is that particular 'nature' that is always kept at a distance, and hidden from view. The second reason lies in the fact that the painter moved excessively close to that part of her body, looking at it closely, more or less in the position he might have assumed while having sex with the model, or we could even argue, while performing cunnilingus. Courbet was not playing at pretending, he was not interested in creating an illusion of reality. If mimesis is the presence of an absence, here the absence is all too present. For Courbet, naturalism begins and ends with reality. There are no deviations whatsoever. In doing so he goes far beyond Caravaggio, who in any case would have been his main point of reference. I am thinking, for example, of the feet painted with extreme realism and placed without 'decorum' in the foreground in the famous *Madonna di Loreto* or *Pilgrims' Madonna* (1604-1606), a canvas still preserved today in the Cavalletti Chapel of the basilica of Sant'Agostino in Rome. Courbet wants to possess painting, a painting of the flesh, and has no intention of psychoanalysing the fear of sex, or containing the original power of female sexuality under the veil of iconography and modesty. That crevice with its warm, reddish fleece anticipates Lucio Fontana's famous cut by a century, also a crevice open to the origin of life and the beginning of the infinite cosmos. But, while the crevice of Courbet's *Origine du monde* seems to come towards us with all the fragrance of reality in painting, that flesh of the material that conceals nothing but carries in its presence the warm fleece of the shearling, the 'crevice' of Fontana's *Spatial Concept* opens inwards, asking us to make a metaphysical effort to go beyond the surface of the painting and discover a different kind of realism, in keeping with the new cosmological perspective intuited by the artist in infinite spatiality. Incidentally, here we should recall how for many scholars Fontana's cut should be related to an opening in the garment in Piero della Francesca's *Madonna del Parto* [*Madonna of Parturition*]. That slit in the fabric of the Virgin's cloth would be, in translation, the one opened in Mary's body to receive the infinite divine nature, the fruit of the miraculous embrace with God sheltered in his mother's womb, that incarnate God who is the origin of everything.

II

But let us return to the painting, dated around 1866. The image of the *Origine du monde* is cropped so as to universalise the woman's body; here the woman belongs to everyone, the woman is the wife, lover and mother of everyone. She has no face, she cannot be recognised, except through certain intimate details that only the one who has approached that woman lying on a bed can have knowledge of. She is not individualised. She is both subject and object of the gaze, of desire. The body comes out of the painting: a large part of her lies before us and lives beyond the perimeter of the frame. But she does not lie still. She seems to have shifted slightly to one side; an imperceptible move at the height of pleasure, or perhaps she is in a deep sleep and turning over like certain sleeping nymphs. A glimpse of one breast, the right one, is allowed, while the other remains covered by a sheet. The nipple is turgid, magnetic. The origin of the world is exclusive and the vulva is invasive. Courbet's formal-conceptual work relies on a dual movement that is both perspective-iconic (the vanishing point at infinity is reversed, the V here is reversed) and spatial-plastic (the body is not in the box, the frame does not contain the body). Or rather, the frame does not contain desire. The painting distances the object of desire. Art, like the woman, remains mysterious. The gaze is ensnared in a game that pushes beyond, well beyond touch. The title hinders the desire for possession. It imposes something sacred that curbs the impulse to penetrate the crevice. This game of concentration and subtraction, of enticement and inhibition, is also found to some extent in *Étant donnés*, Marcel Duchamp's last work, a staging that has inspired a river of words. Let us return to Courbet, to consider the way he places the viewer (man or woman, no matter, their function is ecumenical) in a performative position. We are pushed to look at far too much and much too closely. It is not a question of proximity to the painting, but to the subject, which we reduce to an object of morbid desire. Courbet,

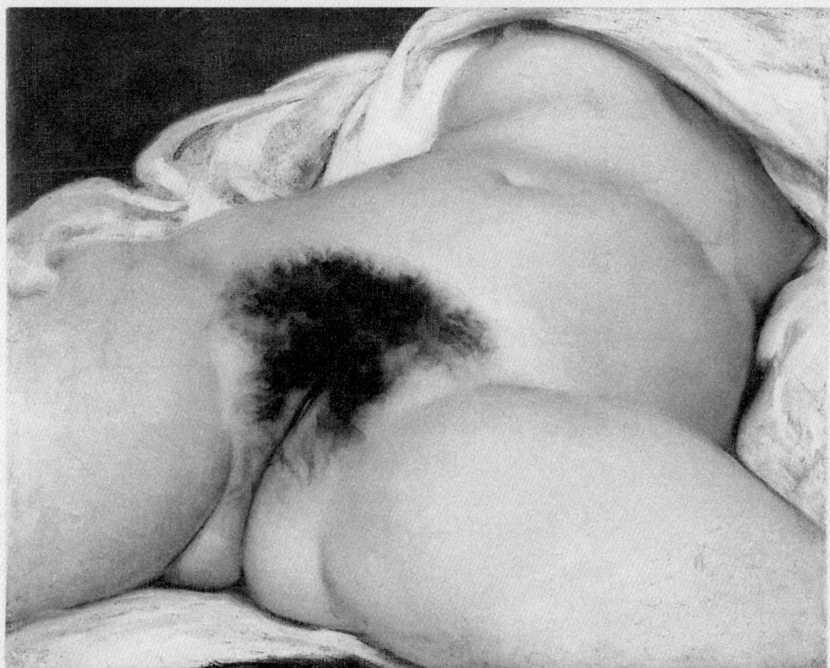

Gustave Courbet,
L'origine du monde, 1866,
Musée d'Orsay, Paris

but perhaps the work itself, hence art, is playing with us. If we look at the subject, we lose sight of the painting. By remaining dazzled by the subject we lose sight of the velvety part of the painting. If, on the other hand, we indulge in the haptic sensation of the pictorial touch, we shift too far to the side of the object of desire, to the carnality of the image. The origin of the world is offered and taken away; its mystery, here the mystery of painting, is too great and inviolable. After all, our position is the same as the person who is painting a 'sacred' image and wooing a real person. It is a sensitive contemplation, the result of which is a painting that makes itself felt. The result is not imitation, but something else. Painting begins its journey towards new dimensions, distancing itself from photography (1926), which may, however, have been used by the artist. It is that same art of photography that Courbet attacks with the same violence and patience with which he attacks the most academic neoclassicism.

We must, however, look at another work to better understand Courbet's personality. It is a painting executed in 1855, *The Painter's Studio: A Real Allegory Summing Up Seven Years of My Life as an Artist*. At the time, Charles Baudelaire must already have been an artistic and moral reference for Courbet, as he stands isolated at the back of the room, absorbed in his reading, while in the centre of the space, the artist, recognisable by his dark beard, paints from real live in front of his fans. He is finishing a landscape: large dark trees, a blue sky in the background, a few clouds at sunset. That painting on the easel actually looks like an open window in the middle of the studio. It is as if Courbet's art were gutting the walls of the studio to go out into nature. A completely unclothed model is admiring the vigorous brushstrokes, the "wild and patient determination". It is as if the painter were forced between the canvas and the woman, between the green of the forest and the pink of her complexion, between the thickness of the painted material and the fleshiness of her skin. A kind of dance is established between the woman, the artist, the palette, the paintbrush and the landscape painted in the centre of the Studio: each element of this universe is closely connected to the other, in a meaningful embrace that joins the blue background of the sky and the female 'rump'. It looks like a whirlpool, a love spiral, a performance between fields of intensity to transcend limits, and all the artist's friends have been invited to attend. It could even be said that between Courbet's left shoulder and the model's pubis there is an interlocking, almost as if the woman's belly acts as a backrest to the painter's eagerness and at the same time provides him with the right respite. Ultimately, we understand that the artist needs the presence of the woman, the contact with her flesh in order to access the open air through painting. He wants to re-enter mother earth and mother-woman, to make intimate contact with both like an infant or an animal. Painting is a sexual act aimed at reaching the origin of the world and life without distinction. *L'origine du monde* encompasses all this, and seals the pact between the artist, woman and reality. Only through the experience of sexuality can one arrive at ground zero of reality, as close as possible to life, to being in the world like an animal in a clearing.

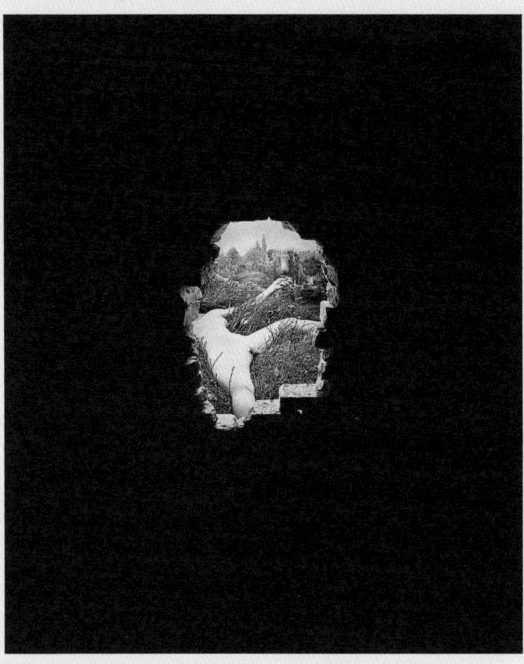

Marcel Duchamp,
Étant donnés, 1946–66
mixed media assemblage
Philadelphia Museum of Art,
Philadelphia

Courbet loves the woman then and loves her crevice. He sniffs her out and penetrates her with his realist painter's gaze as he would a deer or a roe deer, which he has portrayed in the middle of clearings, among large lichen-covered boulders, about to drink from a stream. He rests his nature-loving gaze on the crevice, similar to when he sniffs the wind that smells salty, admiring the great waves that plough the North Sea. Only by doing this, by becoming animal and child, does he succeed in painting the image of eternal femininity from life, removing it from all idealism in order to exhibit it 'really', without mediations (except those regarding the pictorial material), in its powerful and perturbing truth. The down, that at first glance covers the hollow of the pubis like a turf, is more animal than vegetable, a fleece in fact. It is as if a brush had combed and ruffled that fur, as if it had passed over it, caressing its surface, ruffling the tufts. Fragrant, icastic, the vulva is a given natural feature, like the entrance to a cave, the thicket of a forest, an inlet, a stormy sea, a sky pouring with rain. The female sex shows itself openly to the gaze. In this open-ing-crevice lies the mystery of origin. If there is something sacred, it is here. Opening up before the artist-lover is the mystery of the birth and death of humanity: the mere naturalness of life. In other words, when Courbet painted *L'origine du monde*, he performed with the nature of sex as if it were a rain-soaked meadow. He was inside the landscape contemplating the origin of life, not outside. Between the viewer and the image there is only painted matter, and it is this that makes the painted thing. And so, the naked truth of love stripped of all false idealisation resurfaces in the freshness of living flesh, of the painting-imprint, and does so with the original power of a primordial intercourse. An inter-course that can only be consummated by the artist-hunter-lover as a function of life and art. After all, there is heroism in this image of sex. That of life and art in its eternal, daily battle against death.

L'origine du monde [The Origin of the World] by Courbet

Lucio Fontana and the Apocalypse of Space

Marco Fagioli

I

Seeing sculptures such as the *Group de trois hommes* (*Trois hommes qui marchent*), 1943-49 by Alberto Giacometti and *Concetto spaziale. Natura*, 1959-69, by Lucio Fontana together in the same exhibition has a strange effect; it creates a kind of apocalyptic face-to-face encounter with the fate of sculpture itself, its beginning and its end. Giacometti and Fontana are both *primitives*. For them being a primitive is not a historical condition but a profound disposition of the soul, an outstanding feature of their existence. They enclose the alpha and omega of sculpture in their works and therefore in contemporary life, dragging it out of the contingent and returning it to that *origin of the absolute* that characterises the ever-present angst in their work.

In his critical review of Lucio Fontana, Enrico Crispolti - writing about the *Manifiesto Blanco,* drafted in Spanish in Buenos Aires in the autumn of 1946 by the group of artists gathered around the *Arte concreta-Invención* - pointed out that Fontana, still "working in a figurative art with an expressionist accent", had "substantially inspired the text" but had not participated in its drafting. Crispolti referred to the testimony of Thomas Maldonado, who claimed that the *Manifiesto* had been "a playful provocation" by Fontana "against the concretist group", because Fontana, "although working in a very different figurative terrain, however problematic, followed it with great interest and sympathy". On the other hand, Maldonado was also very close to him conceptually, recalling that "he had served in the ranks of European abstractionism", and indulged "in turning a blind eye to his neo-baroque sculptures of the time"[1].

This interpretation therefore insisted on the *neo-Baroque* character of Fontana's sculptures in Argentina (after his *abstract* phase, culminating in his solo exhibition at the Galleria del Milione in Milan in January 1935), and therefore on a stance that differed from the ideas he would inspire in the *Manifiesto Blanco*. However, certain small terracotta sculptures, such as *Rosa; Pescado, Coquilla, Mariposas*, all from 1946, testify to how the sculptor was already working on his new concept of space.

On rereading Lucio Fontana's poetics today, from the *Manifiesto Blanco, First Manifesto of Spatialism*, Milan, 1948, *Second Manifesto of Spatialism*, 1948-early 1949, to the *Proposta di un regolamento del Movimento Spaziale [Proposal for Regulations]*, 1950, one is struck by the rigour and prophetic vision of the artist in anticipating the end of the traditional idea of physical and geometric space and establishing an atomic, or as he called it, "nuclear" conception that went beyond the history of the idea of space that underpinned European art from the Renaissance to Cubism.

----

1   E. Crispolti, *Lucio Fontana. Catalogo ragionato di sculture, dipinti, ambientazioni*, Skira, Milan 2006, vol. 1, pp. 56-58, pp. 108-14, p. 98, no. 105.

Fontana's Spatialism arrived in the mid-20th century, after Albert Einstein had already revolutionised the notion of space and time with the Theory of Relativity at the beginning of the century, and after the great historical avant-gardes had shaken and destroyed the foundations of the Western painting tradition. Of these, it was Futurism, with its idea of movement, that anticipated the new idea of space. And yet Spatialism represented what today appears to be a decisive revolution in the languages of modern art.

The *Manifiesto Blanco* states: "The peaceful, gentle life has come to an end. Speed has become a constant in the life of mankind. The artistic era of colours and static forms is coming to an end. Man is becoming less and less responsive to fixed, motionless images. The old static images no longer satisfy the modern man who has been shaped by the need for action, and a mechanized lifestyle of constant movement. The aesthetics of organic motion have replaced the out-moded aesthetics of fixed forms […].

We present the substance, not the marginality of things. We represent neither man nor animal nor other forms. These are manifestations of nature, mutable in time, changing and disappearing according to the succession of phenomena […]. We move towards the material and its evolution, the generating sources of existence. We take the material's very energy, its need to be and to develop. We postulate an art free of any aesthetic artifice".

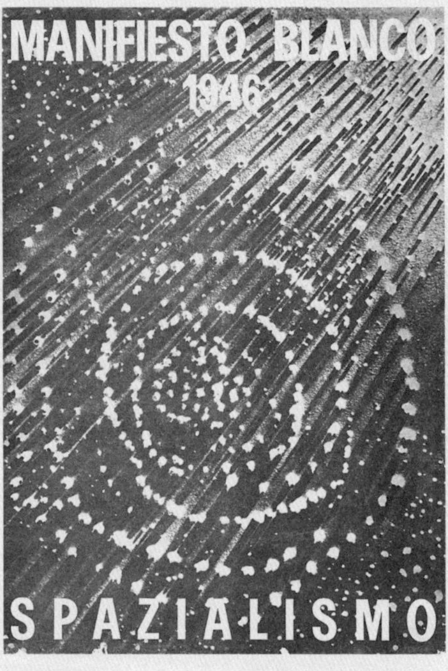

Manifiesto Blanco 1946
Spazialismo
engraving, artist's book,
artist's book in slipcase
48,7 × 33,5 × 2,5 cm
D 9520
Sprengel Museum, Hannover

This was not so much a declaration of poetic intent as an existential statement, almost the affirmation of a phenomenological principle of artistic language. Starting with the physical conception of the world, it also involved the inner psyche in a common revolutionary synthesis, where image and conscience became a total and inseparable unity: "The subconscious, that magnificent well of images perceived by the mind, takes on the essence and form of those images and harbours the notions that make up man's nature. Thus, as the objective world is transformed, what the subconscious identifies with is also transformed, and this produces changes in man's mode of conception. The subconscious determines the historical legacy of pre-civilized states and the manner of our adaptation to new lifestyles. The subconscious shapes, composes and transforms the individual. It gives him a sense of order, which comes from the world and is adopted by the individual. All artistic concepts arise from the workings of the subconscious. Plastic art developed from its original base of natural shapes. The manifestations of the subconscious adapted easily to natural forms as a consequence of the idealized conception of existence. Our material consciousness, that is, our need for things which are easily verifiable, demands that art-forms should flow directly from the individual and that they should assume a natural form. An art based on forms created by the subconscious and balanced by reason, constitutes a true expression of existence and is the synthesis of a moment in time. The position of the rational artists is false. In their effort to privilege reason and to deny the workings of the subconscious, they succeed only in rendering them less visible". [2]

The *Manifiesto Blanco,* in a nutshell, contained all the later developments in Fontana's art and can now be considered one of the major theoretical events of modern art for its importance as a rupture with the established codes of artistic language. In affirming the apocalypse of the Renaissance conception of geometric-perspective space, in openly assuming Einstein's idea of the space-time relationship, in the total implosion between physical space and inner psychological space, the authors did not look kindly on the tradition of objective painting established up to the 20th century, and were therefore against the idea of the reasoning on which it was founded: "Reason does not create. In creating shapes, it is subordinate to the subconscious. In all of his activities, man uses all of his faculties. Their free development is fundamental for creating and interpreting a new kind of art. Analysis and synthesis, meditation and spontaneity, construction and sensation are all values which come together to work in union; and their development in experience is the only way to achieve a complete demonstration of being. Society suppresses disparate energies and integrates them into a greater unified force. Modern science is based on the progressive unification of all its elements. Humanity weaves together its knowledge and its values in an historic process which has developed over hundreds of years. A new, integrated art flows from this new state of consciousness, in which existence is shown in its totality. After several millennia of analytical artistic development, the moment of synthesis has arrived. Prior to this moment, specialization was necessary. Now however, this specialization amounts to a disintegration of the unity we envisage. We imagine synthesis as the sum total of the physical elements: colour, sound, movement, time, space, integrated in physical and mental union. Colour, the element of space; sound, the element of time and movement, which develops in time and space. These are fundamental to the new art which encompasses the four dimensions of existence. Time and space. The new art requires that all of man's energies be used productively in creation and interpretation. Existence is shown in an integrated manner, with all its vitality".[3]
With the *Proposal for Regulations*, dated 2 April 1950, the importance of the *Manifesto Blanco* was openly accepted by all the spatial artists who signed it, and Fontana was recognised as the movement's founder. The first article of the regulation in fact stated: "Lucio Fontana is recognised as the initiator and founder of the Spatial Movement in the world". The sculptor had returned to Italy in April 1947, where he created works such as the *Scultura spaziale [Spatial Sculpture],* 1947, and the *Concetto spaziale [Spatial Concept],* "*Uomo atomico [Atomic Man]",* the former exhibited in Venice in 1948, and the latter in 1954, true manifestos of his new spatial vision.

---

2   *Manifesto Blanco,* in Guido Ballo, *Fontana: idea per un ritratto,* Turin, 1970, pp. 185–89.

3   *Manifesto Blanco,* cit., p. 189.

The *Apocalypse* of the space is the condition in which Fontana places man, who is immersed in modern life. Before Einstein's Theory of Relativity, physics was based on the conception of an absolute space and time, and the image built on this conception had been established from Copernicus and Galileo to Newton. Fontana had posed the problem of defining space as a fundamental problem of knowledge of the universe and life, but he had posed it as an artist and not as a scientist.

In his numerous statements and interviews, as well as the various Spatialism manifestos, no reference was made to the history of modern physics, but he obsessively insisted on the problem of space as being central to the artistic experience.

Newtonian mechanics continued to rule physics until 1905. After the development of Maxwell's equations and Lorentz's studies, the principle of absolute time failed Einstein's Theory of Relativity . The theory of *special relativity* starts with the principle that if the speed of light is a constant, then time and space are variables, so that time and space are united in a new concept called *spacetime*. Fontana's work, albeit in a "fantastically" artistic way, moves against the backdrop of this profound revolution, even if he never explicitly states this: the poetics of each artist never corresponds to scientific theories, but often reworks certain ideas of time in an imaginative way.

In the *Second Spatial Manifesto*, 1948, signed by Fontana with Gianni Dova, Beniamino Joppolo, Giorgio Kaisserlian, Milena Milani and Antonino Tullier, the *apocalypse* of classical space is combined with the *utopia* of a new universe: 'The work of art is destroyed by time. When, then, in the final burning of the universe, even time and space will no longer exist, no memory will remain of the monuments erected by man, although not a single hair of his head will have been lost.

But we do not intend to abolish the art of the past or stop life: we want the painting to come out of its frame and the sculpture out of its bell jar. It is as though the aerial expression of the art of one minute lasted a millennium, in eternity. To this end, with the resources of modern technology, we will make artificial shapes, rainbows of wonder, luminous writings appear in the sky.

With radio and television, we will broadcast new artistic expressions.

If, at first, enclosed in his towers, the artist portrayed himself and his wonder and saw the landscape through the glass, later, descending from the castles into the cities, breaking down the walls and mingling with other men, he saw the trees and objects up close. Today, we spatial artists have escaped from our cities. We have broken our shell, our physical cortex, and looked down on ourselves from above, photographing the Earth from the rockets in flight. With this we do not exalt the supremacy of our minds over this world, but we want to recover our true face, our true image: a change anxiously awaited by all creation. *The spirit spreads its light; in the freedom we have been given*".

And yet in Fontana's later work, this enthusiasm for a new world seems to fade into a more theological vision of Space, in the expectation of a liberating Apocalypse:

"By now, there is no longer any measure in space. You see, now, the infinite... in the Milky Way, by now, there are billions of billions.... The sense of measurement, of time, is gone. Before, it might have been so... but, today, it is certain, because man speaks of billions of years, of a thousand and a thousand billion to reach ... and, then, here is nothingness, man himself who is reduced to nothing [...] Once man gets it into his head [...] that he is nothing, nothing, nothing, really, he is pure spirit, he will no longer have material ambitions [...] man becomes like God, becomes spirit. Here is the end of the world and the liberation of matter, of man. [...] man will become a simple being, like a flower, a plant, and he will live only in his intelligence, in the beauty of nature, and he will purify himself of blood, because he lives in the midst of blood all the time [...] And my art is also all about this purity, this philosophy of nothing, which is not a nothing of destruction, but a nothing of creation, you understand? And the cut - really, the hole, the first holes - was not the destruction of the painting [...] it was really a dimension beyond the painting, the freedom to conceive art through any medium, through any form. Art is not painting, sculpture, alone: art is a creation of man, who can transform it into anything... as it can also end because such exceptional events will happen... Art will seem too elementary: it will be surpassed by man's intelligence and other activities will take over and replace art"[4].

II

In reconstructing the artist's entire and complex – yet essential – expressive approach, Crispolti described Fontana's second phase of spatial works, the "holes" of the 1958-1967 period, as follows:

"In the meantime, already between the late 1950s and early 1960s, Fontana developed other 'series' of works, linguistically differentiated according to specific imaginative strands. These were the other 'holes', initially close to the 'inks' with the large, almost monochrome aniline backgrounds filled in more fully, where the holes themselves are arranged almost circumscribing images or in free constellation. In the early 1960s, the natural canvas was also a support for the even warp patterns of 'holes', which almost outline an image, or are free; but the 'holes' themselves sometimes become tears. However,

---

4   C. Lonzi, *Autoritratto*, Bari, 1969, pp. 319-322.

in the early 1960s, apart from more freely inventive departures in the form of constellations, the new 'holes' were generally arranged according to profiles or outlines of 'forms' or patterned coordinates"[5].

Fontana is never decorative: his forms are always structural. They obey a conception of space that is no longer geometric, Euclidean, but cosmic, a space that is unlimited and reliably infinite, not measurable, and yet rigorously structured.

In his *Fogli di poetica spaziale [Sheets of Spatial Poetics]*, 1951-1952, some of which were rightly reproduced by Guido Ballo in his 1970 monograph, Fontana outlines the foundations of his conception of space-cosmos in an almost aphoristic way. "No form can be spatial, because any form is contained in space in all but one of its dimensions. Colour, the element of space, sound the element of time and movement that develops in time and space. These are the fundamental forms of the new art that contains the four dimensions of existence"[6].

These are almost cryptic utterances by Fontana, at times difficult to transfer from the field of artistic thought to that of physics and geometry, yet they are profoundly fascinating and part of a new way of conceiving space, in its implications that are not only scientific but also philosophical, typical of 20th-century thought, in the troubled course of a century that revolutionised the complete image of the world. A course that runs from science to philosophy and that forces art into a continuous pursuit, a continuous questioning of its foundations. His *Concetti spaziali [Spatial Concepts]* are a testimony to such labours, but at the same time a powerful cry for the vitality of art, the tangible manifestation of its strength. Fontana wants to affirm that artistic language is not the child of a "lesser god", but that it moves with the same force as the other two, and that his "holes" and "cuts" warn of the terrifying nature of art in a world of science.

In the realisation of this new conception of space, Fontana is second only to Boccioni and the Futurists, to whom he pays avowed homage: "Spatial art is consistent only with the sculptural dynamism of the Futurists – Boccioni's *Bottiglia in movimento [Bottle in Motion]*, 1910 – anticipates all the evolutionary and creative movements of contemporary world art. We pay homage to Arp, Klee, Kandinsky, Mondrian, Calder, but we recognise the creative genius of Boccioni"[7].

These are statements, such as the letters to Giampiero Ciani in 1949, which further clarify the presuppositions of Fontana's art, his criticism of Cubism – "Cubism, deformation, disfigurement if you like, intelligent

---

5   E. Crispolti, *Lucio Fontana*, cit., p. 70

6   G. Ballo, *Fontana*, cit., p. 125, nos. 140, 143.

7   *Perché sono spaziale*, 1952, in *ibidem*, p. 111.

human forms" – and the exaltation of Boccioni's plastic dynamism, the only recognised historical antecedent, also for the established need to exit from the work and move out into the environment, into space; he also feels with Boccioni the tendency "toward vital energy [...] but he feels estranged from Cubist reconstruction"[8].

But Fontana's "holes" also contain within them a profound existential value, also present in his informal phase with his experiments in monochrome painting; it is no coincidence that the *Spatial Concept* series was also called *Attese [Expectation]* by the artist, signalling its psychological significance.

Crispolti emphasised the importance of certain guiding ideas of the programme, such as those regarding the "evolution of the medium of art" and the use of new media, "such as radio, television, black light, radar"[9].

And again, when it was stated that "the invention conceived by the Spatial Artist is projected into space', it brought upheaval to the traditional codes of the arts. Even the historical avant-garde movements, notably Cubism and Futurism, transcended the spatial boundary in which the work, painting and sculpture had hitherto been constrained: an anthropocentric space, measurable to the naked eye, founded on the application of a Renaissance perspective. If the Impressionists had then delivered the first great blow to this conception, through the affirmation of the atmospheric-sensorial primacy of vision, nevertheless the representation of forms had remained within established codes. With his new conception of sculpture, asserted with a sculptural dynamism, Umberto Boccioni had demolished the idea of a closed space, a limited and measurable universe: Fontana, albeit with different premises, took this new vision of space to its extreme consequences. According to Crispolti, "the Spatial Artist no longer imposes a figurative theme on the spectator, but places him in the condition of creating it himself", and it is "precisely in relation to such an operative implication of new technologies" that "Fontana's formulation of the "holes", canvases (the very first, paper on canvas), initially monochrome,

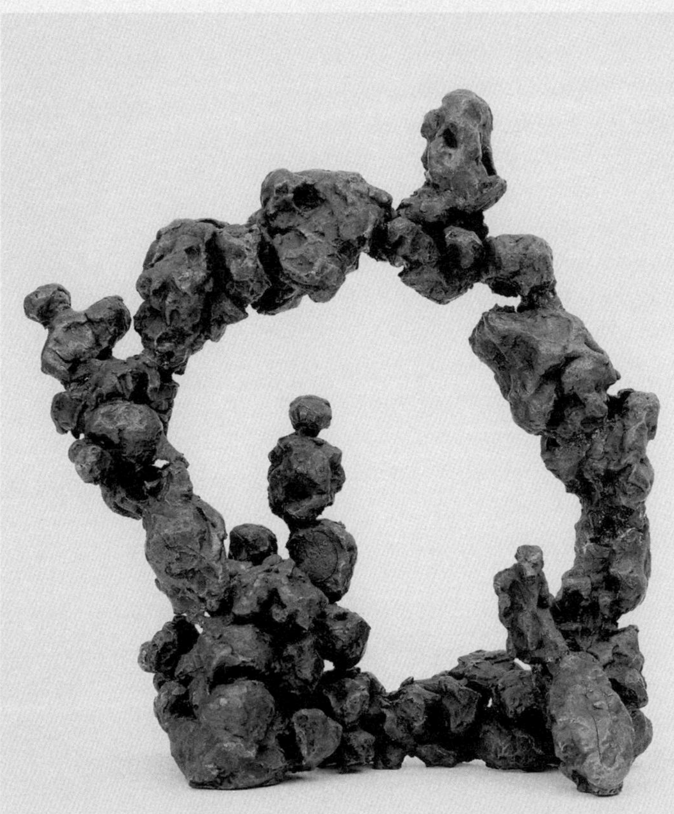

Scultura spaziale
1947
bronze
56 × 52 cm
47 SC 1
Courtesy Fondazione
Lucio Fontana

---

8   *Ibidem*, pp. 111-12.

9   E. Crispolti, *Lucio Fontana*, cit., p. 60.

perforated with constellations of holes, is situated. In fact, some of them were initially used by Fontana to project 'moving light images' as part of television experiments by RAI-TV in Milan on 17 May 1952".

In the *Manifesto tecnico dello Spazialismo (Noi continuiamo l'evoluzione del mezzo nell'arte) [Technical Manifesto of Spatialism (We continue the evolution of the medium in art)]*, written on the occasion of an international conference on Proportions at the 9th Milan Triennale, in 1951, Fontana further specified his conception of space, founded on "an art based on new techniques and mediums; Spatial Art, for now, neon, Wood's blacklight, television, the 4th ideal dimension of architecture [....] The real conquest of space made by man, is the *detachment from the earth, from the horizon line*, which for millennia was the basis of his aesthetics and proportion".

This conception of the quest for a dematerialised space, reduced to "pure gesture" and therefore "not immortal but eternal, undoubtedly shapes the direction that was later pursued, between the late 1950s and throughout the 1960s, by the daring and vividly ground-breaking works of Manzoni and Yves Klein (who, by extremes, are descended from Fontana's lineage: consciously and with Fontana's esteem in return) and then by what was called specifically 'conceptual art'"[10].

III

In the essay *Handling Space*, which introduced Fontana's exhibition at London's Hayward Gallery, October 1999, Sarah Whitefield put forward the fascinating hypothesis that the idea behind Fontana's cuts first originated at the time he created the Christ for the Castellotti family tomb in 1935 at the Monumental Cemetery in Milan.

Whitfield's interesting hypothesis, whether valid or not, raises the very complex problem of the history of Fontana's formal language, from his Argentinean origins to his experience as a student with Adolfo Wildt at the Academy of Fine Arts in Milan in 1927, his relationship with Edoardo Persico's rationalist architecture group introduced to him by Fausto Melotti, the abstract experience from 1934 with the sculptures in the Salone della Vittoria for the VI Triennale in Milan, 1936, again with Persico, the sculpture project for the pavilion of the International Exhibition in Paris in 1937, and the glazed terracotta pieces of the late 1930s.

However, there is no doubt that the series of cuts, the first *Concetto spaziale, Attese*, dating back to 1958, originated when he fully assumed a new conception of space, described in the manifestos of Spatialism,

---

10   *Ibidem*, p. 60.

the result of a close confrontation with 20th-century physics. However, the manifestos never mention the scientific theories of spacetime and quantum physics that laid the foundations of modern physics, from Albert Einstein with his 1905 theory of "special relativity", which "redefined the concept of measurement, and abolished the idea that space, time and mass were to be regarded as absolute quantities", and that "space and time are inseparable from one another, and spacetime and mass become relative to the observer", to Max Planck, who in 1900 outlined the "law of black body emission", the foundation of quantum theory.

Therefore, the group of bronze and terracotta sculptures created in 1959-60 and titled *Concetto spaziale, Natura*, is an important example of the "spatial revolution" introduced by Fontana towards the middle of the century.

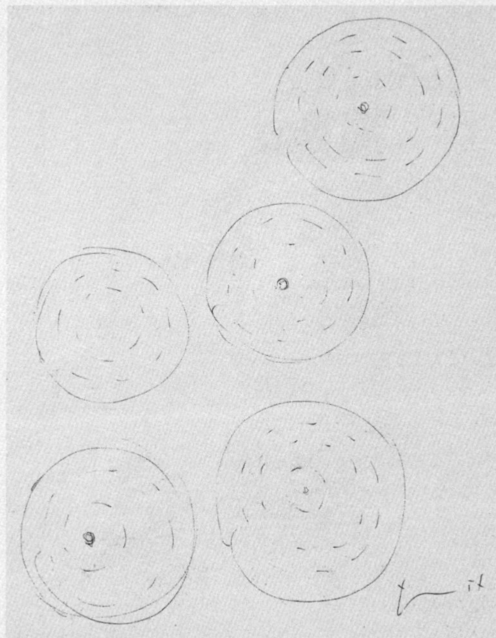

Lucio Fontana, *Studi per Concetto spaziale*, 1957, black ballpoint pen on paper, 32 x 25,5 cm, 57 DSP 83 Private collection

In the years to follow, Fontana developed this new conception of space with his mature and specifically spatial language, responding to the situation determined by the new avant-gardes and the Informal movement, along a line that runs from the *Attese* (cuts) to the *carte [works on paper]* and the *quanta*.

In the exhibition space at the 1966 Venice Biennale, which he designed himself, Fontana created a setting that was all white, which "[…] the cuts barely cracked, with an obvious conceptual and almost metaphysical revelatory significance, representing the culmination of this type of operative experience. For Fontana, white represented the 'purest colour, the least complicated, the easiest to understand', the one most immediately responding to 'pure simplicity', 'pure philosophy', 'spatial philosophy', the 'cosmic' to which he aspired in these last years of his life"[11].

In an article published on 24 June 1966 in the Florentine newspaper *La Nazione*, *Difendo I miei tagli [I Defend my Cuts]*, the artist once again rigorously stated the spatial character of his research: "Art cannot keep pace with the progress of these phenomena and consequently is transformed. Perhaps it will encroach – if it has not already crossed the boundaries – on other disciplines; perhaps it will no longer be art. However, it is already a private affair and I deny in the strongest possible terms that it could ever be a something popular. Besides, whether or not it is doesn't interest me. From here, I believe, comes the lack of a case against contemporary art for the alleged imputation. The public is unable to immediately comprehend such a complex expression of an individual sensitivity.

---

11   E. Crispolti, *Lucio Fontana*, cit., pp. 78-79.

It has never been able to. It is enough to think that even certain political events are only understood fifty years later; we sometimes only come to know the meaning of certain formulas worked out by scientists – and to use them – many years after the death of the person who worked them out. Yet here we are in the field of exact sciences!

As for me personally, I would like to point out that mine is no longer really painting; it is, if anything, a manifestation of plastic art. The cuts and holes? Ah, yes, that is my quest beyond the usual plane of the canvas, towards a new dimension. Space. A gesture of breaking beyond the limits imposed by habit, custom, tradition, but – let me be clear – developed in the honest knowledge of tradition, in the academic use of chisel, pencil, paintbrush, colour".

In an interview he gave to Daniela Palazzoli in October 1967, Fontana stated the principles of his research as follows: "First of all, I wouldn't call them paintings; I no longer called the works I did in '46 paintings, but from the very beginning I called them 'spatial concepts' and this is because for me all painting lies in the idea. The canvas served and serves to document an idea. What I do now are just variations on my two basic concepts: the hole and the cut. At a time when people talked about 'planes': the surface plane, the plane of depth, etc., my act of making a hole was a radical gesture that broke the space of the painting and said: after this we are free to do what we want. The space of the painting cannot be enclosed within the limits of the canvas but must be extended to the entire environment. In what way, and in how many different ways, I don't know because unfortunately I won't be able to live to the year two thousand, but the important thing was to bear witness to this need. Then there were the environments with neon light, the spatial environment organised by Cardazzo in '49 and so on"[12].

Guido Ballo was the first to grasp the predominantly linguistic nature of Fontana's art: "Fontana, however, did not subscribe to any abstractionist poetics: moreover, unlike others, while composing abstract works, he continued to create figurative ones at the same time. This attitude, which dampened any fanaticism, could not appear orthodox to other abstractionists: but with the distance of time, instead it is now understandable that for Fontana it was a matter of linguistic enrichment, of other research possibilities, of experimentation, without, for this reason, fixating on one single approach or on the mythical contrast between abstract and figurative, as if they had to become two new irreconcilable genres. In short, for Fontana the signifier could exclude the meaning of representation as experimental research, but only temporarily, and vice versa, the figurative meaning could yield to the signifying purity of line, colour, rhythm, and material expressiveness"[13].

---

12   *Ibidem*, p. 121.

13   G. Ballo, Fontana, cit., p. 55.

In the end, the artist's existential component was not extraneous either. He based his research on this condition, as he stated in 1968: "[...] figurations of man in space, this anguish that seeks forms and has not yet found them, the fear of getting lost. This tracing of holes would indicate man's path in space. These forms would be those of inhabitants of other worlds. I put myself in a position not of the artist, but almost of a scholar, of a researcher who closes himself off from the world"[14].

However, beyond the "existential" component, in all its phases, Fontana's research is still essentially "linguistic": this almost consubstantial need that distinguishes his works persists in the Fontana of the figurative 20th-century sculpture presented at the Hall of Honour of the 6th Milan Triennale in 1936, in the "baroque" Via Crucis, as well as the "abstract and informal" and finally "spatialist" work of the *Concetti spaziali*.

If one of the foundations of *linguistics* is the concept, extremely linear in its essentiality, that every system of *communication* – and artistic expression is still considered one of these systems today – is based on "a set of structures in relation to one another", all of Fontana's research corresponds to this principle even when this is masked by the emerging *gesture*.

---

14   Lucio Fontana, interview by Luigi Grassi, in Caffeclub, year II, Issue no. 5, Milan, January -February 1968, p.

From the Places
of the Origins
to the
"Non-places"
of the Cosmos

Paolo
Campiglio

THE (BLACK) MAN AND THE (PINK) WOMAN IN THE FIRST TERRESTRIAL LOVES

In December 1930, the 31-year-old Lucio Fontana showed his anti-graceful *Uomo nero [Black Man]* (1930), now the undisputed sign of the primitivist turn, in the group exhibition *Opere e studi di artisti lombardi noti e giovanissimi* at the Galleria del Milione. The monumental piece even surprised the show's curator, Edoardo Persico, and the younger painters gravitating around the *ruche* of via Solferino 11, with whom the artist had showed his work until not long before. It appeared obvious to everyone that Fontana, who had just finished his apprenticeship with Wildt at the Accademia di Brera, had abandoned the stylism of his master and had also distanced himself from the soporific Maillol-style atmosphere of the academy (in that short period, between 1928 and 1929, which Persico would identify as the artist's classical period). He had embarked on an entirely independent phase of inquiry unlike anything else going on in the Italian art world in those years, aside from the inspirations he shared with other young artists like Aligi Sassu, Renato Birolli (who showed at the group exhibition), Giandante X and others.[1] His "restarting" from scratch, after the experiments in style, appeared to be the first decisive step in erasing and rebelling against an art that sought to engage, in one way or another, with history, evoked in Waldemar George's *Appels d'Italie* exhibition at the Biennale of that year. Instead, he intentionally tapped into a prehistoric or a-historic dimension, for now merely imagined.

In those first investigations, which began in 1930 and continued over the next few years, especially in his drawings, the motifs of inspiration appear to have been the first terrestrial loves of men and women – the isolated male figure, the female nude in a desert landscape, the man and the horse, the woman and the horse, the virgins. Primitive loves, core instincts, not experienced nostalgically. The atmospherics of these pieces allude to a time in which there is no awareness of an afterwards, and the "waiting" figures (a condition that takes on meaning in the light of the best-known appellative that the artist would use for his "cuts") are mute presences in an anti-history dilated within an undefinable time frame. The old primitivist myth dear to Matisse and to German Expressionism (in the more suggestive themes of the nude in a natural landscape, of bathers and wild animals), stripped here of any symbolist connotation, represents just an initial idea for an inquiry into another meaning of "origin". The notion of origin was certainly a reappraisal of the dominion of the instinct, the allusion to the sexual sphere as a vital element, but at the same time it was a questioning of his own linguistic abilities, a journey à rebours.

––––––––––––

1   Raffaello Giolli, one of the closest observers of the young Lucio Fontana in the 1930s, reviewed two solo shows held by Giandante X in 1928 and 1929, first at the Galleria Micheli and then at the Galleria Bardi, organised with the encouragement of Pier Maria Bardi himself. Giolli published two different articles in *Emporium*, including illustrations of his work. R. Giolli, *Cronache milanesi*, "Emporium", 1928, Vol. LXVIII, n. 403, p. 56.
R. Giolli, *Cronache milanesi*, "Emporium", 1929 , Vol. LXX, n. 415, p. 59.

Having stripped away every superstructure, Fontana felt like the man performing the first ever creative gesture by tracing a line in the sand. His intention was to relate his every act to the essence of making art, implicitly asking himself what meaning it now had to model material, paint a surface or draw a form. It was a question with no answer for now. The spare, unbroken line graphically generating those squat human figures and those desert landscapes of beaches in sea horizons – the places of a millenary existence imagined in his many studies on paper – translates in a plastic way into the act of scratching "tablets", namely surfaces in coloured plaster or cement, with a burin, performing a distinct and prehistoric gesture.

Uomo nero is the all-round three-dimensional solution that seems to derive from or precede the ideas left on paper: it is a kind of incunabulum, a mute, "waiting", seated figure that is apparently the result of a mass of material angrily thickened to create the form, an attempt at representing man by way of cubic volumes. But in its concreteness, it is actually a form devised to express a pure plastic "concept". The work represents an act of rebellion against modelling and the aura attributed to it by critics in those years; in drawing on the unconscious, it reveals the adoption of techniques derived from Surrealism, such as the scratched signs, the infatuation with Cubist methods, the abstraction of a black, tarry colour; and finally, in Persico's view, it seems to be a test run for calling into question the very instruments of the avant-garde, as he would note in 1936.[2] The ready equivalence between the search for origins and instinct would lie at the heart of Persico's interpretation of a primarily expressionist Fontana, as also appears evident from the contemporary reflections of Piero Torriano, who was an assistant of his at the journal *Casabella*. "One of the most characteristic aspects of the modern aesthetic conscience", Torriano noted in 1932, "is the one determined by the desire to link artistic creation to its original act, reducing it to a primitive expressive core shorn of all the artificial superimpositions left by an excess of culture and experience". Referring to Fontana as one of the young artists that exemplified this tendency, he described him as "instinctive, who in his work seems only to aspire to the embryonic three-dimensional fact that is still all expression".[3] In truth, as Crispolti amply reiterated, for Fontana the implicit concept of the origin, insofar as it was a reduction to the essence, entailed abstraction as the means for questioning the ponderal volume of matter, above all in the use of pronounced colour fields, almost as if to deny it, as the artist himself would later admit: it is what Crispolti calls the *levity or essentiality* of Fontana's approach.[4] From the start he was attracted

---

2   "The taste for influences in Fontana seems to be not so much an aesthetic pleasure (…) as it is a strict and controlled critical search for the reasons of European art". E. Persico, "Lucio Fontana", republished in E. Persico, *Destino e modernità. Scritti d'arte (1929–1935)*, edited by E. Pontiggia, Medusa, Milan 2001, p. 168.

3   P. Torriano, "Cronache d'arte. Due giovani", *Casabella*, January 1932, p. 53.

4   "The most authentic and original measure of his creative imagination can easily be seen,

by abstract, artificial colours, by what we would now call "Pop" tonalities, which, as was noted at the time, made his three-dimensional concepts look like "sugar sweets", accentuating their unnatural and sometimes frivolous nature.[5] This function was performed by his tarry, unreal black, with its tendency to cancel out any shadow, the blinding pink, the pure, reflecting gold, the bright red, the deep ultramarine blue, the sky blue and white, which enveloped the plastic forms. Fontana would subsequently arrive at a finer and more dazzling solution in his ceramic work in Albissola, its endless reflections capable of liquifying matter. As if to bear out that right from his early inquiry into the a-historicity of the gesture and the conceptual essentiality of the line his work was bound up with a chromatic and almost mental abstraction of pure light. This would come to maturity first with the well-known suite of abstract sculptures in coloured and scratched reinforced concrete from 1934–35 and then with his first experiments in ceramics. It would subsequently reappear, with an altered sign, in the first nuclear "spatial concepts" (1949) with gilt, blue or purple fields, before returning many years later in the better-known "spatial concepts" of the 60s, especially in the "Oils", with brightly coloured paint pastes of pinks or whites.

As regards Fontana's approach to the theme of man-woman as the origin of life, it is curious to note that *Uomo nero*, though it has an emblematic value, seems to have a rival in a later, "violently red and gold coloured" female "version" in the monumental bas-relief of *Vittoria* (1932). A rough figure also seated on a rock, it was later realised in bronze for the Monument to the Fallen in Erba, designed by the young architect Giuseppe Terragni. A plaster cast of the figure, shown at the artist's second solo exhibition at the Galleria del Milione in December 1931, once again surprised Persico. "A disconcerting work", he admitted, "a point of arrival in Fontana's art, the solution to a series of pondered experiments (...)."[6] Then there is *Amanti* (1933), the lost relief in coloured cement exploring the ambiguous theme of love, also recurrent in the drawings of this period, where the man is often a mute and apparently characterless figure alongside the woman. Functioning as a "sign" on the façade of the experimental *Casa del sabato degli sposi* of Portaluppi and the BBPR at the Fifth Triennale of Milan, it was not just an experiment in a possible dialogue between the work and the transparent surfaces, white walls and crystals of early Italian rationalism. It also represented the

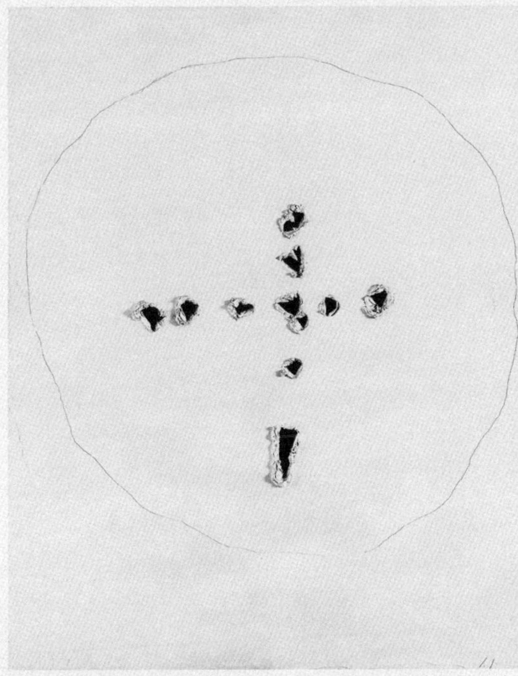

Concetto spaziale, 1962, oil, gashes and graffiti on canvas 146 × 114 cm
62 O 32
Courtesy Fondazione Lucio Fontana

I believe, in terms of levity, essentiality, the acuteness of the project: in a process that stems from the particular mental formulation". E. Crispolti, "Viatico per il Centenario", republished in Enrico Crispolti, *Carriera Barocca di Fontana*, edited by P. Campiglio, Skira, Milan 2004, p. 222.

5   R. Crippa, "Mostre d'arte", *Libro e moschetto*, 20 February 1931, p. 4.

6   E. Persico, "La Vittoria di Fontana", in Persico, *Destino e modernità*, p. 116.

From the places of the origins to the "non-places" of the cosmos

atavistic and simultaneously contemporary atte-
station of the male-female relationship, a black
man and in all likelihood a dazzlingly pink woman,
intertwined and inseparable, as if to reaffirm the
origin of humanity in the notion of the couple.
Or the coloured concrete of the *Bagnante [Bather]*
(1933), the reclining black figure conceived for the
machine à habiter of the *Villa-studio per un ar-
tista* by Figini and Pollini for the same exhibition,
which displayed a strident contrast between the
wild and almost brutal sensuality of the "girl" and
her bathing costume, with its fashionable, colour-
ful stripes and abstract motifs offering an ironic
distraction from any primitive thesis, as if to li-
ghten the original reference with a note of taste.

The connotations of his plastic and graphic output
from then on revolved around the female portrait.
In his busts or in the full, lying-down figures he
exploited a rapacious instinct to render the intimate eroticism, the sensuality, the wild and irra-
tional side, the aristocratic air. His partiality for the
female gender would become proverbial over the
years, but the female portrait was primarily understood by the artist, like
the origin, as the means to a liberation from the narrow conventions of
language and from the prejudices of contemporary society. We need only
think of the aristocratic sensuality of *Paulette* (1938), in which the baroque
ceramic material seems to elude the coming into focus of the person with
its crude black and white tones. Actually, though, it skilfully renders the essential features, the psychology of a emancipated girl bubbling with vitality.
In this regard, it is worth referring to the picture Raffaele Carrieri painted
of the early Fontana in recollections dating to 1931: the thirty-year-old
was certainly not the gruff Arturo Martini-like sculptor, locked away in
his studio, or the hermetic Sardinian, Mario Sironi. Instead, he cloaked
himself in an exotic aura, and in his friend's eyes he became the elegant captain of a steamship, a mysterious adventurer, the Argentinian
who on nights out loved the dance shows of the Viennese ballerinas.
Fontana had just returned from Argentina: he looked like the captain of a
rich steamship. His grey suits went down in history, as did certain thick
buckskin gloves, inseparable from his hands. Meeting Fontana coincided
with the debut at the Teatro Lirico of Schwartz's first Viennese company.
Fontana didn't miss a single performance of *The White Horse Inn*. I think
the ballerinas kept an eye on him. The presence of the Argentine was imposing. He preferred to keep quiet: then his eyes seemed to be new nails
emerging from the solid head. We knew little about him. Born in Rosario di
Santa Fe from Milanese parents, he had studied sculpture at Brera under
the supervision of Wildt. He had worked a lot in Argentina, but none of us
had seen a single photograph of the sculptures he had produced there.
Fontana didn't talk much about these things. Partly out of insolence, and
partly because, even then, he liked doing more than talking (…) one of

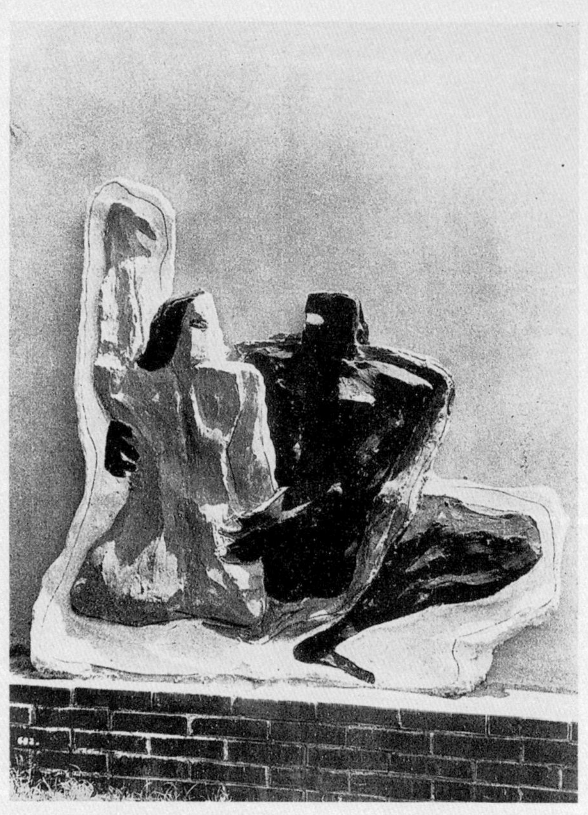

Amanti, 1933,
coloured cement
33 A 1
V Triennial (1933)

Fontana's greatest gifts was that he was likeable. A virile likeability that left no room for rest. In everything he did the temperature exceeded the normal voltage.[7]

Assuming that *Uomo nero*, conceived as an emblematic "beginning", represents "the void", to use a definition dear to Fontana, that it signifies the apparent antinomy between concept and matter, or rather the intent, not yet clear in the artist's mind, to get round the notion of volume by emphasising volume itself, the subsequent *Concetto spaziale* or *Uomo atomico [Atomic Man]* (1947), created some time later as a companion piece for the ring sculpture *Scultura spaziale [Spatial Sculpture]* (1947) – an imaginary non-place of a cosmic planet, almost without gravity – becomes an emblem of the "concept" of space introduced following the writing of the *Manifiesto Blanco* (1946) and in concomitance with the first Italian manifestos of the *Spaziali*, which anticipated the discovery of the "hole". Space was the infinity of the cosmos as "elsewhere" in the era of the future. The work was still a mass of black matter (still painted reinforced plaster), though distributed along essential lines to form the limbs, and it bears signs of manipulation; but insofar as it is an agglomerate of nuclei, it belongs to an idea of a future human existentiality in the new atomic era, in an imaginary cosmic corollary: it seems to be a silhouette of an indeterminate time.

On the threshold of a second new beginning, that of the perforated spatial concept, Fontana transposed the idea of the origin as a metaphor of erasure to the multidimensionality of an imagined and infinite cosmos. From the earthquake-riven palaeolithic deserts of the 1930s he moved on to the idea of the first nucleus of matter and life, already explored in sketches and drawings dating to his years in Argentina. He did this through a crucial series of steps that led him to the atom, a new metaphor of erasure but with an essential energetic connotation of vital projection. Arising from this new perspective of the reduction and demonstration of primary energy was the above-cited series of nuclear gouaches, with extensive gold and blue blots, or with violet and red shades, shown in 1949 at the Galleria Libreria Salto in the context of a series of exhibitions devoted to the protagonists of Milanese abstractionism, but initially conceived as preparatory studies for his *Ambiente spaziale a luce nera [Black Light Space Environment]*.

Pertaining to this problematic – the demonstration of a nucleus of primary, vital matter, that is at once an act of negation of matter itself (the manifestation of the "void") – are the "spatial" ceramics. Almost corroded and burnt, and presented as residual fragments of dead

---

7   R. Carrieri, "Primo incontro con Fontana", *Epoca*, VI, 1955, p. 226, partly republished in "Memorie dell'altro ieri: Lucio Fontana", *Epoca*, 22 September 1963, p. 100. Carrieri's recollection is of 3 November 1931, the date of the debut of the operetta *The White Horse Inn* (*Im weissen Rössl*) at the Teatro Lirico. Cited in P. Rusconi, "Uomini neri", in *Fare storia dell'arte. Studi offerti a Liana Castelfranchi*, Jaca Book, Milan 2000, pp. 261–64.

planets, he developed them between 1948 and 1949 in a new and wholly experimental phase of acceleration of the Albissola experiment: a kind of large sphere marked by primordial vortexes impressed with force, a spiral form resting on the floor, a nucleus of greenish matter and an imposing whirling black cube (also called *El quadrado*, which recalls his first *Uomo nero*), these latter works acquired by the collector Adriano Pallini for his Ospedaletti villa.[8] What's more, the allusion to a spiral-shaped gesturalism, evident in the vortexes of ceramic material and in the concomitant appearance of the first perforated papers, could relate, as primary gesture, to the phenomenology of the galaxy and to the sign scratched on the sand of the first man on earth. Recalling the provocative presentation of one of these pieces as the National Exhibition at the Galleria d'Arte Moderna in Milan in May 1948, his friend Mario Radice remarked:

"But if we were to strip his ceramics of their fine enamels and iridescences what might we think today? We ask this question having in mind a strange, monochrome "fossil" piece by Fontana shown at the National Exhibition in via Palestro. A piece that looks like one of these ceramics but seems to have been struck by lightning and carbonised, corroded, we might even say killed [...]".[9]

There is no doubt that these episodes underpinned the subsequent Nature Sculptures. After seeing the works when they first went on display at the Palazzo Grassi in the exhibition *Dalla Natura all'arte* in 1960, Marcello Venturoli described them as "swollen and blind" seeds. These too were originally in black-painted terracotta, produced around ten years after the nuclear drawings and in concomitance with the conceptual extremisation of the act of the "holes" in the most decisive and absolute formula of the monochrome "waits", as if to reiterate the possibility of such a cancellation through matter as well. The solution would appear to contradict the absoluteness of the spatial concepts on canvas, as Fontana also admitted, yet these "30 very large balls in terracotta with large slashes and holes" are also "the void! the death of matter (...) the pure philosophy of life".[10]

He conceived of a spheroidal form – a large seed or a hypothetical cell – and then made a deep furrow in the mass, which seems to separate the form in two halves or valves in a horizontal or vertical direction, alluding to the molecular genesis of life. The show at the Palazzo Grassi seemed

---

8   These are the *Ceramiche spaziali* catalogued as 49SC3, 49SC4, 49SC5 and 49SC6, the last of which is now in the collection of the Centre Pompidou in Paris. See E. Crispolti (ed.), *Lucio Fontana*, catalogue raisonné, vol. 1, Skira, Milan 2004, p. 215.

9   Mario Radice, "Giornale delle Arti. Lucio Fontana", *Corriere di Milano*, 28 May 1948, p. 3. The spiral ceramics of 1949 were then presented in the exhibition *Scultura all'aperto. Premio di scultura città di Varese*, as demonstrated by the catalogue. *Premio di scultura "Città di Varese"*, Villa Mirabello, Varese, 2 September – 10 October 1949, cat., n.n. p.

10   Letter from Lucio Fontana to Jef Verheyen on 28 September 1960, in P. Campiglio, *Lucio Fontana. Lettere 1919–1968*, Skira, Milan 1999, p. 179.

to allude to the incubation of a birth: a show that might be understood, today, as a full-blown environment in which everything contributed to suggesting an essential and barbarous "poverty": an earth floor; the ochre-coloured walls and ceiling, roughly painted and, in the middle of the room, freely distanced from each other but illuminated by a sulphurous light, seven large nature sculptures in fireclay. Six of these were coloured when cold with a greyish lampblack and are as opaque "as the epidermis of a shark", and they rested on rough wooden crates used as bases. The seventh "nature" was left in its bare, uncoloured state. On the walls were the "waits", characterised by a single slash and a monochrome *Concetto spaziale* with a simple motif of perforations.

In truth it was what the artist called the "pure philosophy of life" that became the dominant theme in the last decade of the artist's output, the fruit of a line of thinking that slowly came into focus over the years; based on doubt, the artist moved towards it in stages, but, as has been seen, it was always present in his creative universe. In other words, as Crispolti made clear, his convictions contained not just an intimate allusion to the life inherent to his every gesture, a constant feature of every form of his production, but also the consequent reference to the mystery of genesis. Whether it related to the first loves of man and woman, the imagining of an "atomic man", the genesis of life in his secular world remained a question that he tried to answer without resorting to the grand philosophical schemes of the past, but with an optimistic and almost pragmatic projection into the future, into a world finally freed, thanks to genetic science and new technologies, from the need to explain the origin of life by resorting to divinity. In the artist's modest view, the development of human intelligence would soon lead to the possibility of generating life in a laboratory, to the development of genetics (which did then occur). At that point man would in a certain sense have "replaced" divine thought, being able to do without it. Fontana had already alluded to this concept in a letter to his friend Charles Damiano in 1960:

Get ready then for the prayers you will have to say on your knees in front of my NATURE SCULPTURES. They will roll around the world's galleries sowing terror and the freedom of matter in art! The wait for pure intelligence. In a thousand years we will be similar to God. Original sin will have finished for man, and we will return to how he created us, similar to him. I am thinking of writing a manifesto that will give priests and communists something to meditate about!![11]

In the artist's thinking there was the conviction that the development of what was then defined by media-divulged science as the "living cell" could lead, over time, to the generation of a human being. Only then would the progress of humankind be comparable to God, because

____

11   Letter from Lucio Fontana to Charles Damiano on 7 August 1960, in G. Gaggiotti, *La visione verticale*, Morlacchi editore, Perugia 2019, pp. 132–133.

there would for the first time be the possibility to generate life without necessarily resorting to the sexual act, thereby overcoming the material condition of human beings, traditionally associated with original sin. This theologically influenced secular thinking began to gain ground in his creative world: the cell is the concrete possibility of future life imagined in purity, in the absence of any material implication. On the basis of this conviction, the Nature Sculptures, like the "waits", could be understood in metaphorical terms as necessary and entirely imaginary anticipations of a future human condition based on immateriality, in a kind of ataractic limbo. Hence also the use of the term "waits" as premonitory signs of a utopian "pure intelligence". A condition that the artist intuited in the 60s to be a necessary and almost retaliatory path to take by a society overly bound to material requirements.

THE END OF GOD AND THE "PILL"

At this point the thread linking the phenomenology of the Nature Sculptures to the later *Fine di Dio* (1963) series can be clearly grasped. In the latter, the oval form alludes to the "mandorla" in which God is represented in the Christian tradition, and also to the idea of the egg – recurrent in his ceramic output at the time – as a metaphor of genesis. According to this reading (though the artist has offered different and sometimes contradictory and discordant interpretations of the series), the "end of God" signifies not just the exhaustion of the idea of representing God, but a moving beyond the conception of the divine act to explain the origin of life. It was the theme of the end of God as "end of the world" that Fontana tried to clarify when speaking to Carla Lonzi in 1967:

At a certain point God gives a scientist, or a hundred scientists, the faculty to create pure spirit, and so, once the cell is created, matter ends: man becomes like God, he becomes spirit. So, we have the end of the world and man's liberation from matter. (…) Man will thus become a simple being, (…) and will only live on his intelligence, on the beauty of nature, and will purify himself of blood, because he lives continuously in the midst of blood. Maybe he will no longer kill animals, he will create pills and live artificially… because he is still a cannibal, isn't he? … Men will no longer kill each other, wars will end. It will take hundreds and perhaps thousands of years, but science will lead to that.[12]

Fontana's philosophy of the void, arising above all from the "waits", would appear to stem from an intimate palingenetic hope and an optimistic faith in science, that the creation of life in a lab might lead to a kind of definitive foregoing of material needs, to immateriality as the human condition linked to the utopia of purity. In this regard, the impromptu hypothesis formulated by Pierre Rouve in the presence of Fontana's

---

12   P. Campiglio, "Milano, 10 ottobre 1967, Carla Lonzi intervista Lucio Fontana", in *Lucio Fontana. Sedici sculture*, Silvana Editoriale, Milan 2007, p. 38.

provocative series shifts the emphasis onto the dramatic interpretation of the eternal contrast between the finite and the infinite:

His work represents the image of complex man of modern times, torn between the impulse to flee from the straitjacket of sterile conventions and the inability to attain the peaceful ripose of transcendental convictions. It is not a pure whim that has prompted Fontana to give to his latest series of calm and vibrant works the Nietzschian title of "Fine di Dio". Yet this transcending torments the artist no less than it does nuclear physicists and dodecaphanic composers: only this impossible *Absolute* can tie together the confused and contradictory experiences scattered throughout our lives. Deprived of this continual cohesive, our existence is reduced to being an incoherent mosaic of fragments, a frenetic succession of fractures that inexorably mark our inner existence. Fontana reflects this gap against the ineffable background of an ungraspable transcendence: reality is not enough for him and is to be avoided – but the transcendent is just an unattainable attraction. And Fontana finds himself up against the surprising task of giving us the artistic representation of the collision between two absences. (...) The infinite and the Infinite Void. Grasping an instant of this is to shudder in desperation. Perhaps this explains why there is such a condensation of terror around these craters of desperation that open in the consoling calm of colour. But this chromatic exquisiteness is not fortuitous. It is the mark of modern man playing at being hopeful.[13]

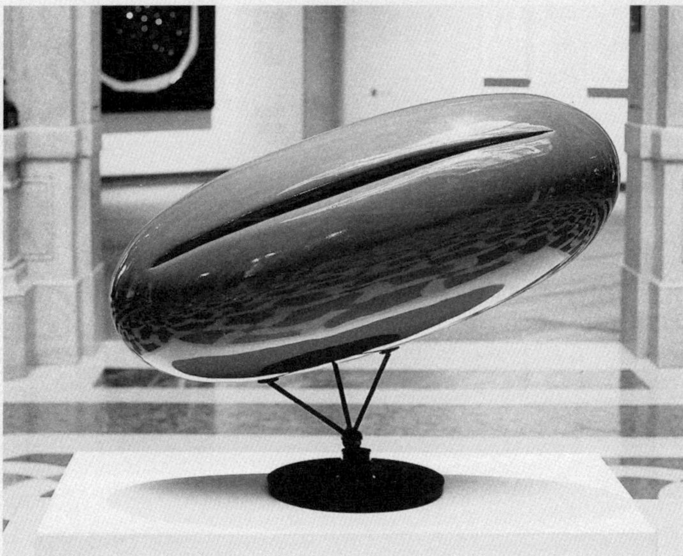

Concetto spaziale, 1967
lacquered and cut metal, red,
h 128, diam. 49 cm
67 SC 5
Intesa Sanpaolo Collection
Gallerie d'Italia, Milano

Corresponding to the optimistic faith in a future palingenesis of humanity that transpires from his every creative act, not just in the 60s but also retrospectively in all the gestures that Fontana described as acts of "fecundation" of matter, was a polemic vein about the achievements of science, interpreted by the artist as being contrary to life or as unjustified interruptions of the birth of man in contemporary society. This stance surfaces in particular in Fontana's final series of "ellipses" and "ovular missile sculptures", produced in metal in 1967, which also include a very large work lacquered in red and marked by a single horizontal slash, which the artist always referred to as the "pill".[14]

---

13   P. Rouve, *Lucio Fontana. Peinture. Sculpture*, catalogue of the exhibition at the Gimpel Hanover Galerie, 21 May – 15 June 1963; E. Crispolti, *Lucio Fontana. Fine di Dio*, Tornabuoni / Forma edizioni, Florence 2017.

14   This is the only exemplar of *Concetto spaziale*, 1967, general catalogue 67 SC 5, in Crispolti, *Fontana*, catalogue raisonné, vol. 2, p. 908.

From the places of the origins to the "non-places" of the cosmos

Realised as a kind of design object, with a spherical pedestal that can be oriented to change the inclination and position of the oval in the space, the work was cited in a later interview given to Tommaso Trini, effectively the artist's final public declaration. From it one can glean that it was an ironic allusion to the female contraceptive pill, which was already widely available in the United States:

I called it "the pill" because I make a joke of things. But the pill has already produced more deaths than a nuclear war. Think of how many thousands of women take the pill and how many thousands of beings are not born. So, instead of erecting a monument to Glory, to the victory of Samothrace, I made this egg with a slash that is a monument to the pill, which today is as socially important as the victory of Samothrace, as a war won or lost.[15]

The equally ironic and grotesque interpretation of the myth of Fontana offered by a young Ugo Nespolo is therefore not entirely out of place. He presented him as being ultimately a gentleman of a bygone age, an impenitent and adventurous "knight", in the artist's film shot between 1966 and 1967 with Enrico Baj. The film, edited as a frenetic "collage", is entitled *La galante avventura del cavaliere dal lieto volto* (1966/67) and has a pop soundtrack. It was shot in the garden of Baj's villa at Vergiate, not far from the village of Comabbio to which Fontana had retired. This was the ideal setting for the sequences with artists dressed up as characters from former times, wearing Risorgimento military uniforms and waving implausible patriotic flags, in tribute to his friend's poetics of the "generals". Fontana and Baj clumsily pursue a woman, but she eludes their insistent requests, finally merely displaying, without modesty, her nudity in a kind of grotesque performance *en plein air*.

*Concetto spaziale,
La fine di Dio*, 1963,
oil, gashes, holes, graffiti
and sequins on canvas,
178 × 123 cm
63 FD 28
Courtesy Fondazione
Lucio Fontana

---

15   T. Trini, "Ultima intervista a Lucio Fontana", in *Burri e Fontana 1949–1968*, Milan, Skira 1996 (Prato, Museo Pecci, 13 April – 30 June 1996), p. 68.

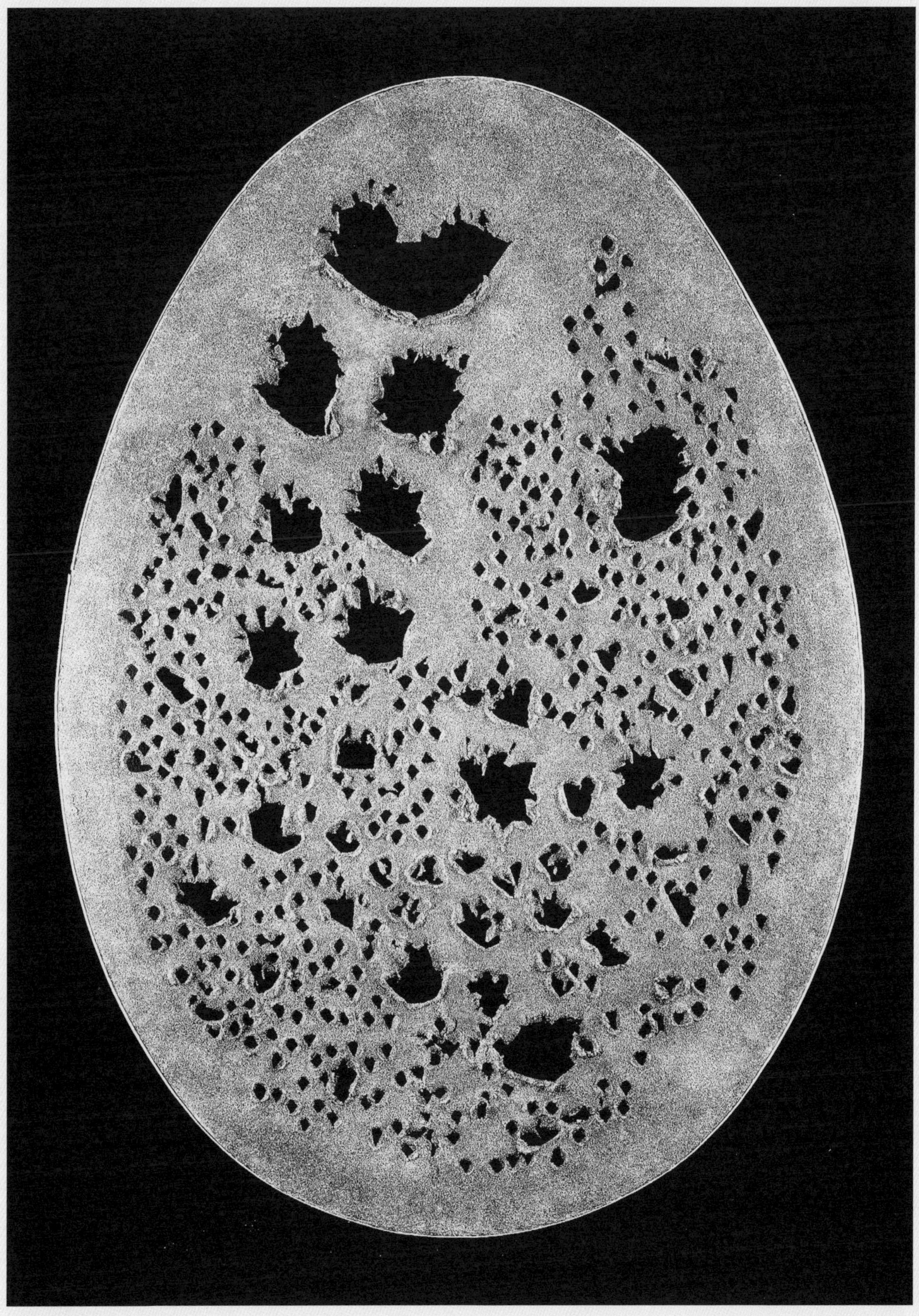

From the places of the origins to the "non-places" of the cosmos

Anthropophagous Fontana: from the Beginning to the End[1]

Andrea
Bruciati

'Primordial and primeval' is a hendiadys of two terms that emblematically intersect in Lucio Fontana's work over the course of his career, following a sinusoidal path. From the *Uomo Nero* [*Black Man*], (1929) to the contemporary unicellular scratched tablets,[2] the geological beginning and start of human history coincide in the artist's work, almost as if the universe's physical Big Ben were inseparable from the biological origin of the world. Using a scale that goes from amoebic structure to sidereal representation, and so where the beginning forms a whole with the end, Fontana unfurls the most innovative ideas of the manifestos through signs and an apparently basic, archaic language.[3] Almost prehistoric forms, floating in para-Surrealist amniotic liquids, are inevitably partnered with geographic cosmographies, in accordance with a vitalistic anthropophagous approach[4] in some ways similar, in terms of the richness of linguistic results, to that of Picasso. Worlds that came into alignment following Fontana's rejuvenating experience in Argentina[5] (*Accademia Altamira* and *Manifiesto Blanco* are the unavoidable link between prehistory and future, including terminologically[6]) and the tragedy of war, and were expressed in all of Fontana's thought thanks to an image world made up of cosmogonies, nebulas and galaxies. From the revolutionary pierced white screens[7] (*Concetto spaziale* [*Spatial Concept*], 1949) to the magmatic ceramic works (*Ceramica spaziale* [*Spatial Pottery*], 1949), from the Giacomettian sculptures like *L'uomo atomico*

---

1 This essay developed out of my text 'Ecce Homo: il pensiero di Nietzsche e Lucio Fontana', in A. Bruciati (ed.), *Ecce Homo: l'incontro fra il divino e l'umano per una diversa antropologia*, exhibition catalogue, Tivoli, Villa d'Este, 25 June – 6 November 2021, Gangemi, Rome 2022, pp. 102–113.

2 Here, I am specifically thinking of the two *Tavoletta graffita* from 1931 (E. Crispolti, *Fontana. Catalogo ragionato di sculture, dipinti, ambientazioni*, Skira, Milan 2006).

3 'There was always something primary in the imaginative genesis …, primary and hence also essential', E. Crispolti (ed.), *Centenario di Lucio Fontana*, exhibition catalogue, Milan, multiple venues, 23 April – 30 June 1999, Charta, Milan 1999, p. 14.

4 I believe that the parallel exploration in Brazil and Argentina linked to the contemporary thought of Oswald de Andrade and Martìn Fierro deeply influenced that aptitude for shaping an identity through superimpositions and gaps, which was read in Europe solely as immanentist experimentation carried out in accordance with a form of phenomenological *varietas* (Edoardo Persico emphasised the 'taste for influence' and 'capacity to continually convert' while Enrico Crispolti wrote of imaginative actualism and phenomenological activism). See, respectively: E. Persico, *Lucio Fontana*, Edizioni di Campo Grafico, Milan 1936; E. Crispolti 2006. On this subject, see my forthcoming publication, but also see Paulo Herkenhoff 'L'ottica dell'invisibile. Voglia di spazio: Fontana / Brasile', in P. Herkenhoff (ed.), *brazil Lucio Fontana*, exhibition catalogue, Rio de Janeiro, Brazil, Sao Paulo, Centro Cultural Banco do Brasil, November 2001 – April 2002, Charta, Milan 2001, and Enrico Crispolti 'The Latin Axis in the Twentieth-Century Avant-Garde', in I. Candela (ed.), *Lucio Fontana: on the Threshold*, exhibition catalogue, New York, MET, 23 January – 14 April 2019; Bilbao, Guggenheim Museum 17 May – 20 September 2019, MET, New York 2019.

5 See: Dominique Liquois 'Fontana, l'Argentine et la Modernité' in B. Blistène (ed.), *Lucio Fontana*, exhibition catalogue, Paris, Centre Georges Pompidou, 13 October 1987 – 11 January 1988, Center Georges Pompidou, Paris 1987, Lorena Mouguelar, 'Lucio Fontana en Argentina: relecturas', in *Separata*, no. 15, X, 2010, pp. 38–55) and Andrea Giunta 'The War Years: Fontana in Argentina' in Candela 2019.

6 See: A. Bruciati, 'Podriamos hacer un arte nueva: neoavanguardia e "grado zero" in Lucio Fontana', in G. Cortenova (ed.), *Lucio Fontana metafore barocche*, exhibition catalogue, Verona, Palazzo Forti 26 October – 16 March 2002, Marsilio, Venice 2002, pp. 157–171.

7 On the monochrome, see: A. Bruciati, *Dal monocromo all'achrome: l'opera bianca in Lucio Fontana e Piero Manzoni*, Lettere e filosofia, aa. 1996/97, Università degli Studi di Udine, Udine 1997.

[*Atomic Man*] and *Scultura spaziale* [*Spatial Sculpture*] (1947-1948) up to the amalgamation in the subconscious space of the *Ambiente spaziale a luce nera* [*Spatial Environment in Black Light*] (1949) and the pierced, swelling matter of *Il pane* [*Bread*] (1950). His contemporary production in gouache on paper is also of clear and relevant interest (*Ambiente spaziale* [*Spatial Environment*], 1948, which was included in the exhibition at the Galleria del Naviglio in 1949[8]), where once again the globular shape and circular, cosmic, energising dimension of the colour are what confirm the parallel exploration within his drawing practice. The intersections between painting and sculpture that register this continuous osmosis in biological forms in fact date to the 1950s:[9] unicellular elements and geological outlines now poetically unfurl on the surfaces of the canvases, ink or plaster, and on the stems with a fossil, cosmic, future-possible nature that sprout genetically modified from the soil.[10] The cuts were a phenomenal consequence and accompanied this production: they, too, were immediately partnered with existentialist or organic actions.[11] The cut was a kind of 'break the shell' god and transformed the spatial concept into anticipation: it is as if there were a kind of operating vital need; space, heavy with spatial tensions, needed to react to those same tensions.[12] What is clear is that, like the holes, they were an anthropological act through a renewed 'natura naturans' as is clear in the *Nature* [*Natures*], terracotta 'balls' made in the summers of 1959 and 1960 in Albissola and presented in the exhibition *Dalla natura all'arte* at Palazzo Grassi.[13] That exhibition was a kind of

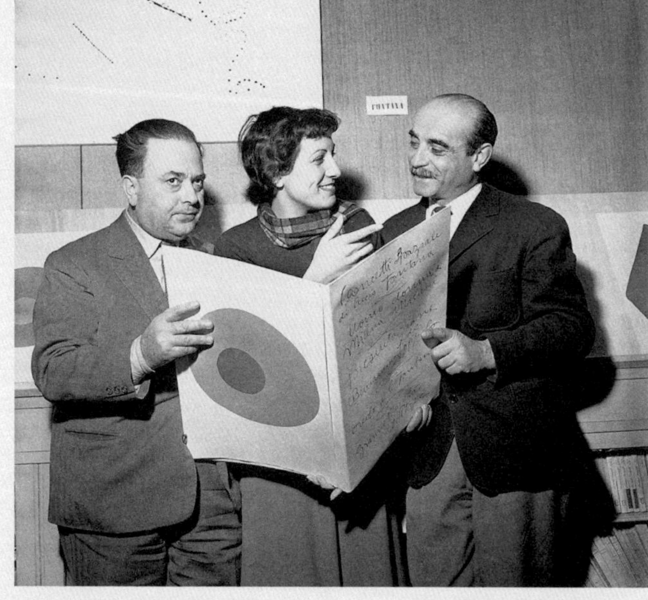

Beniamino Joppolo, Milena Milani and Lucio Fontana at the *Arte Spaziale* exhibition at Galleria del Naviglio, Milano, 1952

---

8   L. M. Barbero (ed.), *Lucio Fontana. Catalogo ragionato delle opere su carta*, Skira, Milan 2013, vol. II, p. 519.

9   G. Ballo, *Lucio Fontana, in XXIX Biennale Internazionale d'Arte*, exhibition catalogue, Venice, Giardini della Biennale, June–October 1958, pp. 19–22.

10   Here, I am referring to the evocative work *Concetto spaziale* from 1952, which was presented outdoors on grass that insinuated itself into the lamellar composition, as if it were a cosmic flower fermented by the union with the planet Earth. On the cultural context, see: S. Petersen, *Space- Age Aesthetics: Lucio Fontana Yves Klein and the Postwar European Avant-Garde*, Penn State University Press, Penn State University 2009.

11   Here, I am referring to his first solo show in Paris, at the Galerie Stadler between March and April 1959. See the review: G. Limbour, n.t., in *Les Lettres Nouvelles*, 8 April 1959.

12   'He opens the surface of today to the dimensions of the future: piercing the given, or granted, space, he pierces the time of its own constituted being', Pier Luigi Tazzi, *Trent'anni dopo: Lucio Fontana*, in P. Herkenhoff 2001, p. 213.

13   *Dalla natura all'arte*, exhibition catalogue, Centro Internazionale delle Arti e del Costume, Palazzo Grassi, Venice, 1960. Two of the *Nature* were presented in June at the Musée Rodin in *Sculpture italienne contemporaine, d'Arturo Martini à nos jours* and then again on 9 November 1961 at the Iris Clert Gallery in Paris, in the exhibition *Concetti spaziali de Fontana: sculptures "nature" 1959-1961*. S. Bignami, J. Galimberti, *Lucio Fontana e l'artventure parigina*, Scalpendi, Milan 2014, p. 27.

Andrea Bruciati

summary and result of his artistic path thus far. As we read in a letter he wrote to his friend Jef Verheyen: "I made almost thirty very large terracotta balls covered with cuts and holes, I am really happy, it's nothingness! The death of matter, it's pure philosophy of life! Good."[14] At first, these glazed terracotta sculptures were like stones with one flat side or complementary 'bivalve' forms that together formed a single sculpture. They later became balls, the artist's unofficial name for them: both types, along with *Scultura spaziale*, various high-temperature ceramics, *Il pane*, Baroque canvases and an *Attesa* with a single, decisive, assertive cut. The 'balls', placed on bases rather than on the floor, like alien eggs, and an amniotic installation made of fabric and rope that was later destroyed completed the artist's section at the Venice exhibition, where Fontana's selection of works took the form of a precise, detailed project, expressed in a way at once both metamorphic and harmonious: an environment where nature makes itself into a womb and source of all human action, where civilisation is merely the result of a natural process in which Art substantialises its origin.[15] The *Nature* evoke both the cosmic imagination of the manifestos and the primary anthropological act, represented by the abyss of the hole, so often mentioned by Fontana.[16] As Marcello Venturoli observed: "The key to the sculpture lies in their threatening vitality, part vegetable, part animal: these inflated, blind fruits, full of a lymph that stretches their surface like a skin, the solids and voids on the also round body of which almost seem to make them breathe, were attacked and in a certain way profaned by the artist. Palm-length marks made with a piece of wood, he inflicted gashes and wounds on these lives, longitudinal tears that seem to have been made with a giant tin opener. What remain are eyes and throat, fissures and lips open in the blindness of this living matter, so helpless and terrible in its protest.[17] On the one hand, a kind of Dionysian explosion;[18] on the other, an almost

---

14   P. Campiglio (ed.), *Lettere 1919 – 1968*, Skira, Milan 1999, Lettera 197, pp. 179–180. In reality, more than forty of them were made (E. Crispolti 2006).

15   The documentary produced by the Istituto Luce is especially evocative: https://patrimonio.archivioluce.com/luce-web/detail/IL3000090155/1/dalla-natura-all-arte.html?startPage=0#n.

16   'Matter is accepted in all its ponderability and develops into a primeval emblem, originary mass that the artist shapes, or better, marks like a functional figural theory of reality itself (cosmological and more properly human), in its globality. The "hole" that becomes vortex, that plunges deep, is like a material spring that marks an entrance in life … or the "split" that cuts these round "balls" (hypothetical artificial satellites, but that – still – have a lunar face) is an ancient gesture of capture, trace of will and call, like it is in a certain way the – religious, exorcistic – sign that country folk often make on massive loaves of bread, instrumentally manipulated almost just like Fontana manipulates these "natures". And, on the other hand, "natures" in that they refer to a cosmogonic force that moves all things, like primary energy, that is in the mass and nourishes it, dynamises it, gives it meaning, transforming it from brute inertia into modifying force', E. Crispolti, *Omaggio a Lucio Fontana*, Carucci, Assisi-Rome 1971, p. 183.

17   M. Venturoli, 'Suggestive opere a Palazzo Grassi nella mostra "Dalla Natura all'arte"', in *Paese Sera*, 16-17 July 1960. See: L. Hochtin, 'Les 'Ballons' de Lucio Fontana', in *XXe siècle*, a. XXIII, no. 16, May 1961, pp. 87–89; E. Crispolti, *Erotismo nell'arte astratta e altre schede per una iconologia dell'arte astratta*, Celebes Editore, Trapani 1976.

18   'He became interested in earth with the soul of a primitive man, using the techniques of today's kilns as a means – however ephemeral – of replacing the fire of the ancient kilns. His ceramics and his sculpture – linked by a style submitted to the compassion of their material – give off a geological feeling, the illusion of the fruit that a volcano would produce if it were

Jungian search for the origin of everything,[19] towards a path that seeks to return to the origin and thus found a new metaphysics. As Emilio Villa during that period: "Here, the marriage between man and nature excludes all forms of domination and introduces an allure that comes from the sprout or seed, going back to the original meaning of the Greek word *phýsis* as sprout, spring, gush of becoming, and not as orderly kingdom of already existing and known beings."[20] In his interview by Carla Lonzi, Fontana himself explained: "I was thinking of those works, of the moon with these… holes, this atrocious silence that fills us with anguish, and the astronauts in a new world. And, so, these… these immense things have been there for billions of years… the arrival arrives, in a deadly silence, in this anguish, and leaves a vital sign of its arrival… these were the still things with a sign of wanting to make inert matter live, right."[21] The sign is the cut (which is a split) or the deep hole with which Fontana took possession of the matter and made it dynamic in a sensual, erotic relationship. The rending of the canvas led to the negation of the representation, but it did not cause total destruction; in fact, it aspired to being constructive. This became clear three years later at the opening in Zurich on 21 May 1963 of the exhibition *Lucio Fontana. Peinture, sculpture*,[22] in which the artist debuted the oval paintings he had named *finediddio* (*endofgod*) in a letter to Enrico Crispolti the previous January.[23] In the introductory text, Pierre Rouve defined them in Nietzschean terms as a symbol of the modern overcoming of the dialectic between reality and transcendence.[24] The oval paintings were represented in the catalogue

---

prey to a rule. Only Sumerian and Iranian earth – in their contact with the millennia – can give off this impression', G.M. Lo Duca, 'Artisti italiani a Parigi: Corbellini, Fontana, Gherardi', *in Emporium*, LXXXVII, no. 519, March 1938, p. 160; G. M. Lo Duca, 'Cronache parigine. Parigi e Lione: artisti italiani', in *Emporium*, LXXXXVII, no. 528, November 1939, p. 336. 'Fontana's material is incandescent, rich in mineral lumps and azonic substances: you could find a diamond in the middle of these statues. … Everything that ferments in the earth has become plastic image … the material frees itself from the usual patterns and lives autonomously, it progresses before our very eyes, it is a continuous metamorphosis.' R. Carrieri, 'Le maioliche geologiche di Lucio Fontana', in *L'Illustrazione italiana*, Milan, 8 January 1939, pp. 63–64.

19   One notes the archaic power in the review of Iris Clert's Paris show, set up like an extraterrestrial environment, all blue, cold and lunar, immersed in composer Yannis Kenakis's *Métastases* (C. Rivière, 'Au-delà de la forme. Fontana la matière menaçante', in *Combat*, 20 November 1961, p. 7), where José-Augusto França observes: 'They are like delayed explosions, mines full of explosives, exploded buoys that transport us into the water's depths … And it is still a space beyond space, an interior space, just barely illuminated, mysterious, that encloses an ancient threat'. J. A França, 'Fontana' in *Aujourd'hui. Art et Architecture*, no. 34, December 1961, p. 45.

20   A. Tagliaferri, 'Parole silenziose', in B. Corà, A. Tagliaferri (eds.), *Emilio Villa. Opere e documenti*, Skira, Milan 1996 p. 16.

21   C. Lonzi, *Autoritratto*, De Donato, Bari 1969, p. 389.

22   P. Rouve, *Lucio Fontana. Peinture, Sculpture*, exhibition catalogue, Zurich, Gimpel Hanover Galerie, 21 May – 15 June 1963, Zurich 1963. For an analysis of the critical review and the 'Ova' type, see the volume edited by Enrico Crispolti and, specifically, the fundamental text by L. P. Nicoletti, published by Tornabuoni Art. E. Crispolti (ed.), *Lucio Fontana*. Fine di Dio, Forma, Florence 2017.

23   See Letter from L. Fontana to E. Crispolti on 17 January 1963, in E. Crispolti, *Carriera 'barocca' di Fontana. Taccuino critico 1959 – 2004 e Carteggio 1958 – 1964*, Skira, Milan 2004, p. 346.

24   This was a survey exhibition featuring forty-one works: fifteen ceramic sculptures, both matte and glossy, twenty-six *Concetti spaziali*, eighteen of which four-sided with cuts, holes

with reproductions of a green work and a pink one, the colours of which were deliberately the same as those predominant at the beginning of the series, as also evidenced by the larger number of pink and green ovals on view in the exhibition. On 11 June of the same year, Beatrice Monti della Corte opened *L. Fontana. Le ova* at the Galleria dell'Ariete, Milan.[25] The walls of the gallery's large main space were hung with seven green ovals and three pink ones, while a series of *Nature* were arranged on the floor, like in other solo exhibitions of the artist's work. The second, smaller room presented a few ceramic ovals, described by Marco Valsecchi as 'large terracotta ovals with a split, tearing and perforation'.[26] As reported by Dorfles, he was the one to advise Fontana against naming the oval paintings for the exhibition *Fine di Dio*, finding the title to be 'too inflated', 'vaguely irritating',[27] and to be replaced with *Concetto ovale* (*Oval Concept*), as found in the catalogue. However, the ambiguity of the original title remains in his introductory text: among the various interpretations of the oval shape, he privileges the eschatological one of resurrection and the esoteric one of 'alchemical melting pot', at the same time interpreting the oval painting as a reference to 'natural form', striving in its 'absolute organicity, its constant imprecision' for a 'metamorphosis that has always been implicit to it'.[28] He is probably referring to the *Manifesto tecnico dello Spazialismo* (1951) in which the oval is selected among the experimental shapes of a utopian modern architecture opposed to the laws of physics and proportion.[29] This exegesis is also in line with Beatrice Monti's exhibition design, the dominant colours of which evoked, in the first room, a setting partway between arboreal and epidermic that alluded to a fecund world of images also evoked by the *Nature*, described by Michel Tapié two years earlier as 'concretised magic of a metaphysics of eroticism'.[30] The idea of a

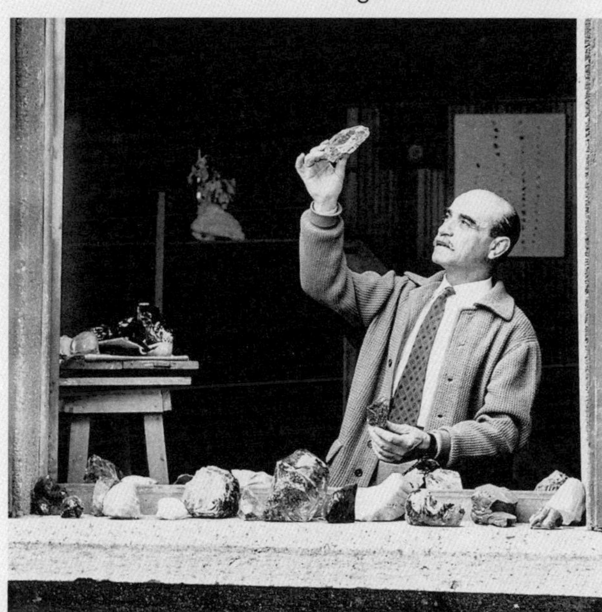

Lucio Fontana in his studio in Milan, 1960s

---

and stones and eight oval-shaped (three green, three pink, one black and one white). The selection of works is illustrated in the catalogue with photographs by Ugo Mulas and Carlo Orsi of a *Concetto spaziale rosso* (1962), various ceramic sculptures (1962) and two oval paintings.

25   *L. Fontana. Le ova*, introduction by G. Dorfles, exhibition catalogue, no. 96. Galleria dell'Ariete, Milan 1963.

26   M. Valsecchi, 'Fontana', in *il Giorno*, 7 July 1963. Also see M. Lepore, 'Mostre d'arte', in *Corriere d'informazione*, 4 July 1963.

27   G. Dorfles, 'Ho squarciato 10 tele come il muro di una prigione', in *Bolaffiarte*, March 1972.

28   *L. Fontana. Le ova* 1963.

29   'I saw a design for an egg-shaped house, another tossed onto a field not giving a damn about divine proportion' in *Manifesto tecnico. Noi continuiamo l'evoluzione nell'arte*, read in 1951 by Lucio Fontana at the first International Conference on Proportion in the Arts at the 9th Milan Triennale. See: A. Sanna (ed.), *Lucio Fontana. Manifesti, scritti, interviste*, Abscondita, Milan 2015.

30   M. Tapie, *Devenir de Fontana*, Edizioni d'Arte F.lli Pozzo, Turin 1961.

rebirth returned the following year in the monograph published by Misuzu in Japan, where the expression used, 'end of art', similar to the title of the series, leads one to suspect that the artist might have been making a provocative comparison between God and art.[31] The term 'end' implies the expectation of a future experimental era, dominated by spatialist premises and free from social aims. 'As in thought as in spiritual need', he stressed in a longer English version of the letter sent to the editor of the Japanese monograph, Takiguchi Shuzo, which the latter transcribed in a letter to the artist dated the following June. The translation in this text of 'fine dell'arte' (literally, 'end of art') as 'An End to Art' indicates a possible correspondence to the 'Fine di Dio' ('End of God') through the treatment of the title, being placed between quotation marks and using English-style capital letters. Moreover, the use of the preposition 'to', instead of a categorical 'of', reveals a constructive vision for art that, although having reached a terminus, is projected towards change.[32] In the most important iconographic meaning of the *Ove*, the gash is an evolution of the cut on metal: the gashes reference another dimension, one that is far more physical and corporeal, and the physicality of something that would be otherwise incomprehensible without the formulations of the 'balls', which were indeed arranged alongside. Unlike his previous work, the gash brought Fontana into a fully materialistic dimension, such that "the holes and cuts on the thick layer of homogeneous paint aspire to be even more torn, lacerations that destroy its homogeneity and return the flat surface to organic principles".[33] These gashes opened up a new dimension and offered the possibility of going beyond the closed, static image, as well as hope for a dimension of becoming, growing and developing. These ideas are perfectly translated by the shape: "The egg, the sprout, the embryo of a new being: but also the spiritual matrix, the microcosm… The giant egg:

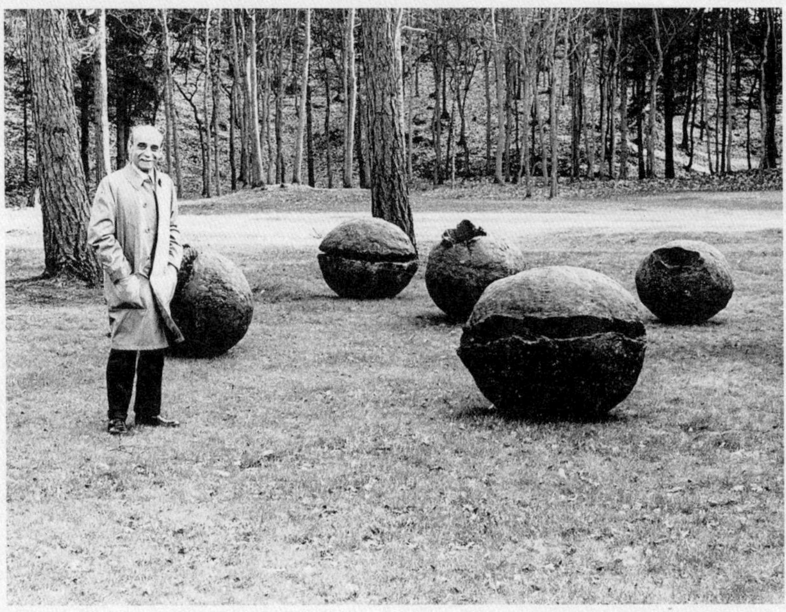

Lucio Fontana with some works from the series "Nature", Kröller-Müller Museum, Otterlo, 1962-63
Ph. Ad Petersen

---

31   'Anticipation of a new historical moment, encouraged by "La fin de l'art (pas la mort de l'art)" experienced by the factual situation in which: "L'art n'a plus de raison sociale, les conquetes de la science et de l'espace (Spatial Era) sont en train de bouleverser toutes les esthetiques rhetoriques.' Letter from L. Fontana to M. Akai, 16 May 1964, in *Galleria dell'Ariete records 1955-1993*, RL, GRI, Los Angeles, Accession no. 990058. See: E. Crispolti 2017.

32   Letter from Takiguchi Shuzo to Fontana, 19 June 1964, in Archivio Beatrice Monti della Corte, Donnini. The curator transcribed the English version of the statement, sent by Fontana in an earlier letter, asking him to send it to him in Italian for the publication. See: E. Crispolti 2017. For the review of the exhibition, see: S. Takiguchi, 'Fontana', in *Arte Contemporanea*, 25, Misuzu, Tokyo 1964.

33   G. Cortenova 2002, p. 94.

synonym of the World and of Creation. Forming and formative force that is no longer that of the Sphere of the perfect circumference but that of a sphere that collapses, flattens, stretches downwards."[34] This egg can easily be the symbol of an always present, always fertilising, always fertilised divinity, and also the symbol that replaces an old, by now drained, worn and spent image; in place of the holy icon comes the holy egg. Once again, the beginning of a new semanticity, that of an eternal symbol, forever renewing itself in the diversity and multiplicity of its interpretations.[35]

<hr>

34   F. Gualdoni, P. Campiglio, *Lucio Fontana e Milano*, Electa, Milan 1996, p. 35.

35   G. Mascherpa, C. De Carli, *Lucio Fontana e il sacro*, exhibition catalogue, Milan, Centro San Fedele, March – April 1986, Federico Motta Editore, Milan 1986, p. 9.

A Memorandum of the Gestures of Lucio Fontana

Luca Pietro Nicoletti

The best-known and most eloquent photographs of Lucio Fontana in his studio are all by Ugo Mulas. Among these is a series of 1964 shots dedicated to the famous "cuts". It was the most famous and icastic act of his entire career, becoming the foundation on which the current vulgate was built, and these shots immediately took on an unavoidably iconic role.[1] Mulas himself later revealed the deception behind that series: for Fontana, he recounted, it did not feel right to slash a canvas for the camera lens, on the grounds that he would not have been able to concentrate enough to give the right intensity to that primal action that characterised his work. And yet there was no shortage of previous occasions when the artist had let himself be photographed or filmed, demonstrating his speed and readiness in creating a series of slashes on a large canvas; or the patient work of applying the rich and sumptuous material of the "oils", followed by the lightning-fast creation of a slash and the equally immediate drawing, traced with a pointed tool on fresh paint.

It is the gesture itself, in its simplicity as a primal action, that holds together such complex and ramified work as Fontana's, which moves simultaneously as though on several gaming tables. More than for other artists, the good basic rule for deciphering the modes of the Informal is crucial here, that of identifying the trajectory of the hand gesture underlying the impression of a stroke or sign, and to learn to recognise it in every possible variation of the medium and tool.

A similar consideration must be behind a little-known text by Giulio Carlo Argan on the painting of Hans Hartung, written for a Roman exhibition in the winter of 1969. In his usual comparison of dialectically opposed polarities of poetics, Argan cited Lucio Fontana to explain the specificity of the German painter's style. According to the scholar, Hartung's gesture could have been seminal for Fontana's "cut", which brought a greater and more ground-breaking phenomenological complexity to that graphic motif: "Lucio Fontana, who was able to accurately interpret the meaning of the act behind that which gives life to Hartung's sign, has translated it into an actual slash, which breaks through the usual screen of the canvas and traumatically modifies the physical space. But just as Hartung excludes the *before* of symbolic meaning, he also excludes the *after* of reification. His swordplay has no secret stabs, and his painting, while being presented as an action, purposefully remains on a speculative level".[2]

This is not a neutral observation, because it implies an interpretation of Fontana's work, and his most iconic and recognised gesture, in terms of

---

1   For an orientation on the relationship between Fontana and Ugo Mulas: Miriam Criscione, Mulas, Ugo, in *Dizionario Lucio Fontana*, edited by Luca Pietro Nicoletti, Quodlibet, 2023, pp. 375-376. See also: Ugo Mulas, Lucio Fontana, Achille Mauri, Milan 1968; Idem, *La fotografia*, Einaudi, Turin 1973; Ugo Mulas. *Intrecci creativi*, (London, Robilant + Voena 4 March - 24 May 2019) edited by Francesca Pola, Marsilio, Venice 2019.

2   Giulio Carlo Argan, in *Hans Hartung*, (Rome, Galleria "Il Collezionista", 11 November - 8 December 1969).

pure painting, thereby momentarily disregarding the repercussions of his copious sculptural production and particularly his ceramics. Alongside his already established reputation as a sculptor, in fact, Fontana established himself as a painter only after his return to Italy from Argentina in 1947. During the 1950s, in particular, he made a rapid and progressive metamorphosis in conjunction with his association with art dealer Carlo Cardazzo and the exhibitions at his galleries in Venice, Milan and Rome. Fontana transferred much of his experience in the plastic arts to the new medium, to the extent that it could be said that his approach was that of a sculptor approaching painting, with experimental readiness and great versatility in using techniques and combining them.

As Enrico Crispolti stated in 1963, "Fontana's research always moves in a series of fertile alternatives, while remaining faithful to his own ideological core, which at a distance is exceptional". For this reason, he commented in 1968 in "Arte Illustrata" and then in the monograph *Omaggio a Fontana* [Homage to Fontana] in 1971, "The tradition of the most authentic and genuine, humanly and intellectually daring avant-garde, in Italy and beyond, has a kind of symbol of its own in Fontana, one that is more alive today than ever before, and not only in his latest imaginative and creative formulation, but in the very body of his work, whose character assumes a distinct historical significance"[3].

Moreover, this phase coincided with his approach to the demands of Informalism, which he approached without the biases of someone who had come exclusively from a painting background. Fontana immediately felt the canvas to be a plastic surface, and he manipulated that surface, going so far as to violate the integrity of the support with holes and slashes and, at the same time, modelling the material in relief with the same verve he used in ceramics. He subverted the artisanal practices but without renouncing strictly manual work. It was precisely this that enabled him to be bolder in his unrestrained approach to the support as a diaphragm that could be subjected to a certain number of processes, that would have an equal number of corresponding gestural acts.

Therefore, it will be necessary to sketch out, sooner or later, a history and above all the fortune of Fontana's "gestures" in his individual cycles, or in the units that were more clearly identified by critics during his lifetime and after his death, in order to understand how they entered the lexicon and culture of the interpreters. From cycle to cycle, as we have tried to do with the *Fine di Dio [End of God]*[4]. But as one could just as fruitfully trace this in the *Nature* of the *Teatrini [Little Theatres]* and the

---

3   Enrico Crispolti, L'avventura di Fontana, "Arte Illustrata", a. I, nos. 7/12, July–December 1968, p. 58.

4   See Luca Pietro Nicoletti, *The Story of the End of God in Art Criticism of the Sixties and Seventies/ Cronaca della Fine di Dio nella critica fra anni Sessanta e Settanta*, in *Lucio Fontana. Fine di Dio (1963-1964)*, edited by Enrico Crispolti, texts by Luca Massimo Barbero, Enrico Crispolti, Luca Pietro Nicoletti, Caterina Toschi, with the collaboration of Duccio Nobili, Forma, Florence 2017, pp. 124-177.

small cycle of "oils" dedicated to Venice, Fontana, with a burning sensitivity, was playing on the heartstrings and perhaps the spirit of his own time, with a vitality and exuberance that could hold together the most eclectic proposals and methods that were at times most contradictory.

And perhaps this is precisely why his work has had such a broad impact. In fact, Fontana's success warrants a look at how the art of the following generations was affected, from conceptual additions to the basic principle of his visual offering and true iconographic derivations, as well as a vast range of moments of transversal harmony. For example, certain "cuts" made to some of Alberto Burri's "sacks" point in this direction (e.g. the one in the Cerruti collection, now at the Castello di Rivoli). However, one cannot help but reflect on the profound harmony, beyond the occasions of direct collaboration, between certain gestures entailing the appropriation of space through the subtraction of matter - all the way to the deep intrusion into the earth with an act of explicit appropriation made in the *Nature* – and Francesco Somaini's "wound" sculpture, penetrated by incandescent gashes that pass through it from side to side. And with Leoncillo too, as already partially noted, the point of contact cannot be limited to the problem of coloured ceramics[5], nor even to the simple "baroque" sensibility of plasticity, but has a more penetrating depth.

This is all due to Fontana's recourse to a repertoire of elementary gestures that run through different materials and contexts, from modelling to painting to installations in space, as iconographically recognisable but morphologically varied trajectories: holes, cuts and etchings, in fact, are a feature of his work from graffiti tablets to the "oils", from the *Attese* [Expectations] to the "nature", from drawing to the luminous arabesque of neon, all the way to the functional ceramics, where holes and furrows run across the surface of vases and ovoid sculptures. When Enrico Crispolti introduced the 2006 annotated catalogue, he reiterated the presence of "primary structural constants of imaginative design"[6], featured from time to time in experiments that differed in medium and technique, and with a "lightness in the designation", that is, an "intervention that marks the material but is not steeped in it, or conditioned by it"[7], but on the contrary, uses it as a tool to synthesise a "cursive drawing script"[8]. In Crispolti's interpretation of Fontana, this statement justified the central role of drawing as a moment of apprenticeship in

---

5   See Enrico Crispolti, *Fra Fontana e Leoncillo: un tramando di scultura "colorata"*, in Fontana - *Leoncillo. Forma della materia*, (Milan, Fondazione Carriero, 6 April - 9 July 2016), edited by Francesco Stocchi, Fondazione Carriero, Milan 2016, pp. 23-39; *Barocco e Barocchetto. Materia e colore nella scultura di Lucio Fontana e Leoncillo Leonardi*, (Umbertide, Fa.Mo Museo Rometti, 22 September - 20 October 2018), edited by Lorenzo Fiorucci, first-hand accounts by Enrico Crispolti, Bruno Toscano, contribution from Lisa Hockemeyer, Editoriale Umbra, [Foligno] 2018

6   Enrico Crispolti, *Lucio Fontana. Catalogo ragionato di sculture, dipinti, ambientazioni*, with the collaboration of Nini Ardemagni Laurini and Valeria Ernesti, Skira, Milan 2006, p. 28.

7   Ibid., p. 28.

8   Ibid., p. 32.

pure gesture detached from any practical applications, as a moment of fine-tuning a repertoire of strokes and a series of operations aimed at becoming familiar with manual expressions to be then applied to painting, sculpture or drawing.[9] For this reason, the discussion on the role of the gesture is central to the interpretation of Fontana's work, and this acquired a new impetus once the focus was on drawing. It is no coincidence, on the other hand, that in the publicity of the time, shots that focused on the artist's hands were especially popular, and featured prominently, for example, in the two important monographs by Ballo in 1970[10] and Crispolti in 1971[11]. Moreover, his training as a sculptor played a decisive role in this, and some aspects of his "plastic writing"[12] derive from this.

In 1963, (and the later editions of that text in 1968 and 1971[13]) Crispolti had pointed out the "desire for an absolute lyricism, not as a personal confession, but rather as an extreme, and I would say objectively, a sublimation of expressive depth, a reduction to the act of a pure configurative gesture, but always replete with all its freedoms, all its necessities, a pure presence of human creativity, almost a transcendental formal response – in phenomenological consonance – to the very rhythm of life itself"[14]. According to Guido Ballo, on the other hand, the importance of the gesture was to be attributed to a revival of Surrealist automatism. In his opinion, Fontana was one of the first admirers of it after the initial phase of André Breton's movement, a movement that at the same time was the necessary historical premise "for the exaltation of the sign-gesture and action painting"[15]. "Fontana," wrote Ballo, "became more and more inorganic. He was one of the first to invent the tendency towards the "continuous". He made this gesture as pure emotion, in a spatiality that became mobile, or suggested the idea of mobility, but without geometries, without fixed relationships, as a pure act of living"[16]. Ballo also emphasised a crucial aspect of Fontana's graphic work, which lends itself to a broader interpretation: "the joy of moving the stroke, of realising oneself in the sign without regrets or backtracking or making corrections"[17]. Lara Vinca Masini, on the other hand, insisted on the concept of the "duration" of the gesture and its action within a given "field", transformed into

---

9   Francesco De Bartolomeis, *Segno antidisegno di Lucio Fontana*, Edizioni d'arte Pozzo, Turin 1967; *Concetti spaziali*, edited by Paolo Fossati, Einaudi, Turin 1970.

10   Guido Ballo, *Lucio Fontana. Idee per un ritratto*, Edizioni Ilte, Turin 1970.

11   Enrico Crispolti, *Omaggio a Fontana*, Beniamino Carucci editore, Rome-Assisi 1971.

12   See Enrico Crispolti, *E se fosse stato soltanto scultore? Un interrogativo e qualche considerazione sulla sua scrittura plastica*, in *Lucio Fontana scultore*, edited by Filippo Trevisani, Electa, Milan 2007, pp. 31-32

13   See Luca Pietro Nicoletti, *Crispolti, Enrico*, in *Dizionario Lucio Fontana*, cit.; Idem, *Aspetti dell'arte contemporanea*, Ibid; Idem, *Omaggio a Fontana di Enrico Crispolti*, ibid.

14   Crispolti, *Carriera «barocca» di Fontana*, cit., p. 51.

15   Ballo, *Lucio Fontana. Idee per un ritratto*, cit., p. 86.

16   Ibid., pp. 22-23.

17   Ibid., p. 98

a "space-beyond". Everything, on the contrary, is played out precisely in the "arc of duration of the existential gesture" to arrive at the holes, the true moment of transcending a "baroque imagination". This is even more evident in the extreme simplification of the "cuts", which represent "the accentuation of the concept of 'duration' of the gesture, which descends inexorably and perfectly, causing a scanning of the surface that engraves, according to harmonic relationships with the measurements of the size of the surface itself"[18]. The same critical reflection, moreover, varies widely depending on whether the attention is focused on the act of piercing (Ballo), of drawing and moving the modelled material in ceramics or on canvas (Crispolti), or rather confirms the central role of the razor's slashing, documented by Mulas' photo reportage.

In any case, in each version, the peremptory aspect of a gesture inflicted without any uncertainty is confirmed, with a constant rhythm that leaves no room for second thoughts or regrets, and that even registers a trace of the speed of execution on the material, something typical of informal and gestural poetics, but with a disruptive innovative action that goes so far as to violate the integrity of the surface.

At the same time, as Maurizio Fagiolo Dell'Arco pointed out in 1966, "Fontana needs to close the action, to delimit the space of the research: which cannot be that which is included in the actual frame of the painting"[19]. This principle was implicitly reiterated in 1977 by the curators of the exhibition regarding a possible museum dedicated to Fontana by the City of Milan (which was never realised). For the cover, they chose to publish the cold-coloured terracotta tablet *Concetto spaziale. Il pane* [Spatial Concept. Bread], a flattened rectangle riddled with holes created by the awl sinking into the soft material with the same speed seen in some sheets of paper filled with dots of ink emulating the "holes" of the future: the holes are surrounded by a large circular mark traced with a single movement, as if to circumscribe an operational space distinct from the extension of the available field. With a simple preliminary gesture made with a pen or awl, especially in the case of *Pane* [Bread], which chronologically coincides with the season of the "holes", Fontana established a hierarchy within the spaces that marked a point of exit from the formal equivalent of the informal *all over*, like a containment fence that curbs the risk of dispersing the dissemination of the holes.

Over time, this gestural motif, heir to the graffiti on plaster or cement of the 1930s (and the related drawings), was developed in an iconographic sense as a proper frame (for example in the 1961 cycle dedicated to Venice) or in

---

18   Lara-Vinca Masini, *Lo spazio-oltre*, "NAC", 31, 15 February 1970, pp. 12-13 (republished in Idem, *Scritti scelti 1961-2019. Arte architettura design arti applicate*, edited by Alessandra Acocella and Angelika Stepken, Gli Ori, Pisa 2020).

19   Maurizio Fagiolo Dell'Arco, *Lucio Fontana*, in Id., *Rapporto 60*, Bulzoni, Rome 1966, pp. 75-84.

a meandering engraving, the result of a fluid movement of the hand on the canvas, in the case of the "oils" and the *Fine di Dio* [End of God].

The first ground-breaking act in his research, however, had come with the invention of "holes": canvases attacked with an awl from the front and back to create series of holes in neat rows or in random order, forming geometric figures, vortices, or simply sparse assemblages that could resemble sidereal space. The choice to illuminate these works with grazing light contributed to this effect. Sometimes he would even back-light them to enhance the quality of the surface and make it resemble an astronomical or lunar landscape.

Along these lines, Fontana began to apply sand and sequins to the canvas, fragments of coloured glass or stones, accentuating the impression of cosmic imagery. Within a few years, those impregnable forms began to take on a more defined appearance, a geometric compositional framework reminiscent of concretism in abstract painting, but enriched with abundant layers of material, creating distinct cords or planes between a figure as a conglomerate and a more expansive background. The holes, meanwhile, continued to act as a counterpoint to the manipulation of the canvas, and of various materials that made up a complex palimpsest, consisting of layering and erasures, of ripples of colour above all useful for their plastic quality, but then covered with another (generally darker) colour that unified the entire surface, as in the so-called "baroque" paintings.

The graphic interventions that burst onto the surface of the "inks", on the other hand, should be interpreted differently. They mark a point of convergence, in the handling and the medium, between painting and drawing, which in this case enriched the texture of a discourse in which perimeters and holes continued to hold a visual dialogue. After the layering of matter in the "baroque" works, together with the coeval "plaster works", the "inks" are a moment of rarefaction and a reduction of expressive elements. In fact, aniline allowed for a transparency unprecedented up to that time, giving an impression of floating shapes and a return to an atmospheric tonalism. However, this did not mean that Informalism in the strict sense of the word was automatically superseded, since using the pen more or less boldly was comparable to other *autre* experiences, such as that of Wols. At the same time, the "inks" mark one of the points at which drawing and inventing on canvas were most closely related: the partial overlapping of the tools used, in fact, makes the graphic equivalents of the "inks" very close to the same signs present in the actual paintings. In fact, the transition took place in the study of forms and their interconnection, which was then retranslated into a new medium with new expressive possibilities.

It is here that the point of greatest continuity with the "oils" of the early 1960s can be identified. In developing the silhouettes perfected in the "plaster works", which become wide perimeters around the central slash (or pair of slashes), here the artist arrived at creating open figures, with clear allusions to genitalia, a reference to erotic imagery. It is no coincidence that in 1969, Crispolti himself introduced his article on eroticism in abstract art, published in "Opus International", with the reproduction of a detail of a laceration on the canvas from a *Fine di dio* [End of God], visually illustrating what he meant by "explicit sexual symbol" in the case history analysed by the essay.[20]

However, there is no lack of cases in which oil was used to outline simpler frames, even combined with cuts and inserted glass, which hark back to certain perimeters of the "hole" season. This is confirmed by the drawings with which Fontana studied the progression of the engravings, executed according to a principle analogous to that found in the graffiti on plaster or cement in the 1930s and the studies for the lozenges of "plaster works" and "inks". Unlike the latter, however, in the case of the "oils", the circular sign does not circumscribe an outline but describes an open path, with deliberately jagged contours, as if wishing to graphically describe the beaten profile of the "nature", where the erotic allusion was also made. Following these principles, and taking advantage of the fluidity of the colour and the new material, Fontana also devised other images of the sign, from short, rapid tangles to broader interweavings that seem to recall the patterns of the neon ceilings, and certain "portraits", such as that of Iris Clert, where the colour was covered with a golden pigment that recalls the "baroque" sensibility of the previous decade.

The advent of the "cuts" put an end to this dialectical relationship, introducing a new vein that concentrated on a few gestures and their rhythmic and paratactic progression, with a precision in the slit that catalyses attention without leaving room for other possible comprimarios (while remaining open to targeted hybridisations). However, this had not prevented a migration of that gesture, at least on an iconographic level, from the first *Attese* to some of the "nature". Gradually, however, the impression of intervention by hand began to disappear from Fontana's work in the 1960s. The advent of water-painting, well before the enamel lacquering of the "object-paintings" of the last five decades, led to the application of solid surfaces, rendered homogeneous by the uniform and imperceptible application of paint by means of a mechanical instrument, which would not have been possible with the human hand.

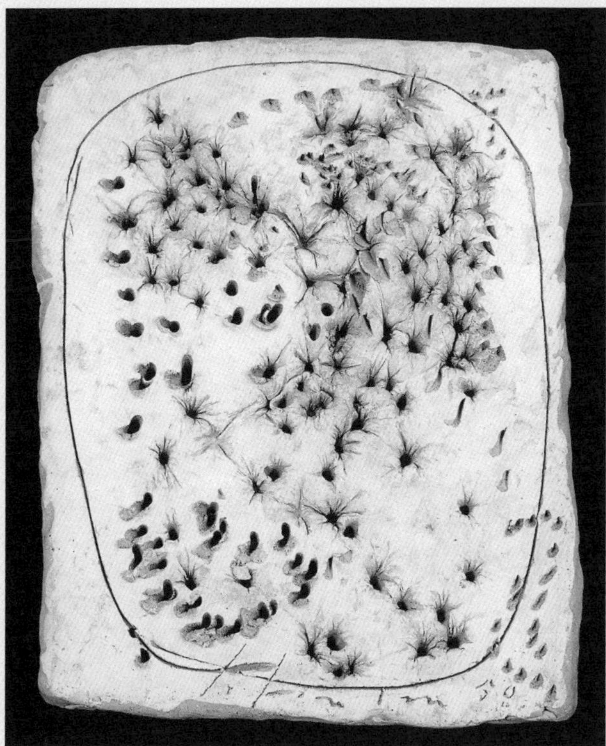

Concetto spaziale. Il pane,
1950
engobed terracotta,
holes and graffiti
42 × 33 cm
50 SC 3
Courtesy Fondazione
Lucio Fontana

---

20   Enrico Crispolti, *Erotismo nell'arte astratta e altre schede per una iconologia dell'arte astratta*, Celebes, Palermo 1976, p. 22.

Lucio Fontana.
L'origine du monde

Lauretta
Colonnelli

The title, *L'origine du monde*, references the notoriously explicit picture painted by Gustave Courbet in 1866. So explicit that it remained secret for a hundred and twenty-two years, until 1988, when it was shown for the first time at the Brooklyn Museum in New York, in a small exhibition entitled *Courbet reconsidered*.

The work is now on display at the Musée d'Orsay. It was unveiled on 26 June 1995, before the animated gaze of the guests attending the grand event. Also present was the culture minister Philippe Douste-Blazy, who studiously tried to avoid being filmed alongside the image of the torso of a woman with her legs open and her vulva slightly parted beneath a dark bush of pubic hair. This extremely realistic representation of female genitalia was unthinkable and unsettling in an age when the conventions of the artistic nude demanded that eroticism be covered by a chaste yet evocative veil.

But what has *L'origine du monde* got to do with Lucio Fontana, famous for his *Tagli* ('cuts') on white canvas, which he named *Concetto spaziale* ('Spatial concept'), often adding the word *Attese* ('expectations' 'waits') as well? The Italo-Argentine artist had embarked on his perforated *Concetti spaziali* in 1949, which he generically called *Buchi* ('holes'). And he had initiated Spatialism, where the picture is no longer the picture, and sculpture is no longer sculpture.

Artists had actually begun to go down this path many centuries earlier, as painters strived to produce sculpture with a brush and sculptors strived to paint with a chisel. Giotto, who highlighted his images with chiaroscuro, paved the way, together with the Renaissance masters who had developed perspective, Brunelleschi and Masaccio being among the first. "There seems to be a hole in the wall", Vasari had exclaimed, looking at Masaccio's fresco of the *Holy Trinity* in the church of Santa Maria Novella in Florence. And Donatello had produced his celebrated *stiacciati*, small marble panels with a relief of sometimes just a few millimetres. The first appeared between 1415 and 1417, in the predella of his statue of *Saint George*, and it marked a radical turning point in the history of sculpture. The artist succeeded in dissolving the insuperable barrier of the background, sending the viewer's gaze soaring beyond the saint on horseback in the act of striking the dragon, beyond the fearful princess with her hands joined in prayer, beyond the glimpse of arches on the left, all the way to the tree-filled plain and the ridges of the hills and the clouds in the sky, lightly scratched on the marble.

In various interviews, Lucio Fontana went about explaining his line of inquiry by referring to the beginning of the history of painting, when nature was depicted in two dimensions. Artists later began to study three-dimensionality and, following the discovery of perspective, representations of reality became more natural and closer to the real.

The day eventually came when this three-dimensionality was no longer enough, because human knowledge had expanded, leading to the discovery of the fourth dimension, of the cosmos, of infinity. "The discovery of the Cosmos is a new dimension, it is the infinite: so when I pierce this canvas, which was basic to all the arts, then I have created an infinite dimension, an X that for me lies at the very base of all Contemporary Art", Fontana explained.[1]

At the end of 1958, as he neared the age of seventy and while the first astronauts were preparing to go beyond the earth's boundaries and land on the moon, the artist passionately embraced the novelties of the technique and its cosmic and futuristic openings, beginning the *Tagli*. However, he left no written record of how he executed these cuts, which were always vertical. What we do know comes from the only two people who worked with him in his studio: the designer Nanda Vigo (Milan, 1936) and the artist Hisachika Takahashi (Tokyo, 1940).

Fontana always chose Belgian linen canvas, prepared with an application of cementite on both the front and rear to ensure that the whole surface was impregnated. The canvas was then attached to the frame and coloured, usually with a water-based paint, the same kind used on walls in domestic interiors. This was readily available, cheap, dried quickly and yielded a smooth surface with invisible brushstrokes.[2]

At this point Fontana was ready to cut the canvas, to open a passage through and beyond his surface.

This final gesture, the most important, was also witnessed by the great Ugo Mulas, who captured it in a sequence of photographs.

Occasionally a long time elapsed before Fontana decided to make the incision. He waited until the canvas was dry but not too dry, otherwise the laceration would lack precision. He used a sharp Stanley knife and cut in a downward direction at moderate speed. This had to be done with a very steady hand; a poorly executed cut was impossible to correct and the long process of preparing the support would all have been for nothing. After making the slit, he glued a strip of thick black gauze to the rear side of the two edges of the cut so that the wall on which the picture would then hang could not be seen. The lips of the incision were then adjusted by hand to obtain the characteristic slightly concave shape that distinguished them all.

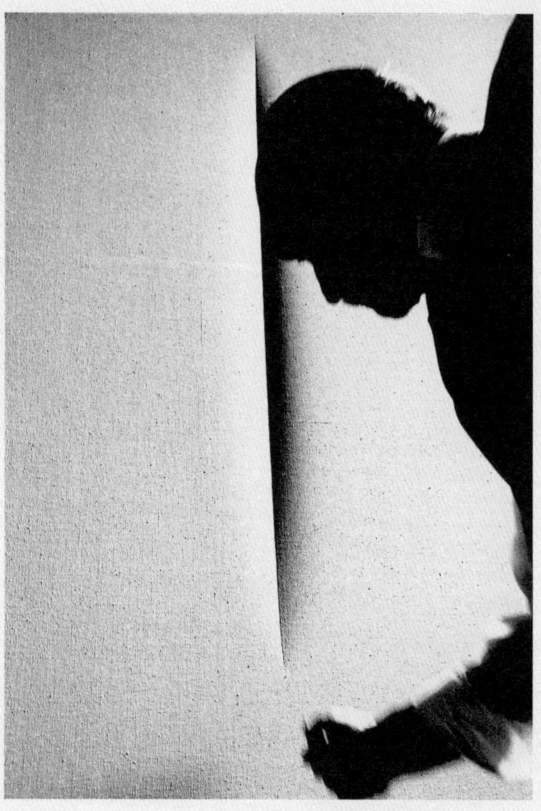

L'Attesa,
Milan, 1964
Photograph Ugo Mulas
© Eredi Ugo Mulas

---

1   C. Lonzi, *Autoritratto*, De Donato, Bari 1969.

2   P. Gottschaller, *Lucio Fontana. The Artist's Materials*, J. Paul Getty Museum Publications, Los Angeles, USA 2012.

Lauretta Colonnelli

Finally, he signed the rear, often adding a sentence relating to memories, states of mind, small everyday events, expressions of love for his wife: "I love Teresita", or "It's going to be cold tomorrow" or "How can politicians possibly not understand?" or "I'm waiting for the gardener of the soul" or "I'm tired of thinking". These inscriptions have been interpreted as a ruse devised by Fontana to foil counterfeiters, the idea being that any subsequent appraisal would establish the authenticity of the handwriting.

In interviews he reiterated that with his *Tagli* he wanted to gaze within the cosmos, sinking deep into a mysterious and endless perspectival vision.

But to critics, who in the 60s kept asking him how the first *Taglio* had come about, he confessed one day: "The idea came to me from V's c..t". Who his friends knew well, "because she was a very active (and very fine) artist, and had been (or was?) Piero Manzoni's girlfriend. A fascinating and very creative girl, and particularly uninhibited for the times".[3] Historians would later concur: "Fontana proposed to go beyond the limits and compactness of the canvas, to open it as the sex of a woman is opened. It is a valid point of view to see an erotic impulse in Fontana's gesture, as has often been done. In a climate of paradoxically calm and tense rigour resembling a measure of deliberate apnea, the spotlessly monochrome canvas is stretched over the square of the frame, and then the artist's hand falls upon it, cutting it in the centre with a quick, imperious stroke of the razor, from top to bottom, in a peremptory 'wound'".[4]

Fontana's subject in *Concetto spaziale* and Courbet's in *L'origine du monde* therefore seems to be the same. So too does the two artists' inquiry into the mystery of female genitalia and the primitive forces that enabled not only the birth of life on earth but also the creation of the universe, and even artistic creation. "The woman's sex is the Alpha and Omega of the world, the origin and the end", wrote Alexander Dumas fils, one of the few who managed to see Courbet's painting.[5]

But did Fontana ever have the opportunity to see it?

Probably not. When *L'origine du monde* first went on display in 1988, Fontana had been dead for twenty years. The painting had already exchanged hands many times by then, but always very confidentially and it had remained swathed in mystery. The first mystery was the identity of the model, and scholars made various efforts to give a face to the woman depicted in the work.

In 2011, the historian Gérard Desanges came up with the name of Jeanne de Tourbey, a literary salon host who at the time was the lover of

---

3   G. Politi, "Amarcord", in *ArtsLife*, 12 June 2018.

4   A. Boatto, *Di tutti i colori*, Laterza, Rome–Bari 2008.

5   Alexandre Dumas fils, preface to *L'Ami des femmes*, Paris 1869.

Khalil-Bey, a wealthy Egyptian-Turkish diplomat who commissioned and first owned the painting. But there was no proof, just speculation.[6]

In 2013, one of the world's leading experts on Courbet, Jean-Jacques Fernier, suggested that the model was Joanna Hiffermann, a beautiful red-haired Irish woman who had arrived in France with her partner, the American painter James Whistler, and who also had a relationship with Courbet. He did a beautiful portrait of her, *Jo l'irlandaise*, in 1866, the same year in which *L'origine di monde* was produced.

However, Courbet also portrayed Joanna in *Le sommeil*, a highly sensual image of two naked women lying asleep, intertwined, in an unmade bed. Joanna's red curls are recognisable, but her body is pale white, while the model in the *Origine du monde* has an olive complexion and dark pubic hair, which does not correspond to the Irish woman's hair.

Then, in 2018, the historian Claude Schopp, an expert on Alexandre Dumas fils, happened upon some documents by chance. These related to yet another woman.[7] Schopp, who was studying correspondence between Dumas and the writer George Sand, discovered a letter dating to June 1871, in which Dumas talks about Courbet. The transcription of the manuscript, held in the Bibliothèque Nationale de France, contained the sentence: "With his talent one doesn't paint with one's most delicate and sonorous brush the *interview* of Ms. Queniault of the Opéra, for the Turk who took refuge inside it from time to time – all of it life-size".

Schopp, realizing that the word "interview" made no sense at all in the context, decided to check the original manuscript and found that Dumas had not written *interview* but *intérieur*, the interior visited by Khalil-Bey. For the historian, the phrase was a clear allusion to the French dancer's genitals, and he hypothesised that she had been Courbet's model. Hunting around in the archives of the Opéra, he uncovered photos and documents, and pieced together the whole life of Constance Quéniaux, as her exact name was. She was thirty-eight when she posed for Courbet, had no longer been dancing for six, and she too was a lover of Khalil-Bey. She belonged, like the other women previously thought to have been the model, to the demi-monde of Paris described by the Goncourts: wealthy maintained women who hosted artistic and literary salons and travelled around the city in carriages pulled by horses with roses in their ears.

The letter from Dumas to Sand also revealed something else: the writer had seen the picture. How many other people knew of its existence, apart from the artist and the man who commissioned it? And how had they interpreted it?

---

6   G. Desanges, *La comtesse de Loynes. La belle Ecouteuse*, Editions L'Harmattan, Paris 2011.

7   C. Schopp, *La modella senza volto. Indagine su un quadro scabroso*, Donzelli, Rome 2019.

The thousand and one ways in which that picture was seen has been recounted by the historian Bernard Teyssèdre.[8] Courbet's nude was – and is – interpreted as if it had something more or different about it to the nudes that have alluded and enchanted since classical times. Here one can read an allusion to the infinite, which arouses disquiet and renders female genitalia sublime and mysterious. They are likely to have profoundly disturbed Courbet himself when he was painting it, to the extent that he was unable to give the work a name. The painting went from the artist's studio to Khalil-Bey's large and Orientalizing *cabinet de toilet* under the title of *Tableau X*. It was then covered with a green curtain and only unveiled for private viewing or to show to some special visitor.

After squandering in just three years the fifteen million francs the Turkish diplomat had brought with him to Paris, in January 1868 he decided to sell his sophisticated collection of ancient and modern paintings. But the catalogue, with a preface written by the most celebrated critic of the time, Théophile Gautier, contained no mention of *Tableaux X*.

It is not known from whom, or when, the unnamed picture received its current title. Teyssèdre suggests that it was coined by Jean-Baptiste Faure, a baritone at the Opéra, thought to have secretly purchased the work from Khalil-Bey.

All trace of the painting was effectively lost from 1868. It finally reappeared in Paris on 29 June 1889, when Edmond de Goncourt spotted it in the bric-à-brac of La Narde, who had invited him to come and examine some newly arrived Japanese objects. Edmond was no admirer of Courbet. Far from it. "There is no shadow of a study of nature in this master of realism. Ugliness, always ugliness! Ugliness without its greatest quality, ugliness without the beauty of ugliness!" he had written in his *Journal* on 18 September 1867, after having seen the nude body of the *Femme au Perroquet* in an exhibition.

Around twenty years later, having been to La Narde's shop, he described the visit as follows: "While I was looking in boredom at these mediocre novelties, Narde asked me: 'Have you seen this?' And he unlocked a painting, whose exterior panel shows a village church in the snow concealing a painting that Courbet did for Khalil Bey of a woman's stomach with a prominent black mound of Venus over a half open pink aperture. Before this picture, which I had never seen, I must make respectful amends to Courbet. This stomach is as beautiful as the flesh of a Correggio".

The sentence was censured in the initial publication, and it took exactly one hundred years for it to be reinserted in its rightful place in the *Journal*, in the critical edition of 1989.

---

8   B. Teyssèdre, *Le roman de l'Origine*, Gallimard, Paris 1996.

But there is no trace of the new title in the diary. It cropped up for the first time during the First World War, when the painting entered the collection of the Hungarian baron Ferenc Hatvany, who later sold it to the psychoanalyst Jacques Lacan in 1955.

Lacan was encouraged to buy it by George Bataille, a scholar of eroticism, who admired the picture but was too poor to purchase it. Lacan, who had married Bataille's former wife, Sylvia, kept *L'origine du monde* in his study, covered by a panel painted at Sylvia's request by André Masson. This was certainly not out of prudery on the part of the owners, she said, but in order not to disturb the neighbours or the cleaning lady.

Bataille equated eroticism with mysticism and the height of contemplation, and his thinking comes to mind when listening once again to the words of Lucio Fontana: "My cuts are above all a philosophical statement, an act of faith in the infinite, an affirmation of spirituality. When I sit down to contemplate one of my cuts, I sense all at once an enlargement of the spirit. I feel like a man freed from the shackles of matter, a man at one with the immensity of the present and of the future."

He began to add to the appellative "Tagli" that of "Attese" to indicate a pause in time, a pure and absolute space further and further away from the accidentality of matter, a state of erasure and at the same time of construction. It is the wait for a future imagination.

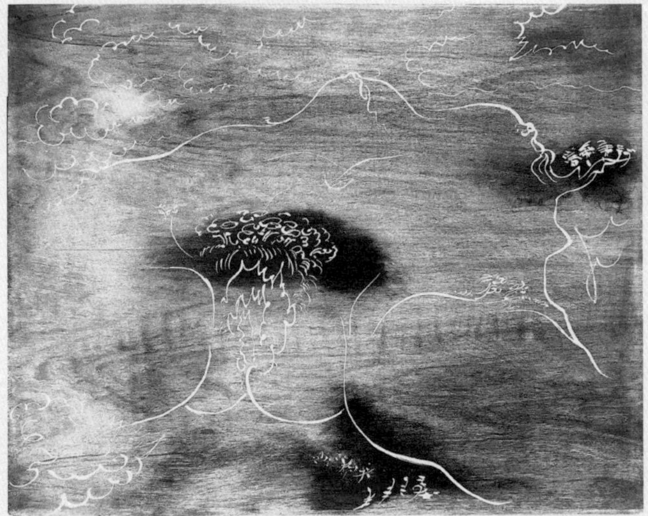

André Masson,
*Cache pour L'origine
du monde de Gustave Courbet*
Institut Gustave Courbet,
Ornans

"These 'waits' give me peace!!! In many years of work this is the happiest moment for me!", he wrote to his friend Mario Bardini on 21 February 1959.

A year later he began doing the ink drawings of female nudes on display in this show. The bodies are not in pose but move freely in the space and seem to alter it.

They call to mind the *Disegni proibiti* ('prohibited drawings') of Auguste Rodin, published for the first time in 2017, exactly a hundred years after the French sculptor's death and kept secret until then.[9] Fontana therefore never saw them.

Rodin too was over fifty when he embarked on this new season of creativity in 1894. He did his drawings between one sculptural work and another, and with no intention to sell them. They were not sketches for

---

9   *Rodin. I disegni proibiti*, texts by Nadine Lehni, preface by Catherine Chevillot, Rizzoli arte, Milan 2017.

Lauretta Colonnelli

works to be realized in three dimensions. Rodin was simply setting himself a challenge: he wanted to capture the continual flux of movement, the evolution of human nature in space.

The critic Claude Roger-Marx, who witnessed some of those sessions, recalled how Rodin "seemed to obey the orders of an unmoving and superhuman force". He allowed his hand to run blindly over the sheet, without looking at the lines he was tracing. Visual contact with the model was never interrupted. Rodin himself explained this. Everything, he said, "must flow naturally from my eye to my hand… Look! What is this drawing? Not once in describing the shape of that mass did I shift my eyes from the model. Why? Because I wanted to make sure that nothing evaded my grasp of it. Not a thought about the technical problem of representing it on paper could be allowed to arrest the flow of my feelings about it, from my eye to my hand. The moment I drop my eyes that flow stops."

The women came into the studio in turn and were instructed not to pose but to act naturally and forget that someone was portraying them.

Around thirty of these drawings have foreground depictions of female genitalia. In one, entitled *Baccante*, the voyeuristic effect is enhanced by a touch of reddish-brown watercolour.

But there is no evidence that Rodin ever saw *L'origine du monde* by Gustave Courbet.

Lucio Fontana. *L'origine du monde*

Crossing Space, Time and the Material: Lucio Fontana and the Experience of Reality

Paolo
Tozzi

When looking at a spatial concept by Fontana, one runs the risk of being dominated by two extreme and opposing sensations. One is the disturbing simplicity of the object we are observing. The other is the cumbersome presence of an enigmatic conceptual apparatus underlying the work. In both cases, we risk losing the immediate and tangible sense of the experience of looking (but it could also be the experience of touching, or of hearing if the works were made of sound), which consists of moving from a cognitive plane of the founding elements of reality (namely, space, time and matter), to a symbolic plane of the same. That is, the cuts, the holes, the cavity that Fontana imprints in space, time and matter, open up a passage that takes us from the instantaneous and limited experience of reality to the cultural and symbolic consequences of unveiling reality itself. To visualise this passage, what I propose here is a comparison between what happens in Fontana's canvas and what happens in the astrophysicist's sky. In both cases, we are faced with both a physical and symbolic crossing of an invisible (and totally unexpected) boundary that leads us to a radical rethinking of the image of the world. Let us see how.

The canvas of the painting, the support for the image, is a privileged place for the accumulation of symbolic meanings. It is too easy to say that an artist has total freedom when faced with an empty canvas. In reality, the artist will inevitably come up against layers of meaning from which he will find it very hard to free himself, and which influences every single action he makes on the canvas, as well as the canvas itself. In this respect, the canvas is not so dissimilar to the vault of heaven, which for mankind has always represented the essentially two-dimensional support on which light signals from the non-terrestrial world appeared. Even after the lower spheres were unhinged, after the Copernican revolution, the Universe beyond the solar system remained enigmatic, of an unfathomable depth, a place that was fully three-dimensional, but still symbolically tied to our centrality (because the abandonment of geocentrism never really eliminated anthropocentrism). The universe could not be travelled through and was not referable to human experience. The last "sphere", that of the embedded, immobile stars, was still perceived as a black screen on which lights of an unknown nature appeared.

In the 1920s, this black screen was irreparably torn. On 26 April 1920, in a timely and memorable event remembered as the *Great Debate*, the two astronomers Harlow Shapley and Heber Curtis confronted each other on the distance of the so-called *nebulae* and the true size of the Universe[1]. A few years later it was Edwin Hubble who proved that Curtis was right, that the Andromeda Nebulae, and in general the other known *nebulae*, are much more distant than all the other stars in the Milky Way and are

---

1   R.W. Smith, *The Expanding Universe, Astronomy's 'Great Debate' 1900-1931*, Cambridge University Press, Cambridge 1982.

therefore galaxies like our own[2]. This discovery opened the window on an expanding Universe of dimensions unthinkable until a few years before, populated by galaxies each containing hundreds of billions of stars, and distributed at distances of several billion light years. What was torn apart was the idea of a single Universe-island thoughtfully gathered around us, and with it the ancient cultural and symbolic references that had become entangled in the fabric of the celestial vault, and that the end to geocentrism had failed to banish.

The astrophysical research that led us to conceive the expanding Universe is a very different undertaking from an artistic creation, and we must recognise that the gesture of tearing the canvas has nothing in common with the way that scientific procedures are carried out. But this genuinely performative gesture actually has very similar implications from a cultural point of view. The question "what is behind the canvas" is as idle a question as "what is behind the sphere of fixed stars" was. It is idle because until the 20th century, there were no conceptual or technological tools that could meaningfully answer this question. The large ground-based telescopes, the ability to analyse the spectra of faint objects such as *nebulae*, and the revolutionary vision of space-time proposed by Einstein's General Relativity[3], offered the possibility of imagining a space beyond the Milky Way, a space that had not been even remotely conceivable before, and of making it a place open to human exploration (in terms of observations at least). Science, after all, can be seen as the ability to visualise and describe a space, or a phenomenon that one cannot directly experience[4]. Behind the canvas, however, there is no observable reality. But there is a symbolic space that can be conceived. And, perhaps more importantly, there is an absence of prior signification, and this immediately opens up the creation of new cultural and symbolic references. To give an example, perhaps the most immediate one, the cuts and holes break away from the consolatory idea of space as it is experienced in everyday life, that is, as a mere support on which, and in which, matter appears and moves. And, immediately, the way we *occupy* space is an act that must be remodelled on the basis of a model of reality that is antithetical to the previous one. That space can be bent as if it were a physical object, Einstein showed us, causing a real culture shock. But now we can see distorted space-time directly in the spectacular gravitational lensing images[5] that we have collected with the Hubble Space Telescope[6] and,

---

2   E. Hubble, "Extragalactic nebulae", *Astrophysical Journal* 1926, 64, pp. 321–369.

3   A. Einstein, "Die Grundlage der allgemeinen Relativitätstheorie", Annalen der Physik 1916, 49, pp. 769–822.

4   An aspect of science set out very clearly in C. Rovelli, *Che cos'è la scienza. La rivoluzione di Anassimandro*, Mondadori, Milano 2009.

5   https://hubblesite.org/contents/articles/gravitational-lensing (last visit April 2023)

6   https://hubblesite.org/

more recently, with the James Webb Space Telescope[7], to the point that the curvature of space is a concept that has entered common parlance. The fact that the canvas is not a neutral support for an image but is itself capable of taking on a form and becoming an intermediary between our gaze and an elsewhere, is something we can see directly in the works of Lucio Fontana. This elsewhere, by the mere fact that it exists, and has finally been revealed, forces us to rethink our cultural and symbolic references.

Although these juxtapositions are based on analogies between the scientific and artistic worlds, we want to emphasise the significance of the operation, rather than the analogy itself. That is to say, speaking of the distortion of space in scientific terms (as in general relativity) or in symbolic terms (as in Fontana's cuts) has the same effect: it opens up the crisis of man in relation to the contemporary, expressing in a way that is by now irrevocable that immediate human experience and its reassuring product, common sense, do not in themselves represent any foundation of reality, neither on a physical nor on a symbolic level. These operations, which come out of extremely different contexts such as scientific research and contemporary art, thus prove to be radically similar. We can go further in the quest for this unity of intent. For example, by daring to cross the cut on the canvas.

A not insignificant detail is that behind the cut or pierced canvas is blackness, the absence of light and colour. The celestial vault is also dark. Long before we discovered the abysmal distances at which galaxies are distributed, mankind had to come to terms with this seemingly familiar darkness, which we confidentially call night and which we consider a simple consequence of the Earth's rotation. But the darkness hides a secret. Because in a Universe that extends infinitely in time and space, and is full of galaxies, and therefore of stars, darkness should not exist. On the contrary, the entire celestial vault should be bright in every direction, more or less like the surface of the Sun: an image as unnatural as it is monstrous, to the point of being disconcerting and paradoxical. Yet scientific thinking leaves no way out: if the stars are infinite and have existed since time immemorial, the sky must necessarily appear that way. This is none other than Olbers' paradox, a scientific idea that played an important role in the birth of cosmology[8]. There are two ways to

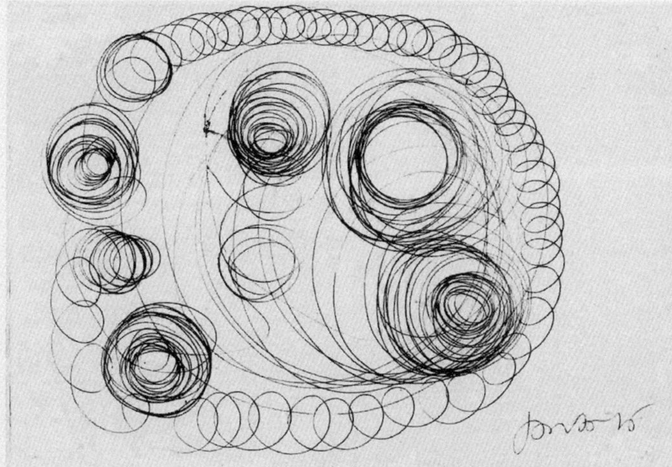

Concetto spaziale
1946
ballpoint pen on paper
20 × 27,5 cm
46 DSP 46
Private collection
Courtesy Gió Marconi
Milano

---

7   https://webb.nasa.gov/

8   E. R. Harrison, E. R., *Darkness at Night: A Riddle of the Universe*, Harvard University Press, 1987.

solve the paradox and explain the darkness of the night. The first is that the stars are confined to a limited region of the Universe around us, as in William Herschel's[9] reconstruction, and that therefore beyond an (unnatural) cosmic boundary, there are no more stars, but just darkness and emptiness. But this model of the Universe, as we have seen, was swept away by Edwin Hubble's discovery. The second is that the Universe has not always existed, but had a beginning. Yes, because looking far ahead also means looking back in time[10]. And here is where darkness finds its natural explanation: when we count the light of the stars at great distances, for example greater than 10 billion light years, we find that there are fewer and fewer stars and galaxies, as if we were approaching an era when stars and galaxies themselves had not yet formed. And indeed, we are approaching the Big Bang, the limit beyond which we can no longer find time or space. The Big Bang[11] is a concept that entered popular culture decades ago, and it is still how we astrophysicists call the cosmological models by which we describe the Universe. Over recent months, the James Webb Space Telescope is revealing the most distant galaxies ever observed by mankind. That is, the first galaxies formed after the Big Bang, emerging from a dark and homogeneous Universe. At present, the most distant galaxy ever observed[12] corresponds to a temporal distance of thirteen billion four hundred million years, just over three hundred million years since the Big Bang[13]. The flickering lights that we can now capture against the dark background of the celestial vault tell a story of creation and evolution. This, in the end, was the meaning of that darkness: the existence of an origin of time and space itself. What was believed to be the mere absence of our Sun, turns out to be the consequence of the evolutionary process that underlies our Universe. Ultimately, life itself would not be possible if the Universe did not evolve as it did in the Big Bang cosmology.

It is all too easy at this point to push the analogy further at the suggestion of Lucio Fontana's own words: "The discovery of the cosmos is a new dimension, it is infinity, so I make a hole in this canvas, which was the basis of all the arts, and I have created an infinite dimension. [...]

---

9   W. Herschel, *On the Construction of the Heavens*, Philosophical Transactions of the Royal Society of London 75, 1785.

10   This is due to the simple fact that the speed of light has a finite value (about three hundred thousand kilometres per second), and when the distances between us and a light source are enormous (distances that we call cosmological), the images brought to us by light correspond to a time earlier than ours, equal to the time it takes for light to reach us. Therefore, it is natural to measure cosmological distances in light years.

11   The Big Bang, according to the most recent cosmological measurements, occurred some 13.7 billion years ago compared to present times. Some of the books on the history of cosmogonic theories and the Big Bang include S. Singh, *The Big Bang Theory*, Fourth Estate, New York 2004.

12   B. E. Robertson, et al., 2023, *Identification and properties of intense star-forming galaxies at redshifts z>10*, Nature Astronomy, in press (https://arxiv.org/abs/2212.04480)

13   Strange as it may seem, three hundred million years is a very short time to form an entire galaxy from the basically homogeneous and isotropic Universe that emerged from the Big Bang. And we are certain that as early as 2023, the record for the most distant galaxy will be broken again..

The idea is just that: a new dimension corresponding to the cosmos. [...] The hole was made to create this void behind it"[14]. And then, in the White Manifesto: "The element of space; sound, the element of time and movement, which develops in time and space. These are fundamental to the new art which encompasses the four dimensions of existence. Time and space.The new art requires that all of man's energies be used productively in creation and interpretation"[15]. And again, even going so far as to suggest an intention of imitating reality: "I thought of these universes, the moon with its holes, the exhausting silence that surrounds us, astronauts in a new world and all these immensities that have been there for trillions of years. Man took his first steps into space in deadly silence and left a vital sign of his arrival"[16]. The silence, the void, the hole crossed by infinity, seem to make room for the appearance of man, who becomes the protagonist not for having passively inherited the Universe, as in a biblical tale, but for having understood it (or more modestly, for having begun to understand it). It almost seems as though Fontana wanted to represent with his artistic gesture the human condition in a cosmological key by retracing the same steps taken by scientific knowledge, in a sort of conceptual mimesis. But let us again refrain from suggesting a facile analogy: in reality, in spite of any similarity, Fontana's gesture remains free and independent of any previous image. The artist is aware of a resonance between his research and astrophysical research, but he keeps the two spheres well separated and avoids any didacticism, however sophisticated and intellectual.

Precisely because of this freedom and independence, Fontana's gesture becomes a tool for questioning the symbolic aspect of scientific knowledge. In fact, we astrophysicists reflect too little on the symbolic value of our research, and the way science modifies our self-awareness as human beings. But when we accept the enigma created by the cut, or the holes in the canvas, we are also ready to reconsider the night as a passage between the human dimension and the cosmological dimension, a mystery that concerns our very existence and that does not lose its archaic and primordial force of attraction even when we replace our human gaze with the power of space telescopes. The technological ability to record the light of the stars that formed at the dawn of the cosmos is no less revolutionary than the revelation we have arrived at, thanks only to our human eyes and human mind, that the darkness of the night is a sign of the origin of the Universe itself.

No artistic research that is as extensive and complex as Fontana's can avoid confronting the essence of life itself. The *natures* seem to reiterate

---

14   Cited in C. Lonzi, *Autoritratto*, De Donato, Bari 1969, p. 169.

15   Cited in the *Manifesto Bianco*, Buenos Aires 1946. Lucio Fontana does not appear among the manifesto's signatories, although its contents are often directly associated with the artist.

16   Cited in the article by F. Vertucci of 24 January 2023, *Cosmogonia di Lucio Fontana*, published at the website https://www.ilsole24ore.com/art/cosmogonia-lucio-fontana-AEQhIoUC

the basic idea of perforation, Fontana's iconic gesture, in volumes that are perhaps even more explicitly reminiscent of cosmic, and at the same time, biological forms. The spherical form, while historically referring to the feminine, cosmically refers to everything that is formed under the action of gravity, which, acting isotropically, always creates roughly spherical celestial objects. But even in the microscopic world, spherical shapes form naturally, this time thanks to the chemical properties of complex molecules. Lipid molecules displaying elongated structures with a hydrophilic and a hydrophobic end, when they aggregate, due to surface tension, naturally form tiny hollow spheres called *micelles*, in which the hydrophobic part faces inwards, leaving the hydrophilic part to protect it against the water-rich external environment. These molecules are still believed to be the ancestral forms from which the first cells developed. It is thought that the chemical reactions that led to the formation of the first complex organic molecules were severely handicapped in the vast and open liquid environment of the primordial oceans. The fortuitous fact that some molecules were trapped within these *micelles*, entering through an opening and remaining locked in, may have greatly facilitated the combinations that eventually led to the formation of the first complex organic molecules. It has been observed in the laboratory that these *micelles*, by creating a selective barrier to the external aquatic environment, are able to grow by incorporating more and more molecules, until they reach a size beyond which it becomes impossible to grow any further. This condition leads to a natural division into two similar micelles. A behaviour that occurs in a purely mechanical and chemical manner, but which appears so close to that of cellular reproduction, and therefore makes it easy to imagine that life developed precisely from these extremely simple and minimal entities. Understanding this mechanism is crucial for exploring the possibilities of life outside the solar system. This is the subject of a field of research, astrobiology, which has grown enormously in recent decades thanks to space missions to planets in the solar system, the study, still in its early stages, of the atmospheres of extrasolar planets, and the laboratory study of samples from comets, asteroids, and soon, Mars. Returning to Fontana's *natures*, the analogy with *micelles* apparently does not add much compared to any other analogy based on the theme of sphericity, the most common form encountered in nature. But going further, the *natures*, cracked or perforated, suggest the creation of an inner space that acquires a primordial reproductive function. Almost an ancestral womb that refers directly to the first closed and protected places, inside *micelles*, where organic molecules probably had the chance to build themselves in a slow process driven by coincidence. As we increasingly find in nature, the sum of many events, extremely simple if taken individually, leads to a growing and surprising complexity[17], following a development that is now described by the physics of complex systems, a subject now also known to the general Italian public thanks to the Nobel

---

17   P. W. Anderson, 1972, "More Is Different: Broken symmetry and the nature of the hierarchical structure of science", *Science*, Vol. 177, Issue 4047, pp. 393–396.

Prize awarded to Giorgio Parisi[18] in 2021. Imaginative as it may seem, a phenomenon of such enormous complexity as life (up to and including intelligent life capable of comprehending the very Universe that generated it) seems to have emerged from the combination of extremely simple processes that organise themselves[19]. Fontana's *natures*, once again disarmingly simple objects, quiver with inexplicable potential, as if at any moment they could start to roll or open up and generate. Understanding how life emerges[20] from conditions of extreme simplicity is the key to understanding whether extra-terrestrial life is widespread or a relatively rare phenomenon. Astrophysical research is currently facing the challenge of analysing the chemical composition of the atmospheres of Earth-like planets. Objects that are impossible to visualise directly, but which can be studied thanks to sophisticated techniques for analysing the spectra of stars that host planetary systems. The subject of life on extrasolar planets is one of the central topics of astrophysical research in the years to come, as indicated in NASA's Decadal Survey[21], a reference document for the development of astrophysical research in the U.S. and internationally.

It may come as a surprise that a profound understanding of such disparate (but intimately related) scientific topics can pass through the experience of contemporary art. But this surprise stems from a cultural misunderstanding that is unfortunately well rooted, especially in the Italian cultural sphere. Namely, the thought that in order to understand science, it is necessary to have technical expertise, without which we are all at the mercy of a narrative written by a few experts. This caution strangely falls away when we are faced with art (especially contemporary art). It gives us an unjustified jolt of self-confidence that makes us feel capable of easily making evaluations and positioning ourselves in relation to art. Practically speaking, we feel empowered to handle the symbolic plane with ease, while we feel excluded (not without a certain resentment) from the technical and cognitive plane.

It is difficult to overestimate the negative consequences of this misunderstanding for democratic society, which must necessarily be based on shared knowledge, including scientific knowledge, in order to function. The only solution here is to learn to see the symbolic and cognitive planes simultaneously, and to understand how society and its elements, including

---

18   For an introduction to the work of Parisi, see G. Parisi, *In un volo di storni. Le meraviglie dei sistemi complessi*, Rizzoli, Milano 2021.

19   For a simple introduction to self-organisation in physics and biology see: http://www.scholarpedia.org/article/Self-organization (data ultima visita aprile 2023)

20   P.L. Luisi, *The Emergence of Life: From Chemical Origins to Synthetic Biology*, Cambridge University Press, Cambridge 2002.

21   The two reference documents can be found online at:
https://nap.nationalacademies.org/catalog/26141/pathways-to-discovery-in-astronomy-and-astrophysics-for-the-2020s
https://www.nationalacademies.org/our-work/planetary-science-and-astrobiology-decadal-survey-2023-2032

science and art, function. In other words, learn from the outset that it is not necessary to be a scientist to understand science, just as it is not necessary to be an artist to understand art. But it is necessary to understand how science works, and to understand how art works. Both of these aspects are, unfortunately, not part of the cultural preparation of Italian citizens.

Yet, it is enough to observe how children, right from primary school, demonstrate that they naturally have analytical minds, and are able to immediately acquire the scientific method, just as they are able to grasp the symbolic value of the artistic gesture and distinguish it from a banal process of imitating reality. We are too busy with fragmented and immediate skills and miss the opportunity to cultivate those citizens of tomorrow, who we will need, including contemporary scientists and artists. Upending the meaning of those all too familiar and misused quotes by Picasso (like all extemporaneous quotes), the problem is not that of the child who has to struggle to still be an artist when he grows up. The problem belongs entirely to society, which has the task of saving children from the trivialisation of the market, from the standardisation of ugliness, from alternative pedagogies peddling bogus libertarian themes, and so on. Today Lucio Fontana's cuts look out from museum walls, or from the flattering showcases of the contemporary art market, but we must realise that these are not the only places where his works can live. The best place for art is in the hands of those who are able to learn new gestures and new points of view, just as the artist did.

I am most grateful to John R. Brucato, Research Director at INAF- Arcetri Astrophysical Observatory, Florence, for discussions on astrobiology and the emergence of life, and to Guido Risaliti, Full Professor at the University of Florence, for discussions on extragalactic astrophysics and cosmology. I am also indebted to my wife Rita Filomeni, whose sensitivity as a poet helped me put into words the muted reflections of my profession.

Concetto spaziale
1950
gouache on canvassed paper
48 × 33 cm
50 DCSA 4
Courtesy Fondazione
Lucio Fontana

Paolo Tozzi

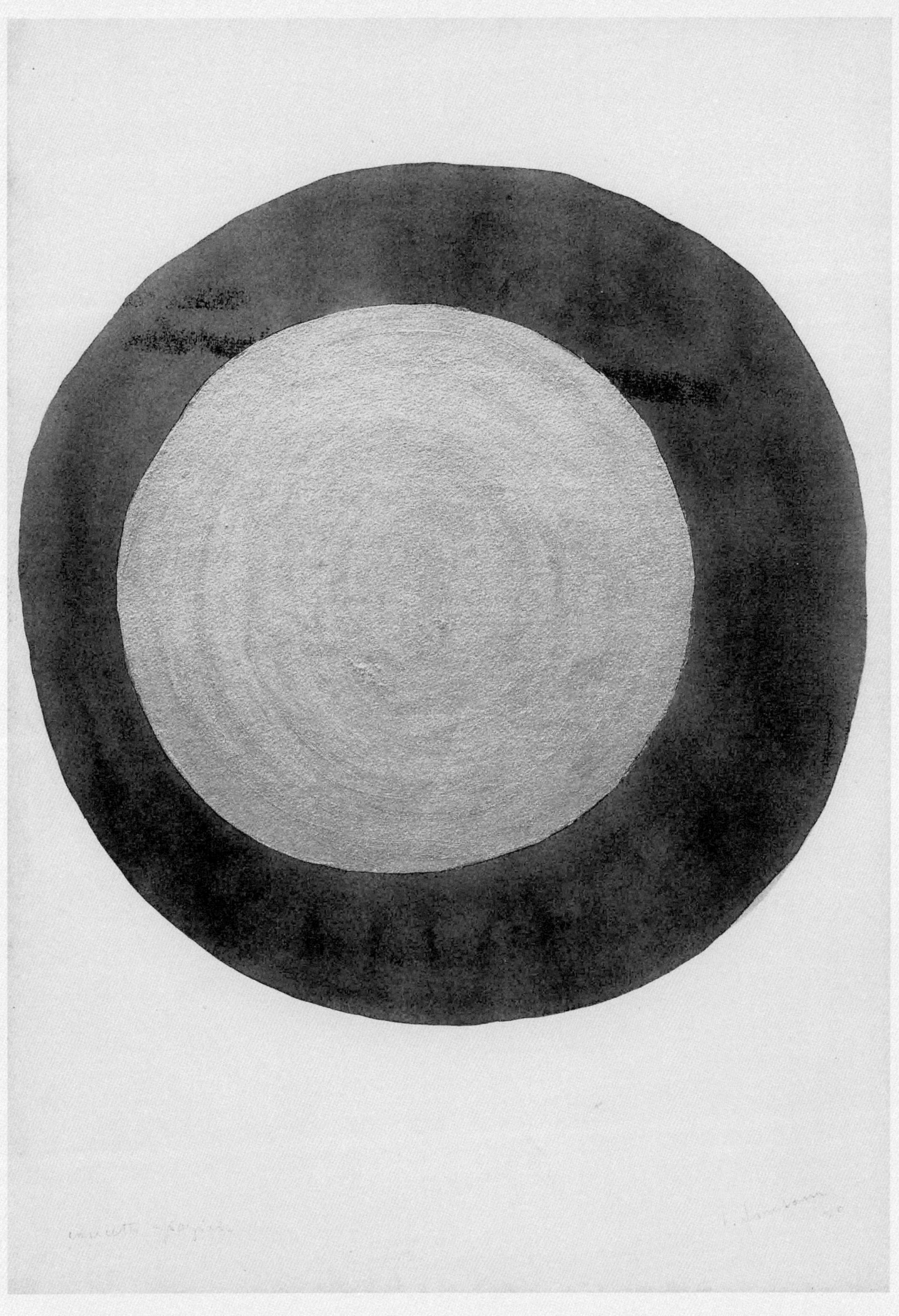

Lucio Fontana

Giorgio Verzotti

When the Centre Georges Pompidou in Paris devoted a major retrospective to Lucio Fontana in 1987, "postmodern" aesthetics were very much to the fore, having brought about the crisis in teleological visions of history, the famous "grand narratives" about which Jean-François Lyotard had recently written.

As far as art history was concerned, one of the criteria for evaluation that the age sought to call into question was what at the time was called the ideology of the avant-garde, a concept best summarised by the expression "tradition of the new" successfully coined by Harold Rosenberg to define the essence of the artistic avant-garde, its primary driving force.

The tradition of the new had effectively swept away and replaced, at least until the 80s, every other tradition, and art had been based for decades on a temporality substantiated by movements and trends which set out to contradict, as the very reason for their establishment, previous movements and trends. *Antipassatismo* or "anti-pastism" was for a long time an essential attribute of contemporary artistic output.

However, the 80s also saw the decline of such a conception. The finalistic vision of history on which it basically depended, and the associated absolute faith in progress, began to be called into question. Tradition, the past and the associated values made a comeback (this happened with the various European "returns to order" in the early post-war period, suitably reconsidered in those years): nothing was ever "superseded" and one thing coexisted with another, and they related to and relativised each other. The criterion of innovation became part of a universe of meanings in which it was no longer the dominant attribute. Progress was significant in art, but equally so was regress and stasis.

In 1987 Lucio Fontana seemed to be the figure who fit in most appropriately with a reading suited to the demands of the age. In the light of an evolutionistic ideology, how in fact might Fontana's work be appraised? As a long process of refining, of experimentation, of perfecting techniques and of bringing into focus the line of thought that culminated in Spatialism? With his investigation of space Fontana did in fact play the role of the innovator and established himself as an undisputed master for later generations. However, Spatialism was not all he had to offer.

His work overall, and his entire output prior to this "major" phase, cannot only be read in the light of the ground-breaking gesture of perforating the pictorial surface. There is more.

By his very nature, Fontana eludes unequivocal definition. Far less can he be labelled as an experimentalist who, at the end of the 40s, "finally" found his way. Fontana never participated in the spirit of the avant-garde, in the sense that he never complied with the restrictions of programmes, groups and programmatic manifestos, despite having written more than one himself. Fontana was receptive to what was new without ever adhering to the ideology of the new. His story must be viewed as the co-presence of tradition and innovation, with an ability – and this was absolute – to give fresh meaning and pertinence to every language, every signifying practice. His was a discontinuous story, one of fractures, returns, moments of suspension. Opposition, the most exemplary denial of one-directional coherence, stirs in his practice in response to every supra-historical point of view posited as a criterion for the attribution of historic value.

During the 1930s Fontana was active on two fronts, figuration and abstraction – two expressive practices which, after the Second World War, became discriminating and totalising choices in Italy. The 30s laid the foundations for this conflict: the hegemony of figurative painting and sculpture, which the Fascist regime would try to use as a platform for consensus-producing art, was countered by the line of resistance of geometric abstraction. Both these positions were underpinned by demanding programmes regarding the social role of the artwork. On the one hand, the Novecento group, and then Martini and Sironi; on the other, the abstraction championed in the writings of Carlo Belli and by the (also commercial) organisation represented by the Galleria del Milione in Milan. Even back then, Fontana dissolved the very essence and reason of that dichotomy, thereby calling into question its purported epochal necessity. He pursued lines of inquiry transgressing both choices. The portraits, busts and statues of this period, from at least 1931 onwards, remain extraneous to the a-temporal aura presumed to surround the figures of establishment art, but in their antinaturalistic use of colour they are at the same time far removed from anything anecdotal. The gold of the faces rescues them from the clutches of pure description, but also distances them from the Masaccesque golden age that seduced exponents of the Novecento movement. A distinctive feature had already come into play in his work: the scratches, the linear incisions in the material that define the figure by rendering the profile. This feature recurs in the scratched tablets, also produced in 1931, where Fontana first experimented with abandoning referentiality.

The sculptures realised in the course of 1934 and shown at the Milione the following year also represent a moment of lucid radicality. They still prompt reflection today about how the status of the artwork can exist even though its nature remains undecidable. Painting, sculpture, articulations in space, the poetics of colour: Fontana's "foray" into the abstract and his move to counter any fundamentalist poetics. Geometry yes, but not a priori, so as not to conceal its origin in the organic, exhibited as a badge of honour. Sculpture yes, but almost reduced to two dimensions, flattened, deliberately without volumetric prominence. These darting, agile forms constitute one of the most important moments in European art in this decade, precisely because they did not derive from a programme that had been drawn up a priori, but which established their own programme – in the sphere of the undecidable itself.

After his abstract endeavours, however, Fontana did not "move forwards". If anything, he went back to another line of inquiry consigned to history, that of Medardo Rosso – a blow to the evolutionism underpinning the auto-legitimising discourse of the avant-garde movements. How should Fontana's great work as a ceramicist be judged? As a regressive act? Compared to what, to which direction or path considered (and why?) to be the main one? The important thing was to verify everything, to transform everything into working practice. The ceramics produced at Albisola and Sévres enabled the artist to engage with the material and to attain the maximum expressiveness with his ability to manipulate material, with a touch that cut surfaces and with his skilful use of the colour of glazes. Yet his themes were based on more traditional topoi, mainly the still life – nothing that by definition involved an "expressionism", a torment, an agitation of the spirit and of the hand. There is all this though, to the extent that the ceramics can be seen as precedents for the poetics of the *informale*, just as the blot in the figurative tablets of the early 30s already had a fully autonomous value in the signification of the image.

The works are not regressive, then; on the contrary, they are premonitory. With the aid of Medardo and by referencing the Baroque, Fontana "preceded" something that would only become the leading style of the age in the 1950s. By contrast, in the 50s, right in the middle of the early Spatialist work, we find the airy and nimble ceramic modelling from the 30s in a commissioned work, the models for the fifth door of Milan Cathedral. Returning to stylistic features which in theory were already obsolete with respect to his own evolution, Fontana actualised the religious monument, stripping it of magniloquence and working with temerity: another unpredictable "place of beginning".

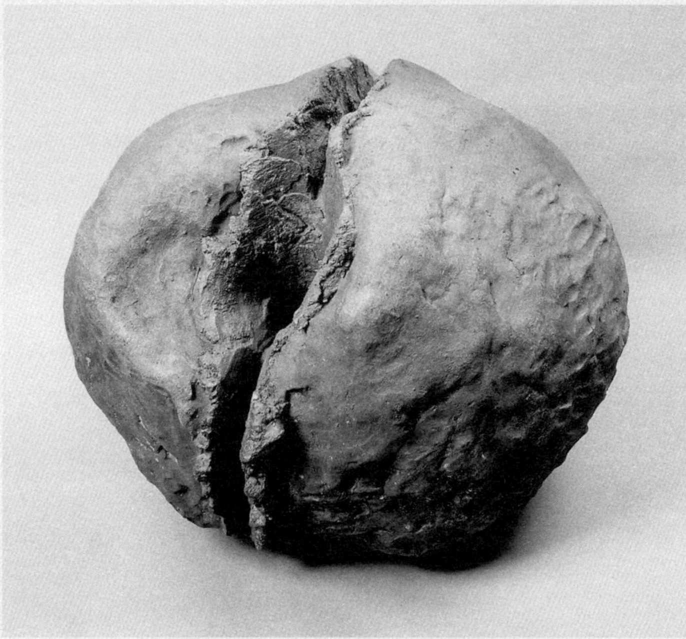

Concetto spaziale. Natura
1959-60
bronze
60 × 57 × 57 cm
59-60 N 10
Courtesy La Gaia, Busca

In the same year, 1951, and in the same place, the Triennale of Milan, Fontana showed these projects together with what until then had been his most innovative work, the tangle of neon installed above the staircase of honour of the venue in Milan. It seems to offer a reminder that the origins of the most advanced work in terms of the involvement of the environment and the viewer lies in manual skills, in doing, in the squiggle that is the project of the work. Spatialism originated from ceramics: the *Scultura Spaziale* [Spatial sculpture, 1947], which appears to be an instance of Art Brut, is a phenomenology of the hand that sketches and assembles. From a formal point of view there is a coherent continuity in Fontana. His sculptural self, for example, induces us to read the perforated, slashed, cut canvases as plastic events. From a conceptual point of view, however, this continuity is broken by intervals, studded with absences and non-consequentialities. The years of his second sojourn in Argentina (to avoid being called up again, having fought in the First World War) were a long interval in which the artist produced completely traditional sculptures, albeit sometimes ruffled by a certain restlessness. But after returning to Italy, the theme of space "exploded": announced by the series of drawings executed during the sea voyage to Milan and openly declared in his Manifiesto Blanco (which, note, he did not sign), it ushered in a new phase in which the artist became a passionate champion of the new.

Aside from the environments, where it was investigated positively as reality, the Spatialist line of inquiry was negatively articulated. It was based on and started with what denied and was in contrast with it, positing itself as problem. Inscribing space in a two-dimensional work, and reuniting two incommensurable entities, was the extreme wager to which Fontana devoted himself with the awareness of someone tacking an issue for the first time – an open question that others addressed after him, taking his solutions as a point of departure. Spatialism turned Fontana into a "conceptual" artist, not just because his works are invariably called *Concetto Spaziale* [Spatial Concept] but above all because their distribution in the purely eidetic dimension, as an expression of pure thought, changed their function: no longer just works to observe, but indexes alluding to a further dimension, which Fontana himself described very well in an interview with Carla Lonzi, included in her famous book, *Autoritratto*.

This is the Lucio Fontana thematised in the Pompidou exhibition thirty-six years ago, as conveyed through the choice of works and the critical contributions in the catalogue: an artist who rejected any form of dogmatism and was open to the most disparate expressive possibilities, not due to a conscious or, what would be worse, an ideological choice, but due to his temperament and an instinctive impatience. Just one aspect failed to emerge in the role assigned to him, and that is the sensuality of his work. This is very much in the foreground in the Florence exhibition, a sign of how times and criteria of evaluation have changed, leading to a reconsideration of what was once viewed as secondary or marginal.

In fact, not only does Fontana elude unambiguous definition; his work also oscillates between high and low, between the most rarefied abstraction and the impulses of carnal desire, with his customary unsnobbish nonchalance.

Right at the height of his most abstract work, which resulted in the *Concetto Spaziale, Attesa* [Spatial concept, Waiting], Fontana instilled sensuality into his output. Enrico Crispolti pointed this out back when he compiled the General Catalogue, the works from the 60s without holes or cuts but outright slashes, inflicted on dense, thickly painted surfaces, and which clearly have erotic allusions; these deep gaping holes in the centre of the canvases, accompanied by filaments and slight scratches in the paint are allusions to the vagina. In the same decade he produced some female nudes, which the Paris curator, Bernard Blistène, examined at the Fondazione Fontana but decided not to show. These same works can be seen at the Museo Novecento: far removed from the elegant effects of the "main volante", to use the term employed by Fanette Roche-Pézard to describe the corpus of drawings.[1] Here the watercolour mark is pronounced, a little rough, even when it is an airy pink, almost akin to the eroticised scratch and in any case generating a "summarised" figuration, as Argan called ancient, coarsely summarising Roman painting. We do not know what Fontana thought of these works on paper, probably relating to a more private sphere and which in his own time would certainly have surprised admirers of the Spatialist master. But they unquestionably transmit the same tension that guided the artist to his most revolutionary works.

––––––––––––––––

1   F. Roche-Pézard, "Fontana ou la main volante, essai sur l'oeuvre graphique", in *Lucio Fontana*, Editions du Centre Pompidou, Paris 1987, pp. 74 ff.

Lucio Fontana

Lucio Fontana.
The Dark Depths
of the Infinite

Letizia Fuochi

The Neapolitan writer Erri de Luca reminds us that in Hebrew, the word for *female* is *nekevà*, from the verb to carve, cut or engrave: in fact, female means incision, fissure, the fissure out of which life comes[1]; a primordial passageway where coming into the world is like being blinded by another dimension, a dual dimension, the space-time dimension where the inaccessible cosmological past is first connected and then directed towards the expansion of the universe. The search for the beginning and the absolute can be frightening for anyone who tries to approach the great secret without resorting to invaluable tools such as religion or the ability to transform imagination into art. And there is no certainty that anyone possesses both of these tools. But if those touched by the gift of faith trust and rely on the unknowable, those who succeed (also or only) in transforming the supreme mystery into artistic expression have the opportunity and perhaps also the responsibility to give our senses and intellect a conceptual heritage of inestimable value. My pleasure, my enjoyment, my ambition will be to try to inspire - through literature, mythology, poetry and music - a little curiosity and some food for thought on both the magmatic principle of life and the importance of myth and archetype in its complexity. An ancient midrash – a traditional method of biblical exegesis, in which the text is explained in a way other than its literal meaning[2] – reveals that we find what we are seeking and seek according to who we are[3]: The great Italo-Argentine artist Lucio Fontana is no exception in this.

The audacity and realism with which Gustave Courbet painted *L'origine du monde* [The Origin of the World] in 1866, still continues to seduce anyone who lays eyes on this painting. The fact that it is devoid of any kind of historical, poetic or literary artifice makes it disarming. *"On ne peint pas de son pinceau le plus délicat et le plus sonore l'intérieur de Mlle Queniault de l'Opéra* [One cannot paint the intimate parts of Mademoiselle Queniault with one's most delicate and musical brush]" the younger Alexandre Dumas is said to have written in his letters to George Sand, referring to Constance Quéniaux, a well-known dancer at the Paris Opera, as the model for the scandalous canvas. Words of astonishment? Of disappointment? Or admiration for a work that because of the painter's artistry and skill, fully escapes the stigma of pornography? And what can the connection between the 19th-century canvas and the title of an exhibition on Lucio Fontana in 2023 possibly be?

In the grand theatre of eroticism, so to speak, the act of spying on other people's sexual encounters or scenes gives the viewer undeniable pleasure; and in depicting these situations, authors of erotic literature

---

1   E. De Luca. *Le sante dello scandalo*, Giuntina, Florence 2011, p. 8.

2   A. Unterman, *Dizionario di usi e leggende ebraiche*, Laterza, Bari 1994.

3   L. Kushner, *In questo luogo c'era Dio e io non lo sapevo. Sette commenti a Genesi 28,16*, Giuntina, Florence 1994.

often introduce a second-hand voyeurism: the keyhole, daguerreotype postcards of the belle époque, or literary devices such as those used in *Souvenirs d'une Puce* [*Autobiography of a Flea*][4], from 1887, the point of view of a flea in the mattress... promiscuity, on the other hand, always entails risks, depending on the times, places, and situations.

But what is the difference between eroticism and pornography? The difference - explains the French-Armenian writer Sarane Alexandrian, author of the famous *History of Erotic Literature*[5] –does not exist per se. What is important is to distinguish between the erotic and the obscene: pornography is the pure and simple description of the pleasures of the flesh, eroticism is the same description re-assessed according to an idea of love and social life. All that is erotic is perforce pornographic, but with something more; the poem of Eros sings of splendour, delight and beauty; in obscenity, on the other hand, the flesh is debased, lumped in with vulgarity. "One cannot make love in drawing rooms", wrote Pier Paolo Pasolini, "nor in beds. What is needed is a grassy patch in the suburbs, a piece of desert, the steppe, the heath, in short, all the places where the grass is scarce, burnt and hot", in other words, where love is pure instinct and voluptuousness, without inhibition.

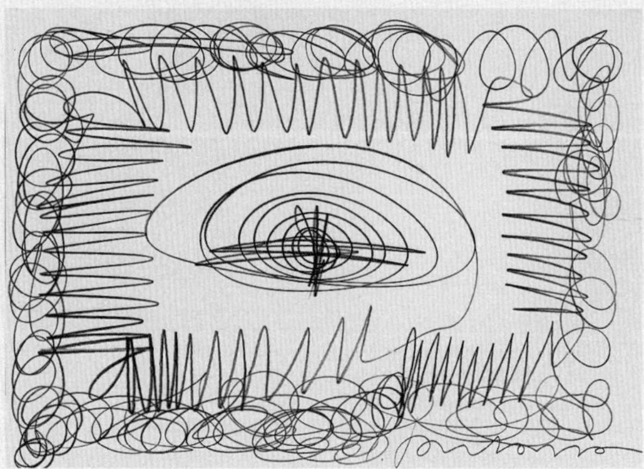

Concetto spaziale
1958
pencil and tempera
on cardboard
49,7 × 67 cm
58 DSP 41
Courtesy Fondazione
Lucio Fontana

It was the female nudes in India ink on cardboard drawn between 1960 and 1964 by Lucio Fontana that brought to mind these thoughts of Pasolini, where the hot fusion of pleasure, combined with savage instinct, bring the impulses of life out of the primordial earthly mud as well as the subterranean dimension of the chthonic depths, that of the visceral, invisible, almost frightening earth. Luckily, this woman of Fontana's does not seem to be born from Adam's rib, but from his own matter, fertile, generative and dark.

A powerful, black energy in which holes, cuts, fissures, lumps of pitch, dark, irregular meteor-like stones disrupt time and space: "generative sources of existence are matter and its evolution", Lucio Fontana explained in the Manifiesto Blanco [White Manifesto] of 1946. "We use what is true and natural in man. We reject the false aesthetics invented by speculative art. We will draw closer to nature than ever before in the history of art. Our love of nature does not compel us to copy it. The sense of beauty which we get from the shape of a plant, or a bird, or the sexual feelings aroused by a woman's body, are developed and elevated in man according to his sensitivity". No aesthetic research, no ethical

---

4   C. Hill, W. Wallace, *Erotikon. Un'antologia universale dell'arte e della letteratura erotica*, Taschen, Cologne 2001.

5   Alexandrian, S. *Storia della letteratura erotica*, Rusconi, Milan 1990, p. 6.

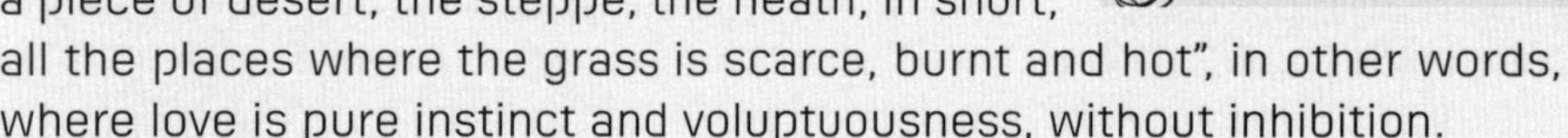

Letizia Fuochi

perspective, but a burst of expressive power that brings the observer into contact with this innovative viewpoint that strives to stimulate new intellectual transitions that become a means for inspiring thought.

"The themes of mythology, science and space exploration have fascinated me since childhood. And they are somehow connected with the music I write", stated Vangelis in 2016, the Greek musician and composer whose style - short melodic phrases and solemn symphonic arrangements – is said to have marked the junction between the cosmic music of the 1970s and the new age of the 1990s, to the point of radically influencing the global electronic scene. The propagation of sound in Vangelis' music (as in his album Albedo 0.39, whose title refers to the measure by which the reflective power of a celestial body is calculated, and specifically, 0.39 is the Earth's albedo) drew my attention to Fontana's Concetti Spaziali [Spatial Concepts]: those drawings in pencil, oil pastel, ballpoint pen, graffiti, rips and tears, capturing the sound wave of movement, as if it were a multiplying and unstoppable source in boundless space. "The work of art is not eternal. Man and his creation exist in time: when man is finished, infinity continues", the Italo-Argentine artist reiterated. "As our point of departure we shall take the earliest artistic experiences. Prehistoric man, who first heard the sound made by striking a hollow object, found himself captivated by the rhythm. Driven by the power of the rhythm he must have danced into a state of euphoria. For primitive man, sensation was everything – the sensation of nature, wild and unknown, the sensation of music and rhythm. We intend to develop that original characteristic of man".

Those works by Lucio Fontana that are certainly less well-known to the general public, where the female generative force is as alive in the artist's mind as it is in nature, the cosmos and the fertile body of the earth, call for a mythological and archetypal reference. In contrast to the cosmological vertigo, and in the attempt to understand the chthonic dimension - to which I already referred earlier – are the words of the Italian philosopher Giorgio Agamben in his column *Una Voce* for the publisher Quodlibet dated 28 December 2020 and on that occasion dedicated to Gaia and Chthonia: "The Latin term corresponding to *chthon* is not *tellus*, which designates a horizontal extension, but *humus*, which implies a downward direction (not by chance *humare*, meaning to bury), and it is significant that the name for man was taken from it (*hominem appellari quia sit humo natus*). That man is 'human', namely, of the earth, in the classical world does not imply a connection with Gaia, with the surface of the earth looking skyward, but first and foremost an intimate connection with the chthonic sphere of depth". In classical Greek, the earth had two names: *gaia*, the face of the earth that turns skyward, the land from the surface and upwards, and *chthōn*, the outer face of the underworld, the land from the surface downwards that cannot be cultivated and from which no nourishment can be drawn. In the myth of Persephone - the daughter of Demeter and Zeus, abducted by Hades - in the verses attributed to Homer we read of a transition between the upper and lower worlds: "[...] the earth opened up with wide roads in the plain of Nisa, and there arose from it the god whom many men welcome, the son of Kronos, who has many names, with his immortal horses. And seizing the goddess, on his golden chariot, reluctantly, in tears, he dragged her away". Chthonia evokes the idea of a gateway and a passage, the journey to the world of the dead that we are all destined to make, swallowed up by that same earth that generates life and prolificates it. In Rome, according to one legend, it was Romulus himself who dug the *mundus* - the so-called *mundus cereris*, a pit in the shape of an inverted womb - to symbolise not only the act of founding a new city, but also a primordial womb, a source of life and a passageway connecting the world of the living with the chthonic world of the dead. "The ancient city is founded on the *mundus*, the world, because men dwell in the opening that unites the celestial earth and the subterranean earth, the world of the living and the world of the dead, the present and the past, and it is through the relationship between these two worlds that it becomes possible for them to direct their actions and find inspiration for the future", Agamben explains. "Not only is man connected by his very name to the Chthonic sphere, but his world and the very horizon of his existence also border on the recesses of Chthonia. Man is, in the literal sense of the term, a being of the deep".

The origin, the end, the Alpha, the Omega, light, darkness, the observation point of a keyhole, the cut in a canvas that reveals the infinite beyond the infinite; the magma and meanderings of the universe, sound, silence, Lucio Fontana's spatialism has no boundaries. True to his name, Fontana's spatialism carries a wellspring within it: the flourishing and purifying spring of those who continue to ask questions, knowing that the real answer will be yet another threshold to be investigated.

Studies for
"Concetti spaziali"
1957
ballpoint pen on paper
32,5 × 25,5 cm
57 DSP 85 r e v
Private collection
Courtesy Gió Marconi
Milan

Letizia Fuochi

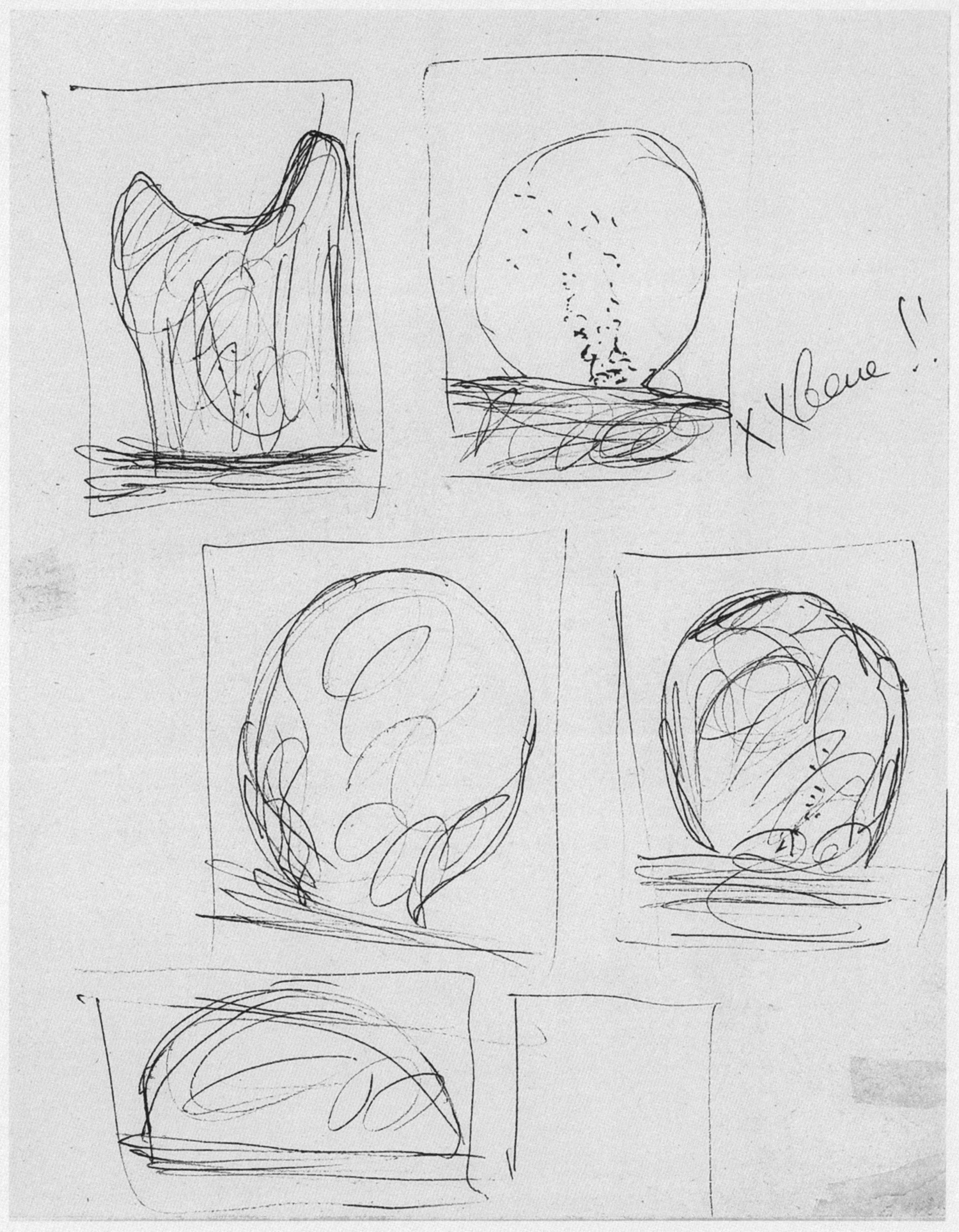

Lucio Fontana. The Dark Depths of the Infinite

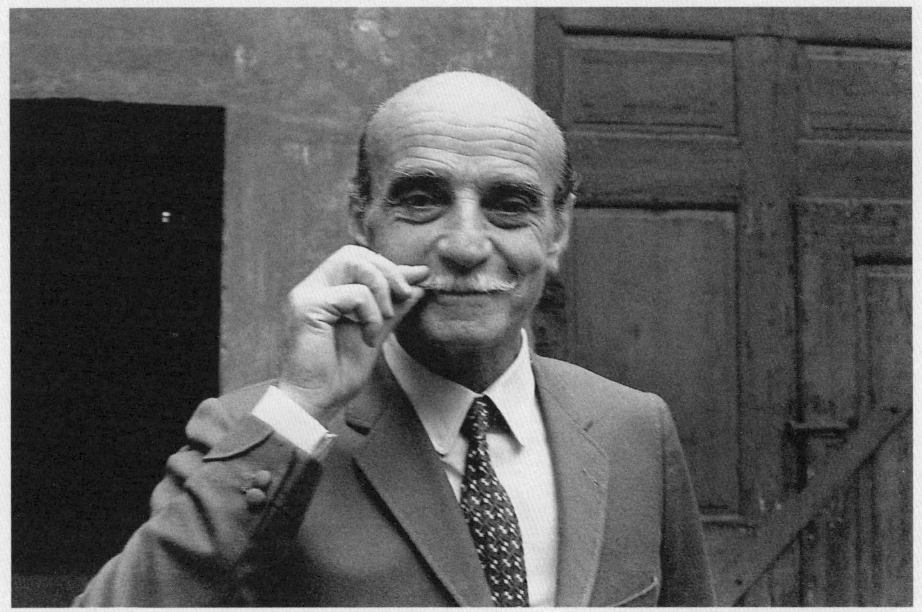

Lucio Fontana
in the courtyard
of his studio in Palazzo
Cicogna, Corso Monforte 23,
Milan, September 1967
© Archivio Fotografico
Enrico Cattaneo

Biography

1899
He was born on 19th February in Rosario di Santa Fe to parents of Italian origin. His mother, Lucia Bottini, was a theatre actress and his father, Luigi, was a sculptor who went to South America in 1890.

1906–1913
After spending his early childhood in Argentina, he was taken to Italy by his father, who by then had married Anita Campiglio.
Entrusted to the care of his uncle Tino Nicora, he first attended the "Torquato Tasso" boarding school in Biumo Inferiore (1906-1911), and then the three-year program at the technical school of the "Ballerini" Archiepiscopal College in Seregno.

1914–1915
Simultaneously enrolled in the School of Building Masters at the "Carlo Cattaneo" Technical Institute and the Art Secondary School attached to the Brera Academy of Fine Arts, he began his apprenticeship in the studio of his father, who had moved to Milan in the meantime. He was then admitted to the architecture department of the Secondary School of Applied Arts and Industry at Castello Sforzesco.

1916–1921
After the outbreak of the First World War, he enlisted as a volunteer, fighting on the front line as an infantry second lieutenant. Wounded in the Karst, after a few years he returned to Milan where he graduated as a building surveyor.

1922–1926
Having returned to Argentina, he began working in the family business. Following the recognition he received in the competition for the creation of a memorial frieze dedicated to Louis Pasteur for the Faculty of Medicine at the University of Rosario (1924), he abandoned commissioned sculpture to pursue a strictly artistic career, setting up his own business. In these years he obtained his first important commissions.

1927–1929
He returned to Italy and settled in Milan.
He attended Adolfo Wildt's sculpture course at the Brera Academy of Fine Arts, where he graduated at the end of 1929, presenting the work *El Auriga* (1928). Works such as *Eva* (1928) and *Vittoria fascista* [*Fascist Victory*] (1929) date back to these years, marked by the teacher's influence, as well as some important creations for the Monumental Cemetery in Milan (Mapelli Chapel, 1928; the Berardi Tomb, the Pasta and Locati Loculi [*Burial niches*], 1929). Through his friendship with Fausto Melotti, he also established contact with some young representatives of rationalist architecture.

1930
He exhibited *Eva* and *Vittoria fascista* at the 17th Venice Biennale and took part in the group exhibition "Studi di artisti lombardi noti e giovanissimi" at the Galleria del Milione in Milan, where he presented *Uomo nero* [*Black Man*] (1930), in plaster covered with tar, which departed from Wildt's teachings and ushered in a new, more openly experimental research into the representation of the human figure. That same year, he moved to his home-studio to Via Edmondo De Amicis and met Teresita Rasini, who would later become his wife.

1931–1934
He held his first solo exhibition ath the Galleria Il Milione. He continued to experiment with painted bronze and plaster sculptures, including *Signorina seduta* [*Seated Young Lady*] (1934), possibly inspired by his sister-in-law Jole Bonifacini Fontana, which was presented that same year at the 5th Exhibition of the Sindacato Interprovinciale delle Belle Arti di Lombardia, where the artist won the Tantardini Prize for sculpture with *Il Fiocinatore* [*The Harpooner*].

1935–1936
After years of experimentation, marked by important departures towards geometric abstraction and the use of different techniques and materials (from polychrome terracotta to plaster, bronze, cement and wire), he forged closer relations with the artists and intellectuals involved with the Galleria Il Milione, where he held the first exhibition of 'astract' sculpture in Italy. In March 1935, he was one of the artists featured in the "First Collective Exhibition of Italian Abstract Art", organised in Turin at the studio of Felice Casorati and Enrico Paulucci. Close to the artists supported by Edoardo Persico, he joined the Parisian Abstraction-Création movement. In the meantime, he moved his house and studio to Via Guglielmo Pepe, in a building designed by architects Terragni and Lingeri, and began to concentrate intensively on ceramics. He worked in Giuseppe Mazzotti's factory in Albissola Marina, a meeting place for artists and intellectuals also thanks to the influence of Giuseppe's second son, known as Tullio d'Albisola. The first monograph dedicated to his work, written by Edoardo Persico in 1935, was published in 1936.

1937
He moved to France, where he met the critic Lionello Venturi and got to know some important members of the international avant-garde. Committed to a personal experimentation in the field of ceramics, he stayed in Sèvres, where he was employed as a sculptor and continued to develop a personal style involving complex forms and daring colours. He took part in the Universal Exposition in Paris.

1938
Having returned to Italy, he doubled down on his work as a ceramist, also supported by Tullio d'Albisola. In the pieces from this period, he investigated the potential of volumes by first shattering the forms and using intense colours, which created an articulated interpenetration between the work and the space. Some important creations date back to this phase, as well as, among others, the sculptures *Paulette*, *Donna sdraiata* [*Reclining Woman*] and *Cavalli marini* [*Seahorses*] , which were purchased by Alberto Della Ragione probably at the Galleria Genova, where the artist's ceramics were exhibited from January 1939.

1939
He continued to work as a ceramist and became involved with the Corrente group, with whom he exhibited at the end of the year.

1940

Among others things, he made several full sculptures in coloured mosaic and inaugurated the *Volo di Vittorie* [*Flight of Victories*] frieze on the ceiling of the *Sacrario dei martiri fascisti* [*Fascist Martyrs' Memorial*] in Piazza San Sepolcro in Milan.

At his father's request, he returned to Argentina, where he remained stranded due to Italy's joining the war.

After taking part in the competition for the *Monumento Nacional a la Bandera* [*National Monument to the Flag*] in Rosario de Santa Fe, he continued to work mainly on figurative pieces, including *La mujer del marinero* [*The sailor's wife*], *Donne al balcone* [*Women on the balcony*], and *Mujeres ante el espejo* [*Women before the mirror*] .

1941–1945

He received numerous important accolades, both from the public and from critics. In the years that immediately followed, he became a professor of model-making at the Escuela de Artes Plasticas in Rosario and of decoration at the Accademia di Bellas Artes "Prilidiano Pueyrredòn" in Buenos Aires, where he moved in 1943. That same year, 14 of his drawings were published in Milan to illustrate a story by Tullio d'Albisola. Again in Buenos Aires, in 1945, he also obtained the chair of model-making at the Escuela Nacional de Bellas Artes "Manuel Belgrano".

1946

Together with Jorge Rornero Brest and Jorge Larco, he set up "Altamira, Escuela libre de artes plàsticas" in Buenos Aires, which became an important cultural hub also frequented by young people from the Madì Group.

In the Argentinean artistic avant-garde circles, the document *Manifiesto Blanco* [White Manifesto] developed and brought together the theses inspired by Lucio Fontana's theories. This was drafted by Bernardo Arias, Horacio Cazenueve, Marcos Fridman and also signed by Pablo Arias, Rodolfo Burgos, Enrique Benito, César Bernal, Luis Coli, Alfredo Hansen and Jorge (Amelio) Rocamonte.

In the same year, the term *Concetto Spaziale* [*Spatial Concept*] appeared in a group of drawings by the artist, a title that would accompany much of his later work.

His father Luigi passed away.

1947

He returned to Milan and settled on Via Castelmorrone 37. He went back to working as a ceramist in Albissola. In December, the first *Manifesto dello Spazialismo* [*Manifesto of Spatialism*] was published, signed by Lucio Fontana, critic Giorgio Kaisserlian, philosopher Beniamino Joppolo and writer Milena Milani.

1948

He published the second *Manifesto of Spatialism*, signed together with Gianni Dova and Antonino Tullier. This manifesto reiterated the need to move beyond the art of the past, making "painting come out of its frame and the sculpture out of its glass bell jar".

He participated in the 24th Venice Biennale and as well as the exhibition in Rome, "Abstract Art in Italy".

1949

On 5 February, he inaugurated *Ambiente spaziale a luce nera* [*Spatial Environment in Black Light*] at the Galleria del Naviglio, a work that invites us to experience space in a different way, starting with the installation of suspended phosphorescent elements in a black room, illuminated by Wood's black light. In Spring, he held a solo exhibition of drawings at the Libreria Salto in Milan, fundamental for his later research. He also worked on his first experiments, which later merged into the series of the *Buchi* [*Holes*] (1949-68): these were works on which the artist made holes with an awl, at first in the form of a vortex and

later in a more regular structure, conceived as openings to a further space.

1950

He exhibited his ceramics at the Galleria Il Milione and took part in the 25th Venice Art Biennale with a solo exhibition. He signed the third *Manifesto dello spazialismo. Proposta di un regolamento* [*Manifesto of Spatialism. Proposal for a regulation*], along with Milena Milani, Giampiero Giani, Beniamino Joppolo, Roberto Crippa and Carlo Cardazzo.

He took part in the competition organised by the Veneranda Fabbrica del Duomo for the fifth door of the Milan Cathedral, winning later second prize *ex aequo* with Luciano Minguzzi.

1951

The models submitted to the competition for the fifth door of the Duomo were shown at the 9th Milan Triennale, where the artist set up a large neon motif on the monumental staircase and read the *Manifesto tecnico dello Spazialismo* [*Technical Manifesto of Spatialism*].

In November, he signed the fourth *Manifesto dell'arte spaziale* [*Manifesto of Spatial Art*].

1952

On 9 February he married Teresita Rasini in Milan. A few days later, he exhibited his *Buchi* for the first time at the Galleria del Naviglio as part of the "Arte Spaziale" exhibition. He also began work on the *Pietre* [*Stones*] series (1952-56). These were canvases mostly covered with oil paint, on which the artist then used an awl and affixed fragments of glass paste. Because they protruded from the canvas, they expanded the spatial research into new physical and imaginative possibilities.

As one of the signatories of the *Manifesto del Movimento Spaziale per la Televisione* [*Manifesto of the Spatial Movement for Television*], he took part in the production of experimental RAI broadcasts, in which he combined *Buchi* with light projections. He moved his studio to 23 Corso Monforte.

1953

In collaboration with architect Luciano Baldessari, he created a ceiling of "holes" for the cinema in the Breda Pavilion and a ceiling of "holes" with neon elements for the cinema in the Sidercomit Pavilion (Finsider) at the 31st Milan Trade Fair.

1954

He participated in the 27th Venice Biennale with works created between 1930 and 1952. In collaboration with Luciano Baldessari, he signed a ceiling for the Breda Pavilion at the 32nd Milan Trade Fair. He also began working on *Barocchi* [*Baroque works*] (1954-57) and the *Gessi* [*Plaster works*] (1954–58) series. The experiments conducted in these years reverberated with telluric images, which translated the processes governing the origin of life and its unfolding on Earth and in the cosmos into germinating matter.

1955–1957

His research attracted growing interest, both nationally and internationally. His numerous exhibitions in Italy and abroad included, for example: the solo exhibitions of ceramics organised in Milan, at the Galleria San Fedele, and in Rome, at the Galleria dello Zodiaco (both in 1955); the group exhibition organised at the Galleria del Naviglio to celebrate 10 years of the Spatialist movement (1956); the Fourth International Biennal of Lithography in Cincinnati (1956); he had exhibitions at the Galleria Rotta in Genoa, the Galleria del Naviglio, the Galleria Selecta in Rome, the Galleria il Prisma in Turin, and the Galleria Il Cavallino in Venice (all in 1957).

1958

He exhibited with Piero Manzoni and Enrico Baj at the Galleria Bergamo in Bergamo. He also participated in the 29th Venice Biennale, where he presented some *Baroque works*, sculptures on a stem, *Gessi* and *Inchiostri* [*Inks*] (1956-59). He signed the seventh *Manifesto tecnico dello Spazialismo*. Towards the end of the year, he began to make clean cuts in the surface of his works, initiating the *Tagli* [*Cuts*] series (1958-68).

1959

He exhibited the *Tagli* at the Naviglio Gallery and the Galerie Stadler in Paris. He was featured at Documenta 2 in Kassel and had his own retrospective curated by Enrico Crispolti, organised first at the Galleria L'Attico in Rome and later at the Galleria Notizie in Turin. He started the *Quanta* series (1959-60), wall-mounted combinations of shaped canvases which often had cuts in them. He also continued to work on *Buchi*, *Carte* and ceramics, and in Albissola, he produced the first terracottas of the *Natura* [Nature]cycle (1959-60), works that recall the "cosmic imagination" that the artist often alluded to and that in the following years would be translated into bronze.

1960

Featured in numerous exhibitions, he exhibited *Tagli* at the Galerie Schmela in Düsseldorf. He also participated in the "Monochrome Malerei" exhibition in Leverkusen and in the travelling exhibition "From Nature to Art", organised at Palazzo Grassi, Venice, where he exhibited some *Natura* pieces and created the spatial environment *Esaltazione di una forma* [*Exaltation of a Form*].
A relentless experimenter, he began to concentrate on the *Oils* [*Oils*] series (1957-68), canvases with a thick material layer of paint, in which he made holes or lacerations.

1961

Some *Olii* inspired by the city of Venice were exhibited at the exhibition "Art and Contemplation" at Palazzo Grassi and shown again for the first solo exhibition organised in the United States, at the Martha Jackson Gallery in New York. On the occasion of the Expo "Italia 61", he collaborated with architects Gian Emilio, Piero and Anna Monti to create the "Hall of Energy Sources", for which he designed a neon ceiling. He also participated in the creation of the mosaics for the Lungomare degli Artisti promenade in Albissola Marina, inaugurated in 1963.

1962

The impressions from the New York metropolis reverberated in the conception of a new cycle of works, the *Metalli* [*Metals*] (1961-68): flat surfaces of mirrored sheet metal in which the artist made cuts and gashes. Works from the new series were presented in June at the Galleria dell'Ariete in Milan.

1963

At the centre of numerous exhibitions in Italy and abroad, he continued his untiring research into the potential of the different mediums and their intersections, launching *Fine di Dio* [*The End of God*] series (1963-64): oval canvases on which a monochrome paint had been applied, sometimes embellished with sequins, and which appear to have irregular holes torn in them. The works in this new cycle, which the artist himself considered to be an extreme breakthrough towards the infinite and the germinating nothingness, were originally called "ova". First exhibited at the Galleria dell'Ariete in Milan, with a text in the catalogue by Gillo Dorfles, they were presented in 1964 at the Galerie Iris Clert in Paris, with the title *Les œufs célestes*.

1964–1965

He began work on the *Teatrini* [*Little Theatres*] series (1964-66), monochrome canvases pierced by holes onto which shaped lacquered wooden frames were applied, a way for the artist to investigate new possible spatial shapes.
He exhibited at the Tate Gallery in London, in Hanover (with Burri, Capogrossi, and Dorazio), in Buenos Aires, and New York (1964). He also had solo exhibitions at the Galleria Notizie in Turin and the Galleria Blu and Galleria Apollinaire in Milan (1965).

1966

He had solo exhibitions at the Walker Art Center in Minneapolis, the Marlborough Gallery in New York and the Galerie Alexander Iolas in Paris. At the 33rd Venice Biennial, he had a room created in collaboration with Carlo Scarpa: a labyrinthine oval space, illuminated by a white light and containing white canvases pierced by a single cut, which won him the painting prize.

1967

Featured in numerous exhibitions, both solo and otherwise, he presented his *Ellissi* [*Ellipses*] (1964-67) at the Galleria Marlborough in Rome: these works consisted of monochrome lacquered wood panels pierced with holes, which, in line with the new technical achievements, were executed by machine by Sergio Tosi, based on an executive drawing by Fontana. He also designed numerous spatial environments (for the Stedelijk Museum in Amsterdam; for the exhibition "The Space of the Image", curated by Tommaso Trini at Palazzo Trinci, Foligno; for the Galleria del Deposito in Genoa).

1968

He left Milan to move to Comabbio (VA), where he restored his father's house. There he designed a spatial environment for the 34th Venice Biennale and another in the form of a white labyrinth for Documenta 4 in Kassel. He died on 7 September in the Santa Maria clinic of the Ospedale di Circolo, in Varese.

Bibliography

1869
A. Dumas figlio, prefazione a *L'Ami des femmes*, Paris 1869

1931
R. Crippa, *Mostre d'arte*, in "Libro e moschetto", 20 February 1931, p. 4

1932
P. Torriano, *Cronache d'arte. Due giovani*, in "Casabella", January 1932, p. 53

1936
E. Persico, *Lucio Fontana*, Edizioni di Campo Grafico, Milan 1936

1938
G.M. Lo Duca, *Artisti italiani a Parigi: Corbellini, Fontana, Gherardi*, in "Emporium", LXXXVII, no. 519, March 1938, p. 160

1939
R. Carrieri, *Le maioliche geologiche di Lucio Fontana*, in "L'Illustrazione italiana", Milano, 8 January, 1939, pp. 63-64
G. M. Lo Duca, *Cronache parigine. Parigi e Lione: artisti italiani*, in "Emporium", LXXXXVII, no. 528, November 1939, p. 336

1948
M. Radice, *Giornale delle Arti. Lucio Fontana*, in "Corriere di Milano", 28 May 1948, p. 3

1955
R. Carrieri, *Primo incontro con Fontana*, in "Epoca", VI, 1955, p. 226

1958
XXIX Biennale Internazionale d'Arte, exhibition catalogue (Venice, Giardini della Biennale, June-October 1958), pp. 19-22

1959
G. Limbour, s.t., in "Les Lettres Nouvelles", 8 April 1959

1960
Dalla natura all'arte, catalogo della mostra (Centro Internazionale delle Arti e del Costume, Palazzo Grassi, Venice), 1960
M. Venturoli, *Suggestive opere a Palazzo Grassi nella mostra "Dalla Natura all'arte"*, in "Paese Sera", 16-17 July 1960

1961
J. A França, *Fontana*, in "Aujourd'hui. Art et Architecture", n. 34, December 1961, p. 45
L. Hochtin, *Les 'Ballons' de Lucio Fontana*, in "XXe siècle", a. XXIII, no. 16, May 1961, pp. 87- 89
C. Rivière, *Au-delà de la forme. Fontana la matière menaçante*, in "Combat", 20 November 1961, p. 7
M. Tapié, *Devenir de Fontana*, Edizioni d'Arte F.lli Pozzo, Turin 1961

1963
M. Lepore, *Mostre d'arte*, in "Corriere d'informazione", 4 July 1963
L. Fontana. Le ova, introduction by G. Dorfles, exhibition ctalogue, no. 96. Galleria dell'Ariete, Milan 1963
Memorie dell'altro ieri: Lucio Fontana, in "Epoca", 22 September 1963, p. 100
P. Rouve, *Lucio Fontana. Peinture, Sculpture*, exhibition catalogue (Zurigo, Gimpel Hanover Galerie, 21 May – 15 June 1963), Zurich 1963
M. Valsecchi, *Fontana*, in "il Giorno", 7 July 1963

1964
S. Takiguchi, *Fontana*, in "Arte Contemporanea", 25, Misuzu, Tokyo 1964

1966
M. Fagiolo Dell'Arco, *Rapporto 60*, Bulzoni, Rome 1966

1967
F. De Bartolomeis, *Segno antidisegno di Lucio Fontana*, Edizioni d'arte Pozzo, Turin 1967

1968
E. Crispolti, *L'avventura di Fontana*, in "Arte Illustrata", a. I, no. 7/12, July-December 1968, p. 58
Lucio Fontana, intervista edited by L. Grassi, in "Caffeclub", year II, n. 5, Milano, January-February 1968, p. 15
U. Mulas, *Lucio Fontana*, Achille Mauri, Milan 1968

1969
Hans Hartung, catalogo della mostra (Rome, Galleria "Il Collezionista", 11 November - 8 December 1969)
C. Lonzi, *Autoritratto*, De Donato, Bari 1969

1970
G. Ballo, *Lucio Fontana. Idee per un ritratto*, Edizioni Ilte, Turin 1970
P. Fossati (edited by), *Concetti spaziali*, Einaudi, Turin 1970
L. V. Masini, *Lo spazio-oltre*, in "NAC", 31, 15 February 1970, pp. 12-13

1971
E. Crispolti, *Omaggio a Lucio Fontana*, Carucci, Assisi-Rome 1971

1972
G. Dorfles, *Ho squarciato 10 tele come il muro di una prigione*, in "Bolaffiarte", March 1972

1973
U. Mulas, *La fotografia*, Einaudi, Turin 1973

1976
E. Crispolti, *Erotismo nell'arte astratta e altre schede per una iconologia dell'arte astratta*, Celebes, Palermo 1976

1986
G. Mascherpa, C. De Carli, *Lucio Fontana e il sacro*, exhibition catalogue (Milan, Centro San Fedele, March-April 1986), Federico Motta Editore, Milan 1986

1987
B. Blistène (edited by), *Lucio Fontana*, exhibition catalogue(Parigi, Centre Georges Pompidou, 13 October 1987 - 11 January 1988), Center Georges Pompidou, Paris 1987

1990
S. Alexandrian, *Storia della letteratura erotica*, Rusconi, Milan 1990

1994
L. Kushner, *In questo luogo c'era Dio e io non lo sapevo.*

**245
/**

Sette commenti a Genesi 28,16, Giuntina, Florence 1994
A. Unterman, *Dizionario di usi e leggende ebraiche*, Laterza, Bari 1994

1996
Burri e Fontana 1949-1968, exhibition catalogue (Prato, Museo Pecci, 13 April - 30 June 1996), Skira, Milan 1996
B. Corà, A. Tagliaferri (edited by), *Emilio Villa. Opere e documenti*, Skira, Milan 1996
F. Gualdoni, P. Campiglio, *Lucio Fontana e Milano*, Electa, Milan 1996
B. Teyssèdre, *Le roman de l'Origine*, Gallimard, Paris 1996

1997
A. Bruciati, *Dal monocromo all'achrome: l'opera bianca in Lucio Fontana e Piero Manzoni*, Lettere e filosofia, a.a. 1996/97, Università degli Studi di Udine, Udine 1997.

1999
P. Campiglio, *Lucio Fontana. Lettere 1919-1968*, Skira, Milano 1999
E. Crispolti (edited by), *Centenario di Lucio Fontana*, exhibition catalogue (Milan, various locations, 23 April - 30 June 1999), Charta, Milan 1999

2001
P. Herkenhoff (edited by), *Lucio Fontana. Brasil*, exhibition catalogue (Rio de Janeiro, Brasilia, Sao Paulo, Centro Cultural Banco do Brasil, November 2001 - April 2002), Charta, Milan 2001
C. Hill, W. Wallace, *Erotikon. Un'antologia universale dell'arte e della letteratura erotica*, Taschen, Köln 2001
E. Persico, *Destino e modernità. Scritti d'arte (1929-1935)*, edited by E. Pontiggia, Medusa, Milan 2001

2002
G. Cortenova (edited by), *Lucio Fontana metafore barocche*, exhibition catalogue (Verona, Palazzo Forti, 26 October - 16 March 2002), Marsilio, Venice 2002

2004
E. Crispolti, *Carriera 'barocca' di Fontana. Taccuino critico 1959 – 2004 e Carteggio 1958 – 1964*, Skira, Milan 2004
E Crispolti (edited by), *Lucio Fontana*, catalogue raisonné, Skira, Milan 2004

2006
E. Crispolti, *Lucio Fontana. Catalogo ragionato di sculture, dipinti, ambientazioni*, with the cllaboration of N. Ardemagni Laurini and V. Ernesti, Skira, Milan 2006

2007
Lucio Fontana scultore, edited by Filippo Trevisani, Electa, Milan 2007
Lucio Fontana. Sedici sculture, Silvana Editoriale, Cinisello Balsamo 2007

2008
A. Boatto, *Di tutti i colori*, Laterza, Rome-Bari 2008

2009
S. Petersen, *Space- Age Aesthetics: Lucio Fontana Yves Klein and the Postwar European Avant-Garde*, Penn State University Press, Penn State University 2009

2010
L. Mouguelar, *Lucio Fontana en Argentina: relecturas*, in "Separata", no. 15, X, 2010, pp. 38-55

2011
E. De Luca. *Le sante dello scandalo*, Giuntina, Florence 2011
G. Desanges, *La comtesse de Loynes. La belle Ecouteuse*, Editions L'Harmattan, Paris 2011

2012
P. Gottschaller, *Lucio Fontana. The artist's materials*, J. Paul Getty Museum Publications, Los Angeles, USA 2012

2013
L. M. Barbero (edited by), *Lucio Fontana. Catalogo ragionato delle opere su carta*, Skira, Milan 2013

2014
S. Bignami, J. Galimberti, *Lucio Fontana e l'artventure parigina*, Scalpendi, Milan 2014

2015
A. Sanna (edited by), *Lucio Fontana. Manifesti, scritti, interviste*, Abscondita, Milan 2015

2016
F. Stocchi (edited by), *Fontana - Leoncillo. Forma della materia*, exhibitioncatalogue (Milan, Fondazione Carriero, 6 April - 9 July 2016), Fondazione Carriero, Milan 2016

2017
E. Crispolti (edited by), *Lucio Fontana. Fine di Dio*, Forma, Florence 2017
Lucio Fontana. Fine di Dio (1963-1964), edited by E. Crispolti, texts by L. M. Barbero, E. Crispolti, L. P. Nicoletti, C. Toschi, with the collaboration of D. Nobili, Forma, Florence 2017
Rodin. I disegni proibiti, texts by N. Lehni, preface by C. Chevillot, Rizzoli arte, Milan 2017

2018
L. Fiorucci (edited by), *Barocco e Barocchetto. Materia e colore nella scultura di Lucio Fontana e Leoncillo Leonardi*, testimonies of E. Crispolti, B. Toscano, contributions by L. Hockemeyer, exhibition ctalogue (Umbertide, Fa.Mo Museo Rometti, 22 September - 20 October 2018), Editoriale Umbra, Foligno 2018
G. Politi, *Amarcord*, in "ArtsLife", 12 June 2018

2019
I. Candela (edited by), *Lucio Fontana: on the Threshold*, exhibition catalogue (New York, MET, 23 January - 14 April 2019; Bilbao, Guggenheim Museum 17 May - 20 September 2019), MET, New York 2019
G. Gaggiotti, *La visione verticale*, Morlacchi editore, Perugia 2019
F. Pola (edited by), *Ugo Mulas. Intrecci creativi*, exhibition catalogue (Londra, Robilant + Voena, 4 March - 24 May 2019), Marsilio, Venice 2019
C. Schopp, *La modella senza volto. Indagine su un quadro scabroso*, Donzelli, Rome 2019

2020
L. V. Masini, *Scritti scelti 1961-2019. Arte architettura design arti applicate*, edited by A. Acocella e A. Stepken, Gli Ori, Pisa 2020

2022
A. Bruciati (edited by), *Ecce Homo: l'incontro fra il divino e l'umano per una diversa antropologia*, exhibition catalogue (Tivoli, Villa d'Este, 25 June – 6 November 2021), Gangemi, Roma 2022

2023
Dizionario Lucio Fontana, edited by Luca Pietro Nicoletti, Quodlibet, Macerata

Contents

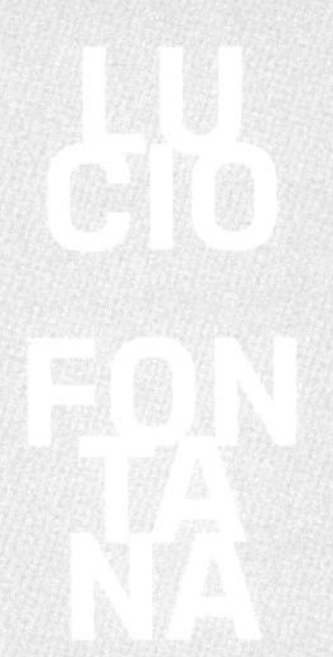

LUCIO FONTANA

The Origin of the World

**2 MARCH
13 SEPTEMBER 2023**

An exhibition promoted by
Comune di Firenze

Artistic direction
Sergio Risaliti

Scientific coordination
Eva Francioli
Francesca Neri – MUS.E
Jacopo Manara

Press office and communication
Costanza Savelloni
Lara Facco P&C
Lara Facco, Claudia Santrolli
Elisa Di Lupo, Comune di Firenze
Sara Camaiora, Comune di Firenze

Social media
Giulia Spissu

Visual Identity
Forma Edizioni

Education department
MUS.E

Graphic prints on display
Litografia Ip srls

Photographs
Serge Domingie

Translations
NTL – Il Nuovo Traduttore Letterario S.c.

Insurance
Aon Spa | Fine Arts, Jewellery
& Private Client Solution

Handling and artworks preparation
Apice Firenze S.r.l.

Condition report
Chiara Valcepina

Lighting installation
Vannetti Andrea S.r.l.

Service audio/video
FD Events S.r.l.

Room set up
Matteo Calviani, Alessio Tirinnanzi

Bases
Galli Mostre

Surveillance
REAR Società Cooperativa

Thanks to
Dario Nardella, Mayor of Florence
Alessia Bettini, Vice Mayor and Councillor
for Culture
Matteo Spanò, President of MUS.E

The lenders
Fondazione Lucio Fontana, Milano
Collezione La Gaia, Busca
Gió Marconi, Milano
Sergio Casoli
Robilant + Voena

And all the lenders who kindly lent works and
wished to remain anonymous

We would also like to thank
Rosa Alba Acquaviva, Silvia Ardemagni,
Alessia Ballini, Claudia Bardelloni, Andrea
Batistini, Nausicaa Bertellotti, Andrea
Bianchi, Laura Barazzini, Andrea Bruciati,
Paolo Campiglio, Mariella Carlotti, Francesca
Cattoi, Laura Chimenti, Elena Chiti, Lauretta
Colonnelli, Silvia Colucci, Rita Corsini,
Deborah D'Ippolito, Silvia Evangelisti,
Marco Fagioli, Gabriella Farsi, Letizia
Franceschini, Francesco Fricelli, Letizia
Fuochi, Manuela Galliano, Marina Gardini,
Susanna Giancolombo, Barbara Lo Giudice,
Maria Grazia Messina, Valeria Morandi, Ilaria
Nerli, Ugo Nespolo, Antonella Nicola, Luca
Pietro Nicoletti, Cecilia Pappaianni, Silvia
Penna, Fulvio Pierangelini, Chiara Pinna,
Franca and Lorenzo Pinzauti, Emanuella
Pisetti, Alessandra Pozzati, Barbara Rapaccini,
Stefania Rispoli, Giancarlo Rizzi, Emilie Ryan,
Cristiano Giulio Sangiuliano, Paolo Sani,
Sandra Santinelli, Lapo Sergi, Margherita
Stabiumi, Chiara Useli, Maria Villa,
Valentina Zucchi

All the offices of the City of Florence involved,
in particular
L'Ufficio del Sindaco, la Direzione Cultura,
il Cerimoniale, le Sale Monumentali

Supported by
Fondazione Lucio Fontana, Milano
Aon Spa | Fine Arts, Jewellery & Private Client
Solution

Credits
© 2023. Foto Scala, Firenze/bpk, Bildagentur
fuer Kunst, Kultur und Geschichte, Berlin
Archivio Patrimonio Artistico Intesa Sanpaolo
/ foto Paolo Vandrasch, Milano
Farabola / Bridgeman Images
© Kary H. Lasch / Booxencounters /
Bridgeman Images
photo © Estate Ad Petersen
Fotografie Ugo Mulas © Eredi Ugo Mulas.
Tutti i diritti riservati
© Institut Gustave Courbet /
Bridgeman Images
© Archivio Fotografico Enrico Cattaneo
© Fototeca dei Musei Civici Fiorentini
© Collezione La Gaia, Busca
© Loris Barbano
© Fabio Mantegna, Milano
© Roberto Marossi
© Francesca Pellacini
© Federico Torra

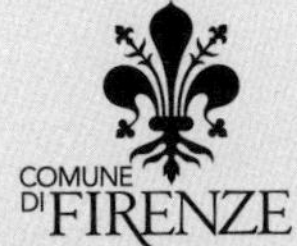
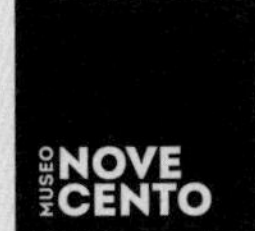
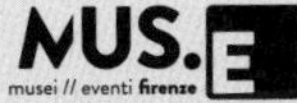

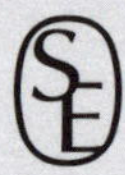

Silvana Editoriale

Chief Executive
Michele Pizzi

Editorial Director
Sergio Di Stefano

Art Director
Giacomo Merli

Editorial Coordinator
Natalia Grilli

Copy Editing
Lorena Ansani

Layout
Mirco Ameglio

Production Coordinator
Antonio Micelli

Editorial Assistant
Giulia Mercanti

Photo Editor
Silvia Sala

Press Office
Alessandra Olivari, press@silvanaeditoriale.it

Silvana Editoriale S.p.A.
via dei Lavoratori, 78
20092 Cinisello Balsamo, Milano
tel. 02 453 951 01
www.silvanaeditoriale.it
Reproductions, printing and binding
in Italy
Printed by Grafiche Antiga, Crocetta del Montello (TV)
in December 2023

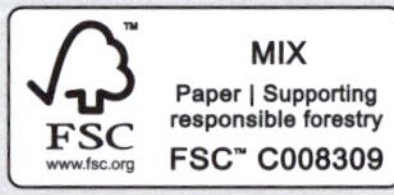